The Green Transformation of Urban Areas in China Under Global Warming

Shouhu Du

The Green Transformation of Urban Areas in China Under Global Warming

四川大學出版社
SICHUAN UNIVERSITY PRESS

国家哲学社会科学成果文库
NATIONAL ACHIEVEMENTS LIBRARY OF PHILOSOPHY AND SOCIAL SCIENCES

Springer

Shouhu Du
Sichuan Academy of Social Sciences
Chengdu, Sichuan, China

Translated by
Heng Du
Ecological Civilization Research Institute
Sichuan Academy of Social Sciences
Chengdu, Sichuan, China

ISBN 978-981-95-1004-7 ISBN 978-981-95-1005-4 (eBook)
https://doi.org/10.1007/978-981-95-1005-4

The Translation of this Book is Sponsored by Chinese Fund for the Humanities and Social Sciences (本书由中华社会科学基金资助).

English translation of the original Chinese edition published by Social Sciences Academic Press, Beijing, 2015

This Springer imprint is published by the registered company Springer Nature Singapore Pte Ltd.
The registered company address is: 152 Beach Road, #21-01/04 Gateway East, Singapore 189721, Singapore

In 2013, Mainly Facilitated by China, the 28th United Nations General Assembly Decided to Designate October 31st as World Urban Day Each Year.

—This Book is Dedicated to World Urban Day

Acknowledgements

This book is dedicated to my father, Professor Shouhu Du, who originally authored the Chinese version of the book. He instilled in me values of gratitude, the importance of purposeful work as a calling, and the idea of turning each day into a celebration of life. Without his support and encouragement, I couldn't have completed this translation project.

The original book has gone through the entire process of being a major bidding project of the National Social Science Fund, being selected into the "National Achievements Library of Philosophy and Social Science", and being selected into the academic translation project of the Chinese Fund for the Humanities and Social Science for the English version. It can be said to have achieved a "grand slam" in applying for National Social Science Fund projects. This is a systematic project, a result of teamwork, and a reflection of the inheritance and promotion of social science spirit across two generations in our family.

Special thanks to the team members of the National Social Science Fund project—Xiaoyan Li, Binbin Wang, Xiyong Chen, Shengzhi Li, Yi Ding, Yousheng Wu, etc.

I am honored to collaborate with Sichuan University Press on this translation project, and I look forward to further cooperation in the future. Heartfully thanks to Ms. Chang Liu, my wonderful editor, whose strict edits have helped shape this book into an academic wisdom.

I would also like to thank Professor Gary Bull from the University of British Columbia in Canada, Professor Christian Azar from the Chalmers University of Technology in Gothenburg, Sweden, Mr. Peter Hesseldahl, Editor, digital transition, Mandag Morgen, Denmark, Professor Shuiping Hou and Professor Jiaduo Liu, for their intellectual support and guidance on this project.

I want to thank my team members, Ms. Yazhen Gong, Mr. Shengbo Ge, and Ms. Xiaoqin Jin, for their collaboration in attaining this achievement.

This book is the result of years of many wonderful conversations and enduring relationships with friends and colleagues around the world who have inspired and shared in my life journey including Connie Magalit, Anna Sternbeck, Mattias Iweborg, Par Larshans, Per Porten, Ulrika Engstrom, Duanhua Tian, Notting, Wenfu Song, Qinglin

Wang, Yanhua Ding, Yujian Zhu, Xia Shi, Xiaoyan Guo, Qun Gu, Ying Cao, Qian Yan, Yunjuan Mu, Gengxuan Chen, Yong Liu, Bing Huang, Shaohong Fu, Xu Zhang, Li Liu, Qiuping Deng, Ya Deng, Li Dai, Qian Wang, Randy Kritkausky, Taiyong Chen, Meg Young, Kate Leyland, and all the others whom I treasure as friends.

Many Thanks to Sichuan Academy of Social Sciences, Ecological Civilization Research Institute, Innovation Team of Green Development Research of Sichuan Academy of Social Sciences, and Innovative Green Development of Sichuan Soft Science Research Base for granting me time to concentrate on the translation project.

Last but not least, I want to express my heartfelt gratitude to my mother, my sister, my son, and my pet dog "Laifu" for showing me that love is the ultimate source of enduring power in the universe.

Overview

The advent of the twenty-first century is synonymous with the era of metropolises. The year 2010 symbolized a critical juncture in the trajectory of human evolution, as the global urban populace overtook the rural population for the first time.

With growing socioeconomic development and expanding labor division, to pursue a better life, human society gradually builds cities and develops modernized urban production, lifestyle, and consumption patterns. As cities continue to grow, demands for transportation, energy, construction, and information soar up, which affects atmospheric and water environment significantly and presents increasing challenges for the sustainability of cities. Therefore, cities are the places where modern industrial civilization is concentrated, but they are also the places that suffered from many modern problems.[1] An increasing number of environmental issues are severely threatening the survival and development of mankind while human beings enjoy the happy life with modern cities, such as the eight world-known environmental hazards in the twentieth century, and the large number of urban agglomerations under extensive and lasting smog attack for several consecutive years in North and East China at the beginning of this century.

Urban development is intertwined with the intricate phenomena of urbanization. On the one hand, urban development requires population growth, and on the other hand, a rapidly growing population raises a series of issues including traffic congestion, and inadequate supply of public resources. Although it is difficult for any country or region to avoid these problems, cities in the world have commonly faced a major problem of environment pollution in their urbanization process, as well as conflict between urban development, ecological, and environmental protection. Mitigation of these issues through urban planning and sustainable progression choices have emerged as global challenges to consider.

While environmental pollution and the shortage of resources threatened world cities continuously, global warming joined the game by creating more frequently and more severe calamities associated with climate change. The Fourth Assessment Report of the United Nations Intergovernmental Panel on Climate Change (IPCC) projects that one direct repercussion of global warming will be a rise in sea level by 82 centimeters by the end of this century. The inundation will cause threatens to devastate coastal cities and island nations and regions. Economic calamity awaits 136 of these, including Chinese bustling hubs Shanghai and Guangzhou, with egregious cumulative losses projected to reach 28.21 trillion U.S. dollars. Previous natural disasters such as the triple threat of earthquake, tsunami, and nuclear crisis that devastated Tokyo in 2011, or Superstorm Sandy's assault on the eastern seaboard of America in 2012, underscore this concern.

The reality is that urbanization sits at the heart of environmental problems while paradoxically presenting as a potential solution. Given the current climate change scenario, sustainable cities that reconcile economic, societal, population, resource, and environmental sustainability may be realized through strategies such as the adoption of green and low carbon urbanization models, the green transformation of cities, alterations to production models and lifestyles, strategies focused on energy conservation, and investments into sustainable energy industries.

China's reform and opening up policy have spurred rapid urbanization in the country. China's urban population exceeded its rural population for the first time in 2012. It is widely held that China's urbanization and America's technological innovation are two seminal occurrences of the twenty-first century destined to shape global trends. In the forthcoming decades, China aspires to construct a moderately prosperous society while expediting socialist modernization to actualize the "Chinese Dream"—the great rejuvenation of Chinese nation. In this pursuit, the challenges of economic growth, environmental degradation, and global warming loom large. Meeting these challenges will chart an unprecedented path for urbanization in China, impacting the sustainable development of urban regions and the evolution of its ecological civilization.

Sustainable urban development is multifaceted under global warming, presenting numerous new circumstances and new characteristics. It brings both new challenges and new development opportunities.

First, the intertwining issues of resource shortages, environmental pollution, and climate change compound to create monumental threats to the urban environment. Urban living conditions, quality of life, and residents' health are imperiled by a rising frequency of extreme weather events. Global warming is now a major contributor to mortality, causing an estimated 4.5 million deaths annually.

Climate change—induced loss of species diversity, soil degradation, land desertification, threats to fresh water resources, energy scarcity, rapidly depleting forest resources, deteriorated marine ecosystems, chemical contamination, and waste management issues are further pressing global concerns. Due to global warming, "more people in the world will be more vulnerable to natural disasters and other climate change factors, 250 million will have to deal with the consequences of sea-level rise, 30 million will encounter extreme weather condition and floods, 5 million will be affected by desertification".[2]

Second, cities are both victims of and contributors to global warming due to their extensive resource and energy demands coupled with significant greenhouse gas emissions they produce. Urban carbon emission accounts for three-fourths of the world's total carbon emission. In 2010, energy consumption in China's cities accounted for 80% of the nation's total, and carbon emission took up 90% of the nation's total. It is projected that, by 2020, with its urbanization level reaching 56%, China's cities will see over 11 billion square meters of new civil buildings in need of heating, and an additional consumption of 250 million tons of standard coal and 630 billion kWh electricity as compared to 2004. This increase alone will lead to a substantial increase in the nation's emission of greenhouse gases.

Third, it is of decisive importance and significance in combating climate change to adjust urban spatial distribution, optimize urban economic structure, and change urban development models, lifestyles and consumption patterns to reduce greenhouse gas emission. This is the main undertaker and the enormously promising operating platform in achieving multiple emission reduction target specified by the United Nations Framework Convention on Climate Change, the Kyoto Protocol, and China's Greenhouse Gas Emission Reduction Targets.

Fourth, urban green transformation presents significant opportunities for development. Industrialization and urbanization are common and indispensable elements of human social development. Mankind should not give up industrialization and urbanization just because of negative side including environmental pollution and ecological destruction. Cities will have enormous development opportunities in the course of combating climate change. For instance, Japan's urbanization brought about more than 60% increase of the nation's GDP from emission-reduction related industries alone.

In tackling urban environmental issues within the context of climate change, future cities adopt distinctive development models compared to their current ones. It is crucial for cities to embrace green transformations.

In the process of green transformation, urban authorities should take population, resources, environment, and development into consideration. The goals should be to shape cities into efficient and cost-effective production space, comfortable living space, visually appealing eco-friendly space, and nurturing environments of happiness and harmony for humanity. In China, the target of green transformation, and the goal of ecological civilization is to build Resource-Efficient, Environment-Friendly, and Climate-Resilient city (hereafter referred to as *REEFCR city*).[3]

Building up REEFCR city is a practical model to deploy the green urbanization strategy. It essentially aims to change urban development model, and to achieve green development, recycling development, and low-carbon development. Developing REEFCR city makes a more specific and clear objectives of sustainable urban development and ecological civilization, which is possible for the public and government officials to understand and support. Building up REEFCR city provides a foothold for green transformation of cities in China and serves as a crucial platform for sustainable urban environment and ecological civilization. It is the underlying solution to tackle key challenges such as economic growth, environmental pollution, and global warming within China's urbanization process.

REEFCR city prioritize resource efficient and environment-friendly practices, while also highlighting climate security and low-carbon development. As global warming is both an environmental and energy-related issue, the solution lies in energy-saving and emission reduction tactics. However, climate change requires different strategies than those needed for environmental and energy dilemmas.

Despite the fact that certain countries could directly benefit from tackling domestic environmental pollution, reducing greenhouse gas emissions provides a global benefit at the cost of the country itself, leading to both market and government failures. Cities as a whole, have a huge impact on climate security, although one specific city may have little impact, positively or negatively, on climate security. Cities aiming to contribute to climate mitigation and adaptation must reach a balance between their economic development, life quality, and efforts to curb climate change. Hence, investigating strategies to balance mitigation and development is crucial for cities.

In addition, climate-resilient endeavors also reflect a city's proactive attitude to climate change and its international image of maintaining ecological security. Such cities are most likely to win international respect and achieve collaboration.

Since the mid-twentieth century, many countries in the world have explored the theory and practice of REEFCR city. With an increasing understanding of scientific concept of development, many cities in China have made fruitful progresses in exploring REEFCR city. All of these experiences and explorations, international or domestic, have laid solid theoretical foundation for and accumulated valuable experience in REEFCR city construction and will provide great reference and evidence for the green transformation of urban China.

Priorities and Strategies for REEFCR City Construction:

1. REEFCR City Indicator System

The purpose of an indicator system for the REEFCR city is to monitor, evaluate, and assess urban environment and eco-civilization. The indicator system should not only take the indicators of eco-city, moderately prosperous society, and ecological civilization in account, but also fully include national binding targets such as the ecological red line, energy-saving, and emission reduction that includes the reduction of greenhouse gas emissions, and air quality standards, etc. In order to ensure the accuracy, credibility and instructional role of the evaluation results, the design of the indicator system should be based on well-designed weights assigned to different indicators, the indicator system to reflect differences in resource endowment, carrying capacity, economic development, and major functions among different types of cities. The REEFCR city indicator system should guide the REEFCR city requirements through government decision-making to adjust urban development model.

2. REEFCR City Production Model and Industrial Structure

It is at the core of REEFCR city development to change economic development model and strategically adjust economic structure. International experiences have demonstrated that environmental protection does not necessarily slow down economic development, and rapid economic growth does not have to be achieved at the expense of environmental degradation. The most effective energy saving and emission reduction is structural, i.e. a strategic adjustment in urban economic structure to shift from its high dependence on heavy chemical industry to modernized service industry, and to promote regional economic growth that decouples from intensive energy consumption or high pollution.[4]

To establish the production model of REEFCR city is to implement the REEFCR requirements in all aspects and throughout stages of production activities, detailed as the following:

- To upgrade, renovate, and control traditional industries characterized with high energy consumption and high pollution.
- To phase out backward production models and workmanship.
- To encourage enterprises to use more advanced equipment and technologies to minimize energy consumption and pollution.
- To make strict emission standards and control pollutant emission.
- To close down small-scale, but heavily polluting and energy-intensive factories.
- To centralize and strengthen management of traditional industries, optimize industrial structures, subsidize energy-saving, and emission reduction technologies.
- To improve the proportion of tertiary industries.
- To improve the treating capacity and efficiency of regional environmental protection industries.[5]
- To strongly promote circular economy in cities.

The process of building REEFCR city may hinder local economic development, and create enormous conflicts and difficulties, particularly in cities where primary and secondary industries dominate, and in resource-based cities, and in cities relying on heavy chemical industry. For these cities, it is therefore very important to study responsibilities taken by their local governments in implementing national climate change strategies, and their corresponding policy and funding support from the central government.

3. REEFCR City Lifestyle

REEFCR city development encompasses change of production models, consumption, and lifestyle. Consumption is the basis of human survival and development, an important aspect of social reproduction, and an important foundation for market economy. Consumption determines social production and the change in consumption patterns, and leads the change in social production models. On one hand, optimizing citizen's consumption structures, continuously improving their living standards and enjoying enhanced public services are one of key objectives of a moderately prosperous society; on the other hand, unrestrained consumption and extravagant lifestyle have made the consumption concept and lifestyle of urban residents in China deviate from sustainability, resulting in a big conflict between economic development and energy supply, severely degraded urban environment and decreasing life quality in urban areas in China. Therefore, there is a strong need for increasing the public awareness of the serious consequence and urgency of greenhouse effects and climate crisis. Urban residents need to be encouraged to take their conscious actions in every aspect in their daily life to promote low-carbon lifestyle in urban areas, which will help to turn the concept of rational consumption, green consumption and low-carbon consumption into individual voluntary actions. Eventually, firms and families in cities are mobilized to construct the REEFCR city, i.e. resource-efficient, environment-friendly, and climate-resilient cites.

4. Balanced Economic and Ecological Benefits

A new mindset that protecting ecological environment is to protect productivity and improving ecological environment is to improve productivity must be firmly developed. This means that the old paradigm that looks for "silver and gold mountains" rather than "clean water and green mountains" needs to be shifted to a new paradigm that "silver and gold mountains" and "clean water and green mountains" are both needed. The new paradigm can be further shifted to hold that "clean water and green mountains" can be turned into "silver and gold mountains", which essentially implies a virtue cycle between economic and ecological benefits. The above paradigm shifts not only show that protecting environment helps to improve the soft power of cities, but also indicate that ecological restoration, supply of products and services from ecosystems provide new engines for economic development in urban areas including urban recreational industry, environmental protection industry, low-carbon industry, and new energy industry.[6]

5. REEFCR City Development Through Ecological Economy

The integration of economic development and environmental protection is ecological economy, which encompasses a series of environmental-economic tools for promoting cities' ecological civilization including green taxes, green capital, green insurance, ecological compensation, emission trading, carbon trading, etc.

The design of environmental-economic tools is based on the principle of internalizing externalities of environmental protection, providing incentives and constraints for different stakeholders to conserve resources and protect environment. The environmental-economic tools can help to balance resource conservation and environmental protection objectives, and benefits and costs. They consider resource conservation and environmental protection objectives, while allowing enterprises and regions to have profits. They increase the costs of polluting firms but help firms that protecting environment to earn profits. They help to turn the pressure of environmental protection into motivations, constraints into incentives, and passive responses into proactive actions. Therefore, it is necessary to carry out and improve the carbon trading, emission trading, and ecological compensation mechanisms that have been in place, and fully utilize urban environmental trading platforms and build their capacities for them to play effective roles in constructing REEFCR city.

6. Government Responsibilities in Urban Ecological Civilization

It is one of the most important responsibilities and a crucial public service for the government to guarantee basic quality of living environment. The government should renovate its environmental management in the following aspects:

a. To coordinate national restrictive goals such as energy-saving, emission reduction, and greenhouse gas emission reduction to create a forcing mechanism for adjustment of economic development and economic structures and for a combined momentum of energy conservation, environmental protection, and low carbon.

b. To integrate the building of REEFCR city into the comprehensive city development strategy as important performance evaluation indicators of and proofs for rewarding and punishing government officials at all levels. To this end, a leading institute for ecological civilization of REEFCR cities needs to be established to lead and coordinate urban eco-civilization construction, and improve implementation capacities in REEFCR cities such as tightening environmental law enforcement to substantially change the current situation of high compliance cost but low violation cost.
c. To strengthen environmental impact assessment (EIA) and publicize the EIA results to the general public. Most importantly, before introducing and implementing major projects, the EIA and social risk evaluation systems must be established to safeguard citizens' environmental rights and interests and prevent environmental emergencies from the source.
d. To launch systematic mitigation and rehabilitation projects in urban areas where the health of urban citizens and the eco-environment are threatened.
e. To establish and improve mechanism and contingency plans against disasters in the cities under the context of climate change.

7. REEFCR Eco-Civilization Through Urban–Rural Integration

The comprehensive governance of urban–rural environment is an important component and historic mission in urban–rural integrated reform. Rural environmental governance and protection is not only related to rural development, but also directly related to urban development in specific and the overall development of the whole society.

The externalities and spillover effects of environment protection implies that environmental protection and sustainable development can only be achieved through urban–rural integration. The urban–rural integration should be implemented by setting up eco-friendly villages, eco-friendly townships, and eco-friendly counties as platforms, through which a series of activities will be conducted and goals accomplished, such as integrated plan for urban–rural environmental protection,[7] integrated urban–rural environmental protection structures, full coverage of environmental monitoring facilities through urban and rural areas, establishment of modernized agricultural production system of the resource-efficient, environment-friendly, and climate-resilient standards, development of pollution-free production, and guarantee of food safety.

8. REEFCR City Development Rationales and Principles

Norms that constructing REEFCR cities is rational and a common goal should be developed. It is important to recognize not only that urban pollution is severe and environmental protection is pressing, but also that the environmental protection is complex and challenging. In developed countries such as the United States and the United Kingdom, the work of urban pollution control lasted for 30–50 years at least. China has a much bigger population and is currently at the rapid development stage of industrialization and urbanization. Accumulated urban pollution over a long period of time remains unresolved before new pollution occurs. Therefore, a transformation in the REEFCR cities in China is expected to be a complex and systematic project. It cannot be accomplished within a short period of time due to huge difficulties and challenges. The government and the public should build up a rationale for controlling pollution and coping with climate change tackling, and be prepared for unremitting efforts. Following the principle of government-led, corporate governance, market-driven and public participation, the government, enterprises, and citizens should all take their respective responsibilities. The government is responsible for improving the quality of urban environment through implementation of corporate responsibility for pollution control, advocacy for green and Resource-efficient consumption and living habits and mobilizing people to participate in environmental protection and supervision.

Enterprises need to fulfill their social responsibilities of saving energy, reducing emission, and protecting the environment to internalize external costs of pollution. Urban citizens, as they monitor the government and enterprises' responsibilities for environmental pollution, can also change their consumption and living habits and start from making small changes and participating in the REEFCR campaign.

9. Low-Carbon Economy and Low-Carbon City

Promoting a low-carbon economy and creating low-carbon cities are key aspects of building REEFCR city. A low-carbon economy represents a novel economic class, created as a societal response to climate change, and serves as a future economic model for cities functioning on ecological economies. It is a green development path sought by human society to resolve the conflict between industrial civilization and eco-civilization, and between development and climate change. Low-carbon is becoming the new quality and image of urban competitiveness, and the important demonstration and development trends of modern cities. Low-carbon is also a strong feature of China's new urbanization. China has regarded climate change mitigation as the major strategy for urban economic and social development and has used REEFCR city development as the means to promote the national strategy in coping with climate change. Low-carbon economy and low-carbon cities will not only provide enormous momentum and operational platforms to change urban development model, cultivate low-carbon and green consumption and lifestyle, optimize energy structure and industrial structure, and develop new, low-carbon-based, strategic industries, but will also provide economic, technological, and institutional support for the development of REEFCR city.

Notes

1. Shouhu Du, "Advance Eco-Civilization in Chengdu through REEFCR City Development", *Journal of Chengdu Institute of Public Administration,* Issue 3, 2013.
2. The Fourth Assessment Report of UN's Intergovernmental Panel on Climate Change (IPCC)

3. Shouhu Du, "Advance Eco-Civilization in Chengdu through REEFCR City Development", *Journal of Chengdu Institute of Public Administration,* Issue 3, 2013.
4. Ibid.
5. Keli Liu, "Corner Overtaking: No Better Time than Now—Reviews on the Leaders' Readings for Resource-Efficient and Environment-Friendly (REEF) Society", *Hunan Academy of Social Sciences*, 7th edition, 2009.
6. Shouhu Du, "Advance Eco-Civilization in Chengdu through REEFCR City Development", *Journal of Chengdu Institute of Public Administration,* Issue 3, 2013.
7. Ibid.

Contents

Author and Translator

About the Author

Shouhu Du was born in December 1945 in Qianwei County, Leshan City, Sichuan Province. He graduated from the Mathematics Department of Sichuan Normal University in 1968.

Renowned for his research and academic contributions, he formerly served as the vice director of the Sichuan Academy of Social Sciences. His esteemed roles have also included academic advisor, doctoral supervisor, and director of the Resources and Environment Research Center of the Sichuan Academy of Social Sciences. His expertise is recognized nationally, with his receipt of special allowances from the State Council, and provincial recognition as an academic and technological leader of Sichuan Province. As an active member of the Sichuan Provincial Party Committee and Provincial Government Decision Advisory Committee, he also holds guest professorship positions at the School of Economics and Management at multiple universities, such as Sichuan University, Sichuan Agricultural University, Southwest University of Science and Technology, and Southwest Minzu University. He is the chief expert of the National Social Science Foundation's major project— "Research on Sustainable Development of Urban Ecological Environment and Ecological Civilization Construction in China under Climate Change".

Shouhu Du's primary research interests lie in agricultural economics, regional economics, and environmental economics. He has successfully led numerous national social science fund projects and international collaborative research endeavors. Noteworthy projects include "Research on the Compensation Mechanism for Ecological Environment Construction in Western Regions", "Tracking Survey of 100 Counties (Cities) in China—Investigation of Qu County", and "Research on Consolidating and Enhancing the Effect of Western Development in Ethnic Regions of Sichuan Province". His scholarly work includes the publication of monographs such as "Economic Records of Modern and Contemporary Sichuan Towns", "Environmental Economics", "Road to a Well-Off Society in a Big Agricultural County", and "Research on the Effect of Western Development in Ethnic Areas".

About the Translator

Heng Du was born in December 1975. She received her Bachelor's degree from the Southwest University of Finance and Economics in 1997, followed by a Master's degree from the University of the Philippines Los Baños, in 2002.

Heng Du has been associated with numerous Government and International Nonprofit Organizations. She has extensive experience in community development and poverty alleviation over the years. Her command over English language has made her an excellent translator and interpreter. As part of her portfolio, she has contributed significantly to national, provincial, and enterprise projects and has received accolades, such as the first prize in Philosophy and Social Science Achievement from the Sichuan People's Government.

In the past decade, Heng Du has been actively involved in translating advanced contents relating to climate change, renewable energy, food security, water crisis, AI development, Corporate Social Responsibility, etc. from reputable magazines, such as "Foreign Affairs" and "Futurist". Her translated works have been published in prestigious academic platforms such as "Guangming Daily", "Xinhua Digest", and "Journal of Southwest Minzu University". These translated articles provide the domestic readers with an international perspective and up-to-date information.

List of Figures

List of Tables

List of Columns

Chapter 1
Climate Change: Challenges and Responses

Climate change refers to a long-term global warming trend, flourishing notably from the twentieth century through to the early twenty-first century. *"Global warming means the Earth's surface temperatures have risen by 0.74 °C over the last 100 years. The rate of warming over the last 50 years is almost double that over the last 100 years"*.[1] The study of Berkeley Earth Surface Temperature (BEST) also suggested in 2011 that the Earth's temperature had risen by 0.911 °C since 1950.

Responding to climate change entails addressing anthropogenic global warming rather than naturally occurring variabilities, i.e., as stated in the United Nations Framework Convention on Climate Change, "a change of climate that is attributed directly or indirectly to human activity that alters the composition of the global atmosphere and that is in addition to natural climate variability observed over comparable time periods."

1.1 Climate Change: Scientific Perspectives

Although climate change has undergone a lengthy scientific cognitive process, controversy and uncertainty remain. The focus of controversy is on: is this warming a cyclical fluctuation or a genuine warming trend? Whether global warming is a natural cause or mainly anthropogenic global warming (AGW), that is, whether the contribution of human activities is changing the climate. Whether the policies adopted by the country regarding climate change will have an impact on the country's economy and society?

S. Du and H. Du, *The Green Transformation of Urban Areas in China Under Global Warming*, https://doi.org/10.1007/978-981-95-1005-4_1

1.1.1 *The Five Stages of Scientific Cognition on Climate Change*

First Stage: During the 1970s, the scientific community grappled with perceived catastrophic climate alterations. However, the global warming we recognize today was not their concern; they feared a global cooling trend that might herald a new ice age. This belief was rooted in temperature patterns observed in the mid-twentieth century, featuring a sharp increase between the World Wars followed by a subsequent drop over the next 30-year-period. In examining the long-term context, our climate has always exhibited changes. The Earth has experienced substantial temperature fluctuations since emerging from the last Ice Age 20,000 years ago. The warmest interval occurred over 8000 years ago, after which the climate cooled before transitioning into the so-called "Roman Warm Period" during the zenith of the Roman Empire. This gave way to the "Little Ice Age" approximately 1300 years ago, which lasted until two centuries ago, leading us into the "Modern Warm Period". However, this trend is punctuated by intermittent periods of cooling, such as the slight cooling observed from 1940 to 1975.[2] The global climate began warm once again in the late 1970s.

In 1987, acting on behalf of the United Nations, the Norwegian Prime Minister, Mrs. Brent, oversaw the release of "Our Common Future from One Earth to One World", a report by the World Commission on Environment and Development. The document called attention to the intertwined nature of the environmental, energy, and development crises, emphasizing the need to change conventional development models to meet contemporary and future human needs while preserving Earth's resources and energy. This report served as a primary catalyst for the United Nations' global initiatives to address climate change since the 1990s.[3]

Second Stage: began in 1988, with Dr. Roger Revere, an American marine scientist in the 1950s, proposing a continuous upward trend in the content of carbon dioxide in the Earth's atmosphere. Albert Gore Jr., who previously worked under Roger Revere, and later served as a US senator, reinforced this view during a hearing in Washington D.C. His notion quickly achieved mainstream consensus, suggesting that the escalating levels of carbon dioxide were a significant factor contributing to global warming. One of the key developments was the inception of the Intergovernmental Panel on Climate Change (IPCC) by the United Nations in 1988. The body assembled around 1500 experts to compile a detailed scientific report. Their collective effort materialized in the form of the World Conference on Environment and Development, commonly named as the "Earth Summit", held in Rio de Janeiro. The conference saw the approval of several documents and conventions, including the United Nations Framework Convention on Climate Change. This framework laid the groundwork for international cooperation on tackling climate change and became an environmental constitution of international relevance. The United Nations Framework Convention on Climate Change came into effect on March 1, 1994. It established that the Conference of the Parties would convene annually starting from 1995 to evaluate the progress in managing climate change. In the second report assembled in 1996, a scientist from America unequivocally suggested the finding of substantial evidence drawing a link between global warming and escalating carbon dioxide emissions.

Third Stage: marked by the official introduction of the Kyoto Protocol. In December 1997, the Third Conference of the Parties was held in Tokyo, Japan, and the Kyoto Protocol was adopted. It is stipulated that developed countries should reduce greenhouse gas emissions by an average of 5.2% based on 1990 amount from 2008 to 2012, and developing countries should assume emission reduction obligations starting from 2012. The Kyoto Protocol also establishes three "flexible compliance" mechanisms, creating a combination of addressing climate change issues and developing low-carbon economies, combining the common interests of human society with the special interests of various countries, and utilizing market mechanisms and financial means to respond to climate change.

However, there are still significant differences in understanding global climate change at this stage. The United States Senate still refused to accept the Kyoto Protocol until 1997, due to a large amount of evidence at that time indicating that global temperatures had been higher than at the end of the twentieth century. The new temperature distribution map drawn by American physicist Michael Mann shows that over the past 1000 years, temperature changes have been almost flat, and suddenly rose to record levels at the end. Michael Mann's "hockey stick" climate curve provides evidence for the IPCC, demonstrating the relationship between rising carbon dioxide concentrations and climate change.

Fourth Stage: marked in 2004 by Russia reaching a consensus with the European Union, which led to the ratification of the Kyoto Protocol. Subsequently, the European Union announced various tactics to combat climate change, including unprecedented subsidies for wind turbine construction and pledges to reduce carbon dioxide emissions by 60% by 2050. And these measures are based on the conclusion that global temperatures are continuously rising under the concentration of carbon dioxide, and if humans do not take measures, it will be a catastrophe.

Fifth Stage: people witnessed a significant uptick in the belief that temperature increases over the past 50 years were predominantly attributable to human activities. The likelihood of this increased from 66% in 2001 to over 90% in 2007. The fourth assessment report provided by the Intergovernmental Panel on Climate Change (IPCC) in November 2007 concluded that "global warming is an undeniable fact and is mainly caused by human activities, rather than natural causes, as some people claimed." This further confirms the correlation between human activities and global warming. "Climate change poses a serious threat to the sustainable development of ecosystems and human society, and adapting and mitigating climate change is urgent."

1.1.2 *Debate on the Causes and Responses of Climate Change*

A significant turning point in the understanding of climate change came in 1896 when a Swedish Chemist Nobel Laureate, Svante Arrhenius, postulated the hypothesis of climate change. He posited that "the burning of fossil fuels will increase the concentration of carbon dioxide in the atmosphere, contributing to global warming". From the first release of the IPCC's climate change report in 1990 till the fourth assessment report in 2007, ongoing evidences were constantly emerging to prove that climate change is not only a reality but is intrinsically associated with the impacts of human activities.

1.1.2.1 IPCC's Primary Viewpoints on Climate Change

1. Regarding the causes of climate change: nearly 90% of the global warming we are experiencing today is instigated by human activities. Moreover, approximately 99% of global greenhouse gas emissions are attributed to actions conducted by humans.
2. Prediction of trends and consequences of global warming: If carbon dioxide levels double—increasing from the current level of 280 ppm to 560 ppm—the global temperature is expected to rise by approximately 3 degrees Celsius.[4] Such a rise could be catastrophic, leading to issues such as the rise of sea levels, scarcity of food and water, species extinction, spread of infectious diseases from south to north, conflicts, and wars.
3. The threshold for global warming: The IPCC asserts that the rise in global temperatures should be kept under 2 degrees Celsius and the corresponding greenhouse gas concentrations should not surpass 450 ppm. Greenhouse gases encompass carbon dioxide, methane, nitrous oxide, among others. As different greenhouse gases have varying warming potentials, a conversion to carbon dioxide equivalent, CO_2-e, is necessary. Thus, a reference to 450 ppm covers not just carbon dioxide but also concentrations of CO_2-e, implying that the carbon dioxide concentration must be lower.[5]
4. For an effective response to climate change and ultimately saving Earth, it is imperative that there is a significant reduction in greenhouse gas emissions.

1.1.2.2 Queries Surrounding the Trends and Causation of Climate Change

1. Before the acceleration of human activities, there were warm and ice periods. These periods can be attributed to the repetitive occurrence of warmer times.
2. The upsurge in carbon dioxide concentration does not always match with an increase in atmospheric warming. For instance, following 1940, despite a rapid

increase in carbon dioxide emissions, global temperatures began decreasing from 1940 and continued until 1975.

3. Several studies, including those by NASA, have put forth that natural elements play a significant role in global warming. NASA has suggested that anomalies in solar activity can result in global warming, hypothesizing that roughly half of the global average temperature rise since 1980 can be ascribed to these anomalies. They state that Earth's magnetic field—if altered—could contribute to climate change. Consequently, the global warming experienced over the last 20–30 years can be linked to reduced volcanic activity, which, in turn, increases the quantity of solar radiation reaching Earth's surface.
4. The principal element of greenhouse gases is water vapor, not carbon dioxide. Although water vapor enhances the insulating effect of carbon dioxide, it does not deny the warming effect of carbon dioxide itself.
5. The recent unusually cold winters in the northern hemisphere seem contradictory to the concept of global warming.
6. Some argue the push towards a "low carbon" economy is a ploy to slow the progress of developing nations while safeguarding the industry and employment interests of already developed nations.
7. The question of whether carbon dioxide is the cause of global warming is that the interaction between the comprehensive impact factors of global warming and the laws of climate change have not been expressed, and there is a lack of specific data support, making it difficult to determine whether there is a lag or temporary inversion in the process of climate change.
8. The field of climate change research displays a propensity for data selection bias. An exemplar of this is evident in the IPCC report of 1990. The report acknowledges critical periods of climate change, such as the Middle Ages Warm Period and the Little Ice Age, between 1550 and 1750. However, two articles published by Mann in 1998 and 1999 make no mention of these periods and disregard the climate shifts that occurred before the large-scale emission of carbon dioxide. Further, the IPCC 2001 annual report, of which Mann was the key author, was heavily reliant on Mann's findings. Al Gore also drew conclusions in his report on global warming from Mann's research.
9. Limitations imposed by human technological capabilities hinder an accurate evaluation of long-term climate change. Firstly, despite the Earth boasting a history of billions of years, humans have quantitatively measured key climate parameters such as temperature only in the last century. Secondly, the future climate change predictions based on numerical climate models are still primitive, due to our incomplete understanding of the physical laws and processes of climate change. No existing climate model can accurately predict climate changes for more than a few months in advance. Hence, predictions derived from numerical models for time spans of several years, or even decades, are not entirely reliable and serve merely as reference points.

1.1.2.3 Viewpoints Supporting the Conclusion of Global Warming

1. Global warming is a consequence of an amalgamation of numerous influential factors. As an illustration, during the geological era, the movement of crustal plates altered regional disparities in the Earth's absorption of sunlight and heat, inducing global warming. Another factor to consider is climate changes brought on by alterations in the Earth's rotational orbit. Different causative phenomena may dominate each warming phase, but the human contribution to climate change is undeniable.
2. The delineated physical mechanism of greenhouse gases, which permits the entry of solar shortwave visible light while impeding the escape of longwave radiation from surface heat, suggests a positive correlation between the greenhouse effect and atmospheric carbon dioxide concentration. In the aftermath of the Industrial Revolution, the rapid consumption of fossil fuels led to the release of natural carbon sequestration, which had been accumulated over billions of years. Concurrently, human activities inflicted widespread damage on surface ecosystems that absorb carbon dioxide, weakening normal carbon dioxide absorption and becoming a major contributor to global warming.
3. Although the climate has been warming since the last glacial period, promoting the carbon sink capacity of surface vegetation and marine organisms to absorb carbon dioxide, the carbon sink capacity of surface lags behind the carbon emissions of the "calcium carbonate pump" of volcanoes and oceans, resulting in the rising temperature and the peak of the "Medieval Warm Period". At this time, due to the warm climate, lush land forests, vast area and strong carbon sink capacity, the natural carbon source and carbon sink tend to balance in quantity, but due to the influence of external forces (changes in the earth's orbit), the balance reverses, and the climate reverses into the Little Ice Age (1550–1750). The year 1750 was the beginning of the industrial revolution represented by the steam engine. The time of burning a large amount of mineral energy and emitting carbon dioxide coincided with the end of the Little Ice Age.
4. Although there are issues with the interests of the environmental protection industry, and developed countries are technologically advanced, low-carbon technology has different levels and is also a development opportunity. It is obviously insufficient to infer whether the global warming is occurring from the perspective of industrial interests.
5. Recent cold weather events do not disprove the global warming phenomenon because of its global nature, which precludes generalizations derived from localized temperature variations.

1.1.3 Interdisciplinary Development and Integration by Climate Change

Climate change not only promotes the overall trend of global response to climate change and the gradual formation of major alliances, but also promotes the widespread participation of disciplines other than meteorology, such as physics, chemistry, economics, and law, as well as unprecedented alliances among various disciplines. Climate change has also given rise to new sub disciplines.

1. Climate Philosophy. With the intensification of the climate crisis, various conflicts of interest arising from climate issues have led to a comprehensive political, economic, and cultural game among countries. Addressing climate change necessitates the formulation of a universally acknowledged philosophical framework by governments and societies worldwide.

   Scholars like Shi Jun posit that climate philosophy is an expansion and advancement of traditional environmental philosophy. It should not only guide the resolution of climate issues, but it should also employ such crises in structuring comprehensive global and social systems to ensure the preservation of new connections. Dai Jianping believes that the basic concepts and methods of climate philosophy, the proposal and testing of climate science hypotheses, and the relationship between climate and politics have become urgent issues that philosophers need to consider. Arthur Peterson from the Netherlands deems climate philosophy a field interweaved within science and philosophy, characterized by issues surrounding the essence of climate models, climate ethics, and climate disputes. It primarily stresses the constraints of climate science, using climate science as a foundation to comprehend and predict the potential limits of climate. The specificity of climate philosophy resides in the examination of how climate science acquires reliability and the types of uncertainty that permeate it. Its core issues include the just distribution of carbon emission spaces and the establishment of climate justice within the contemporary population and between contemporary and future cohorts. The philosophical analysis of climate models focuses on their essence, testing, and their experiential relationship.

   The emergence of climate philosophy internationally traces back to the early twenty-first century, whereas in China, climate philosophy research commenced post-2010. It concentrated on key areas such as climate ethics, climate justice, and carbon equity. The employed research methods are mainly interdisciplinary combining theoretical constructs and practical elements. To unravel the core of its complex issues, an in-depth analysis adopting multiple lenses, such as science and technology, politics, economics, and philosophy, is essential.

   In 2001, the Rock Institute of Ethics was founded at Pennsylvania State University in the United States: a pioneering international institute devoted to climate change ethics and policy studies. Later, in 2004, the Ethical Dimension of Climate Change White Paper was collaboratively published by the Rock Institute of Ethics and 16 European and American climate policy research institutions.

In China, the Institute of Climate Change and Public Policy was initiated in 2010, at the Information Engineering University in Nanjing. The institution actively embarks on climate philosophy research, and established the Climate Ethics Research, the Meteorological Philosophy Research, and the Climate Policy Research.

2. Climate Economics. This field emerged in the early 1990s and is primarily concerned with the effects of climate on the economy, the economic aspects of climate change, and the role of economics in comprehending and addressing climate issues. Notable individuals in this field include Nicholas Stern and Nordhaus, with key works comprising the Stern Review, Equilibrium Issues, and Choice and Balance of Global Warming Policies.
3. Climate Politics. This discipline arose in the early twenty-first century. It mainly studies international politics, especially geopolitics, the relationship between global governance and climate change, climate issues and national security, community governance, and justice in political philosophy. Anthony Giddens, David Hickman, and Joseph Smith are renowned contributors in this respect, with notable works including "Politics of Climate Change" and "Climate Change and National Security".[6]
4. Climate Sociology. It emerged in the early twenty-first century. Examining the interactive relationship between climate and society from a sociological perspective, viewpoint, and method, such as the challenges posed by climate change to sociology, and the impact of social systems on climate change. Representative figures include Ulch Beck, James Garvey, and representative works include "Changing for Climate: How to Create a Green Modernity" and "Climate Change Ethics".

1.2 Climate Change: Environmental Perspectives

1.2.1 Global Warming: A Grave Threat to Human Existence

Climate change is an environmental issue, first and foremost because its negative impacts, like other environmental issues, have seriously endangered the living environment, quality of life, and health of humanity.

A primary concern is the escalating trend of global warming which is increasingly posing as a lethal human threat, with climate change and fossil fuel consumption accounting for approximately 4.5 million deaths annually and a projected estimate of nearly 6 million mortalities post-2030. Absence of strategic measures could result in 100 million climate-change related global deaths by 2030. Hence, addressing climate change not only has intrinsic environmental merit but also substantial economic implications today. Strategically mitigating and adapting to climate change could substantially reduce the escalating trend of disease and death rates induced by climate change.

Climate change, secondly, has led to a significant imbalance in key global systems, causing major alterations in the Earth's atmospheric system (atmosphere) and ecosystem (biosphere). This has resulted in species extinction, soil degradation, land desertification, freshwater resource crisis, energy scarcity, decline in forest resources, marine environment degradation, chemical pollution, and waste management challenges.[7]

Climate change inflicts considerable changes in weather patterns, causing notable changes in the frequency, intensity, seasonality, duration, location, and scope of extreme weather events, compared to previously recorded data and baseline knowledge. Over the past two decades, there has been a significant shift in the frequency and intensity of global extreme weather and climatic events. The recurrent incidence of floods, droughts, and snow disasters, precipitated by climatic irregularities, has induced geological catastrophe such as debris flows, hastening the process of land desertification. Affected by climate change, more people in the world will be more susceptible to natural disasters and other climate change factors. 250 million people will have to cope with the consequences of rising sea levels, 30 million people will suffer from extreme weather and floods, and 5 million people will be affected by desertification. The World Wildlife Fund (WWF) predicts that by 2050, global sea levels will rise by 50 cm, flooding coastal cities and island countries and regions, and affecting 136 coastal cities and 28.21 trillion dollars in property worldwide. "Global warming will make cities like Shanghai face more frequent and severe hazards related to climate change."[8] Accordingly, Shanghai, among other cities, is enlisted as endangered.

In 2012, the global extreme climate normalized, and glaciers in the Arctic continued to melt at unprecedented levels. The volume of glaciers decreased by 18%, and 97% of Greenland's ice surface experienced varying degrees of melting. The melting of glaciers has exacerbated global warming, causing many cities and regions to suffer from sun exposure, drought, and floods, a cold wave that has resulted in over 800 deaths in Europe; the eastern United States has encountered a strong storm—Hurricane Sandy, which has affected a wide area with a diameter of 1600 square kilometers, bringing heavy rainfall to the area, leading to blackout, snowfall, 125 deaths, and other systemic damages. In 2012, the highest temperatures in five countries have broken historical records, becoming the 8th warmest year in the world since meteorological records began in 1880. 69,000 regions have broken records for high temperatures, and the level of flood disasters far exceeds the 2011 record. Parts of Africa, Russia, Australia, and China have suffered heavy losses from floods.

Climate change-induced natural disasters present an increasing threat to economic stability. Comparatively, the economic threat from natural disasters between 2000 and 2006 is fourfold that of the 1970s. Concurrently, we observe a sevenfold increase in annual losses and a quadrupling of the number of affected people. Besides, climate change yields severe economic implications. The struggle against drought and water shortage— culminating in crop death—may cause the US GDP to shrink by over two percentage points. The hardest-hit might be third-world countries as they grapple with mitigating diseases and droughts with their limited resources. Predictions suggest that over 90% of climate-change-induced deaths will occur in these countries. Among all affected groups, the poorest subsets in low and middle-income countries face the most severe impact. Their losses have reached an extreme level. Climate change escalates the toxicity of chemicals, augmenting the susceptibility of air and water to pollution. Furthermore, global warming poses a severe threat to the biodiversity of the world's species, translating into significant setbacks for future global development.

1.2.2 Climate Change and Its Typical Externality

Climate change and its response, like other environmental issues, are also plagued by "externality" and "market failure". "We emit a large amount of carbon dioxide, exposing humans and ecosystems to immense danger. We can harm others at will without being responsible for our own actions, as the victims are far away from us in both time and space."[9] Climate change has the typical externality characteristics of environmental problems. How to internalize the cost of externalization is one of the challenges and goals that need to be addressed in responding to climate change.

Modern economic theory believes that perfect competition can allow a market economy to utilize self-regulation to achieve optimal resource allocation. However, there are also some areas in the market economy where market mechanisms cannot fully play their role, such as the "failure" of market allocation resources in areas such as environment and biodiversity. Due to the spillover nature of addressing climate change, like other environmental governance achievements, its consumption is not exclusive, making it difficult for its investment entities to charge consumers based on consumption volume. Personal returns deviate from social returns, thus losing the motivation to address climate change and leading to an unprecedented misallocation of capital in the field of climate change.

Climate governance serves as a public good, providing fundamental global environmental quality. Modern economics believe that the combination of self-interested "economic individuals" and public goods will inevitably result in a "free-rider" phenomenon, without ethical constraints. Due to the fact that the achievements of climate governance, like other environmental governance achievements, climate governance have blurred physical boundaries and are difficult to observe and measure. In addition, for a country, the cost of responding to climate change is borne by the country itself, while the benefits are shared by the whole world, and the benefits of controlling other environmental pollution can be directly reflected in the country. That is the reason why the common choice is "free riding", countries are not willing to pay marginal cost to improve the climate for everyone to benefit from, but only wants to wait for others to act and enjoy the benefits.

1.2.3 Government Failure in Addressing Climate Change

Climate change differs from other environmental issues due to its broad impacts and the complex nature of its resolution. Firstly, climate change is the paramount environmental issue. As global warming is indiscriminate, no country or individual is immune from its effects, making its reach and depth unparalleled by any other environmental problem. Thus, Nicholas Stern, the former chief economist of the World Bank, characterizes the effort to counteract climate change as the most significant "market failure" problem in history. Secondly, "government failure" is also a hindrance to addressing climate change. As a transnational environmental issue, climate change cannot be resolved within a single country. A country's sovereignty limits the control and management of climate change by international authorities. This challenge can only be addressed through international negotiations to establish appropriate regulations and cooperation treaties. Additionally, adaptation, which encompasses the ability to mitigate and respond to climate change, sets it apart from other environmental governance measures. The precedent of carbon dioxide existence over the past 200 years has led to the inevitable trend of rising global surface temperatures in the coming decades, irrespective of the extent or success of emission reduction initiatives.[10] Therefore, beyond "mitigation" efforts aimed at reducing greenhouse gas emissions and augmenting carbon sinks, "adaptation" —the implementation of both engineering and non-engineering measures to address climate risks and fortify our response to extreme climate events– presents another crucial facet of tackling climate change. Fourthly, due to the difficulty in defining the identities, rights, and obligations of the perpetrators and victims, the regional differences in the degree of victimization, as well as the contradictions and conflicts between the pursuit of national interests and global climate governance goals, make it more difficult to achieve internalization of external costs and nationalization of global costs in addressing climate change. In addition, compared to general environmental issues, the harm of climate change and the benefits of governance achievements show a more significant lag, so there is a general lack of urgency in climate governance from the government to citizens. "Since the harm brought about by global warming is not specific, direct, and visible in people's daily lives, no matter how terrifying it may be, most people still stand idly by and do nothing specific. However, once the situation becomes concrete and real and forces them to take substantive action, it will be too late."[11]

The above characteristics determine the difficulty and complexity of addressing climate change.

1.2.4 Is Carbon Dioxide a Pollutant?

A related issue is whether carbon dioxide is a pollutant, which is to some extent synonymous with the question of whether climate change has only a negative impact on human society and no positive impact. In general, sulfur dioxide as well as the emitted heavy metals and atmospheric dust, can cause direct harm to the human body, carbon dioxide is not like above substances. On the contrary, carbon dioxide is a necessary gas for the Earth. Without carbon dioxide, there would be no photosynthesis, and without photosynthesis, there would be no existence of the Earth.[12] Without the greenhouse effect formed by carbon dioxide, the temperature of the Earth will remain below -18°C year-round. It is precisely because of the greenhouse effect that the Earth's temperature is maintained above 15°C, creating an environment for the existence of various organisms. Carbon dioxide is an essential substance for plant growth. When the carbon dioxide is doubled, the crop yield can increase by 40%~130%. At the same time, when the carbon dioxide concentration is increased, the gas exchange required by plants is reduced, the evaporation of water is reduced, and the ability of crops to resist drought, ozone and other pollutants is increased. This is of special significance for agricultural production under the increasing drought and pollution.[13]

However, exceeding a certain threshold concentration of CO_2 in the atmosphere can precipitate negative effects, such as a rise in global temperatures, which outweigh its positive impacts, thus deeming it an environmental pollutant. In 2007, the United States Environmental Protection Agency (EPA) decided to include carbon dioxide as a pollutant. In 2011, the Ministry of Environmental Protection of China issued the expanded urban air mass monitoring standard, which also included carbon dioxide and PM2.5 as pollutants for monitoring. It is in this sense that the reduction of environmental pollution and the reduction of carbon dioxide intersect, so in many cases collectively referred to as emission reduction, but there are differences between them.

Indeed, climate change, reduction of greenhouse gas emissions, and environmental protection are frequently conflated in our theoretical frameworks and policies. For example, some scholars directly use the Kuznets curve for analyzing environmental protection to analyze the trend of greenhouse gas emissions reduction, some scholars analyze carbon tax as a type of environmental tax, and so on. But if issues such as how climate change has become an environmental issue, where they intersect, and so on are not clarified, then there will be a logical break. Therefore, studying climate change as an environmental issue is not an unnecessary task.

1.3 Climate Change: Energy Perspectives

Given the intimate link between the underlying causes of climate change and our main strategies to combat it, climate change is often directly perceived as an energy issue.

1.3.1 Anthropogenic Energy Activities as the Main Contributor of Global Warming

The greenhouse effect theory, which originated from Fourier in France and was later refined by Irish scientist Tyndale, believes that global warming is primarily attributable to human's excessive use of carbon based energy sources (coal, oil, natural gas) since industrial revolution, which rapidly moving the "carbon pool" that originally existed underground into the atmosphere, leading to an exponential rise in the concentration of greenhouse gases represented by carbon dioxide in the atmosphere. It is like wrapping a layer of "blanket" on the surface of the Earth, as it can prevent the thermal infrared rays projected onto the Earth from radiating outward into space, thereby accumulating thermal energy on the Earth's surface and causing the Earth's temperature to rise. More and more scientific research results indicate that the direct cause of global warming is the excessive accumulation of greenhouse gases, represented by carbon dioxide, in the atmosphere. Since 1750, human industrialization has led to an increase in global greenhouse gas emissions. From 1970 to 2004, anthropogenic greenhouse gas emissions increased by 70%, with carbon dioxide emissions increasing by 80%. As a result, the current concentration of greenhouse gases in the atmosphere far exceeds the concentration values measured based on ice core records for several thousand years before industrialization. The concentration of carbon dioxide has increased from about 280PPM before the Industrial Revolution to about 389PPM now (Exceeds the total historical record of the past 160,000 years that can be surveyed).

The carbon dioxide emissions from energy activities account for about 90% of the total global carbon dioxide emissions. Due to energy activities being the main source of carbon dioxide emissions for countries around the world, especially developing countries, the most direct and primary way to address climate change is to reduce greenhouse gas emissions by adjusting human behavior and methods of energy use, reducing fossil energy consumption.

The low-carbon economy directly generated by climate change has found a way out for scientifically handling the relationship between economic development and addressing climate change, and has built a bridge for the transformation of industrial civilization based on carbon-based energy into an ecological civilization of "resource efficient, environmentally friendly, and climate resilient". The primary feature of a low-carbon economy is to reduce energy consumption. The overall requirement is to reduce carbon sources and increase carbon sinks. The main path is to save energy, improve energy efficiency, improve energy structure, and replace the current global energy consumption structure dominated by carbon-based energy with clean and renewable energy such as solar energy, wind energy, nuclear energy, and biomass energy.

1.3.2 Energy Conservation as a Crucial Means to Reduce Carbon Emissions

The famous Kaya formula proposed that carbon emissions are driven by population, per capita GDP, energy intensity, carbon intensity and other factors, which are proportional to energy intensity and economic activities, and inversely proportional to energy conversion rate.

Energy intensity and carbon intensity are two indicators that link energy activities with climate change. The direction of energy intensity is to save energy and improve energy efficiency. Carbon intensity, on the other hand, measures the performance of addressing climate change and reducing greenhouse gas emissions. In addition to improving energy efficiency, it also includes improving the energy structure, increasing the proportion of non-carbon-based energy, and other ways to reduce carbon dioxide emissions and increase carbon dioxide absorption. The decline of energy intensity is the main way to reduce greenhouse gas emissions, and is the key to reduce carbon intensity. However, the reduction of carbon intensity is much more difficult than that of energy intensity, and the reduction of carbon intensity is more comprehensive and efficient than that of energy intensity for achieving the goals of energy conservation, environmental protection, carbon reduction and sustainable development.

Energy conservation and emission reduction play a crucial role in reducing carbon emissions and addressing climate change. In fact, the comparison between energy conservation and emission reduction (reducing greenhouse gas emissions) itself reflects this important position and role.

Energy conservation includes technological energy conservation to improve energy efficiency and structural energy conservation caused by industrial restructuring and upgrading, as well as changes in energy structure.[14] Between 1998 and 2008, the UK economy grew by 28%, achieving its longest period of economic growth in 200 years, but greenhouse gas emissions decreased by 8%. The Organization for Economic Cooperation and Development (OECD) analyzed the reasons for sustainable development in the UK and concluded that "although UK environmental policies have played a significant role in improving the UK's natural and urban environment, a crucial shift is due to the transition of the UK's economic model from industry led to advanced service industry led". In fact, the economic structure of the UK in 2008 has evolved into 0.9% in agriculture, 23.49% in industry, and 75.61% in service industry. The case of the UK fully proves that when viewed with the goal of carbon reduction and addressing climate change, the effect of optimizing and upgrading the economic structure is clearly second to none.

Structural energy conservation also includes reducing carbon emissions by transforming the export-oriented economic structure. Due to differences in output and energy efficiency, there are differences in carbon dioxide emissions from the same product produced in different countries. Developed countries may produce one unit of carbon emissions for a particular product, while in developing countries, due to relatively backward production processes and low energy efficiency, it may exceed one unit of carbon emissions. Under the international trade model of "producing in low-income countries and consuming in high-income countries", it is obvious that it will not only lead to more carbon transfer emissions in developing countries, but also lead to an increase in global total carbon emissions.[15]

1.3.3 Optimizing the Energy Structure as Another Crucial Way to Reduce Carbon Emissions

Another important aspect of structural energy conservation is the adjustment and optimization of energy structure. The first step is to develop non-carbon-based energy sources to replace carbon-based energy sources. Another important reason for the decoupling development of the UK is the significant increase in the proportion of renewable energy to energy consumption in the UK's energy structure during this period, with the proportion of renewable energy generation increasing from 1.81% to 5.54%. Among them, wind power generation accounted for only 0.3% of the country's total electricity generation in 2004 and 1.3% in 2006. In order to achieve the goal of addressing climate change and achieve net zero emissions globally by the end of the twenty-first century, the key lies in the establishment of an energy structure dominated by renewable energy. EU countries have proposed a high target of reducing greenhouse gas emissions by 20% to 30% from 1990 in the second emission reduction period (before 2020), based on the fact that the proportion of renewable energy in the EU needs to increase to 20% to 30% during this period.

The low-carbon adjustment of fuel structure, even if the adjustment is relatively small or replaced within fossil fuels, can still have a suppressive effect on carbon emissions.

Optimizing the energy structure also includes reducing the carbon content in the energy composition. From the perspective of reducing carbon emissions, there is also a substitution relationship within fossil fuels. According to the default factor calculation results based on net calorific value provided by the Intergovernmental Panel on Climate Change (IPCC) of the United Nations, coal that produces equivalent calorific value emits 1.32 and 1.73 times more carbon dioxide than oil and natural gas, respectively. If other factors remain unchanged, the proportion of coal in the energy structure will decrease, while the proportion of oil and natural gas will increase, which is clearly beneficial for reducing carbon emissions. If hydropower or nuclear energy replace coal and reduce China's coal consumption by 1%, China's total greenhouse gas emissions will be reduced by 1.14%; if natural gas or oil are used to replace coal, the carbon emissions will be reduced by 0.46% and 0.28% for each 1% reduction in coal consumption.[16] It can be seen that if other factors remain unchanged, the proportion of coal in the energy structure will decrease, while the proportion of oil and natural gas will increase, then carbon dioxide emissions will inevitably decrease.

Reducing the use of mineral energy, especially coal, not only has a positive impact on climate change, but also plays an important role in resource conservation and intensive utilization. This is because mineral energy represented by coal is a composite resource. If fossil fuels such as coal are used only as fuel, it will not only waste a lot of economic value, but also turn the composite resource into environmental pollution.

The role of energy-saving technologies that improve energy utilization efficiency in reducing energy demand growth and reducing carbon dioxide emissions cannot be underestimated. A convincing case is that during 2006—2011 in China, the energy consumption per unit of GDP decreased by 19.1%, resulting in a reduction of nearly 1.5 billion tons of carbon dioxide emissions.

1.3.4 Challenges and Opportunities in China's Energy Development

In its journey of energy development, China faces numerous challenges including the demand for energy security and climate security. These challenges arise not only from the limited domestic energy supply capacity and environmental constraints, but also from the increasing pressure from developed nations to control emissions in China.

China's energy resource structure is mainly composed of non-renewable energy sources such as coal, oil, and natural gas. However, China's per capita remaining recoverable reserves of oil and natural gas are only 7.7 and 7.1% of the world average, and coal is only 58.6% of the world average.

With increasing industrialization and urbanization compounded by the aspiration to improve the people's quality of life, China's fast-evolving energy demand which has grown at an annual average rate of 5.16% since its economic reform and opening up, poses serious challenges. China's energy consumption surge, by 120% during 2006—2010 (compared to the 20% global increase over the same period) is forecasted to continue.

With the continuous increase in demand, China's domestic energy supply capacity has decreased and its external dependence has continued to increase. In 2010, the dependence on foreign oil exceeded 55%, and coal has become a net importer. The main reasons are, on one hand, there is a shortage of energy resources, on the other hand, China's energy use mode is extensive, energy intensity is high, and energy utilization rate is low (Table 1.1).

In 2010, China's GDP accounted for 9.5% of the global total, while the total consumption of disposable energy accounted for 19% of the global total. In 2010, China's GDP was equivalent to Japan's, but its energy consumption was 4.5 times that of Japan; in 2010, China's energy consumption was comparable to that of the United States, but the total GDP was only 40% of that of the United States.

Table 1.1 Illustrates the comparison of energy intensity among major countries in the world from the year 2005

Russia	12.71	Mexico	2.74
China	9.94	USA	2.62
South Africa	7.19	Australia	2.32
Poland	4.32	Germany	1.66
Canada	4.07	Japan	1.65
South Korea	4.07	Italy	1.52
Turkey	3.54	UK	1.48
Brazil	3.49	World Average	3.37

Note The calculations were based on the GDP data released by the World Bank in 2005 and the energy consumption data released by EP in 2006

Source The table is adapted from "Several Issues on Addressing Climate Change", as published in the Yue Jiang Academic Journal, Issue 6, 2010, by Li Chongyin

In addition, as a major export-oriented industrial manufacturing country, China's energy consumption is heavily integrated into the flow of end products overseas, and the transfer of emissions accounts for a large proportion of China's total emissions. The proportion of China's exports to GDP was 32% in 2008, and the energy consumed domestically for the production of exported products accounts for 1/4 of the country's total energy consumption. In 2007, China's main exports to the United States, the European Union, and Japan accounted for 34.6% of domestic carbon emissions, net export carbon emissions account for 29.79% of domestic emissions.

Driven by rapid economic growth, energy structure, and energy utilization methods, China has become the world's largest emitter of greenhouse gases since 2006. Since 1990, more than half of the increase in global carbon dioxide emissions has come from China. During 2006—2010, the proportion of carbon dioxide emissions from energy consumption in China has increased from 12.9 to 23% globally. China has a high carbon intensity, and the level of Shanghai is three times that of cities such as Bangkok, Tokyo, and Sydney. The carbon intensity in high energy consuming industries such as energy, automobiles, steel, transportation, chemicals, and building materials is higher than that of developed countries.

China's per capita carbon emissions are lower than those of developed countries, but the carbon intensity per unit of output value is higher than that of developed countries, indicating that the production sector is a major energy user and carbon dioxide emitter in China, and therefore a key area for emission reduction. In the field of energy conservation in production, we should encourage the introduction of advanced production capacity, accelerate the elimination of outdated production capacity, accelerate the implementation of key energy-saving projects, and actively promote contract energy management. Strictly control the rapid growth of high energy consumption and high emission industries, and implement energy-saving and emission reduction regulations and standards. Deepen reform, improve long-term mechanisms for energy conservation and emission reduction, such as emission trading. To benefit enterprises that improve energy efficiency and reduce emissions through technological innovation, and to lose high energy consumption and high emission enterprises, thus making the social costs of carbon dioxide and greenhouse gas emissions be shared by corporates.

Make strategic adjustment of economic structure the main focus of coordinating energy security and climate resilient. Accelerate the development of modern industrial systems, gradually increase the proportion and level of the service industry, and vigorously develop strategic emerging industries.[17] Adjust the high emission foreign trade structure, change the vicious cycle of "taking away wealth leaving behind poverty, exporting resources leaving behind pollution". Decrease the proportion of transferred carbon emissions to alleviate the pressure on China's carbon emissions. Fully leverage China's abundant renewable energy resources, increase investment in the development and utilization of renewable energy, and establish a sound institutional mechanism conducive to the promotion and application of renewable energy. During 2011—2015, the proportion of renewable energy in China will increase to 11.4%, and during the following five years, it will increase to 15%. On this basis, accelerating the construction of a sustainable energy system with renewable energy as the main body in China can not only ensure the achievement of the greenhouse gas emission reduction goals that China has promised to the world, but also provide guarantees for China's energy and carbon dioxide emissions to reach their peak and absolute emission reduction.

After energy conservation and emission reduction, China has implemented targets to control greenhouse gas emissions. We should further strengthen the guidance and constraint of these two indicators for the sustainable development of China's economy and society. One is to integrate these two indicators, leverage their synergistic effects of energy conservation, environmental protection, and low-carbon, and form a linkage mechanism for adjusting industrial structure, optimizing energy structure, energy conservation and efficiency enhancement, and increasing carbon sinks. The second is to use the goal of controlling greenhouse gases to lead the goal of energy conservation and emission reduction, and make the goal of controlling greenhouse gases a strategic choice for balancing domestic energy conservation and emission reduction with international climate change response.

1.4 Climate Change: International Political Perspectives

1.4.1 The Rising Focus on Global Climate Governance

Climate change has emerged as a critical issue attracting international attention and deliberations. It prominently features in any major international gathering or exchange.

Global climate governance has significantly restructured international politics. Traditional divisions between developed and developing countries have evolved into a more complicated scenario, marked by the emergence of three major climate interest groups. The developed nations are split into two factions: the European Union and the Pacific Rim powers like the United States, Canada, Australia, and Japan on the other side. Within developing nations, interests are diversified further with the oil-related interests of Gulf countries, the environmental demands of island countries, the collective desire of the Group of 77 and the developmental objectives of the four basic countries.

Climate change has become a crucial determinant in the formulation of economic and foreign policy strategies of major global players. It serves as a tool for developed nations such as the European Union to enhance their international political power. It also emerges as an apparatus by developed nations to establish new trade protection barriers and direct trade globalization.

1.4.2 Overcoming "Prisoner's Dilemma" in Global Climate Governance

Climate governance often faces the "Prisoner's Dilemma", characterized by the conflict between individual and collective rationale. The EU aviation carbon tax policy includes political considerations to increase leverage in negotiations to resolve the European debt crisis, enhance the EU's leadership in addressing climate change and environmental protection, as well as economic considerations to expand its advantage in the carbon emissions trading market and overcome the European debt crisis. However, the unilateral imposition of aviation carbon tax by the European Union will greatly increase the cost pressure on airlines. (Based on the current international carbon emission trading market price, for airlines flying in the EU, an additional cost of 380 million euros will be added in 2012 and eventually passed on to consumers.) It not only violates the rules of fair trade, but also violates the principle of "common but differentiated response" to climate change; it may harm the process and order of global response to climate change, have consequences that contradict climate governance, and even lead to the outbreak of trade wars, disrupting the process of economic globalization. The rational choice to get rid of the "prisoner effect" of climate governance should be to seek a cooperative mechanism to achieve collective rationality of global climate governance on the premise of satisfying individual rationality and taking into account the interests of all climate stakeholders. For example, the Clean Development Mechanism (CDM) established to achieve the emission reduction targets of the Kyoto Protocol for major developed countries is a mutually beneficial and win–win example that not only provides financial and technological support to developing countries, enhances their ability to cope with climate change, but also enables developed countries to reduce emission reduction costs and achieve emission reduction targets.

1.4.3 Principles of Global Climate Governance: Common but Differentiated Responsibilities

Addressing climate change is a quintessentially political endeavor. British scholar, Terry Eagleton, conceived of politics as a process of comprehensive organization of social life, encompassing the associated power dynamics.[18] The organizational structure, power distribution, and the interest-driven dynamics underpin climate change as a primarily political issue.

The world has allocated responsibilities and obligations pertaining to climate change amongst nations on the principles of "common but differentiated responsibilities" and fairness and justice. These principles govern the imposition of firm emission reduction tasks by the Kyoto Protocol on major developed countries during the initial reduction stage and the proposed arrangement of emission reduction tasks subsequent to the Kyoto Protocol, as outlined in the Bali Road Map.

The principle of "common but differentiated responsibilities" aims to establish an equitable distribution of climate benefits and responsibilities. Evaluating the distribution of climate benefits and responsibilities across temporal frames, nations, and generations forms a critical part of climate governance. Ethical considerations demand equal rights to climate resource utilization and climate benefits for all, irrespective of socio-economic status or generation. Overconsumption or pollution of resources necessitates the obligation to provide compensatory measures.

Historically, developed countries have appropriated emission space from developing and marginalized countries, facilitating their industrial and modern development endeavors. These countries are now major stakeholders in climate change matters. Developed nations are responsible for seven out of every ten tons of carbon dioxide emitted since the industrial era, with the cumulative historical per capita emissions in the United States exceeding 1100 tons. Despite achieving industrialization, greenhouse gas emissions in developed countries continue to rise, contributing to half of global carbon dioxide emissions with only 15% of the world's population. In 2004, the per capita greenhouse gas emissions of developed countries were four times that of developing countries, with United States' per capita emissions reaching 19 tons. Therefore, developed countries must uphold their accountability for their substantial carbon emissions. Not only does it bear a significant burden of the cost of climate change interventions, but it also provides late-developing countries with opportunities to capitalize on emission space.

However, with the rapidly advancing industrialization and urbanization within developing nations, their proportionate contribution to global emissions has risen notably. In the year 2004, they were responsible for 42% of the world's emissions, in stark contrast to their contribution of approximately 20% in 1990. Forecasts suggest that by 2030, developing countries will be responsible for over half of the globe's total emissions. This trend is the primary motivator for calls from developed countries for developing nations to share in the responsibility of emissions reductions. It also emphasizes an impending climatic risk necessitating that developing countries take measures to combat climate change, even prior to achieving full industrialization and modernization.

Climate security is indeed a universal need but the capacity to address it varies significantly from countries with greater resources to those with fewer. Genuine equity should be grounded in recognizing these differences. In formulating a system for bearing climate responsibility, comprehensive consideration should be given to factors such as a country's developmental stage, its expected responsibilities, and its actual ability to satisfy these obligations.

"All controversies about climate change are essentially a struggle for interests, a struggle for future emissions control."[19] Under the goal of controlling the global temperature increase by 2 °C, the future space for carbon dioxide emissions in the world will become increasingly scarce resources (approximately 800 billion tons of carbon dioxide), and correspondingly, the competition for its allocation will inevitably become more intense. According to the plan of developed countries, 44% of future emission rights belong to them, which will maintain the long-standing 7.5 times gap in per capita emissions between developed and developing countries at a level of 2.7 times. This plan greatly deprives developing countries of their development rights, and according to this plan, China will purchase emission rights from developed countries before 2020. It clearly violates the principle of "common but differentiated responsibilities" and is naturally subject to resistance, which is also the essence of the controversy at the Copenhagen Climate Conference.[20]

1.4.4 The Concept of Global Governance Presents a New Strategy for Addressing Climate Change

Addressing climate change appears to have reached a stalemate under the constraints of the existing political framework, necessitating innovative political insights for exploring new solutions.

The concept of ceding certain aspects of national sovereignty in order to realize global governance of climate change seems to light a pathway towards resolving the climate change quandary. Derived from the phenomenon of sovereignty division and transfer prevalent in processes of global and regional integration, global governance theory suggests an interplay between global governance, including global climate governance, and national sovereignty that is not zero-sum but rather harmonious and complementary.[21] Achieving this goal, however, hinges on stakeholders' willingness to make necessary concessions and sacrifices within acceptable limits, ensuring that the fundamental interests of the nation, economic development, social stability and the improvement of living standards are not compromised. In essence, it proposes transferring a defined aspect of national sovereignty. Notably, the concept of sovereignty transfer does not denote a division or a transfer of a specific portion of national sovereignty. Rather it implies collective ownership and exercise of this particular power by all concerned countries. Within the context of climate governance, this would materialize as a global consensus on climate change issues leading to specific standards and requirements for energy conservation and emission reduction, which would be stringently adhered to by each country. Of course, this step would limit the authority of the respective governments, and noticeably impact the lives and productivity of the people. Christina Figueres, Executive Secretary of the United Nations Framework Convention on Climate Change, commented that the final agreement reached at the end of The Durban Climate Conference in South Africa, 2011, embodied the result of all participating countries surrendering their individual objectives to unite towards the common aim of promoting long-term strategies to combat climate change.

1.4.5 Amplification of China's Impact in Global Climate Governance

China has shown a significant commitment to global climate governance, contributing constructively to the international negotiation process aimed at addressing climate change. With the ascendance of China's international standing and influence, it has extended its aid to small islands nations, to amplify their responsive capabilities towards climate change. Higher degrees of participation from Chinese overseas energy firms are evident in global climate governance; the approach has been characterized by augmentation of environmental protection protocols in developmental zones.

It is crucial to treat climate change as a prevailing strategy for economic and social development. Essentially, it involves leveraging it as a strategic advantage in propelling the transition to a new model of economic development, readjusting the domestic economic structure, inciting a new industrial revolution, accelerating China's undertakings towards energy conservation and emission reduction. These measures seek to establish a resource-efficient and environment-friendly society, bolstering the construction of ecological civilization. This proactive stance will diminish international scrutiny on China's emission reduction commitments, altering China's reactive status in international climate change negotiations, enabling it to gain a more aggressive voice in the rulemaking process of global climate governance. Enhancement of scientific research aid for climate change is deemed indispensable to fortify national leadership capabilities in climate-related negotiations. Such efforts will facilitate the transposition of scientific outcomes favoring national interests into an international political accord, providing theoretical support for China's domestic measures on climate change.

1.5 Climate Change: Developmental Perspectives

1.5.1 Development Principles and Methods Integration to Combat Climate Change

The development-based approach towards climate change is fundamental. The role of development in mitigating climate change is not confined to retarding growth or deteriorating the quality of life. Instead, it suggests tackling climate change adversities through a developmental lens. Adherents of "post-environmentalism", a product evolving during ongoing efforts to mitigate climate change commonly argue against excessive emission-related activities but the impracticality of these measures makes them unsustainable. Development forms the bedrock of sustainable progression, which is regarded as the key to resolving historical and impending challenges.[22] The productive alignment between environmental protection measures including climate change policies and a nation's developmental stage have been substantiated through both national and international instances. A viable environmental protection approach remains unattainable lacking adequate resources and financial strength.

For developed countries, addressing climate change is a postmodern challenge whereas developing nations confront this issue at a stage in their growth trajectory where industrialization, urbanization, and modernization remain unfulfilled objectives. The World Commission on Environment and Development's report—"Our Common Future—From One Earth to One World" highlights that "without addressing the underlying causes of world poverty and international inequality, efforts to combat environmental issues would be rendered futile." The guideline issued by the United Nations evidently upholds this principle in relation to climate change. Several scholars from developed nations have also advocated the promotion of rapid development throughout Africa, Asia, and Latin America as a foundational measure to lessen the impacts of climate change.

1.5.2 The "Double Decoupling" Development Model—A Potential Reality

Addressing climate change, safeguarding the environment and development are not mutually exclusive. The model of "double decoupling" presents a plausible structure and achievable goal. As per the Environmental Kuznets Curve theory, an inverted U-shaped correlation exists. This section investigates the correlation between environmental pollution and per capita income. Regarding climate change, during the ascending phase of the inverted U-shaped curve, a country undergoes economic growth, resulting inevitably in increased carbon dioxide emissions. However, once the country traverses the apex and begins the decreasing phase on the right side of the curve, a possibility opens for a transition to a "double decoupling" scenario, where economic development and reduced carbon dioxide emissions coexist. A survey conducted by the United Nations on energy and climate change in the first decade of the twenty-first century, including China among many countries, indicates that environmental preservation need not decelerate economic development. Moreover, it highlights that swift economic progression need not always entail substantial environmental sacrifice. "Environmental Change and Urban Responsibility" in July 2010, "We have the potential to reduce energy consumption, curtail greenhouse gas emissions, and achieve an overall reduction exceeding 80%, devoid of creating other economic complications or impeding economic development."[23] Given that it is neither feasible nor desirable for developing nations to sacrifice economic growth to facilitate emissions reduction, the ideal strategy lies in charting a course towards low-carbon economic development amidst the conundrum of economic growth and emissions reduction.

1.5.3 Technology as a Decisive Factor in Climate Change Mitigation

Science and technology are the decisive factors in addressing climate change, and their role may exceed the sum of all other factors.[24] The role of technology in the development and utilization of new energy is evident. At a time when the world is facing both the depletion of fossil fuels and the challenge of climate change, humans have discovered that the energy projected by the sun on Earth every second is equivalent to 50 billion tons of standard coal, and the average solar power received by the Earth is 1367 watts per square meter. In China, if 2% of the Gobi and desert areas are utilized, or if solar power generation devices are installed in 20% of urban buildings, it can generate 2.9 trillion kilowatt hours of electricity annually, which can meet one-third of the current electricity demand in the country. However, science and technology are the decisive factors in the development of new energy sources such as solar energy. Whoever possesses advanced technologies for the development and utilization of new energy resources has the right to develop and utilize such energy, and who can grasp and own such energy resources will take the lead in solving the two challenges of energy security and climate resilient.

On the contrary, addressing climate change itself provides a good opportunity for technological progress. Scholars from the National Museum of History and the University of Cambridge have tracked the history of climate change over the past 2 million years and found that the period of Earth's climate cooling or warming did not hinder human development, while greatly promoted human evolution. The most fundamental reason is that addressing climate change forces technological progress and innovation, providing a driving force and platform for promoting a new industrial revolution, accelerating the construction of an innovative country, and achieving leapfrog development.

In fact, countries and organizations such as the United States and the European Union have seized the opportunity to address technological progress under climate change. The timely launch of the new energy strategy by the United States, the development and research of low-carbon smart energy industries such as superconductivity, smart grids, and cloud computing, provide strong support for continuing to maintain their leading position in the world economy and technological development.[25]

Column 1.1 The EU Gains Comparative Advantage by Promoting Climate Issues

The two oil crises of the 1970s forced Europe to shift towards an energy-saving and low-carbon development model, and concerns about energy and economic security were the initial reasons for the EU's low-carbon transformation path. European countries cannot obtain energy supply through various means like the United States, and can only be forced to embark on the path of reducing dependence on energy imports, conserving the use of fossil fuels, and developing renewable energy. Europe started early in improving energy efficiency and developing low-carbon energy, with a leading level. Through low-carbon constraints, it can weaken the traditional advantages of economic competitors such as the United States, Russia, and Middle Eastern countries or petrochemical energy importing countries, and gain comparative advantages. Promoting the development of the international climate system is also conducive to the EU's advantageous strategy of exporting new energy technologies. The overall nature of climate issues is also conducive to promoting the unity of EU member states and promoting the process of EU integration.

Source: EU gains comparative advantage by promoting climate issues, world Economy and Politics, issue 8, 2012.

Column 1.2 Firewood-to-Oil Project

Wuhan Sunshine Kaidi New Energy Group has successfully developed the 'Firewood-to-Oil' second-generation biofuel project. This technology involves placing wood chips with a moisture content lower than 15% into a vaporizer, decomposing them into gases containing carbon and hydrogen, and then forming hydrocarbon biodiesel under the action of a catalyst. The biofuels produced by the company contain 50% biodiesel, 50% bio aviation oil, and bio-gasoline. Aircraft and cars can use the biofuel as energy without any modification. The price is equivalent to that of ordinary refined oil. The same amount of biomass oil can cover 10% more distance than regular gasoline. Due to its absence of heavy metals, sulfur, phosphorus, arsenic and other elements, its use can effectively reduce environmental pollution.

4.3 tons of branch firewood or crop straw can produce 1 ton of biodiesel. The average cost is 6000 yuan/per ton, of which 52.6% is for raw material expenses. Farmers can earn a profit of 3000 yuan per ton of raw materials. The enterprise has established raw material bases in over 300 counties across the country, mobilizing farmers to participate in energy base construction through investment in technology, capital, management, etc.

Every year, China's agricultural and forestry waste is about 1.2 billion tons, of which only a small amount is utilized, while about 800 million tons are burned or decomposed. If firewood can be converted into oil, the annual production can reach 200 million tons, which is equivalent to the 271 million tons of crude oil imported by China in 2012.

1.5.4 Economic and Technological Support for Scientific Development by Addressing Climate Change

The global response to climate change provides technological and economic support for transforming economic development patterns and sustainable development. Replacing traditional GDP with green GDP, establishing a system for paid use of natural resources and ecological compensation mechanisms, etc., are important statistical, evaluation, assessment systems and institutional mechanisms for promoting the transformation of economic development mode and achieving sustainable development. They are not only significant but also very urgent. However, due to the complexity of environmental factors such as cumulative effects, synthetic effects, and threshold effects, as well as the uncertainty of environmental impacts, it is difficult to establish a corresponding relationship between pollution emission levels and environmental damage doses. This makes it difficult to solve technical problems such as pricing and annual decomposition of natural resources and the environment, thereby hindering the paid use of green GDP and natural resources. The ecological compensation mechanism has entered an operational level and has been slow to advance. The emerging carbon emissions trading, carbon finance, and carbon taxes in addressing climate change may or have already provided inspiration and reference for us to address the economic and technological challenges mentioned above.

1.5.5 Lifestyle and Consumption in a Low-Carbon Society

Changing residents' consumption patterns is a recommended emission reduction measure by the IPCC. In 2001, IPCC proposes that in the long run, changing consumption patterns is more important than implementing emission reduction policy measures alone; in 2008, IPCC also proposed that examples that have a positive impact on mitigation actions include changes in consumption patterns, education and training, changes in residential behavior within buildings, and traffic management needs.[26]

1. Guide public consumption behavior and establish a low-carbon social consumption mode. The public consumption concept and consumption mode are the guidance for enterprise production behavior, and also the social foundation for achieving the transformation to low-carbon development mode. We should regard low-carbon consumption as a social morality, guide, regulate, and restrict the consumption behavior of the public, and advocate healthy, civilized, and moderate consumption methods.[27]
2. The environmental label certification system is conducive to guide residents to choose low-energy products.
3. To awaken public awareness of the serious consequences and urgency of the "Greenhouse Effect" and "Climate Crisis". Establish a conscious awareness, sense of responsibility, and sense of mission to save resources and protect the environment. Starting from the details of daily life, such as paying attention to the recycling of waste batteries, sorting and disposal of garbage, reducing and resisting the use of disposable appliances, learning from and promoting the "Low-Carbon Lifestyle", etc.[28]
4. Developing and taking public transportation and subways is a cost-effective and efficient way of energy utilization. To an extent, people's demand for private cars is more driven by psychological satisfaction than solving practical travel problems. The United States was once one of the countries with the most developed railway facilities in the world. After World War II, in order to support rural development, the government built many roads in the United States, which left railways neglected and many passenger arteries suspended, especially in the western region. In addition, many people in the United States live in suburbs, leading to the prevalence of private cars and the degradation of public transportation, which became an issue in the United States.

1.6 Market Mechanisms for Addressing Climate Change

1.6.1 Theoretical Basis of Market Mechanisms

1.6.1.1 Property Rights as the Optimal Market Measure to Tackle Climate Change

Tim Worstall, a senior researcher at Adam Smith Institute, said, "Climate change can be tackled through market measures". Both the climate change itself and the fact that the UN is to tackle climate change suggest that the market mechanism has failed. However, if an "Artificial Market" is created on the basis of the current market mechanism, i.e. to embed financial instruments into climate-change mitigation. For example, new mechanisms and new markets related to the mitigation will evolve in the market.

Ann E. Carlson, a professor at the University of California, Los Angeles, further proposed that the market-based instruments included a "Cap and Trade Program and

Complementary Policies". Cap-and-trade is so-called property rights. It is necessary to enable public goods to have a clear definition of private property rights so that pollution behaviors (gas emissions), which were originally not tradable and did not have price-discovery mechanism, could have the private property right boundary and become tradable and have a price discovery mechanism before they can be configured to a satisfactory balance by market mechanisms.[29] In addition to property rights, there are restrictions and prohibitions, administrative control methods—technology access standards and administrative approval—and economic methods—carbon tax and environmental tax.

Harold Demsetz (1976) suggests that a primary function of property rights is that of guiding incentives to achieve a greater internalization of externalities. Ann E. Carlson believes that the introduction of property rights allows the market to set a carbon price, and enables gas emitters to decide whether and how to curb emissions. This mechanism is expected to effectively tackle greenhouse gas emissions.

Carbon tax and other economic approaches, reflects the market economic benefit and responsibilities, i.e. the "polluter pays" principle, and forces emission reduction, which may not only slow down the development, but also go beyond what enterprises are willing to comply with. It is difficult for enterprises to make a choice. And the price discovery (cost determination) under carbon tax scheme is often decided by laws and administrative measures, and, therefore, difficult to realize effective benefits that match responsibilities.[30] The property rights method is both mandatory and competitive. Not only does it guarantee that enterprises can choose their favorite emission mitigation, ensures tradability of public goods (environment), and realize the social goal of saving resources and protecting the environment from the bottom up, it helps establish the exit mechanism—enterprises that exit can own the transaction income, thus achieving a smooth transition and guaranteeing mutual development promotion factors.

1.6.1.2 Other Complementary Methods for Property Rights

Ann E. Carlson, after comparing the cap-and-trade program to the complementary policies, suggested that the property rights approach required a lot of complementary policies. The complementary policies include administrative approaches, such as total emission control, pollution emission standards, renewable energy quota systems, emission standards for coal-fired power plants, low-carbon fuel standards, vehicle fuel efficiency standards, and economic methods, such as environmental tax and carbon tax.

Ex-BP CEO John Browne believes that complementary policies can more directly control who must and how to reduce emissions, in order to effectively curb greenhouse gas emissions. This is because "Enterprises can't rely on themselves to achieve emission reduction. They have to implement a credible emissions trading system, and work with the government's strict control of emission caps".

Carbon tax complements the property rights which collectively address climate change. The United States uses carbon tax to complement carbon trading to promote industrial restructuring. The implementation of the carbon tax in combination with market reforms produces twice the amount of emission reductions compared to the implementation of market reforms only, but the former has a smaller impact on economy and causes less increase of the cost of national energy services.[31]

Sweden makes coal and oil more expensive by adjusting carbon taxes policy, while using biomass energy has become a more economical choose. Thus, the use of biomass increased significantly. A large amount of biomass for regional heating comes from forest residues in the forestry sector. Oil and coal are not used in regional heating any more. The regional heating network extends enormously to eliminate the need for oil heating in more households and commercial buildings. These changes happened without demanding people to change their life style or holding businesses morally responsible. Managers at district heating plants never dreamed of becoming environmentalists or activists, nor did they attempt to write any books on environmental issues. But they have led the trend in the transition towards a new energy system. Just like green energy transition promotes environmental practices, environmentalists and enterprises find a common ground on this point.[32]

1.6.1.3 Local-Based Property Rights and Complementary Policies

Tim Worstall also recommends paying attention to the scope of property rights and complementary policies to choose the cap-and-trade program or complementary policies according to different circumstances. When the market is functioning normally, a cap-and-trade program may be adopted over complementary policies if the policymakers are only concerned with ensuring cost-effectiveness rather than other objectives, such as reducing air pollution and creating jobs. But if the market fails and emission reduction cannot be achieved at the lowest cost, complementary policies can come into scene and fulfill its duty.[33]

1.6.2 Carbon Emission Trading

1.6.2.1 Importance of Carbon Emission Trading in Addressing Climate Change

The price mechanism of carbon emission trading will internalize the social cost of carbon dioxide emission, which will encourage enterprises to carry out technological innovation, develop advanced low-carbon technology, and guide investment in its choice of industries and projects to promote the development of low-carbon emerging industries.

Carbon emission trading originated from the notion of emissions trading put forward by economists in the 1970s. With the need of coping with climate change, the idea and practices of emissions trading have extended to carbon emission trading, which aims to control greenhouse gas emissions. The mandatory emission reduction targets called for in the Kyoto Protocol, especially the three "Flexible Mechanisms", have pioneered climate mitigation through market and financial measures. Carbon emission trading is even more widely adopted than emissions trading.

Column 1.3 Emissions Trading

Emissions trading is based on the western economist Ronald Coase's theory of property rights and Arthur Cecil Pigou's offset theory. Its legal basis lies in the principle that both contemporary and the next generation have equal rights in using resources and in dealing with the environment. Whoever wants to use more resources and whoever pollutes the environment should compensate as appropriate.

Emissions trading is a property rights approach to environmental protection—the environmental capacity and emission space are regarded as a type of resource. Its price is decided in consideration of its governance cost, availability, supply and demand, etc., and through market trading, on the basis of clearly determining its property rights.

The main function of emissions trading is to reduce the total amount of pollution emissions to improve the quality of environment. Furthermore, emissions trading promotes technological advancement in pollution control, and reduces the cost of pollution control throughout society.

Emissions trading began in the United States as an economic means and management tool in water and atmosphere protection. In developed countries, such as the United States and Germany, relevant laws and regulations on emissions trading, trading markets, and trading institutions are getting increasingly mature. The U.S. Clean Air Act Amendments of 1990 added regulatory programs for control of acid deposition (acid rain), which officially announced the legal statement of controlling total amount of emissions and the emission trading mechanism, along with curbing sulfur dioxide emissions and the prevention and control of acid rain pollution. In 1990–2006, the U.S. electric power industry's electricity generation increased by 37%, but the sulfur dioxide emissions decreased by 40%, the NOx (nitrogen oxide) emissions decreased by 48%, and the wet sulphate deposition by 25–40% in part of the Midwest and Northeast regions, which shows significant pollution control and environmental effects.

1.6.2.2 International Carbon Emission Trading System

- EU: The European Union Emissions Trading System (EU ETS) was set up in 2005. It is the world's largest carbon trading system serving the 27 EU member states, as well as around 11,000 enterprises—that are in close touch with the EU—from Iceland, Liechtenstein and Norway. Enterprises at each EU member state get 2 billion tons of carbon credit every year through EU ETS, following the cap-and-trade principle and according to the total annual carbon quota. Those who exceed the quota will receive penalties; those who reduce emissions win carbon credits. Carbon quota and carbon credits are tradable in the carbon market as trading licenses. Besides factories, other organizations, including banks, investment institutions, carbon trading enterprises, etc., also participate in the carbon trading market.[34]

- United States: the Chicago Climate Exchange, established in 2003, is the world's second largest carbon trading market, and a mature regional carbon trading system. Its main task is to provide carbon emission trading services for the ten states that undertake voluntary emission reduction, and enterprises that are voluntarily curbing emissions. Six types of greenhouse gases, like sulfur dioxide, are traded.[35] Strict monitoring and measurement systems provide strong support for transactions in the emission market.
- South Korea: the national carbon trading legislation was passed in 2012, which states that companies can buy and sell carbon permits or buy carbon sinks under the United Nations Clean Development Mechanism. Over 450 enterprises have joined the South Korean carbon trading mechanism, and their total emissions account for 60% of the national total. South Korea will officially implement the carbon trading bill in 2015. Under the pressure of strict emission targets, South Korea may establish a world-scale carbon trading market.

1.6.2.3 China's Pilot Carbon Emissions Trading and Advancements

- Progress of Seven Pilot National Carbon Emissions Trading

  Beijing has released a carbon trading scheme, which allocates carbon quotas to 300 enterprises. The trade started at the end of 2013. Tianjin released its carbon trading proposal in February 2013. All the basic elements of Carbon emissions trading have been built, including the development of regional carbon market management, establishment of a carbon trading system registration and trading platform, establishment of a unified monitoring, reporting and verification system, and improvement of the market supervision system. Hubei has included 107 companies into the pilot program. Chongqing's Carbon emission trading is expected to begin in late 2013. Shanghai's carbon financial market proposal is nearing completion.[36] Shenzhen does not have large carbon sources, such as heavy chemical industry, iron and steel industry, and coal-fired power plants, but it has "indirect carbon sources". Shenzhen announced its annual carbon trade target of 30 million tons to assist achieving China's national carbon emission goal.

  The responsibilities and functions of all parties taking part in China's carbon trading system need to be determined and coordinated, along with relevant legal systems during its operation, the cultivation of its third-party certifying agencies, the establishment of the construction, certification, approval, and registration system, the construction of the trading platform, and the making of relevant technical standards. In addition, a sound and effective national carbon emissions trading system is an important indicator and a necessary premise of China's carbon emissions trading.
- The Initial Quota Trading at China's First Mandatory Carbon Trading Market was Successfully Achieved

Shenzhen Energy Group Co., Ltd. sold 20,000 tons of year 2013 carbon emission quotas on June 14, 2013. PetroChina International Guangdong Co., Ltd. and Hanergy Holding Group Limited each bought 10,000 tons, priced at 28 ~ 30 yuan per ton. The total turnover was 580,000 yuan. These two buyers were not among the enterprises included in the Shenzhen Emission Trading Scheme. They participated in the carbon trading as market investors.

Shenzhen's practice in carbon trading is to closely watch the emissions of key industrial enterprises and large public buildings. Their carbon emissions accounted for 40% of the city's total.

Identification of key enterprises: 635 enterprises were determined as key enterprises according to their industrial added value, production size, and energy consumption level. These enterprises' carbon emissions were 31.73 million tons in 2010, accounting for 38% of the city's total emissions; their industrial added value accounted for 59% of the city's total, and 26% of the city's GDP. Their 2013–2015 emission quotas were 100 million tons. In 2015, the average carbon intensity of these enterprises decreased by 32%, as compared with that of 2010, and by 6.68% from 2013 to the next half of 2015, each being higher than the emission reduction target of the whole city in the same period. This will play an important role in achieving the city's emission target and greenhouse gases reduction target for the "12th Five-Year Plan".

The membership scheme encourages the participation of institutional and individual investors. Both for the domestic and international market. The purpose is to encourage environmentally responsible citizens and social organizations to reduce their own carbon emissions and offset the inevitable by buying carbon credits. Thus, the carbon market will be reinforced, and citizens and social organizations can effectively raise carbon emission awareness.

Shenzhen Carbon Trading Market is built in the Qianhai Shenzhen-Hong Kong Modern Service Industry Cooperation Zone, for the purpose of convenient cooperation with Hong Kong to co-build Shenzhen-Hong Kong Carbon trading market, explore cooperation model and supporting measures, and to promote RMB to become the currency for cross-border carbon trading and settlement.

European and American carbon trading products are mainly futures, while Shenzhen is spot. Shenzhen Carbon Trading Market released two types of trading products in its first batch: carbon emission quotas allocated by the National Development and Reform Commission (NDRC) to 635 industrial enterprises and 197 buildings; Certified Emission Reductions (CER)—emission reductions achieved by carbon offset projects. The project owner can trade their products after their application gets approved. Individual investors can open accounts at the carbon exchange, with a threshold of 3000 yuan for initial participation.

In the future, Shenzhen will also incorporate new energy transportation into carbon emission trading management, so as to realize the transition from mandatory use of new energy vehicles to promotion through quota allocation. By 2015, three major sectors, namely industrial enterprise market, construction carbon market and transportation carbon market, will be established to form an all-round and multi-level carbon emission control system.

Column 1.4 Zhejiang Provincial Hongshi Cement Co., Ltd. Develops CDM Projects

Located in Lanxi City, Zhejiang Province, Zhejiang Hongshi Cement Co., Ltd., is a large enterprise mainly producing high-grade cement, ranking the 9th in the national cement industry.

Generating electricity using waste gases is one of the main features of the company. In the past, a lot of waste gases at 350°C or below, mainly carbon dioxide, were discharged from the kiln head clinker cooler and the kiln tail preheater during the process of cement production. The heat emission accounts for more than 35% of the total heat of the clinker firing system. Enormous waste exhaust heat boilers, which are installed in the kiln head and the kiln tail, capture the exhaust from the kiln tail preheater and kiln head clinker cooler in the cement production line to produce low-pressure superheated steam to generate electricity. The boilers are able to generate one third of the annual electricity consumption of the whole company— and, therefore, save 35,000 tons of standard coal and reduce 100,000 tons of carbon dioxide emission.

The company contracted with the Luxembourg MGM Carbon Portfolio Sàrl to develop CDM projects to sell its Emission Reduction Credits (ERCs) earned from waste heat power generation. The 6-year contract states that the total amount of the sale is not less than 1.2 million tons of carbon dioxide equivalent (CO_{2e}) at a price of no less than €8.2 per ton. The total amount of CO_{2e} to be sold is 1,047,500 tons valued at €8,589,900. The first payment of 5.8 million yuan was received before the end of 2009.

Cement industry essentially has high energy consumption and high pollution, posing high credit access threshold. The national credit policy strictly restricts loans to cement industry. However, thanks to its efforts in energy saving, consumption reduction and recycling economy, Zhejiang Hongshi Cement Co., Ltd. won strong support from the financial sector. The company raised 50 million yuan for the construction of the waste exhaust heat power generation system, but there was still a gap of 40 million. Then, with a loan from the agricultural bank of China, the company was able to purchase generators, broilers and related control systems, and its waste exhaust power generation project could be implemented as planned. The company paid off the loan within two years of the start of project because of good benefit and the carbon dioxide emission reduction mechanism.

Source: Emissions trading is approaching, China Equity Exchange website, http://www.cnpre.com/search/news/index.php?modules=show&id=27201.

1.6.3 Carbon Tax

Carbon tax is an important market-based policy instrument. Carbon tax originates from environmental tax, and is one of taxation items. The carbon tax goes in line with the goal of emission reduction. It puts a price tag, which is predictable and gradually increasing, on carbon emissions. Finland, Sweden, Denmark, and the Netherlands implemented carbon tax in the early 1990s, followed by Germany, Britain and France with good results.[37] The introduction of carbon tax in Sweden has reduced the country's carbon emissions by encouraging biomass energy to replace oil for heating. Norway taxed oil and gas drilling projects in the North Sea for greenhouse gases emission, thus, the drilling companies captured carbon dioxide and injected it underground, and realized that it was cheaper than direct air emission. This practice promoted rapid advances in carbon capture and storage technologies.

Column 1.5 Environmental Tax

It is also known as eco-tax or green tax. In a narrow sense, environmental tax is levied on pollutants, following the "polluter pays" principle. In a broad sense, environmental tax not only encompasses the environmental tax in a narrow sense, it includes exemption of other related taxes for the purpose of improving environmental quality and encouraging energy conservation and emission reduction. Therefore, it is also called "environmentally related taxes".

The theoretical basis of environmental tax lies in a proposal by the welfare economist Arthur Cecil Pigou in the early 1900s that, in order to overcome the difference between marginal private cost and marginal social cost caused by negative externalities, the government should levy a fee on the polluter per unit of output equal to the marginal damages.

Environmental tax is generally divided into indirect tax and direct tax. Indirect tax refers to tax levied on discharged pollutants and use of resources. Direct tax refers to the reduction or deduction of indirect tax for the purpose of energy conservation and environmental protection, as well as some tax rebate policies.

Indirect taxes include energy taxes, resource taxes, pollution taxes and transport taxes.

Energy tax is a tax on the use of energy products, such as gasoline, diesel, natural gas and coal. Most OECD countries levy energy taxes, up to 25%.

Resource tax is mainly levied on the exploitation and use of natural resources, like water, forest, etc.

Pollution tax is a tax levied on the actual or estimated emissions of pollutants such as exhaust gas, wastewater, solid waste and noise. The most typical exhaust pollution tax is the sulfur dioxide tax.

Water resource tax and water pollution tax originally belong to two different environmental taxes, but are often collected together in practice. A noise tax is usually levied on an airline or a passenger based on the number of takeoffs or landings or the number of passengers at the airport and the weight of their luggage. Pollution taxes are also imposed on the use of nitrogen and phosphorus fertilizers, livestock manure and pesticides in agricultural production. Transportation tax is mainly levied on the possession and use of vehicles and vessels, mainly according to their energy consumption standards and emission standards.

Source: Design and Implementation of a Carbon Tax System, Guangming Daily, September 14, 2010, by Sun Xiaowei.

1.6.4 Carbon Labeling

Carbon labeling serves not only as a critical market-based approach to addressing climate change, but also as a supportive policy for market mechanisms such as carbon emissions trading and carbon taxation.

Through quantifiable indices, carbon labeling provides consumers with information about a product's greenhouse gas emissions—or carbon footprint—throughout its life cycle, from raw materials acquisition, manufacturing, storage and transportation, to disposal and recycling.[38]

It not only helps to promote transparent source of carbon emissions and encourage enterprises to reduce negative impact on the environment through relevant measures, but also guides consumers to choose products with lower carbon emissions to contribute to reduce greenhouse gas emissions and mitigate global warming.

Essentially, carbon labeling encourages both consumers and producers to take on environmental and climate conservation, relying largely on their social responsibilities and ethical awareness. However, the implementation of carbon labels necessitates the verification of greenhouse gas emissions during production, thus imposing additional costs on businesses that could potentially be passed on to consumers.[39] For consumers, this can promote a modification in consumption habits, while for businesses, this can intensify market competition in the low-carbon economy.

Countries such as the UK, Japan, and South Korea have implemented the carbon labeling mechanism since 2007. By 2011, this practice had been adopted in more than 10 countries and regions worldwide.

1.7 China's Process in Addressing Climate Change

1.7.1 China's Vulnerability to Climate Change

China's susceptibility to climate change is largely attributed to its fragile ecological environment, extensive coastal line, limited per-capita resource endowment, large population, underdeveloped economy, and coal-reliant energy structure. Given that further economic development is required to ensure basic livelihood in China, an inevitable rise in the country's greenhouse gas emissions is anticipated over a specific period of time.

China's *National Assessment Report on Climate Change* outlines the major expected effects of climate change on the country includes the following.

1. Over the past century, the annual average temperature in China has increased by 0.5–0.8 °C, a rate slightly higher than the global average for the same period.
2. Over the past five decades, China has seen a significant reduction in precipitation, leading to drought conditions in many parts of the country.
3. The implications of climate change vary across different regions of China, with the following impacts being the most notable:
   - Southern regions: repeated flooding events;
   - Northern regions: critical water shortage despite high demand;
   - Widespread biological disasters;
   - Coastal Regions: escalating severity and frequency of calamities due to rising sea levels;
   - Increasingly instability in agricultural production;
   - Forest and grassland degradation;
   - Numerous major constructions struggling to meet safety standards and operational objectives.
4. Over the last five decades, the sea level on China's coast has increased by an average of 2.5 mm annually, slightly outpacing the global mean increase.
5. China's mountain glaciers, including the Himalayan Glacier, continue to retreat rapidly. Over the past 50 years, a decline in the extent of sea ice has been observed in both Bohai Bay and the northern Yellow Sea; the Northern Glacier has shrunk by 21% in area, the Tibetan permafrost has degraded significantly, the water levels in inland plateau lakes have risen, and grass yield in the pastures of Qinghai and southern Gansu provinces has decreased.

1.7.2 China: A Pioneering Developing Nation in United Nations Climate Change Advocacy

In 1983, China became one of the 22 member countries of the first World Commission on Environment and Development.[40] In 1992, China participated in the United Nations Conference on Environment and Development, also known as World Summit. Besides, China was among the first group of ten countries signing the Kyoto Protocol. In 1994, China took the lead in developing the National Agenda 21, which prioritized environment protection as the most important issues, including air pollution mitigation and sustainable development in energy industry. The agenda defined resource conservation and environmental protection as fundamental national policies that must be adhered to.

In 2002, the 16th National Congress of the Communist Party of China (CPC) established the goal of building a moderately prosperous society, and made it clear to integrate environmental protection and economic development into the nature-human and human–human relationship. The Scientific Outlook on Development, which is a people-oriented, comprehensive and sustainable development, and a strategy encompassing five aspects including human-nature relationship was brought forward on the third Plenary Session of the 16th CPC Central Committee in 2003.

Hu Jintao said at the meeting of the Central Committee of the Politburo of the CPC Central Committee in 2006: "Human life is precious. China is a socialist country. We shouldn't develop at the expense of spiritual civilization, nor should we sacrifice our ecosystem, let alone human life."

As he spoke at the APEC informal meeting in 2007, "Climate change is a global issue. It is connected with the interests of all parties. All the countries in the world need to collaborate to combat climate change. Helping others cope with climate change is helping ourselves. Only through collaboration can we benefit each other. Developed countries should be aware of their historical responsibilities and existing emissions, strictly fulfill the emission reduction goals determined by the Kyoto Protocol, and continue to take the lead in reducing emissions after 2012. Developing countries should take actions based on their respective situations. They should try to import, digest and absorb advanced cleaning technologies, to contribute to the combat against climate change as appropriate".

In 2007, it is written in the report of the 17th National Congress of the Communist Party of China that we need to strengthen capacity building in responding to climate change and make new contributions to safeguard the global climate.[41]

The "National Plans on Climate Change", which was composed by the National Development and Reform Commission (NDRC) of China in June 2007, made the following explicit statement on China's position and principles in coping with climate change.

1. To reduce greenhouse gas emission. As a developing country, based on the strategy of sustainable development, China will work hard to control greenhouse gas emission through improved energy efficiency, energy conservation, renewable energy development, ecosystem protection and development, and vigorous tree planting.
2. To adapt to climate change. We need to fully consider how to adapt to the climate change that have already taken place, particularly measures to help developing countries to improve their capacities against disastrous climates and events.
3. To promote technological cooperation and transfer. "We need to use technological advancement and innovation to cope with climate change, give full play to leading and fundamental roles of technological advancement in mitigating and adapting to climate change, and promote the development of technologies and speed up to introduce new technologies." This stress the core role of technologies in combating climate change, and emphasize the importance of promoting international technological cooperation and transfer so that the world can share the benefits of global technological advancement.
4. To strictly fulfill China's obligations for the United Nations Framework for Convention on Climate Change (UNFCCC) and the Kyoto Protocol. China, as a responsible State, will fulfill its obligations under the UNFCCC and the Kyoto Protocol.
5. To advocate regional cooperation in climate change. The main legal framework for international communities to address climate change has been set up in the UNFCCC and in the Kyoto Protocol. However, this does not mean excluding regional cooperation on climate change. Any regional cooperation would complement with the UNFCCC and the Kyoto Protocol, rather than replace with or weaken them. The goal of cooperation is to promote practical international collaboration by fully mobilizing all walks of life. In this belief, China will participate in regional cooperation.

1.7.3 China's Further Response to Climate Change

In the span of 2007, China introduced an array of policies and measures in response to climate change.

In June, establishment of National Climate Change & National Energy Conservation and Emission Reduction Leading Group. Former Premier Wen Jiabao was the group leader, and group members included 29 ministers of the ministries and commissions under the State Council. The Ministry of Science and Technology compiled "China's Science and Technology Actions on Climate Change".

In August, seventeen national departments, like the National Development and Reform Commission, the Central Propaganda Department, organized a series of campaigns on energy conservation and emission reduction across China.

In September, the national renewable energy development goal was officially brought forward in the "Medium and Long-term Development Plan for Renewable Energy in China"; during the 15th APEC Informal Senior Officials' Meeting (ISOM), former China President Hu Jintao proposed to establish an Asia–Pacific Network for Sustainable Forest Management and Rehabilitation.

In November, China set up the Emission Reduction Fund. China announced a plan to set up such a national fund in 2007, to receive part of the benefits paid to Chinese companies in accordance with the Clean Development Mechanism (CDM) under the "Kyoto Protocol", and then to provide funding and credit support to China's environmental protection projects.

Former Premier Wen Jiabao announced at the United Nations Climate Conference in Copenhagen that China would enhance voluntary emission reductions, and will set the new target of cutting carbon dioxide emissions per unit of GDP by 40–45 percent by 2020 from the 2005 level.

In September 2010, the Standing Committee of the State Council examined and approved the Decision of the State Council on Accelerating the Cultivation and Development of Strategic Emerging Industries, and decided to list industries characterized with renewable energy and low-carbon in national strategic emerging industries.

In 2010, China began to pilot low-carbon development in 5 provinces including Guangdong, Liaoning, Hubei, Shaanxi and Yunnan Provinces, and 8 cities including Chongqing, Tianjin, Xiamen, Shenzhen, Nanchang, Hangzhou, Guiyang and Baoding Cities.

In October 2010, the Fifth Plenary Session of the 17th CPC Central Committee enacted the "CPC Central Committee Recommendations for the Twelfth Five-year Plan for National Economic and Social Development" (hereinafter referred to as "the Recommendations"), which includes green development and building a resource-conservation and environment-friendly society, and adopts resource conservation and environmental protection as binding indicators. The Recommendations clearly defines the following goals supported by a series of policies including promoting low-carbon development and sustainable development as well as mitigating climate change: by 2015, energy consumption per unit of GDP will be decreased by 16% from 2010 level, carbon dioxide emissions decreased by 17%, the proportion of non-fossil fuel energy in total energy decreased by 11.4%, and resource productivity increased by 15%. The Recommendations also proposes the "*capacity building for adaptation to climate change, especially in response to extreme weather event*". It reinforces that renewable energy industry will become one of key industries to be developed during the "12th Five-year Plan".

In November 2011, the Standing Committee of the State Council adopted the "Work Plan for Greenhouse Gas Emission Control during the 12th Five-Year Plan

Period" (hereinafter referred to as 'the Work Plan'), which determined the overall requirements and key tasks for reducing greenhouse gas emissions in China. The Work Plan lists actively coping with climate change as one significant social and economic development strategy, and considered as one major strategic opportunity to accelerate the transformation of economic development model, adjust the economic structure and promote the new industrial revolution. The Work Plan decomposes the targets and tasks and explicitly specifies carbon-dioxide emission reduction targets per unit of GDP for each province/region.

In November 2011, China also launched carbon emission trading in seven pilot areas, including Beijing, Tianjin, Shanghai, Chongqing, Hubei, Guangdong and Shenzhen. A task force was set up and pilot measures worked out in each of the seven areas. The task forces started to work on carbon emissions trading management, established local monitoring system for the trading and cultivate a trading platform at each area.

In 2012, China issued *"China's Policies and Actions for Addressing Climate Change (2012)"*.

In 2012, NDRC enacted and implemented the Management Measures on Voluntary Greenhouse Gases Emissions Trading, established the basic management framework, transaction procedures and regulatory measures of the voluntary emission reduction trading mechanism, encouraged project-based greenhouse gas emission reduction transactions to ensure that the relevant transaction activities are carried out in an orderly manner. It also issued a "Greenhouse Gas Voluntary Emission Reduction Transaction Validation and Certification Guide" to standardize validation and certification work for smooth implementation of the management measures.

The 18th National Congress of the Communist Party of China (CPC) made it prominently important to construct ecological civilization, which became a crucial part of the "Five-in-One" Overall layout of Socialism with Chinese Characteristics. The 18th National Congress reiterated the fundamental national policies of resource conservation and environmental protection and focused on the following development efforts: promoting green development and recycling and low-carbon development to contribute to global ecological security; advancing energy production and consumption revolution; supporting energy-saving low-carbon industries and new and renewable energy development; developing circular economy; promoting resource conservation and recycling throughout production, circulation and consumption; adhering to common but differentiated principles of responsibility, fairness and self-sufficiency; actively coping with climate change along with international societies.

China witnessed the first "National Low-carbon Day" on June 17th, 2013, with the theme of "practice the low-carbon way and build beautiful homes".

Table 1.2 delineates the progress of Low-carbon city development in China.

Table 1.2 Low-carbon city development practices in China

City	Areas of focuses	Strategy and planning
Shanghai	Comprehensive low-carbon cities; Planned construction of Dongtan Eco-city and Lin'gang New City on the Chongming Island	Focusing on renewable energy, hydrogen power grid, environmental-friendly building, fuel cell bus lines; the Dongtan Eco-city and Lin'gang New City on the Chongming Island are the highlights of low carbon city development in Shanghai
Baoding	Industry-led	Based on the "China Electric Valley and Solar Energy City Programs", Baoding plans to build six industry systems of wind-electricity, photo electricity, electricity conservation, electricity storage, power transmission & transformation, and power automation, and develop low-carbon city through construction of urban ecological environment, low-carbon communities and low-carbon urban transportation system
Tianjin	The Sino-Singapore Tianjin Eco-city is an opportunity for low-carbon eco-city development in the New Development Zone of Tianjin	Tianjin: planning to build a new, low-carbon and recycling industrial system, safe and healthy ecological environment system, beautiful and natural urban landscape system, convenient and rapid green transportation system, recyclable and efficient resource and energy utilization system and livable eco-community model, which is expected to be demonstration among low Carbon eco-city development in China
Shenzhen	Comprehensive low-carbon city development, with the Guangming New Development Zone as a pilot	Working with the Department of Housing and Urban–Rural Development to build a demonstration low-carbon eco-city in the Guangming New Development Zone by optimizing urban spatial structure, improving the green municipal planning, guiding industrial low-carbon development, developing green transportation system, and by focusing on green buildings
Nanchang	Industry-led low-carbon city development	Constructing low-carbon eco-industrial systems, develop semiconductor lighting, photovoltaic units, and service outsourcing industries to build Nanchang into a world-class photovoltaic industry base
Wuhan	Comprehensive low-carbon city development	Exploring low-carbon energy, low-carbon transportation and low-carbon industry development models; establish policy systems that promote resource-saving, low-carbon economic development
Changsha	Industry-led	Constructing a demonstration city of low-carbon economy, focusing on promoting the development of renewable energy vehicles, solar energy utilization, renewable energy, energy-efficient buildings
Zhuhai	Low-carbon buildings and low-carbon communities	Introducing advanced technologies to develop low-carbon buildings; promoting the construction of "green communities"; popularizing low-carbon lifestyles; planting trees on slopes and mountains to increase carbon sinks

(continued)

Table 1.2 (continued)

City	Areas of focuses	Strategy and planning
Jilin	Industrial structural adjustment	Jilin listed as a case study pilot city for low-carbon economic zone; "*Jilin City Low-Carbon Development Road Map*" adopted by the Chinese Academy of Social Sciences developed to explore a structural adjustment sample for heavily industrial cities
Xiamen	Comprehensive low-carbon city development	Exploring low-carbon development models from transportation, construction and production; focusing on the development of LED lighting and solar energy buildings
Hangzhou	Comprehensive low-carbon city development	Proposing 50 new low-carbon policies to develop integrated low-carbon city of low-carbon economy, low-carbon buildings, low-carbon transportation, low-carbon lifestyles, low-carbon environment and low-carbon society
Wuxi	Comprehensive low-carbon city development	Building six complete low-carbon systems, namely, low-carbon regulatory system, low-carbon industrial system, low-carbon city construction system, low-carbon transportation and logistics system, low-carbon lifestyle and cultural system, carbon sinks absorption and utilization system
Chongqing	Industrial structural adjustment	Reducing the proportion of high energy consumption industries, gradually form industrial structures predominated by modern service industries and advanced manufacturing industries, and create low-carbon industry clusters step by step

Source: Li C.S., Ma Z.B., Ma Z.B., Zheng Q., Shao T.R., Zeng H., Case Comparative Studies on *Low Carbon City Development in China and Abroad, Urban Studies, Issue 1, 2011*

Notes

1. The Fourth Assessment Report of UN's Intergovernmental Panel on Climate Change, November 2007.
2. Mingfang Guo, "The Lies Behind Global Warming", *English Digest*, Issue 1, 2008.
3. Tianquan Cheng and Zhi Yang, "Reflections on Several Issues Concerning the Development of Low Carbon Economy", *Economic Perspective*, Issue 9, 2012.
4. The Fourth Assessment Report of UN's Intergovernmental Panel on Climate Change, November 2007.
5. Zhongli Ding, "Climate Change and the Game of Interests Behind It", *Liberation Daily*, April 10, 2011.
6. Chunhai Zhang, "Climate Philosophy Research Boosts Ecological Civilization Construction", *China Social Science Daily*, November 30, 2012.
7. The Fourth Assessment Report of UN's Intergovernmental Panel on Climate Change, November 2007.
8. The 2007 Climate Change Report of the United Nations Intergovernmental Panel on Climate Change.
9. Christian Azar (Sweden), translted by Heng Du, and Ke Du, *Solving the Climate Challenge* (Beijing: Social Sciences Academic Press, 2012), 154.
10. Zhongli Ding, "Climate Change and the Game of Interests Behind It", *Liberation Daily*, April 10, 2011.

11. Giddens (UK), Translated by Rongxiang Cao, *Politics of Climate Change* (Beijing: Social Science Academic Press, 2011), 73.
12. Guoguang Zheng, "Enhancing Adaptation to Climate Change and Ensuring Sustainable Development", *People's Daily*, November 21, 2011.
13. Zuotao Zeng and Xun Wang, "Scientifically Studying the Impact of Global Warming on China's Water Resources and Food Production: A Discussion with Professor Park Shilong et al.", *Science and Technology Introduction*, Issue 32, 2011.
14. Jiankun He, "China's Energy Development and Climate Change Response", *China's Population, Resources, and Environment*, Issue 10, 2011.
15. Ibid.
16. Feng Wang and Genfu Feng, "Factors Influencing the Low Carbon Development of China's Economy and Its Role in Carbon Reduction", *China Economic Issues*, Issue 5, 2011.
17. Jiabao Wen, "Making Energy Conservation and Emission Reduction a Compulsory Task, Compulsory Measures, and Compulsory Indicators", *People's Daily*, September 28, 2011.
18. Guolian Wang, "PM2.5: A Sample for Studying Contemporary Chinese Ecological Politics", *Journal of Qingdao Agricultural University, Social Sciences Edition*, Issue 11, 2013.
19. Zhongli Ding, "Climate Change and the Game of Interests behind It", *Liberation Daily*, April 10, 2011.
20. Chongyin Li, "Regarding Several Issues Related to Addressing Climate Change", *Xinhua Digest*, Issue 7, 2011.
21. Boqiang Lin, "The Impact of Resource Tax Reform", *Economic Daily*, November 1, 2011.
22. Achim Steiner, Executive Director of the United Nations Environment Program, delivered a speech at the World Expo themed forum on "Environmental Change and Urban Responsibility" in July 2010.
23. Ibid.
24. Feng Wang and Genfu Feng, "Factors Influencing the Low Carbon Development of China's Economy and Its Role in Carbon Reduction", *China Economic Issues*, Issue 5, 2011.
25. Jiandong Wu, "Rebuilding the United States through Green Economy: Deconstruction of Obama's Energy Strategy", *Science Times*, January 20, 2009.
26. Feng Wang and Genfu Feng, "Factors Influencing the Low Carbon Development of China's Economy and Its Role in Carbon Reduction", *China Economic Issues*, Issue 5, 2011.
27. Jiankun He, "China's Energy Development and Climate Change Response", *China's Population, Resources, and Environment*, Issue 10, 2011.
28. Jiankun He, "The Only Path to Improve Core Competitiveness", *People's Daily*, October 20, 2010.
29. Managerial Personnel Low-Carbon Economy Manual, Baidu Library available at http://wenku.baidu.com/view/73a8c60d52ea551810a687bf.html
30. Low-carbon Economy, Baidu Library available at http://wenku.baidu.com/view/710de9d284254b35eefd3403.html
31. Hongwan Chen, Lei Zhang, "Thoughts on the Feasibility of China's Current Greenhouse Gas Emissions through Carbon Tax", *Collected Essays on Finance and Economics*, 1st issue, 2019.
32. Christian Azar (Sweden), transIted by Heng Du, and Ke Du, *Solving the Climate Challenge* (Beijing: Social Sciences Academic Press, 2012).
33. Hong Jiang, "Tackling Climate Crisis must Rely on Economic Policies", *Chinese Social Sciences Today*, September 14, 2012.
34. "EU Carbon Trading Mechanism to Follow the Cap-and-Trade Principle", China's National Emissions Trading Scheme available at http://blog.sina.com.cn/s/blog_a0ceca600101cryt.html
35. "The Global Rise of Emissions Trading", International Channel, available at http://news.xinhuanet.com/world/2010-12/08/c_12860186_2.htm
36. "Shenzhen Officially Launched China's Carbon Emission Trading Today", available at http://www.jfdaily.com/a/6338426.htm
37. Xiaowei Sun, "Design and Implementation of a Carbon Tax System", *Guangming Daily*, September 14, 2010.

38. Yingfei Hu, et al., "Experience and Prospect of Establishing Carbon Labeling System in China", *Journal of Economic and Management Studies*, 3rd issue, 2010.
39. Jie Wu, and Qi Jiang, "Carbon Labeling in International Trade", *International Economic Cooperation*, 7th issue, 2009.
40. Tianquan Cheng, and Zhi Yang, "Thoughts on Several Issues of Low-Carbon Economy", *Economic Review*, Issue 9, 2012.
41. Jintao Hu, *Holding High the Great Banner of Socialism with Chinese Characteristics, Striving for a New Victory in Building a Well-off Society in an All-round Way—Report on the 17th Congress of the CPC* (Beijing: People's Publishing House, 2007), 4.

Chapter 2
Sustainable Development of Urban Ecological Environment

2.1 City and Urbanization

City represents a spatial and regional system that integrates individuals, resources, advanced technology and culture, focusing on the centralized utilization of spatial environmental resources for societal advancement. They are pivotal economic, political, and social hubs characterized by vibrant scientific and cultural activity. Cities also symbolize the region's political, economic, and cultural epicenters, hosting a diversified artificial ecosystem where secondary and tertiary industries coexist, independently develop, and spatially conglomerate.

The emergence of cities marks a significant stage in human development. Arguably, the history of human civilization is intertwined with urban development. While human existence spans over 3 million years, urbanization only dates back about 6000 years. German scholar, Spengler, posits that "all great cultures of mankind originate from cities. The world history is a narration of human urban times, highlighting those countries, governments, politics, religions, etc., emanate from, and attach to, the fundamental form of human existence".[1]

Cities first emerged in locations that are today considered cradles of human civilization Egypt, the Ganges Valley of India, and the Mesopotamian Plain. There are four main theories about the origin of cities: the first one is the defense theory, which originates from the function of defending against foreign invasion; the second is the market theory, which emphasizes the functions of commodity exchange and market based on the principle that there is a market before there is a city; the third theory is division of labor, which explores the origin of cities from a sociological perspective; the fourth is temples theory, which explains the origin of cities from a religious perspective.

According to the Istanbul Declaration (1996), issued by the UN Habitat, city planning should enhance humans' living standards with dignity, physical health, safety, happiness, sustainability, and hope. The 2008 Shanghai World Expo also echoed a similar message, highlighting "Cities make people's lives better". Noted

S. Du and H. Du, *The Green Transformation of Urban Areas in China Under Global Warming*, https://doi.org/10.1007/978-981-95-1005-4_2

Professor Stieglitz asserts that the triumph of a city symbolizes the success of a country.

The Mega City Region concept, which emerged at the end of the twentieth century, is poised to gain wide acceptance as a contemporary urban formation in the twenty-first century. In 2010, the number of mega cities with a population surpassing 10 million incremented from 2 to 20. Projections suggest this number is likely to hit 22 by 2015, with 17 of these located in developing countries.

Global cities, urban agglomerations, and urban belts all emerged as new Urban Formations in the late twentieth century.

Column 2.1 Global Cities

The composition of the Global City Index entails a range of indicators including city size, business activity, human capital, information exchange, cultural experiences, political engagement, and the presence of Fortune 500 companies' headquarters. Other significant measures incorporated are the scope of the city's capital market, airport and port throughput, diplomatic presences, research institutions, political organizations, and museums. These indicators serve to evaluate a city's external impact, which is defined by its influence over and degree of integration with the global market, culture, and innovation.

In 2010, the Global City Index's highest ranked cities were New York, London, Tokyo, and Paris. Half of the top ten cities belonged to the Asia Pacific region, namely Tokyo, Singapore, Sydney, Seoul, and Hong Kong. The United States had three cities in this group: New York, Chicago, and Los Angeles. Europe had two representatives: London and Paris.

Seven cities from China placed within the top 65 globally: Hong Kong (5th), Beijing (13th), Shanghai (20th), Taipei (39th), Guangzhou (57th), Shenzhen (62nd), and Chongqing (65th).

2.1.1 *Urbanization*

Urbanization is a process of achieving population, industry, wealth, intelligence, and information gathering in a country or region. It is also a process of advancing lifestyle, production, social, and civilization.

In 1800, the world's urbanization rate was only 3%, reaching 7% in 1850, 15% in 1900, and 30% in 1950. By 2000, the world's urbanization rate had reached 48%, nearly half of the world's total population. By 2006, the world's urban population had increased more than fourfold, surpassing the rural population for the first time. It is estimated that the urban population will exceed 70% of the total by 2050.

Developed countries had completed their urbanization tasks before the middle of twentieth century (Table 2.1).

Table 2.1 Urbanization process in major developed countries in the world

								Unit: %
Country/Year	1920	1950	1960	1965	1970	1975	1980	2000
England	79.3	77.9	78.6	80.2	81.6	84.4	88.3	89.1
France	46.7	55.4	62.3	66.2	70.4	73.7	78.3	82.5
USA	63.4	70.9	76.4	78.4	81.5	86.8	90.1	94.7
Japan	28.0	45.8	53.9	58.0	64.5	69.6	74.3	77.9
Germany	63.4	70.9	76.4	78.4	80.0	83.8	86.4	81.2

Since the end of the twentieth century, urbanization has accelerated in many developing countries, including China. About 90% of global urban growth has occurred in developing countries. The total urban built-up area in developing countries is predicted to triple between the years 2000 and 2030.

Over the past 200 years of urbanization in the world, many theories of urbanization have emerged, and urbanization paths have also had their own characteristics. In summary, the following six modes of urbanization development are the mainstream:

1. The development model upholding isolation between urban and rural sectors, first advances by a United States Berkeley University professor. This analogy likens the urban impact upon rural areas to that of vampires, drawing resources, populations, and wealth, whilst concurrently leaving behind pollution and economic depression.[2]
2. The development model prioritizing urban growth. This is theoretical grounded in the Washington Consensus that envisions an urban and rural developmental approach being driven by financial liberalization, the privatization of assets, and political democratization. However, the once popular urban-focused development model, having faced significant issues such as slum proliferation and social instability, is now seen as unsustainable: land privatization has led to a large number of landless farmers flocking to large cities, resulting in a vicious expansion of the population of large cities. Landless farmers cannot find jobs in cities, creating a large number of slums around the city. 60% to 70% of the land in cities is occupied by slums, resulting in very serious social unrest and deterioration of the investment environment.
3. The "laissez faire" urbanization model, also known as sprawling urbanization. In response to the Cold War's prospect of nuclear conflict, the United States sought to minimize urban centers' size and incentivize outward migration to suburban areas. This, paired with widespread motorization, led to the emergence of low-density "urbanization on wheels". Hence, the spatial density of urban populations has substantially dwindled throughout the United States' century-long process of urbanization. Arable land resource depletion stands as a significant concern, complicating issues following closely tied to an American lifestyle that heavily relies on private vehicles for transport, consuming on average five times more gasoline than counterparts in Europe.[3]

4. The coordinated development model between urban and rural areas bears a reasoned theoretical basis encompassing the distinctive development laws occurring in urban and rural settings. Observing from a production perspective, enterprises characterize the primary urban industry, whereas rural agriculture is chiefly regulated by household management. On the consumption continuum, traditional rural agriculture is a low-cost cycle, maximizing resources effectively with minimal to zero waste production. In contrast, cities and industries represent high consumption linear systems exhibiting remarkable producer and consumer strength but lacking degraders, thus failing to form a circular economy. This urbanization model has been successfully implemented by countries including France and Japan. In France, rural populations cluster within historically structured villages characterized by open fields and pastoral scenery. Specialty agricultural products are produced with distinctive geographical indications and historical accumulations. In contrast, the rural population in Japan has experienced a surge having the service-oriented economy development transitioned from solely agriculture to a green development path which was favorable to them.
5. The urbanization model noticeably represents high energy consumption. A country's energy security can mostly be predicated on its urbanization model. If China chooses the development path of the United States, such as highway instead of rail transit, sprawling city instead of dense city, the consumption of gasoline alone will be equivalent to the current global production.[4]
6. The high environmental impact urbanization model provides a typical example centered around the resource-based city, emerging from resource-dependent developmental strategies. Resource depletion, significant environmental damage, industrial structure adjustment inability, and widespread unemployment are common occurrences. Some cities established in ecologically fragile and sensitive areas also pose serious environmental pressure on already fragile ecosystems.

The significant difference between city and nature lies in city's limited degradation functions in comparison with the aggressive production and consumption activities, which results in substantial impacts on the surrounding environment.

2.1.2 *Urbanization in China*

2.1.2.1 Evolution of the Conceptual Framework Guiding China's Urbanization Strategy

1953: "It's not good to have too big a city", we need to "develop more small towns".

1956: "The scale of urban development should not be too large. In the future, the scale of new cities will generally be controlled within the range of tens to hundreds to thousands of people".

1980: "Control the scale of large cities, reasonably develop medium-sized cities, and actively develop small cities".
1990: "Strictly control the scale of large cities, reasonably develop medium and small cities", "Small town and big strategy".
In 2000, the path of coordinated development between large, small, and medium-sized cities and small towns will become a new driving force for China's modernization drive.
In 2002, the report of the 16th National Congress of the Communist Party of China proposed "adhering to the coordinated development of large, small, and medium-sized cities and towns, and taking the path of urbanization with Chinese characteristics".[5]
In 2012, the report of the 18th National Congress of the Communist Party of China proposed "adhering to the path of new industrialization, informatization, urbanization, and agricultural modernization with Chinese characteristics".[6]

2.1.2.2 The Progress and Urban System Formation in China

Through China's ongoing process of urbanization, a multilevel, comprehensive urban system has been established. This structure is hallmarked by large cities as hubs, smaller and mid-sized cities providing critical support, and small towns forming the foundational layer (Table 2.2).

Table 2.2 The urbanization process in China

Number of national censuses	Year	Urbanization rate (%)	Remarks
1st time	1953	13.26	
2nd time	1964	18.30	
3rd time	1982	20.60	Accelerated urbanization process
4th time	1999	26.23	
5th time	2000	36.09	Transition from controlling the development of large cities to coordinated development of large, medium, and small cities and towns
6th time	2006	44.9	The world's urbanization level has reached 51%, with the urban population surpassing the rural population for the first time
7th time	2010	49.68	
8th time	2011	51.3	The urban population surpasses the rural population for the first time, which is an important milestone in China's urbanization

Urban areas contribute significantly to China's economic output: 60% of the country's industrial added value, 85% of tertiary industry value, 70% of gross domestic product (GDP), and 80% of national tax revenue originate from cities. Consequently, cities now serve as the principal economic, cultural, and political powerhouses of China.

Indeed, the nature of Chinese urban expansion has evolved, shifting from a singular, centralistic growth method, to an approach favoring and a more balanced urban–rural coordination. This resulted in the formation of urban clusters or belts such as the Beijing-Tianjin-Hebei region, the Yangtze River Delta, the Pearl River Delta, the Changsha-Zhuzhou-Xiangtan conglomeration, and the Chengdu-Chongqing urban area.

Despite the impressive contribution of rapid urbanization to reform and development initiatives, certain misconceptions exist. Firstly, based on international experience, the development of Chinese cities coincides with the bottleneck constraint period of the relationship between humans and nature, as well as the relationship between humans and humans. "The economy is prone to imbalance, society is prone to disorder, psychology is prone to imbalance, and efficiency and fairness need to be adjusted and rebuilt." The imbalance in human relationships is manifested as a significant development gap between cities and rural areas, between cities in different regions, and between cities. The urbanization process has led to a rapid increase in the cost of living in urban areas and a significant increase in living standards. The imbalance in the relationship between humans and nature is manifested in some cities' one-sided pursuit of urban scale and development speed, which poses a threat to ecological environments such as water, air, soil, and vegetation. The imbalance in the relationship between people and urban infrastructure construction is manifested in that although Chinese cities invest heavily in roads, public service facilities, underground pipeline network facilities, garbage treatment facilities, sewage treatment facilities, and urban management facilities, overall, they still cannot keep up with the rapid growth of urban population. From the data in Table 2.3, it can be seen that there is a significant gap in urban development indicators between China and some developed countries in the world.

With the acceleration of China's urbanization process, urban environmental pollution, ecological damage, the disappearance of old cities, traffic congestion, housing shortages and other urban "comprehensive diseases" have become prominent. Economic development and ecological protection, new city construction and old city protection, urban construction and urban management, cultural inheritance and innovative development, urban development and regional cooperation have become dilemmas in the deepening process of China's urbanization.

The major challenges posed in China's urbanization revolve around correctly comprehending the relationship between advancing urbanization and orchestrating urban–rural development, regional progression, comprehensive socio-economic development, and harmonious development between humans and nature. A potent push towards the formation of livable cities is demanded.

Table 2.3 Comparison of urban development between China and the G7 Industrial Countries (2005)

No	Comparative indicators	China	G7 Counties	Evaluation
1	Proportion of agricultural output value	13%	2%	China is clearly on the high side
2	Proportion of industrial output value	55%	35%	China is clearly on the high side
3	Proportion of service industry	32%	63%	China is clearly on the low side
4	City ratio	43%	81%	China is clearly on the low side
5	Ratio of cities with a population of over one million to the total population	14%	32%	China is clearly on the low side
6	The proportion of the largest city to the total urban population	4%	16%	China is clearly on the low side
7	Urban income difference (proportion of the lowest income group to the highest income group)	5.3%	11.1%	China is clearly on the high side
8	Commuting time in cities with millions of people(minutes)	47 min	25 min	China is clearly on the high side
9	The ratio of urban housing expenditure to income	55.8%	6.1%	China is clearly on the high side
10	Urban traffic accidents (casualties per 10,000 vehicles)	31	12	China is clearly on the high side
11	Urban transportation mileage (million vehicle kilometers) ratio	165,000 1	998,639 6.1	China is clearly on the low side
12	Total suspended particulate matter in cities (micrograms/cubic meter)	320	45	China is clearly on the high side
13	Urban SO_2 (micrograms/cubic meter)	82	19	China is clearly on the high side
14	Urban nitrogen oxides (micrograms/cubic meter)	88	56	China is clearly on the high side

2.2 Sustainable Urban Development

The concept of sustainable development stems from a profound re-evaluation of the traditional development model, which simplistically equates development with growth, often at the expense of resource exhaustion and environmental degradation. This reorientation represents a significant shift in human development thinking, arguably one of the greatest achievements of human civilization in the twentieth century.

2.2.1 *Ideological Foundations of Sustainable Development*

The core premise of sustainable development is the understanding that Gross Domestic Product (GDP) does not provide an accurate measure of a nation's health or prosperity in the real world, let alone reflect the complex interplay of factors like social empowerment, public governance, and environmental stewardship. In the 1920s, a group of economists began to systematically reflect on the GDP oriented development concept, and the result of a combination of factors such as the "super GDP development concept" and the Human Development Index (HDI), which reflect the emergence of new sustainable development concepts and indicators.

The first Human Development Report released by the United Nations Development Program in 1990 explicitly proposed the concept of "human development". The human development perspective is a normative framework for individual well-being, social arrangements, and policy design and evaluation. From the perspective of human development, development is defined as the process of expanding the range of human choices; its focus is on the quality of life, the substantive freedom and opportunities that people enjoy, and what they can actually do and become; economic development is an important means of human development, but it is not a goal in itself. These ideas and theories have become important sources of ideas and theories for sustainable development.

Column 2.2 Human Development Index (HDI)
The Human Development Index, primarily based on factors such as life expectancy, literacy rate, levels of education, and per capita GDP, serves as a robust measure of human development across different regions. The principal indicators of HDI are: (1) longevity and healthy life; (2) education; (3) a standard of living marked by dignity and respect for human rights. Since 1990, HDI has been utilized to measure levels of human development throughout the world.

In the 2009 Human Development Index, Norway topped the list followed by Japan at 9th place, and the United States ranked 13th. China placed itself at the 92nd spot.

Source: Environment and Human Development: A Literature Review, Journal of Peking University (Philosophy and Social Sciences Edition), Issue 3, 2010, by Liu Minquan and Yu Jiantuo.

In 1987, the then Norwegian Prime Minister, Mrs. Brandt, was commissioned by the United Nations to lead and publish the groundbreaking report of the World Commission on Environment and Development. The report, "Our Common Future from One Earth to One World", produced by the Commission on Environment and Development, made a poignant argument. It suggested that environmental, energy, and development crises are inextricably linked. Given that the Earth's resources and energy fall markedly short of satisfying the demands of human development, existing development models necessitate transformation for the benefit of contemporary and future generations. The report subsequently became a critical theoretical underpinning of the sustainable development concept.

Several landmark conferences have played a crucial role in shaping the concept of sustainable development. The first was the United Nations Conference on the Human Environment held in Stockholm in 1972, and the Symposium on Strategic Approaches to Resource Use, Environment, and Development jointly held by the United Nations Environment Program and the United Nations Conference on Trade and Development in Mexico in 1974. At these two conferences, the root causes of environmental problems were pointed out, principles for addressing environmental issues in development were proposed, and the Declaration on the Human Environment was adopted. The second was the 1992 United Nations Conference on Environment and Development held in Rio de Janeiro, Brazil. This conference discussed the environmental and development issues facing human survival and adopted famous documents such as the Rio Declaration on Environment and Development, Agenda 21, Framework Convention on Climate Change, Convention on Biological Diversity, and Statement of Principles on Forests.

These documents emphasize the following viewpoints: (1) Humanity is at a critical moment in history. If we continue to implement current policies, we will inevitably maintain economic disparities among countries and increase poverty, hunger, disease, and illiteracy worldwide; continuing to worsen the ecosystem of the Earth, which we rely on to sustain life. Otherwise, we will have to change policies, improve the living standards of everyone, better protect and manage ecosystems, and strive for a safer and more prosperous future. (2) Global cooperation for common development requires all humanity to change their economic activities and fairly meet the development and environmental needs of present and future generations. (3) the global efforts for sustainable development can be truly realized only when human demands from nature are phase equilibrium with human rewards from nature; only when human efforts for the present are phase equilibrium with human efforts for future generations; only when human efforts for the development of this region are phase equilibrium with human efforts for the co construction and sharing of other regions.[7] (4) The concept of sustainable development is that in the process of economic and social development, it is neither stagnant nor detached from development, but rather simultaneously preventing and controlling environmental pollution, addressing climate change issues, and taking the path of coordinated economic, social, and environmental development.

In 1994, China issued a national sustainable development action, and in 1996, sustainable development was elevated to a national strategy. Entering the twenty-first century, China has proposed a scientific development concept centered on "people-oriented, comprehensive and coordinated sustainable development", which enriches and develops the concept of sustainable development.

The 2012 National Report on Sustainable Development in China proposes that the goal of promoting sustainable development in China is to effectively control the total population, significantly improve quality, significantly improve scientific and technological education levels, continuously improve people's lives, make energy and resource development and utilization more reasonable, significantly improve ecological environment quality, continuously enhance sustainable development capabilities, and basically form a situation of coordinated development among economy, society, population, resources, and environment.[8] The overall idea of promoting sustainable development strategy in China is to make the transformation of economic development mode and strategic adjustment of economic structure a major decision to promote sustainable economic development; make the establishment of a resource-saving and environmentally friendly society an important focus for promoting sustainable development; making improving people's livelihoods a core requirement for sustainable development; taking technological innovation as an inexhaustible driving force for promoting sustainable development, relying on technological breakthroughs and innovation to fundamentally solve unsustainable problems in development; deepening institutional reform and expanding opening up and cooperation with the outside world are the basic guarantees for promoting sustainable development.

2.2.2 *Sustainable Development: Definition and Principles*

2.2.2.1 The Definition of Sustainable Development

The concept of sustainable development was first proposed in the research report "Our Common Future from One Earth to One World" published by the United Nations Commission on Environment and Development in 1987. Later, at the 1992 United Nations Conference on Environment and Development, the concept of sustainable development was outlined in the Rio Declaration on Environment and Development as follows:

1. To ensure that future generations can access natural resources and good living conditions that only a small number of people can enjoy by protecting the environment and fairness.
2. Development should implement conservation in fully respecting the environment and utilizing natural resources, including conserving minerals, energy, water, land, protecting the ocean and atmosphere, and protecting biodiversity; the stock of environmental capital cannot be reduced; when utilizing organisms and ecosystems, it is necessary to maintain their perpetual regeneration.
3. From the perspective of human development, sustainable development should emphasize the sustainability of human quality of life and feasible capabilities, while the sustainability of natural resources, economic development, and production capacity is an important condition and means to achieve human sustainable development, but not the ultimate goal.[9]

2.2.2.2 Principles of Sustainable Development

Equity Principle

Sustainable development advocates for equal rights in the use of resources and the environment for all human beings. This principle focuses on two aspects of fairness. Firstly, the intra-generational equity emphasizes meeting the basic needs of everyone in the current generation and realizing their aspirations for a better life. It particularly advocates for providing impoverished populations and developing countries with fair opportunities for growth and giving priority to poverty eradication. Secondly, inter-generational equity stipulates that the current generation must not jeopardize the future generations' access to the natural resources and environment due to their development requirements.

Sustainability Principle

The core of this principle is that the development of human economy and society cannot exceed the carrying capacity of resources and environment. The economic and social development of humanity must be maintained within the carrying capacity of resources and environment to ensure the sustainability of development. Resources and environment are the foundation of human survival and development, and sustainable development advocates development based on the protection of the Earth's natural system. Therefore, development must have certain limiting factors. For example, human consumption of natural resources must take into account the threshold of resources, and should be based on the premise of not damaging natural systems such as the atmosphere, water, soil, and organisms that support life on Earth. Human beings should adjust their way of life and determine their consumption standards, rather than indiscriminately abusing resources.

Principle of Commonality

This principle recognizes the interdependence and wholeness of the Earth. The diverse history, culture, nature, geography, and economic development levels of different countries and regions necessitate diversified goals, policies, and stages of implementation of sustainable development. The pursuit of sustainable development holds great global significance. However, principles of fairness and sustainability, as encompassed in sustainable development, demand collective compliance by humanity. Attaining the objective of sustainable development necessitates acknowledging the Earth's unity and interdependence, and initiating collaborative global actions.[10] If principles of collectivity are adhered to by all, a mutually advantageous and symbiotic relationship can be sustained not only amongst humans but also between humans and the natural environment, thereby achieving sustainable development.

2.2.3 *Various Associated Concepts of Sustainable Development*

The multi-dimensional changes in the concept of development that began in the 1970s led to the emergence of the concept of sustainable development. At the same time, the concept of sustainable development also showed a trend of quantification and indexing, resulting in a number of concepts and indicators that reflect sustainable development.

2.2.3.1 Urban Ecological Footprint

The urban ecological footprint is derived from the ecological footprint. It refers to how much spatial resources a city needs to support its survival and development, and the smaller the ecological footprint, the less interference it has on the natural environment.[11] The ecological footprint of cities in developed countries is generally several hundred to even a thousand times larger than their own area, while in developing countries, especially some cities with traditional service industries, the ecological footprint is only 10 or even several times larger than their own area. Table 2.4 listed ecological footprint in some cities in China.

Table 2.4 Ecological footprint of selected cities in China

Cities	Year	Per capita ecological footprint(Unit: ha/person)
Beijing	2002	2.91
Deyang	2006	1.61
Yantai	2001	1.47
Macao	2001	2.99
Qingdao	2001	1.89
Xi'an	2005	1.02
Hangzhou	2002	1.77

Source: Environmental Planning Institute of the Ministry of Environmental Protection

2.2.3.2 Ecological Footprint

The concept of the ecological footprint, alternatively known as ecological space occupation, was initially proposed by the Canadian ecological economist William Rees in 1992 and further refined by his doctoral student M. Wackernagel in 1996. It serves as an index and methodology that quantifies the extent of human utilization of natural resources, and measures the ecological carrying capacity that nature provides for humanity.

The ecological footprint is based on the theory that the ecological footprint of any specific population (from a single individual to the population of a city or even a country) is the total area of biogenic land occupied by it for the production and consumption of resources and services, as well as the use of existing technologies to assimilate waste generated. The quantification of ecological footprint is mainly based on two facts: firstly, humans can estimate the majority of resources, energy consumed and the amount of waste generated; the second is that these resources and waste can be converted into the area of biologically productive land for the production and consumption of these resources and waste.

"Bio Productive Land" refers to land or water bodies with biological production capacity, which is divided into the following six categories and assigned corresponding equivalent factors (Table 2.5).

Table 2.5 Types of bio productive land

No	Name	Purpose and characteristics	Equivalence factor
1	Fossil energy land	Land used to absorb waste generated by the combustion of fossil fuels	1.1
2	Cultivated land	Land providing crops such as grain and oil crops and cash crop products	2.8
3	Pasture	Land suitable for the development of animal husbandry	0.5
4	Forests	Artificial or natural forests that can produce wood products	1.1
5	Building land	Including land occupied by human construction of residential buildings, roads, hydropower stations, etc	2.8
6	Ocean	Provided aquatic products	0.2

Note: The use of the same coefficient for fossil energy land and forests is because the area of fossil energy land is calculated based on the newly planted forest area required to absorb CO_2 released from fossil fuel combustion; Considering that construction land generally occupies the most fertile land in the area, it is consistent with the equivalent factor of cultivated land

Source: A Preliminary Study on the Ecological Occupation of Urban Residents' Lives—Case Studies of Beijing and Shanghai, Resource Science, Issue 11, 2001, by Su Yun, Cheng Shengkui, and Xie Gaodi

The key to measurable and quantifiable ecological footprint is the introduction of two key parameters, namely equivalence factor and yield factor.

Equivalence factor: It is to convert the various resources and services consumed by humans for production, as well as the waste generated through the assimilation of existing technologies, into a unified and comparable coefficient of biological productive area.[12]

Yield factor: refers to the ratio of the average productivity of a certain type of bio productive land in a country or region to the average productivity of similar land in the world. Due to the differences in productivity of similar bio productive land among different regions, the actual area of similar bio productive land cannot be directly compared among regions, and a yield factor needs to be introduced for conversion.[13]

The main calculation steps for ecological footprint are as follows:

1. Divide consumption items and calculate the consumption volume of each major consumption item;
2. Using equivalent factors, convert each consumption amount into the area of bio productive land;
3. Convert various types of bio productive land areas into equivalent productive land areas through yield factors.
4. Summarize, add and calculate the ecological footprint area.

Ecological footprints are typically divided into two types: the supply ecological footprint and the demand ecological footprint. The former pertains to the demand side, while the latter is conceptualized from the supply side perspective, signifying the ecological capacity or carrying capacity. The differential between these two types can represent the state and potential for sustainable growth within a given country or region.

Column 2.3 Specific Calculation Formulas for Ecological Footprint and Ecological Carrying Capacity

Ecological footprint: $EF = \sum EFi = \sum \left(Ci/Pi \times Ei\right)$.

Ecological carrying capacity: $BC = \sum BCj = \sum (Aj \times Yj \times Ej)$.

Among them, EF and BC respectively represent the total ecological footprint and ecological carrying capacity of the region (Unit: world hectares);

EFi represents the footprint of the i-th consumer product (Unit: world hectares);

BCj represents the ecological carrying capacity of the j-th land use type (Unit: world hectares);

Ci represents the total consumption of the i-th consumer product (Ton);

Pi represents the world average production of the i-th consumer product (Unit: ton/hectare);

Ei represents the equivalent factor of the land type occupied by the i-th consumer product (Unit: world hectares/hectare);

Aj represents the actual area of land use type j (Unit: hectare);

Yj represents the yield factor of the j-th type of land use (Unit: dimensionless).

Ej represents the equivalent factor of the j-th type of land use (Unit: world hectares/hectare) (Table 2.6).

Table 2.6 Ecological footprint of Deyang City (Year 2006)

Ecological footprint demand				Ecological footprint supply			
Land type	Per capita area (ha/person)	Equivalence factor	Equilibrium area (ha/person)	Land type	Per capita area (ha/person)	Yield factor (2)	Equilibrium area (ha/person)
Cultivated land	0.473	2.8	1.3244	cultivated land	0.062	1.66	0.289
Grassland	0.054	0.5	0.027	Grassland	0.001	0.19	0.00006
Woodland		1.1		Woodland	0.048	0.91	0.048
Waters	0.085	0.2	0.017	Waters	0.004	1.00	0.0008
Fossil fuel	0.196	1.1	0.2156	CO_2 absorption			
Floor space	0.005	2.8	0.014	Building	0.040	1.66	0.187
Total demand area			1.598	Total supply area	0.155		0.524
				biodiversity conservation		12% (1)	0.063
				Total available footprint			0.461

Note 1. According to the report "Our Common Future—from one Earth to one World" by the World Commission on Environment and Development (WCED), it is recommended to set aside 12% of biological production land area for the protection of biodiversity, that is, to protect more than 30 million other species on Earth.

2. In order to maintain the per capita ecological productive area required for various consumption in Deyang City, it is 1.598 hectares per person. However, the actual ecological production area supply in Deyang City is only 0.461 hectares per person, and the ecological footprint required by the population of Deyang City is 61504 km^2, which is more than 10 times its actual area.
3. In the ecological footprint demand, arable land demand accounts for 82.9% of the total ecological footprint demand, and fossil fuel demand accounts for 13.5% of the total ecological footprint demand. It can be seen that grain, vegetables, pork, etc. accounted for a large proportion of ecological footprint in living consumption in Deyang in 2006, followed by coal, oil, electricity, etc. in energy consumption.
4. Overall, the ecological footprint demand in Deyang City is greater than the ecological carrying capacity, with an ecological deficit of 1.137 hectares per person. From the perspective of regional sustainable development, this development model in Deyang City cannot meet various consumption needs through its own production. It is a typical energy and resource supply area that needs to continuously supply energy and resources from other regions. Therefore, in the future development process, Deyang City should focus on adjusting industrial layout, optimizing enterprise production structure, improving resource and energy utilization, vigorously developing circular economy, and effectively implementing energy-saving and emission reduction tasks.

2.2.3.3 Ecological Footprint Assessment of Regional Sustainable Development

1. Evaluation Method of Ecological Footprint Improvement Model.

This method measures the sustainable development status of a region by estimating the size of the bio productive space required to maintain human natural resource consumption and assimilate human generated waste, and comparing it with the ecological carrying capacity of a given population area.

Calculate ecological carrying capacity through yield factors and compare it with ecological footprint to analyze the degree of sustainable development. When the ecological carrying capacity of a region is less than the ecological footprint, it indicates that the region has experienced an ecological deficit and is in a relatively unsustainable state. On the contrary, when the ecological carrying capacity is greater than the ecological footprint, it is an ecological surplus, and the surplus is equal to the difference between the ecological carrying capacity and the ecological footprint. This indicates that the region is in a relatively sustainable state, and the degree of sustainability is measured by the ecological surplus. Please refer to Table 2.7.

Table 2.7 Classification table for regional sustainable development level

Grade	ESI	Regional Sustainable Development Level
1	>0.70	Strong sustainability
2	0.50~0.70	weak sustainability
3	0.30~0.50	Weak unsustainable
4	<0.30	Strong unsustainable

2. Ecological Sustainable Development Index (ESI) Measurement Method.

ESI (Ecological Sustainable Development Index) = Aca/(Aca + Aef).

Among them, Aca is the per capita ecological carrying capacity; Aef is the per capita ecological footprint.

3. The Ecological Footprint and Sustainable Development of China and the World.

The ecological footprint of China is 1.6 Earth hectares per person, which means that the current demand is more than twice the sustainable supply quantity (per capita ecological carrying capacity) of China's ecosystem. According to this calculation, in order to ensure the current lifestyle of each member of China's 1.3 billion population, it is necessary to double the land and water area. Otherwise, the ecological footprint needs to be reduced to 0.8 Earth hectares per person (i.e., China's per capita ecological carrying capacity is 0.8 Earth hectares) in order to ensure sustainable development in China.

2.2.3.4 The "One Planet Living" Philosophy

The "One Planet Living" philosophy centers on adjusting the human ecological footprint to align with the Earth's carrying capacity. This is achieved through modifications in production strategies and lifestyle choices, intending to encourage mankind's sustainable development. As proposed by the United Nations Environment Program's Administrator, "One Planet Living" concept makes sustainable lifestyles attractive and accessible globally, thus fostering a mutually beneficial world built on rational resource utilization.

The concept of "One Planet Living" is based on the understanding that there are a total of 11 billion hectares of biologically productive land on Earth, with a total of 6.2 billion people worldwide, which means that the per capita ecological carrying capacity of the world is 1.8 hectares. The ecological footprint of the UK has reached

6 Earth hectares, requiring 3 Earths to meet its needs. The per capita ecological footprint of the US has reached 10 Earth hectares, requiring 5 Earths to meet its needs. The current average ecological footprint of the world is 2.2 Earth hectares per person, which greatly exceeds the available 1.8 Earth hectares. At the current rate of global use of natural resources and disposal of waste, the world needs to add a complete Earth by 2050. Therefore, a series of measures such as developing low-carbon economy and circular economy should be taken to adjust the ecological footprint of humanity to a level that the Earth can meet. The second is that the ecological footprint of a country mainly depends on factors such as households and energy consumption, transportation, food, consumer goods, services, government, factories, and buildings, so adjusting the ecological footprint should also start from these aspects. Thirdly, compared to ecological footprint, carbon footprint only reflects greenhouse gas emissions, but does not reflect environmental pollution and other factors. Therefore, ecological footprint can more comprehensively measure and guide sustainable development.

2.2.3.5 Equitable and Safe Individual Greenhouse Gas Emission Standards

The fair and safe individual greenhouse gas emission standards were proposed by American scholar Donald Brown in his book "Exploring the Ethical Responsibility of Individuals to Reduce Greenhouse Gas Emissions". The theoretical basis is that the main reason for climate change is that the energy consumption of billions of people far exceeds their fair share of fossil fuels, leading to unsafe levels of greenhouse gases in the atmosphere. Unless everyone accepts the ethical obligation to reduce their emissions to a fair and safe share, it is impossible to prevent the occurrence of dangerous global warming.

Determination of individual fair and safe greenhouse gas emissions share: to prevent dangerous climate change, it is necessary to reduce global greenhouse gas emissions by 60 to 80%. In order to achieve this goal, the fair share of individual safety emissions should be less than 4.5 tons (Tables 2.8, 2.9).

2.2.3.6 Resource-Environment Gini Coefficient

The Gini coefficient of resources and environment is derived from the Gini coefficient.

The Gini coefficient was proposed by Italian economist Gini in 1922. The Gini coefficient is a judgment indicator that reflects the fairness of income distribution. Although thc Gini coefficient is not a concept that can explain all social issues, its warning significance cannot be ignored when defining the relationship between fairness and efficiency through policies and laws.

The Gini coefficient of resources and environment is introduced to evaluate the fairness of resource consumption, pollution emissions, and economic contribution.

Table 2.8 Human carbon footprint in some countries[a] (Year 2004)

Nations	Per capita CO_2 emissions (tons)	Global CO_2 equivalent[b](Billion tons of CO_2)	The required atmosphere is equivalent to the current multiple of the Earth[c]
World[d]	4.5	2.9	2
USA	20.6	132	9
Canada	20.0	129	9
Australia	16.2	104	7
Japan	9.9	63	4
UK	9.8	63	4
Germany	9.8	63	4
Netherlands	8.7	56	4
Italy	7.8	50	3
Spain	7.6	49	3
France	6.0	39	3

Note [a] means calculated based on sustainable carbon budget; [b] refers to the global emissions when the per capita emissions of countries around the world are the same as those of reference countries; [c] means calculated based on a sustainable emission path of 14.5 billion tons of carbon dioxide per year; [d] refers to current carbon footprint
Source United Nation Development Program

Table 2.9 Greenhouse gas emission levels comparison in Chinese cities

	Total emission (10,000 tons)	Average discharge (tons / square kilometer)	Ratio to cities above prefecture level	per capita emissions (ton/person)	Ratio to the average level of prefecture level cities
Cities at or above the prefecture level nationwide (287 cities)	352,000	4800	1	7.9	1
100 cities with the largest economic scale	279,000	9700	2.02	9.7	1.23

Source Project team of the Sichuan Academy of Social Sciences

The Gini coefficient of resources and environment reflects the internal fairness of the allocation of national resource consumption and pollution emissions, which is reflected within a country. If the economic contribution rate of an internal unit is lower than the proportion of its resource consumption or pollution emissions to the national total, it is a violation of the allocation fairness of other units; otherwise, it is a contribution to the fairness of other units.

The Chinese Academy of Environmental Sciences has evaluated the fairness of China's resources and environment based on the connotation of the Gini coefficient of resources and environment, using the green contribution coefficient as an indicator to evaluate the fairness of internal unit pollutant emissions (or resource consumption). The method is to use the green contribution coefficient as the basis for judging unfair factors.

Green Contribution Coefficient (GCC) = Economic Contribution Rate/Pollution Emission Ratio (Resource Consumption Ratio): GCC = (Gi/G)/ (Pi/P).

In the formula, Gi and Pi respectively represent the regional GDP and pollutant emissions or resource consumption; G and P refers to the national GDP and pollutant emissions or resource consumption, respectively.

If GCC < 1, it indicates that the contribution rate of pollution emissions is greater than the contribution rate of GDP, and the fairness is relatively poor; If GCC > 1, it indicates that the contribution rate of pollutant emissions is less than the contribution rate of GDP, which is relatively fair and reflects a green development model.

2.3 Ecological Civilization in Urban Areas

2.3.1 The Evolution of Ecological Civilization Theories

In the mid-nineteenth century, industrialized western nations experienced photochemical pollution incidents in the United States, as well as serious environmental pollution incidents in the UK and Japan. People began to reflect on the drawbacks of industrialization. From the publication of "Silent Spring" in 1962 to "Limits to Growth" in 1972, from the "Conference on the Human Environment" in Stockholm, Sweden, to the United Nations "Conference on Environment and Development" in 1992, and until the convening of the United Nations "World Summit on Sustainable Development" in 2002, all of these marked the international community's search for a model different from traditional industrialization, hoping to embark on a development path that coordinates economic development, social progress and environmental protection. Some scholars have also begun to reflect on industrial civilization from the perspective of social civilization. Paul Birhanan foresaw the imminent emergence of a "post civilization" in his 1971 book *Beyond Civilization.* In 1995, American scholar Roy Morrison officially defined ecological civilization as a form of civilization after industrial civilization in his book "Ecological Democracy". At the same time, western ecological Marxism and eco-socialism are also quietly rising. The systematic ecological Marxist theory was formed with the publication of "Natural Control" and "Limits to Satisfaction" by William Rice of Canada in 1972 and 1976, respectively.[14] In China, in 1984, Ye Qianji was the first to use the concept of ecological civilization. He believed that ecological civilization is a harmonious and unified relationship between humans and nature that benefits both sides, while transforming and protecting nature.

The relationship between humans and nature is an eternal theme in the development of civilization. The relationship between humans and nature always runs through the rise and fall of civilization, and has decisive significance for the direction and fate of civilization. Social progress and economic development must depend on certain environmental conditions, and the ecological environment is the prerequisite and foundation for the development of human civilization.

Ecological civilization is the material and spiritual achievement accumulated in the relationship between humans and nature. It consists of three parts: ecological material, ecological technology and investment, and ecological spirit. The characteristics of the ecological environment determine that ecological civilization has the following characteristics: the physical boundaries of most ecological civilization achievements are fuzzy and difficult to observe and measure. The achievements of ecological civilization construction are closely related to human production and life, and their consumption is not exclusive. The benefits of the construction of ecological civilizations have both spillover and lagging characteristics.

Ecological civilization is the first time in human history that conscious replacement of civilizations. The environmental problems faced by humanity are not short-term disasters, but a systematic trend of diffusion. People have started to work together to solve environmental problems from aspects such as technological development, national legislation, international environmental coordination, and environmental ethics advocacy. It reflects a comprehensive and profound transformation of human values, attitudes, behaviors, and ways of production and life, and is a clear manifestation of another transformation of human civilization. James O'Connor, an American scholar, said that "Watt's steam engine is a victory in the economic field, but it is undoubtedly a disaster in the ecological field". It reflects the profound reflection of contemporary human beings on the achievements and problems of the industrialization road and industrial civilization started from modern Great Britain.

The construction of ecological civilization must be guided by a correct historical view of civilization, and by systematically sorting out the long evolution process of the relationship between humans and nature, revealing the historical truth and laws of the close interdependence between ecological environment and human civilization, providing historical reference for ecological civilization. Environmental history, a study of new history, expects to seek the internal logic between the natural environment and human survival, social development and civilization evolution through a systematic review of the long process of the relationship between human and nature.

Ecological civilization is an attitude and values that are responsible for the future. To build ecological civilization, it is necessary to advocate moderate consumption to ease the tension between human, resource and the environment. Maintaining the coordination between human consumption and environmental supply and recovery capabilities. The economic concept and model of simply relying on consumption to drive production, are contradictory to the construction of ecological civilization.

2.3.2 *The Ecological Civilization Construction Strategy in China*

In 2007, the 17th Congress of the CPC, starting from the goal of building a moderately prosperous society in an all-round way, took ecological civilization as a strategic task for the first time, and put forward "building ecological civilization, basically forming an industrial structure, growth mode, and consumption mode that saves energy and resources and protects the ecological environment".[15] For the first time, ecological civilization, together with material civilization, political civilization and spiritual civilization, has been juxtaposed as an important content and symbol of China's socialist modernization of "prosperity, democracy, civilization and harmony", as a new concept and strategy to achieve harmony between human and nature, comprehensive and coordinated sustainable development.[16]

In 2011, the outline of the "12th Five Year Plan" proposed that with increasingly strengthened resource and environmental constraints, it is necessary to enhance crisis awareness, establish a green and low-carbon development concept, focus on energy conservation and emission reduction, improve incentive and constraint mechanisms, accelerate the construction of resource efficient and environmentally friendly production and consumption modes, enhance sustainable development capabilities, and improve the level of ecological civilization. For the first time, green development and building a resource-saving and environmentally friendly society have been included in the outline, with resource conservation and environmental protection as binding indicators.

In July 2012, former China President Hu Jintao emphasized in his speech at the opening ceremony of the special seminar for major leaders and cadres at the provincial and ministerial levels that promoting ecological civilization construction is a strategic task involving fundamental changes in production and lifestyle. The concept, principles, goals, and other aspects of ecological civilization construction must be deeply and comprehensively integrated into all aspects and processes of China's economy, politics, culture, and social construction. Adhere to the basic national policy of resource conservation and environmental protection, strive to promote green development, circular development, and low-carbon development, and create a good production and living environment for the people.[17]

In October 2012, the 18th National Congress of the CPC proposed to put ecological civilization construction in a prominent position and become an important part of the "Five in One" overall layout of the cause of socialism with Chinese characteristics, striving to build a beautiful China and realizing the sustainable development of the Chinese nation. "Building ecological civilization is a long-term plan that is related to the well-being of the people and the future of the nation. Faced with the severe situation of tighten resource constraints, severe environmental pollution, and ecosystem degradation, it is necessary to establish an ecological civilization concept of respecting, conforming to, and protecting nature. The overall requirement for building ecological civilization is to adhere to the basic national policy of resource conservation and environmental protection. Adhere to the policy of prioritizing conservation, protection, and natural restoration. Efforts will be made to promote green development, circular development, and low-carbon development, forming a spatial pattern, industrial structure, production methods, and way of life for resource conservation and environmental protection, reversing the trend of ecological environment deterioration from the source, creating a good production and living environment for the people, and contributing to global ecological security".[18]

In 2012, ecological civilization entered the Resolution of the Eighth National Congress of the Communist Party of China on the Constitution of the CPC (Amendment). The conference agreed to include the construction of ecological civilization in the Party Constitution and elaborate on it, so as to improve the overall layout of the cause of socialism with Chinese characteristics, clarify the strategic position of ecological civilization, and promote the cause of socialism with Chinese characteristics.

At the 6th Collective Learning Conference of the Central Political Bureau in 2013, Xi Jinping emphasized that we should have a clear understanding of the urgency and difficulty of protecting the ecological environment and controlling environmental pollution, and the importance and necessity of strengthening the construction of ecological civilization. With a highly responsible attitude and responsibility towards the people and future generations, we will effectively control environmental pollution and improve the ecological environment, striving to move towards a new era of socialist ecological civilization, and creating a good production and living environment for the people.

Firmly establish the concept that protecting the ecological environment is protecting productivity, and improving the ecological environment is developing productivity. Never sacrifice the environment for temporary economic growth. We should firmly establish the concept of ecological red lines. In terms of ecological and environmental protection, we should not take a step beyond the limit, otherwise will be punished. To establish a system of accountability, those who make blind decisions regardless of the ecological environment and cause serious consequences should be held accountable, and their responsibility should be pursued for life. Strengthen the promotion and education of ecological civilization, enhance the awareness of conservation, environmental protection, and ecology among the people, and create a good atmosphere of caring for the ecological environment.

In the congratulatory letter to the annual meeting of the Guiyang International Forum on Ecological Civilization, Xi Jinping emphasized that "moving towards a new era of ecological civilization and building a beautiful China is an important part of realizing the Chinese Dream of great rejuvenation of the Chinese nation. China will adhere to the principles of respecting, conforming to, and protecting nature, implement the basic national policies of resource conservation and environmental protection, and more consciously promote green development, circular development, and low-carbon development. Ecological civilization will be integrated into all aspects and processes of economic, political, cultural, and social construction, forming a spatial pattern, industrial structure, production mode, and lifestyle that saves resources and protects the environment, leaving a production and living environment with blue sky, green ground, and green water for future generations".[19]

2.3.3 The Implementation of Ecological Civilization Construction in China

Firstly, establish a regulatory and policy system for the construction of ecological civilization. With the Party and the government taking the construction of ecological civilization as the Party's program and national strategy, China has introduced a series of laws, regulations, and policies. During the 11th Five Year Plan period alone, more than 100 national and local laws and regulations related to ecological civilization construction have been introduced.

Secondly, carry out energy conservation and emission reduction work. The 11th Five Year Plan began to take energy conservation and emission reduction as a binding indicator. National energy consumption per unit GDP decreased by 19.1%, sulfur dioxide emissions decreased by 14.29%, and chemical oxygen demand emissions decreased by 12.45%. The average annual growth rate of energy consumption of 6.6% supported the average annual growth rate of the national economy of 11.2%. The elasticity coefficient of energy consumption dropped significantly, the contradiction between energy supply and demand was alleviated, and the emission of major pollutants was effectively controlled.[20]

Thirdly, develop a circular economy. The 5th Plenary Session of the 16th Central Committee of the Communist Party of China proposed the development of circular economy. In 2005, the State Council issued the "Several Opinions on Accelerating the Development of Circular Economy". During the 11th Five Year Plan period, a unique circular economy development model has gradually emerged. The comprehensive output rate of China's main resources has increased by about 8%, the energy output rate has increased by 23.6%, the water resource output rate has increased by 34.5%, and the industrial water resource output rate has increased by 58.0%. In 2010, the comprehensive utilization of industrial solid waste was 1.52 billion tons, and the comprehensive utilization rate of industrial solid waste increased from 55.8% in 2005 to 69.0%. The total consumption of steel scrap in the steel industry reached 86.7 million tons; the recycling rate of renewable resources has increased by nearly 30 percentage points over the past five years. Developing circular economy has become an effective way for China to take the path of new industrialization, promote structural optimization, and transform the mode of economic development.

Fourthly, promote ecological protection. During the 11th Five Year Plan period, a series of policy documents for ecological protection were released, including the "Outline of the National Key Ecological Function Protection Zone Plan" and the "National Ecological Function Zoning". National afforestation increased by 9.6%; the protection rate of natural wetlands reached 50.3%, an increase of 5 percentage points. The area of national land nature reserves accounts for 14.7% of the national land area, and the trend of ecological deterioration has been controlled.

Fifth, actively respond to climate change. Since the 11th Five Year Plan period, China has incorporated combating climate change into its medium to long-term economic and social development plan. In 2007, a national plan to address climate change was formulated and implemented. In 2009, binding targets for greenhouse gas emissions reduction were established. By adjusting the industrial and energy structure, saving energy and improving energy efficiency, increasing carbon sinks, and other means, greenhouse gas emissions have been effectively controlled. In terms of adapting to climate change, by improving the ability of key areas to adapt to climate change, the adverse effects of climate change on agriculture, water resources, and public health have been alleviated.

2.3.4 *Domestic Scholars' Theoretical Research on Ecological Civilization*

Since the 17th National Congress of the Communist Party of China proposed the construction of ecological civilization, especially the 18th National Congress of the Communist Party of China, which placed ecological civilization construction in a more prominent position and became an important part of the overall layout of the "Five in One" promotion of socialist modernization with Chinese characteristics, the theoretical research on ecological civilization in China has been deeply promoted, resulting in a large number of theoretical achievements.

Chen Ruiqing and others believe that ecological civilization is a development stage of human civilization after primitive civilization, agricultural civilization, and industrial civilization, and is an aspect of social civilization. Civilization corresponds to barbarism. On the basis of industrial civilization, adopt a more civilized attitude towards nature, build and protect the ecological environment, and improve and optimize the relationship between humans and nature. Ecological civilization is a way to improve people's lives and achieve sustainable development, and is a form of civilization built on the basis of advanced productive forces. Ecological civilization should not remain at the ecological level and cannot be understood as ecology within the discipline of ecology. It is a higher form of civilization than primitive civilization, agricultural civilization, and industrial civilization, pursuing a higher level of harmony between humans and nature, environment and economy, and humans and society.

Yu Muchang and others believed that the juxtaposition of ecological civilization with material civilization, spiritual civilization and political civilization is a development concept. Wen Chuanhao and others believe that the construction of ecological civilization mainly includes advanced ecological ethics, developed ecological economy, sound ecological system, basic ecological security, and a good ecological environment. Different from material civilization, spiritual civilization and political civilization, ecological civilization is the concrete embodiment of the relationship between human and nature, human and social ecology, the civilization of the relationship between heaven and human, involving system civilization, cognitive civilization, material civilization and mentality civilization. The construction of ecological civilization can be divided into subsystems such as ecological consciousness, ecological ethics, ecological morality, ecological behavior, ecological industry, ecological system, ecological society, ecological management, ecological culture, ecological economy, and ecological political construction.

Ecological civilization is a modern ecological value, and its core value is that human beings treat ecology well and protect themselves. Ecological civilization is a re-understanding of the relationship between humans and nature based on a profound reflection on the values of industrial civilization, which unilaterally exaggerates the role of the main body and opposes humans and nature, believing that humans are the masters and owners of nature.[21] From the perspective of ecological civilization, the human understanding and transformation of the external world are infinite and also limited; human needs are infinite and limited; the subjectivity of humans is not infinite, but finite. The relationship between humans and nature is not conquest or being conquest, but rather a harmonious coexistence.

From the perspective of civilization development stage, ecological civilization is a higher development stage than agricultural civilization and industrial civilization; it is a civilization that inherits the ideas and customs of agricultural and industrial era, but has qualitative differences.[22] Ecological civilization is a civilization that considers how to use human power reasonably after mankind have a strong ability to transform nature. Ecological civilization is a transcendence of existing civilization, which will lead humanity to abandon the utilitarian and materialistic hedonism formed during the industrial civilization period, and to avoid lose-lose tragedy of both ecology and humanity.

Wen Chuanhao and others believe that ecological civilization is a reflection on past civilizations, especially industrial civilization. Agricultural civilization and industrial civilization developed at a stage that human force was at a disadvantageous situation comparing with natural forces, which featured by material, rational, and offensive characteristics, emphasizing sensibility, balance, coordination, and stability. Ecological civilization replaced anthropocentrism with the concept of ecosystem, and denied the material hedonism and the plunder of nature formed since the industrial civilization. The construction of ecological civilization needs to absorb traditional ecological ideological resources, but it is by no means a return to agricultural civilization. Ecological civilization and industrial civilization are not opposing forms of civilization. Industrial civilization is the closest form of civilization to ecological civilization. The development of industrial technology has provided a complete, rich, and comfortable material world for the survival and development of human society.

Ecological civilization is also a scientific concept of development, a worldview and methodology for development. Ecological civilization is guided by sustainable development, with the main task of building resource efficient and environmentally friendly production, lifestyle, and consumption methods. The goal is to coordinate economic development with population, resources, and environment, so that people can produce and live in a good ecological environment, and achieve sustainable economic and social development. Ecological civilization is related to the vital interests of the people, the survival and development of the nation and the country. Ecological civilization is an important indicator of the coordination and sustainability of development, which can best reflect the level of civilization and development of a country and region.

Ecological civilization also includes industries, management, technology, economy, methods, and other related aspects that enhance the level of energy conservation and environmental protection, and the ability to respond to climate change. Ecological civilization is both a hard power and an important soft power. The quality of the ecological environment determines the resilience of a country's economic development. The positive effects of ecological factors will promote the development of productivity, while conversely, they will hinder the development of productivity. Ecological civilization is an important guarantee for maintaining national ecological security and preventing it from becoming a "weakness" or bottleneck in economic development.

Wen Chuanhao and others believe that ecological construction does not equal the construction of ecological civilization. In addition, it also includes the formation of energy-saving consumption models, the development of ecological industries, and the establishment of ecological civilization concepts.

Ecological creation is not equivalent to the construction of ecological civilization. Building an ecological province and ecological county is only the first step of ecological civilization. The second step is to utilize the effectiveness and foundation of ecological construction, shift the focus of ecological province building towards ecological rich province, and promote the comprehensive and coordinated development of the province's economy, society, culture, and other fields on the basis of ecological rich province, in order to truly achieve ecological province building.

2.3.5 Foreign Scholars' Perspectives on the Strategy for Constructing China's Ecological Civilization

The proposal of ecological civilization at the 18th National Congress of the Communist Party of China is a positive response of the CPC to the development law of social civilization and people's ecological demands. The Chinese government has elevated the construction of ecological civilization to a strategic task and basic national policy, which is not common worldwide.[23]

Developing industrialized countries should fully understand the results of industrialization experiments conducted by leading countries in history, take the lessons from the last century seriously, and take cautious actions.

The Chinese government and scholars have made transforming the economic development model an important aspect of ecological civilization. China's emphasis on ecological civilization has also inspired European and American scholars to reflect on ecological culture and ecological spirit.

The core value of capitalism is to create more material wealth in the most efficient way. However, many Americans realized as early as the 1960s that the culture we promote has exceeded the carrying capacity of the environment. In the 1970s, both the public and the government responded those callings positively, but hindered by some big companies, as the change would reduce their profit margin.

For capitalist countries, development is endless, and once the pace of development slows down, there will be serious economic and social crises arise. The pursuit of ecological civilization is not endless and rapid development, but to meet the basic material needs of everyone as much as possible. When this goal is achieved, society needs to slow down its development speed. We have only one Earth, and our limited resources cannot sustain endless development. Our existing resources are sufficient to support everyone's basic needs for food, housing, transportation, and healthcare, but they are far from meeting everyone's demand for luxury goods. Therefore, a reasonable and balanced allocation of resources is crucial for achieving ecological civilization and promoting sustainable development.[24]

China is still a developing country and a populous country, slowing down development to recuperate is almost impossible. But in the long run, China's emphasis on ecological civilization construction will definitely be beneficial to the development of the world. One challenge faced by China's ecological civilization construction is how to educate the public to recognize their mission: to produce the vast majority of essential goods in a sustainable manner.

For a long time, we have criticized the prevalence of consumerism, but we have failed to curb its spread. The modernization of education has weakened the inheritance of classical values and alleviated resistance to consumerism. Chinese culture has always advocated harmonious coexistence between humans and nature, and this value has been passed on from generation to generation. China is likely to combine its ancient wisdom to curb the trend of consumerism.

2.3.6 Establishment of Ecological Civilization Infrastructure

The construction of ecological civilization should establish and improve corresponding institutional mechanisms to provide institutional guarantees.

2.3.6.1 Evaluation, Reward and Sanction System

According to the requirements of the 18th National Congress of the Communist Party of China, "resource consumption, environmental damage, and ecological benefits should be included in the evaluation system of economic and social development, and a target system, assessment methods, and reward and punishment mechanism that reflects the requirements of ecological civilization should be established".[25] A financial incentive system that is conducive to the construction of ecological civilization should be established.

2.3.6.2 Land and Spatial Development Protection Mechanism

The construction of regional ecological civilization requires selective incentives to promote collective actions for cross regional ecological civilization construction. The integration of regional ecological civilization construction cannot be formed solely by the power of the market. The "free riding" behavior of beneficiaries of ecological civilization construction often makes it difficult for the ecological construction of a single region to receive cooperation and cooperation from neighboring regional governments under the existing system. The integration of regional ecological civilization construction is constrained by the behavior of various ecological entities and cannot achieve "collective action".[26] The construction of a cross regional ecological civilization integration system requires collective action from the central government to local governments. Two types of "selective incentives", social sanctions and social rewards, are essential. They can be used to mobilize potential groups. The essence of this social incentive is that "they can treat individuals differently: disobedient individuals are excluded, and cooperative individuals are invited to participate".

2.3.6.3 Resource Usage and Payment System

Ecology is resource, and ecology is also capital. Utilizing ecology requires payment. Not only do we need to demand the ecological environment, but we also need to invest heavily. If we want to maintain the sustainability of this investment, we need to ensure the reasonable return of ecological investors through institutional innovation, and the system of paid use of resources can effectively motivate people to engage in ecological investment and increase the value of ecological capital.

Most resource-based products are not renewable. Due to long-term unreasonable resource prices, resource waste and low efficiency in resource allocation have been caused. The issue of resources has become a practical bottleneck for the sustainable development of China's economy and society. Treating all resource-based products as capital and as a precious asset bestowed upon us by nature. Only by fully recognizing the importance of each resource, paying for its use, giving resources a reasonable price, and imposing reasonable taxes and fees can we ensure that resource-based products are not abused.[27]

2.3.6.4 Ecological Compensation System

By creating a regional ecological compensation mechanism, it can serve as an extremely effective mediator to ensure that the rights to survival, development, and environment are aligned. How to calculate the value of regional ecological service functions and, based on this, calculate the ecological compensation values of different regions is a key issue in establishing a sound ecological compensation mechanism.

2.3.6.5 Ecological Protection Accountability System

The key is to establish binding norms for the construction of ecological environment protection by governments at all levels, and to achieve the goal of decomposing and implementing the total emission control indicators of major pollutants and other ecological indicators layer by layer to various regions, departments, key industries and units, ensuring the completion of binding indicators. Linking environmental protection with the selection and appointment of cadres. Officials who cause serious environmental accidents shall be strictly held legally responsible, especially criminally responsible. Establish an ecological audit system for the departure of local leaders and cadres, to assess whether their economic decisions and personal achievements during their tenure have been made at the expense of the ecological environment.

2.3.6.6 Environmental Damage Compensation System

Rejecting the concept of "human centeredness". The anthropocentric approach emphasizes the economic value of resources while ignoring their ecological value when dealing with ecological environment issues, focusing on contemporary people's economic interests and comfortable lives to ignore the survival and development of future generations. This has led to intergenerational inequality, ultimately leading to natural control over humanity — the Earth's ecology is becoming unable to support human survival. Therefore, "the intrinsic value or goodness of the ecological environment must be recognized conceptually, and this value comes from the nature of the ecological environment itself to meet the needs of human survival and development, rather than the creation of human labor".

2.3.7 *The Goal and Path of Building Ecological Civilization*

2.3.7.1 The Transformation from "Economic Individual" to "Ecological Individual"

Ecological civilization requires a re-examination of the relationship between humans and nature, so that moral relationships are no longer limited to between humans, but expand to the natural realm. Morality not only includes the norms of behavior between people, but also the norms of behavior between people and nature. We need to transform from an "economic individual" who pursues maximum benefits to an "ecological individual" who maximizes the overall system benefits, including ecological benefits, as the value judgment standard and behavioral basis. Transforming pure economic benefits into ecological and systematic benefits. Correspondingly, social moral standards should not only be norms of behavior between individuals, but also extend to norms of behavior between humans and nature. Let the concept of ecological civilization be firmly established in the entire society. Implementing the task of building a good ecological environment to every unit and family has become a conscious action of the entire society.

2.3.7.2 Transition from Economic Growth to Sustainable Development

Free from the mindset of "economic growth equals development", replace it with sustainable development models and methods, and consider the coordination of economic development with population, environment, and resources, as well as the unity of economic, social, and ecological benefits.[28] Considering both the current and future development needs, without sacrificing the interests of future generations to meet the interests of contemporary people. Not only should we arrange current development, but we also need to create better conditions for future development, shifting from a development model that wastes resources and pollutes first to a development model that is resource saving and environmentally friendly, and from only emphasizing economic development to a combination of economic development, resource conservation, and environmental protection.

2.3.7.3 Transformation in Production and Lifestyle

Building a spatial pattern, industrial structure, growth mode, and consumption mode that is conducive to resource conservation and environmental protection. Transforming from an extensive economic growth model of "low efficiency, high input, high emissions, high pollution, and non-circulation" to a growth model of "low input, high output, low consumption, low emissions, recyclability, and sustainability"; optimize the industrial structure, shift from relying mainly on the secondary industry to driving the coordinated development of the primary, secondary, and tertiary industries; especially, it is necessary to develop modern service industries and energy-saving and environmental protection industries that are conducive to resource conservation and environmental protection. The circular economy has formed on a large scale and the proportion of renewable energy has significantly increased; the shift from mainly consuming material resources to mainly relying on technological progress, improving the quality of workers, and innovating management. The transformation towards a civilized, economical, moderate, reasonable, and circular way of life and consumption patterns.[29]

2.3.7.4 Transition from "Dilemma" to "Mutually Beneficial Scenario"

The prominent contradiction between economic development and the ecological environment is a common issue in the rapid economic development stage of various countries. In the vast developing countries that are currently in the stage of post modernization, there may be some conflicts between economic development and environmental protection, which require paying a price that developed countries no longer need to pay. Therefore, it is particularly important and difficult to handle the relationship between the construction of ecological civilization and the construction of material civilization. For latecomer countries, including China, which are currently undergoing rapid industrialization and urbanization, the economic development, environmental damage, and global warming issues experienced by developed countries must be faced simultaneously, manifested in a compressed and concentrated state. This is the particularity and difficulty of building ecological civilization in these countries.

Economic construction and ecological environment protection are a "dilemma" contradiction, and in dealing with and handling this contradiction, we should overcome the misconceptions formed by the two perspectives. One is the "cost theory", which holds that environmental pollution is an insurmountable stage of industrialization and modernization, and a price must be paid.[30] The issue of resource conservation and environmental protection is a postmodern issue, raised by wealthy countries and people as a "luxury demand". The reason why this "pollution first, treatment later" and "economic priority theory", which goes against ecological civilization, still prevail and have a market, has its profound ideological and social roots. One reason is that economic growth is the organizational principle of society, and the public mainly judges a government based on how fast the country grows under its governance; furthermore, the benefits brought by economic growth are immediate, while the benefits of ecological environment protection are mainly future. Another viewpoint is the "zero growth" theory, which uses stopping economic and social development to achieve a good ecological environment. This viewpoint is not feasible in both theory and practice, mainly because seeking environmental protection by abandoning economic growth will lose the material foundation of environmental protection and ultimately deviate from the goal of sustainable development.

The correct choice is to find a junction between economic development and ecological environment protection. Addressing ecological environmental issues in economic development and developing the economy within the carrying capacity of the ecological environment. The construction of ecological civilization is not opposed to the construction of material civilization, but is unified to sustainable development, changing "dilemma" into "win–win" situation.[31]

2.3.7.5 Internalization of "Externality"

"Externality" refers to the phenomenon whereby the "benefits" or "costs" associated with ecological governance are often transferred to society and future generations. These costs or benefits from one country or region often spill over to others. As such, establishing and improving systems and mechanisms conducive to ecological protection through comprehensive legal, economic, and administrative measures, coupled with awareness and educational initiatives, are crucial. Promoting the internalization of external costs and the commercialization of social costs is an essential task in the process of constructing an ecological civilization.

2.3.7.6 The Overall Coordination of Domestic and International Situations

The construction of ecological civilization in modern countries should have an international perspective, adhere to the overall planning of both domestic and international situations, combine domestic and international ecological environmental issues, combine domestic ecological civilization construction with international environmental issues such as global warming and energy crisis, and jointly implement. We should not only absorb and draw on the positive achievements of ecological civilization construction in other countries around the world, but also adhere to the characteristics of our own ecological civilization construction based on our own reality. In response to global warming, we must not only assume "common but differentiated responsibilities" and contribute to protecting the global climate, but also utilize the advanced concepts, systems, technological and economic means of the world, especially developed countries, to address climate change, improve our own ability to mitigate and adapt to climate change, and provide opportunities and institutional mechanisms, financial and technological support for building ecological civilization in China.[32]

2.3.7.7 Further Reformation

The construction of ecological civilization essentially means the restructuring of social development structure and various social relations, including relations of production. The key to solving China's ecological problems lies not in the environment itself, nor entirely in environmental governance methods and technologies, but in reforming and compensating for a series of institutional deficiencies.

2.3.7.8 Theoretical Research Reinforcement

Strengthen the theoretical research on ecological civilization, and enrich and improve the theoretical system of socialism with Chinese characteristics with a complete and systematic concept of ecological civilization. Strengthen the research on "ecological view" in Chinese traditional culture, Marxist "ecological view", ecological Marxism and eco-socialism. Deeply analyze the relationship between industrial civilization and capitalist economic crisis, political crisis, and institutional crisis, combined with China's practice of reform and opening up and the construction of ecological civilization, create a theoretical system of "ecological civilization concept", and use it as the guiding ideology for China's future economic and social development and environmental protection.[33]

2.3.7.9 The Ecological Culture Construction Promotion

Strengthen the guiding position of the concept of ecological civilization and strengthen the construction of ecological culture. Establish correct values and development concepts, enhance the coordination of development, and promote the achievement of sound and rapid economic development. Strengthen the construction of ecological culture, improve the ecological civilization quality of the entire nation, and promote the comprehensive development of humanities. Advocating ecological ethics, popularizing ecological awareness, gradually elevating ecological awareness into national consciousness, mainstream ideological trends, and fashion concepts, forming a trend of paying attention to ecology, protecting ecology, and rational consumption. Constructing a systematic ecological and cultural system with Chinese characteristics; strengthen and promote ecological culture domestic and abroad, take the lead in international public opinion, enhance China's cultural soft power, and improve international status.

2.3.8 Government's Responsibility in the Construction of Ecological Civilization

The 18th National Congress of the Communist Party of China placed ecological civilization in a prominent position, requiring it to be integrated into all aspects and processes of economic, political, cultural, and social construction. Xi Jinping has been repeatedly emphasized that with a highly responsible attitude and responsibility towards the people and future generations, we will effectively control environmental pollution and improve the ecological environment, strive to move towards a new era of socialist ecological civilization, and create a good production and living environment for the people. Firmly establish the concept that protecting the ecological environment is protecting productivity, and improving the ecological environment is developing productivity.[34] Never sacrifice the environment for temporary economic growth. All demonstrate the heavy responsibility and important position of the government in the construction of ecological civilization.

In addition to political responsibility, moral responsibility, legal responsibility and administrative responsibility, ecological responsibility is also an important responsibility of the government. Traditional public management regards maximizing economic development as its primary goal, rarely considering environmental issues, and even at the cost of sacrificing the environment. Ecological civilization requires full consideration of the value of environmental ecology, taking the path of technological progress, improving efficiency, and saving resources, treating nature fairly, scientifically developing and utilizing it reasonably, and maximizing the ecological balance of nature. These responsibilities should undoubtedly be borne by the government.[35]

Firstly, the government's ecological responsibility towards the market. The market is a key link in the ecological chain, with broad space for government's action. Standardize the standards for enterprises to produce green products; pay attention to the development and utilization of renewable resources; set prices for green products; help enterprises to carry out green marketing, etc.

Secondly, the government's ecological responsibility to the public. Establishing the concept of "intra generational fairness" and using nature as a medium to achieve common development among same generation.

Finally, ensure the institutional supply for the construction of ecological civilization. (1) Levy environmental tax and ecological compensation tax. Environmental taxes can not only regulate people's economic behavior, reduce pollution, but also raise funds for the national public finances; introduce green tax laws such as the "Environmental Tax Law" to provide legal protection for environmental taxes. (2) Promote the legal construction of ecological protection. Many conflicts of interest related to environmental resources have exposed the shortcomings of administrative control measures, and it is necessary to promote the coordinated development of society, economy, and ecology through legal means. The government should establish and improve laws and regulations for ecological protection as soon as possible. (3) Incorporate ecological education into compulsory education. Enhance public environmental awareness, establish a green education mechanism, carry out education on environmental protection knowledge in primary and secondary schools, and enhance students' awareness and sense of responsibility to protect the environment. Offering environmental courses in non-environmental majors in universities, strengthen education on environment and sustainable development for government administrators; promote laws and regulations related to environmental protection in rural areas, and disseminate the information of environmental pollution and harm to human health caused by the use of pesticides, fertilizers, plastic films, and various pollutants emitted by township enterprises. (4) Developing ecological economy, including developing ecological agriculture, ecological industry, ecological tourism, etc.[36]

2.3.8.1 Ecological Agriculture

Ecological agriculture refers to agriculture that can save energy, protect natural resources, improve the ecological environment, and provide pollution-free food. The development of ecological agriculture is mainly achieved through the development of green food, organic food, and ecological agricultural tourism. The way out for animal husbandry, vegetables, fruits, and aquaculture to improve market competitiveness is to ensure that their development is integrated into the ecological track. Ecological agricultural tourism is the optimization and adjustment of ecological tourism products. Through the cross infiltration of the first and third industries, the integration of agriculture and tourism, and an interactive mechanism is established between the two industries. It not only organically combines tourism activities such as sightseeing, vacation, entertainment, and participation, enriches the forms of tourism products, but also plays a positive role in reducing the risks of tourism development investment and achieving cross industry development of tourism.

2.3.8.2 Ecological Industry

Apply modern science and technology to establish a comprehensive industrial production system that is multi-level, multi-structured, multifunctional, and utilizes industrial waste as raw materials to achieve circular production and intensive management. The first step is to build an ecological industrial park, where several enterprises or different subsidiaries within a business group gather in a certain area, respectively assuming the roles of producers, consumers, and restorers, and establish an industrial chain network structure with multiple layers of material and energy utilization, a virtuous cycle, high conversion efficiency, and good economic and ecological benefits. Secondly, it is to develop a circular economy, and thirdly, to implement a green certification system that meets international standards. Through green certification and the use of green labels, green products can smoothly enter the international market.

2.3.8.3 Ecological Tourism

Ecological tourism is a special tourism activity featured with ecological science and education and popular science. It emphasizes the development of tourism while addressing the relationship between human and nature. To develop ecotourism, firstly, it is necessary to make good development plans and implement orderly development. Secondly, it is necessary to strengthen publicity and education to make ecological justice and ecological obligations conscious actions and moral norms of the whole society. Thirdly, it is necessary to strengthen the construction of ecological demonstration areas and provide ecological protection for special and concentrated areas such as forests, water sources, species, and wetlands.

2.3.9 Measurement of Ecological Civilization

Since the 18th National Congress of the Communist Party of China, there has been an accelerating trend in the theoretical exploration and practical promotion of the indicator system for ecological civilization construction in China. Henan, Guiyang, Xiamen and other places have also established local ecological civilization evaluation standards. Taking a comprehensive view of these indicator systems, we mainly refer to the indicator systems in three fields. Firstly, the indicator system for the construction of ecological counties and provinces formulated by the State Environmental Protection Administration; the second is the indicator system for building a moderately prosperous society in the country; the third is the indicator system for the construction of new rural areas. Highlight three key points: first, ecological protection and environmental governance; second, improving people's living standards and quality; the third is to solve the problems of agriculture, rural areas, and farmers. In terms of methodology, the system analysis method is mainly used to construct an evaluation index system for ecological civilization construction from aspects such as economic development efficiency.

Overall, these indicator systems mainly have the following shortcomings: (1) single indicators and lack of comprehensive and systematic analysis. The design and assessment mainly focus on economic and ecological environmental protection, but there are too few indicators for social progress. (2) Basically qualitative indicators or reference indicators; (3) Overall, there are too many reference indicators, which makes the assessment lack operability; (4) The assessment indicators and methods have not been combined with the ecological and economic functions of the administrative region where the assessment is conducted in the main functional areas of the country and region; (5) Emphasis is placed on energy conservation, emission reduction, pollution control, and environmental protection, while ecological construction is lacking or even overlooked. The content of ecological construction only stays at the level of ecological protection. This is not conducive to fully utilizing existing human science and technology to quickly restore and rebuild the ecosystem, let alone providing ecological services for human production and life in the short term.

Column 2.4 Ecological Civilization Ranking in China

"The Study on Regional Differences in Ecological Civilization in China" mainly uses the measurement formula of ecological civilization level:

EEI = GDP/regional ecological footprint.

Among them, EEI is the regional gross domestic product corresponding to the unit ecological footprint generated by the region, which is directly proportional to GDP. Under certain conditions of ecological footprint, the higher the GDP, the greater its level; in inverse proportion to the ecological footprint, the smaller the ecological footprint, the higher its level, given a fixed regional gross domestic product.

Measure the current development status of ecological civilization in various provinces and cities across the country, and form the following order: Beijing, Shanghai, Guangdong, Zhejiang, Fujian, Jiangsu, Tianjin, Guangxi, Shandong, Chongqing, Sichuan, Jiangxi, Henan, Hunan, (after are provinces that below the national average line) Hubei, Hainan, Anhui, Shaanxi, Heilongjiang, Jilin, Qinghai, Hebei, Liaoning, Xinjiang, Yunnan, Gansu, Inner Mongolia, Guizhou, Ningxia, Shanxi.

There are 14 provinces, cities, and autonomous regions with ecological footprints higher than the national average, among which Shanxi, Inner Mongolia, Ningxia, Liaoning, and Shanghai are the five provinces and cities with the highest ecological footprints; there are 16 provinces, cities, and autonomous regions below the national average, with Guangxi, Sichuan, Jiangxi, Anhui, and Chongqing being the lowest. The highest Shanxi is 4.5 times higher than the lowest Guangxi.

2.4 Cities and Ecological Environment

2.4.1 The Harmonious Coexistence Between Cities and Nature as a Fundamental Prerequisite to the Harmony Between Humans and Nature

2.4.1.1 The Impact of Cities and Urbanization on the Ecological Environment

From an ecological perspective, cities are an artificial ecosystem composed of nature, economy, and society. They have important functions such as material transformation, energy flow, and information transmission, but at the same time, the most prominent contradiction between humans and nature happens in the cities. The biggest difference between urban and rural areas is that the degradation function of cities is too weak, and the production and consumption functions are too strong, so cities have a significant impact on the surrounding environment.

Urbanization is a fundamental transformation of human capital, land capital, and other resource utilization methods, which will have a profound impact and change on the ecological environment. On the one hand, urbanization promotes the intensive utilization of resources and improves the efficiency. Urbanization characterized by population aggregation provides opportunities for the concentrated discharge and treatment of various environmental pollutants, which helps to reduce the level of pollution emissions per unit of population. In the long run, urbanization drives economic development, which will bring about an increase in technology (especially pollution control technology) and people's demand for environmental services, thereby promoting the improvement of environment.[37] On the other hand, urbanization also means the intensive use of land, water, and other resources in relatively small spaces, leading to high-density emissions of pollutants that exceed the absorption and degradation capacity of local nature, and can have a huge negative impact on the urban environment and ecosystem.

1. Impact on water environment: one is the excessive exploitation and utilization of water resources, especially groundwater; the second is the pollution of the surface and groundwater, and the intertwined effects of these two aspects. According to the European Environmental Protection Agency, 60% of European cities with a population of over 100,000 have varying degrees of groundwater overexploitation. Over extraction of groundwater is also very serious in Asian cities. The groundwater level in Bangkok, Manila, Madras and other cities has dropped significantly. Excessive exploitation of groundwater can lead to decreased water levels, dry wells, high pumping costs, land subsidence, saline water intrusion, and land salinization.[38] Many cities around the world have experienced subsidence during periods of rapid economic development, such as New York, Tokyo, Mexico City, and others.

Column 2.5 Urban Land Subsidence in China

According to a geological survey report released by the Ministry of Land and Resources in 2012, more than 50 rapidly growing cities across the country are suffering from large-scale land subsidence problems. Although the subsidence rate is relatively slow, the problem is already severe in cities such as Shanghai, Beijing, and Xi'an. The largest cumulative subsidence in the central area of Shanghai has exceeded 2 m. As of 2009, there were 79,000 square kilometers of land with a cumulative land subsidence of over 200 mm across the country.

The most serious subsidence areas in China are the Yangtze River Delta, North China Plain and Fenwei Basin. The National Land Subsidence Prevention and Control Plan approved by the State Council in 2012 requires that the subsidence trends in the above three regions be curbed by 2015 and the nationwide subsidence trend be curbed by 2020.

China is in the process of large-scale urbanization, and the shortage of land resources requires buildings to be built higher. The increasing urban population also requires more water sources, so the development of groundwater has become a trend. The construction of high-rise buildings and the extraction of groundwater are the main causes of urban land subsidence, which in turn accelerates the rate of building collapse and increases the maintenance costs of infrastructure such as railways, drainage systems, power grids, and communication networks.

The response measure is to limit the development and use of groundwater, and for areas with severe settlement, surface water can be injected into the ground. Shanghai spends billions of yuan annually to stop the trend of land subsidence by injecting water underground. But this method is too expensive.

Source: China's urbanization needs to shift to building a new rural area with ecological balance, People's Daily, http://ezheng.people.com.cn/proposalPostDetail.do?id=734263&boardId=1.

2. The impact of cities on the atmospheric environment. The industrial development in cities and surrounding areas will bring about a large amount of dust, sulfides, nitrogen oxides, and other toxic substances emissions. The widespread use of fossil fuels in power generation and transportation also further causes air pollution in cities. The Los Angeles photochemical event in 1943 in the United States, the smoke event in London in 1952, and the Max Valley event in Belgium in 1930 are all typical events of urban atmospheric pollution.
3. The impact of cities on local climate. Due to intensive industrial activities, traffic congestion, and severe air pollution, especially in cities where buildings are mostly made of stone and concrete, their high thermal conductivity and capacity, coupled with their own blocking or weakening effect on wind, form the "heat island effect" and "cold island effect" of the city, leading to changes in the local climate of the city.
4. The impact on land resources. The impact of the sprawling urbanization model on land resources is particularly prominent. During the Cold War, the United States proposed to reduce the size of cities and induce people to go to the suburbs due to

concerns about atomic bomb prevention. In addition, the United States subsidized large-scale highway construction, resulting in low-density urban sprawl. This discrete, frog-jumping-like urban development has resulted in a large amount of farmland and green space being used for real estate development and road traffic construction. Between 1982 and 1992, the United States lost an average of 277.5 Mu of agricultural land per hour, with approximately 2.43 million Mu lost annually, equivalent to 0.1% of the arable land area in the United States.[39]

2.4.1.2 The Impact of Cities and Urbanization on Greenhouse Gas Emissions and Climate Change

Pan Jiahua believes that cities are the main battlefield for creating wealth, as well as the main places for energy consumption and greenhouse gas emissions. In the process of urbanization, urban construction and urban lifestyle have brought about a large amount of greenhouse gas emissions, which have a huge impact on global warming. Cities are the main consumers of resource and energy, and also the main emitters of greenhouse gases. Urban carbon emissions account for 60–80% of the world's carbon emissions. In addition, due to urbanization, a large amount of farmland has been transformed into cement land, and the ground has hardened, causing strong reflection of sunlight, which is also an important reason for global warming.

The rapid urbanization in China has led to a significant increase in urban housing, transportation, and other infrastructure construction, as well as a rapid increase in energy resource consumption. China's energy structure was dominated by fossil fuels, the advancement of urbanization inevitably leads to a continuous increase in carbon dioxide emissions, making cities a huge source of greenhouse gas emissions (Table 2.10).

Table 2.10 Greenhouse gas emission trends in Chinese cities (2006)

Type	Total emission (100 million tons)	Proportion in China (%)	Average emissions per square kilometer (tons/square kilometer)	Ratio to national level	Per capita emissions (tons)	Ratio to national level
Nationwide	54	100	540	1	4.1	1
Cities above prefecture level (287 seats)	35.2	65	4800	8	7.9	1.9
100 cities with the largest economic scale	27.9	52	9700	16.2	9.7	2.4

2.4.1.3 The Origin and Thought of Urban Green Transformation

At the beginning of the Industrial Revolution in the eighteenth century, cities rapidly expanded and the natural environment of cities underwent tremendous changes, prompting humans to pay attention to the living environment of cities and explore the relationship between cities and the ecological environment.

At the end of the nineteenth century, E. Howard in England published the theory of "Garden City" (1898), and began to use ecological theories and methods to study cities. In the nineteenth century, British biologist P. Geddls' *Urban Development* (1904) and *Evolving Cities* (1915) combined environmental, health, housing, municipal engineering, and urban planning into development considerations. R. E. Park of the United States published *Cities: Several Suggestions for Human Behavior in the Environment* (1916), which applies certain laws that govern natural biological communities, such as competition, symbiosis, succession, and dominance, to urban research. The Athens Charter of 1933 stipulated that the purpose of urban planning was to ensure the normal functioning of the four major activities of human habitation, work, recreation, and communication, further clarifying the concept of an organic complex of urban environment. At the beginning of the twentieth century, a group of foreign scholars represented by Parker's *City and Human Ecology* (1952), R. Carson's *Silent Spring* (1962), and the Club of Rome's *Limits to Growth* (1972) applied ecological ideas to the study of urban ecology, laying the theoretical foundation of ecological cities.

The "Man and the Biosphere Program" launched by UNESCO in the 1970s proposed to study the factors that affect the health of urban ecosystem and the harmonious relationship between man and land, analyzed the causes of urban environmental problems, and first proposed the concept of Eco City. In 1984, the "Man and the Biosphere Program" proposed the five principles of ecological city planning, and in the same year, Richard Register, an American urban ecologist and chairman of the Association of Eco city Builders, proposed the principles of building ecological cities. Yanitsky, an ecologist of the former Soviet Union, proposed that the ideal model of eco city is that technology and nature are fully integrated, human creativity and ecological benefits are maximized, residents' physical and mental health and environmental quality are protected to the maximum, material energy and information are used efficiently, and the ecological cycle is a kind of ideal habitat for human beings.[40] Register also believes that an Eco City is an eco-healthy city, which is compact, energetic, energy-saving and harmonious with nature. Cities are places where modern industrial civilization can be concentrated, but they are also places suffering from many modern problems brought about by industrial civilization, including environmental pollution, resource and energy shortages, and so on. "The quality of human life largely depends on the way we build cities, the density and diversity of urban populations. The higher the urban population density and diversity, the less reliance on mechanized transportation systems, and the less consumption of natural resources, the smaller the negative impact on nature."[41]

In the 1930s, Rank Wright, the leader of American modern architecture, put forward the idea of "Broadacre City" in view of the rapid development of the automobile industry at that time. He advocated that the cities in the future would no longer be concentrated, but spread to the suburbs, and adopt a decentralized urban layout. However, Soleri, a student of Frank Wright and the father of American ecological architecture, criticized Frank Wright's viewpoint. He said, "I hate my teacher because he promotes the extraordinary development of the automotive industry, and the 'patching' biofuel strategy is useless". Soleri believes that "humanity is facing a crisis, cities are devouring the Earth and consuming energy. Perhaps 10 Earths are enough to sustain, and humanity should completely change this way of life." "As the natural organism evolves, it will also become increasingly complex and become a more compact or miniaturized system. Just like a city, it also operates like a living system." Soleri first proposed the concept of building a linear city and conducted a 40-year-experiment on the "Lean Linear Arterial City" in the desert of Acosandi, located more than 100 km north of Phoenix, Arizona.

In China, Ma Shijun and Wang Rusong put forward the theory of social-economic-natural composite ecological systems theory, believing that cities are typical social-economic-natural composite ecosystems. Comprehensive social-economic-natural composite ecosystem research should be carried out to identify and solve the problems faced by industrial city, such as population, traffic congestion, unreasonable industrial layout, and insufficient natural resources.

2.5 Resource-Efficient, Environment-Friendly, Climate-Resilient (REEFCR) Cities: Models for China's Urban Green Transformation

2.5.1 The Target Model of Urban Green Transformation in the Context of Climate Change

Climate change poses the most significant environmental threat to humanity currently. It will profoundly affect the survival and development of human being, and is intrinsically linked to considerable economic and social development subjects and the essential interests of the people. Many new situations, new features, new challenges and new requirements have emerged during urban sustainable development under the context of climate change. In response to the green transformation of cities, population, resources, environment and development should be coordinated, and the goal model should be to build a "Resource-efficient, Environment-friendly and Climate resilient" city (referred to as REEFCR city).

The REEFCR city is a city that aims at protecting the ecological environment, combating climate change, maintaining the security of energy resources and other common challenges facing the world. It integrates people, cities and the earth, integrates economic, ecological and environment sustainability, and featured with energy conservation, environmental protection and low carbon. It is a city transformed from an industrial civilization to an ecological civilization.

2.5.2 Key Characteristics of REEFCR City

The first feature of a REEFCR city is its emphasis on ecology, a concept proposed by the "Man and Biosphere Program" sponsored by UNESCO. This ecological focus leads to the inherent respect for, conformity to, and preservation of nature. The city is considered a life system, composed of subsystems such as energy, water, transportation, land, food supply, waste recycling, and usage. Ecological theories, methods, and natural laws like competition, symbiosis, and succession are integrated and implemented throughout the city's plan, structure, lifestyle, construction, and governance. This integration aims to achieve optimal harmony between urban society, economy, culture, and nature, ensuring smooth material transformation, energy flow, information transfer, and symbiosis.

The ecological city also aims to address the scarcity of the necessary symbiotic relationships between urban functional blocks and the multilevel usage functionality of materials and energy in traditional urban development models. This prevalent model neglects inter-departmental coordination, exhibiting a low diversity, poor self-regulatory ability, and strong dependence on the ecological environment due to the individualistic focus of each industry on their specific production rather than the overall city function. However, proliferation and optimization through the REEFCR model pave the way for a synergetic and symbiotic urban systems' operation. In the urban ecosystem, a novel urban form is conceived, geared towards enhancing three core components: the health of the urban material metabolism process, the information feedback process, and the ecological evolution process.

The second feature of REEFCR city is the emphasis on recycling. The main reason why the traditional urban development model has a negative impact on the ecological environment is that the material circulation and energy flow system of cities and industries are basically linear rather than circular, which is high consumption. Human beings in cities extract a lot of resources from nature, and export a lot of materials and energy in the form of waste. Cities have powerful producers and consumers, but no degraders. Recycling is to transform this high resource consumption and linear development mode, with the efficient utilization and recycling of resources as the core, and through the construction of circular enterprises, circular industrial parks, circular industrial chains and other ways and forms, to achieve the combination of the small cycle within the enterprise, the middle cycle of the park and the big cycle of the whole city. The reduction, reuse and resource utilization will run through all links and the whole process of production, life, circulation and consumption in the whole city.

Column 2.6 Reclaimed Water Development and Utilization in Beijing

Recycled water, also known as reclaimed water, relates to urban sewage that has been treated to meet certain water quality standards for beneficial use. Recycled water has become the second water source in Beijing.

Beijing, one of the world's most populous cities, also grapples with severe water scarcity. Despite the internationally recognized warning line for water shortage being 1000 cubic meters of water resources per capita, Beijing's supply is merely around 100 cubic meters.

Continuous droughts over the last 12 years since 1998 have resulted in a 20% decrease in Beijing's yearly average precipitation, compared to the multi-year average. Water from the "two basins" of Miyun Reservoir and Guanting Reservoir decreased by 79%. The groundwater level of emergency water sources in Huairou, Pinggu, Changping and other places drops by 3–5 m annually, approaching the mining limit. While the water source is decreasing, the population is increasing rapidly. In 2010, the resident population was 19.61 million, and the urban population exceeded the planned target of 18 million in 2020 10 years ahead of schedule. In recent ten years, Beijing's total annual water resources have been 2.6 billion cubic meters, while the annual water consumption has been 3.6 billion cubic meters, with an annual water deficit of 1 billion cubic meters. The shortage of water resources has become the first bottleneck of Beijing's economic and social development. The water of the Yangtze River from Danjiangkou in the South to North Water Transfer Project is just a drop in the bucket to ease Beijing's water dilemma.

The first reclaimed water plant was built in Beijing in 2001. From 2001 to 2010, the utilization of renewable water in the city increased from 210 million cubic meters to 680 million cubic meters, and the proportion of water supply increased from 8 to 20%. The total utilization reached 3.36 billion cubic meters, which basically achieve the goal of "fresh water for living, recycled water for production".

The reclaimed water plant transformed brown smelly water into colorless and tasteless water through activated carbon adsorption, odor oxidation and other procedures by using "ultrafiltration membrane", MBR, "reverse osmosis treatment" and other technologies.

The utilization ways of reclaimed water are:

Industry: centralized water consumption and stable consumption. Since the First Thermal Power Plant and Huaneng Thermal Power Plant used recycled water as industrial cooling water in 2003, by 2010, all 9 thermal power plants in the city had used recycled water, and the industrial use of recycled water reached 140 million cubic meters in 2010.

Agriculture: Since 2006, 580,000 mu of reclaimed water irrigation areas have been built in Daxing, Tongzhou and other farmland. In 2010, more than 300 million cubic meters of recycled water were used for agricultural irrigation.

Landscape river: 210 million cubic meters. Renewable water has not only stopped the trend of ecological deterioration of rivers, but also stopped the sharp decline of water sources caused by pollution. Yongding River is the "mother river" of Beijing, it is also the largest river and the first polluted river in Beijing to decline its water supply. Yongding River's Beijing section has been cut off for 30 years, and the use of recycled water that makes Yongding River come back to life. If it is to be built into a "green ecological corridor" according to the plan, the irrigation water demand of the Beijing inland river section alone will be 130 million cubic meters, equivalent to one tenth of the annual domestic water consumption in the urban area. In addition, renewable water is widely used in car cleaning, road dust control, plants irrigation, municipal miscellaneous, etc.

The development and utilization of reclaimed water alleviates the two major contradictions of water resource shortage and water environment deterioration, and creates new water sources while eliminating pollution.

There are 52 main rivers within the Sixth Ring Road in Beijing, with a total length of 520 km. Historically, these rivers have undertaken the dual task of flood control and pollution discharge. Before the 1990s, 400 million cubic meters of sewage was directly discharged into the river channel every year, because no sewage treatment plant was built. In addition, the water body's self-purification capacity was reduced because of droughts. In summer, the river and lake burst into waterbloom, which was fishy and dirty. Strengthening sewage treatment is the fundamental way to improve water quality of rivers and lakes. According to the distribution of Tonghui River, Bahe River, Qinghe River, Liangshui River and other rivers, Beijing has built large-scale sewage treatment plants. By 2010, the city's annual sewage treatment capacity will reach more than 1.1 billion cubic meters. The sewage treatment rate can reach 82%, and the central urban area can reach 95%.

The drainage of Beijing has gone through three stages: "sewage collection, natural discharge", "sewage collection, standard discharge", and then "sewage collection, standard treatment, and renewable water use". During the "Twelfth Five Year Plan" period, all the sewage treatment plants in the central urban area of Beijing will be upgraded to renewable water plants. All the new sewage treatment plants will be built as renewable water plants. The sewage treatment rate in the central urban area will reach 98%, and the utilization rate of renewable water will reach 75%. The reclaimed water will be introduced into the Yongding River and Chaobai River in the upstream to conserve the water source. The upstream and downstream of urban water will make a large cycle, which will not only fill the gap of water resources, but also fundamentally improve the quality of water environment.

Source: "Quenching Thirst" using "Wastewater"—Investigation on the Development of Reclaimed Water in Beijing, Democracy and Legal Network, http://www.mzyfz.com/cms/benzhousheping/shepingzhuanqu/shehui/html/1239/2011-11-04/content-202742.html.

The third feature of REEFCR city is the emphasis on low carbon. Low carbon refers to a city wherein the economy is primarily driven by low-carbon industries, residents are consciously practicing low-carbon lifestyles, the government strives towards building a low-carbon society, and the city is characterized by "low energy consumption and emissions, low pollution, high efficiency, and high productivity".[42] The cornerstone of a low-carbon city is energy conservation and enhancing its efficiency. By establishing energy-efficient enterprises, households, communities, buildings, government entities, developing energy-saving, energy-efficient and novel energy technologies, optimizing land use and energy, realizing low-carbon and recycling industrial layouts, establishing green transportation systems, and promoting green buildings and green consumption, the total urban energy consumption and associated greenhouse gas emissions can be significantly reduced.

Low-carbon practices have progressively become a new metric of urban quality and representation. The shift towards a low carbon economy is an indispensable move given increasing international pressure, ongoing domestic development, and the urgent need to curtail greenhouse gas emissions through urbanization in China.

Column 2.7 Baoding's Integration of Low Carbon Ideals in Urban Development
Baoding has 25 county-level units and 2 development zones under its jurisdiction, making it the prefecture level city with the largest number of counties in China. With a total area of 22,000 square kilometers and a total population of 11.62 million, 80% of them are in rural areas. Baoding has few resources and fragile ecological environment; it is also the ecological barrier of Beijing Tianjin and Baiyang Lake.

Baoding strives to explore a low-carbon development model with energy conservation, the promotion and application of new energy and the reduction of carbon emissions as the main indicators, which help Baoding to be ranked first in the province in terms of economic growth and financial growth.

"Addition and subtraction": addition means to develop new energy and energy equipment industry, and subtraction is energy conservation and emission reduction. Combination of industrial low-carbon and lifestyle low-carbon. Walk out a road of industrialization and urbanization that meets the requirements of ecological civilization development and has its own characteristics.

In 2006, Baoding put forward the development goal of accelerating the development of new energy and energy equipment manufacturing industry and creating "China's Electric Valley".

In 2007, Baoding proposed to promote the popularization and application of new energy in urban infrastructure and residents' lives, and build a "Solar City".

In 2008, Baoding proposed the goal of building a low-carbon city in the key areas of economic and social development.

Industrial development: compared with 2005, the sales revenue of new energy industry in 2011 increased from 6 billion yuan to 45.3 billion yuan, an increase of more than six times. It has initially formed six industrial systems, namely, photoelectric, wind power, power saving, power storage, power transmission and transformation, and power electronics, and has become a world-class new energy equipment manufacturing cluster.

In terms of new energy utilization, Baoding comprehensively carried out the solar energy transformation of urban public lighting, and cultivated and built a number of low-carbon demonstration communities and low-carbon demonstration projects. By the end of 2011, the courtyard of all Party and government organs in the urban area, more than 90% of the main roads, 85% of the garden green space, all the traffic lights, and some living quarters and major tourist attractions have completed the transformation of solar energy application.

New energy industry base with new energy and energy equipment industry as the main content has formed six industrial clusters, namely, photoelectric, wind power, power saving, power storage, power transmission and transformation and power automation equipment.

40% of the residential areas in the urban area have completed the transformation using solar energy, the traffic lights at the main intersections are all changed to solar power. Diangu Building, the world's first five-star hotel powered by photovoltaic, was completed and put into use. The building replaced the traditional glass curtain wall with photovoltaic glass curtain wall that made it a power station with 0.3 MW installed capacity. The annual power generation is 340,000 kWh. The first solar photovoltaic integrated fire station in China - Lekai North Street Fire Station was officially put into use on July 29, 2011. The station is constructed by Yingli Group with an investment of 60 million yuan. The facade is installed with full glass solar cell module curtain wall. Yingli "Panda" single crystal high-efficiency battery modules are used. The installed power generation capacity is 250 kilowatts, the annual power generation capacity is 300,000 kWh, 120 tons of standard coal is saved, and 312 tons of carbon dioxide is reduced.

Source: Incorporating the concept of "low-carbon" into urban development thinking, Economic Daily, February 6, 2012, by Li Qian.

2.5.3 *Conceptual Categories within REEFCR City*

2.5.3.1 Eco City

Eco city refers to the urban development model with high economic efficiency, social harmony and ecological virtuous circle. It is a compound ecosystem with reasonable structure, efficient function and coordinated development. Eco city is a sustainable subsystem with fair carrying capacity share in the global or regional ecosystem. It is a composite system of natural harmony, ecological equity and economic efficiency based on ecological principles. It is also an ideal human settlement environment with its own human characteristics, which is natural and artificial coordination, and harmony between people.[43]

Countries aiming to develop Eco cities include the UK, France, Germany, Sweden, the Netherlands, Norway, Iceland, Spain, Italy, Slovakia and Bulgaria in Europe; China, Japan, South Korea, India, the United Arab Emirates, Jordan and the Philippines in Asia; America and Canada in North America.

2.5.3.2 Low Carbon City

Low carbon city is founded on the concept of a low carbon economy, prioritizing controlled energy use and carbon dioxide emissions notwithstanding rapid economic development. Coping with climate change is the direct reason for emergence of low carbon city, and the fundamental reason is the change and transformation of the city's production and lifestyle, development model. Urban citizens take low-carbon life as their concept and behavior characteristics, and government management takes low-carbon society as its construction specimen and blueprint, which will lead to a three-dimensional spatial pattern formed by low-carbon urban life, compact urban space and recycling of material life. The compact development of urban space promotes the economization of urban land use. The high-density population will ensure the shaping of diversified and complex functions of urban areas, greatly reduce the density of urban traffic construction and various indicators of urban construction, improve the efficiency of development and utilization of land and other resources, guide the transformation of community construction from extension type to connotation type according to the urbanization process, and maintain the combination of high-density compact development and the construction of new mixed function communities.

Column 2.8 Copenhagen—A Bicycle City

Copenhagen aims to become the world's first carbon neutral city by 2025. By 2015, the city's carbon dioxide emissions will be reduced by 20% on the basis of 2005, and by 2025, the carbon dioxide emissions will be reduced to zero. The most important measure and guarantee to achieve this goal is to promote bicycle. The urban traffic has formed a sequence of bicycle first, public transport second, and private cars last. Bicycle transportation has become a kind of city culture. The International Cycling Union named Copenhagen the world's first "bicycle city" from 2008 to 2011. When President Clinton of the United States visited Copenhagen in 1997, an official gift from the Copenhagen municipal government was a specially designed bicycle named "City Bicycle No. 1".

In order to promote bicycle transportation, many supporting systems have been established. The frequency of traffic light changes in the city is set according to the average speed of bicycles, so as to ensure that you can ride bicycles at a constant speed, and the green light is almost unblocked all the way. The second is to improve infrastructure, build more and safer dedicated roads and parking lots for bicycles, which makes car parking a more difficult and costly choice. Provide good bicycle transportation service. There are more than 100 free bicycle parking spots in the city. You can rent the bike at the price of DKK 20. When you return the bike to any parking spot, you can get back the deposit. However, if the bicycle is not parked in the specified area, the fine will be up to 1000 Euros.

Source: Copenhagen's 50 Measures to Build Low Carbon Cities—Denmark's Full Contact with Climate and Energy, China Net, http://www.china.com.cn/fangtan/zhuanti/2009-07/08/content_18092404.htm.

Column 2.9 Low Carbon Expo

Shanghai World Expo Park, located on a site previously polluted by industrial activities, exemplifies the integration of urban redevelopment with environmentally friendly initiatives. This development led to the simultaneous promotion of factory relocations, carbon emission reductions, and ecological improvements. All pavilions use advanced energy conservation and low carbon technologies, such as the London Zero Carbon Pavilion Shanghai Expo gathering the latest energy conservation and emission reduction technologies from various countries and industries, and its operation is fully supported by renewable energy. It also vigorously promotes green travel, so that the concept of low carbon can be popularized in the whole society.

2.5.3.3 Elegant Living City

Elegant living cities are characterized by comfort and health. American journalist James Russell first put forward the concept based on the impact of climate change on cities and vice versa. The focus is on the gradual transformation of the city itself and the change of the behavior of urban residents. The energy consumption of urban housing should be gradually reduced, and eventually the energy output should be greater than its consumption.

2.5.3.4 Environmental Protection Model City

In 1997, the Ministry of Environmental Protection of the People's Republic of China proposed and launched the activity of creating a National Environmental Protection Model City. The important sign of a model city is that the quality of the urban environment has improved significantly, and the goal of "blue sky, clear water, green land, quiet and clean" has been achieved. As of 2010, 71 cities and 5 municipalities directly under the Central Government have built National Environmental Protection Model Cities.

In 2008, the standard rate of water quality in the water environment functional areas of national environmental protection model cities was 4.96 percentage points higher than the national average level of cities; the excellent air quality rate is 30.90 percentage points higher than the national average level; the disposal and utilization rate of industrial solid waste and the centralized disposal rate of medical waste were 3.14 and 20.58 percentage points higher than the national urban average; the centralized treatment rate of domestic sewage is higher than 28.92 percentage points; the harmless treatment rate of domestic waste was 25.77 percentage points higher; the green coverage rate of the built-up area is 3.58 percentage points higher. The average satisfaction rate of the urban public with the urban environment was 78%, 16.83 percentage points higher than the national average.

2.5.3.5 Compact City

Compact city planning is a conceptual framework and strategy for sustainable and low-carbon urban development, intimately connected to urban form and city structure planning. It is the reflection of the western society on the "urban disease" caused by the blind and disorderly expansion and spread of cities in the past hundred years, such as the lack of land resources and environmental degradation. It is a revolutionary change in the concept and mode of urban construction of the traditional "decentralized city" in western society. It is also an inevitable choice for carbon emission control and reduction of urban form change in the world.

Compact cities include controlling disorderly development and sprawl, saving land resources, limiting the unlimited expansion of cities, increasing urban density, and efficiently reusing developed land. It advocates the combination of public transport and pedestrian system to lead urban development. As the scope of urban development is limited, urban construction land is reduced, it leaves ample space for the ecological and natural environment. The complex urban centers at all levels improve the urban functions, facilitate information exchange, and enhance production and research and development.

Column 2.10 The Implementation of Compact City Principles in the UK and the US

The construction of compact cities in Britain is led by the government. After the Second World War, the United Kingdom had experienced the process of anti-urbanization, advocated the rural urban lifestyle, and expanded the city to the suburbs to alleviate the dilemma that private car owners accounted for more than 70% of the urban population at that time, and the city was overly dependent on cars. The British government's "Sustainable Development UK Strategy" (1994) proposed the development principle of creating a convenient living environment and saving energy, and proposed to redevelop, utilize and maintain the nature of abandoned urban centers. In 1999, the development and urban regeneration policy, including the development of compact cities, was put forward, which clearly proposed the requirements for controlling traffic carbon emissions, guiding the compact use of land, and improving urban density. Under the leadership of the government, the concept and model of compact city have been implemented in urban reconstruction and new development zones in Britain. As a result, London has controlled the outflow of population, and the population has returned to the city. The transportation relying on cars has been greatly improved, and the low-carbon effect of new development zones has been shown.

The United States has the highest dependence on cars and the largest number of private cars in the world. It is also the country with the largest traffic energy consumption. The population of the United States accounts for 4.7% of the world's population, transportation energy consumption accounts for 1/4 of the world's total, and carbon emissions account for 1/3 of the world's total. The United States is also the country with the largest urban sprawl in the world. Marked by the "Wise Growth Policy" put forward by the American Planning Association (APA) in 1994, the urban development model of the United States has changed to a green and compact direction, such as to develop TND, which is the traditional neighbor development model; advocate TOD (Transit-oriented Development Model).

In recent years, the theoretical research on compact cities in Japan, including the establishment of mathematical models, has been carried out in depth in response to the problems of population reduction, childlessness and aging. Promote the concept and model of "compact city" in large-scale urban regeneration movement and in urban regeneration areas and new development areas.

The discussion on "compact city" in China: "The current urgent problem is to reflect on the concept and development mode of urban construction, and explore the urban development path that conforms to China's national conditions and ecological civilization construction. At present, China has 15 million people entering the city every year, and this trend will continue in a certain period of time, which further requires mixed land use functions in cities and even regions, and vigorously promote the compact land saving development model."[44]

Adopt compact urban spatial structure, and realize appropriate spatial mixing in land use, so as to reduce traffic distance and traffic volume, and improve urban infrastructure and efficiency. In combination with the compact urban structure, the urban transportation system of public transportation priority is adopted, and the complete bicycle transportation system and humanized walking space are available to reduce the energy consumption in the transportation process.[45]

2.5.3.6 Lean Linear Arterial City

The Lean Linear Arterial City has prominent features like compact space and multi-functions, contributing to the preservation of natural space. It was first proposed by Soleri, widely known as the father of American ecological architecture, and first carried out the experiment of building a "Lean Linear Artery City" in Acosandi, the United States.

In the 1960s, Soleri began to take the form of plant growth as the structural model of urban planning, and proposed to build a compact and continuous Eco City belt composed of interconnected urban modules. He proposed to use a huge high-rise building structure to densely place urban elements such as residential areas, commercial areas, harmless industries, streets, squares, parks and green spaces inside and outside the huge building clusters, and to form a long string of urban ecological building modules to bring the city into the countryside, so as to avoid people swarming into the city, crowding and chaos for survival and development.[46] This simple and orderly urban layout can not only provide a large number of people with the needs of urban life, but also enable people to closely integrate with the nature of the "long string" buildings.

The "Lean Linear Artery City" can realize the huge reduction of energy demand through the construction of highly dense three-dimensional cities. Each city module will make full use of local natural resources, and can generate some energy and raw materials for local use and consumption.

Column 2.11 "Lean Linear Artery City" Laboratory in Soleri

"Lean Linear Artery City" comes from the original intention of Soleri to fundamentally reconstruct the chaotic urban planning into a dense, integrated, three-dimensional city, so as to support complex activities that can maintain human civilization. The "Lean Linear Artery City" conceived by Soleri is that the parallel construction of a multi-functional tower with more than 30 floors along the coast of the Linear Central Park will integrate multiple functions of daily life. People can quickly reach the office or shops in a few minutes by walking or by using bicycles, elevators or transport buses, thus saving daily traffic time. On both sides of the city, there will be large farms, farmland, mountains, lakes or forests. People can easily switch between nature and the city, and animals can live in harmony with people.

To make his dream come true, Soleri settled down in Arizona in 1956, established his own Foundation, and bought nearly 350 hectares of land to begin the experiment of building a "Lean Linear Artery City" in the town of Acosandi in 1970. Although the town's construction has only reached the expected scale of 2% by 2010, the town also has distinctive characteristics of respecting the environment and paying attention to ecology. The town refused cars. It takes about ten minutes to walk to every corner in the city. Each building unit has multiple functions, and all living needs can be completed in a three-dimensional space. The conventional power grid is used to meet most of the electricity demand, but the windmill, solar energy and circulating water are also fully used to provide renewable energy. Thousands of volunteers have come here to participate in academic seminars, conferences and experimental activities. Every year, tens of thousands of visitors from all over the world come here to share the Eco City experience.

2.5.3.7 Garden City

The concept was first proposed by British scholar Howard in 1902. It intended to find a new path of urban development to resolve the contradiction of big cities, and coordinate the relationship between cities and villages, people and nature. It has become the concept of new city construction in the future. In 1918, Osborne put forward the concept of "New City", which enriched the idea of "Garden City".[47] From 1903 to 1919, Britain successively built two "Garden Cities". The construction of new towns around the world is rooted in the theory of "Garden City", which forms the basic experience of the construction of new towns around the world. Both Xi'an and Chengdu have proposed the goal of establishing Garden City in urban construction.

Notes

1. Yue Yu, and Haiyun Wang, "Urban Diplomacy and Image Communication in the Context of Subnational Behavior", *Youth Journalist*, Issue 33, 2012.

2. Baoxing Qiu, "New Urbanization: From Concept to Action", *Administrative Management Reform*, Issue 11, 2012.
3. Ibid.
4. Ibid.
5. Zemin Jiang, *Selected Works of Jiang Zemin* (Beijing: People's Publishing House, 2006), 546.
6. Jintao Hu, *Unswervingly Advancing Along the Path of Socialism with Chinese Characteristics and Striving to Build a Moderately Prosperous Society in an All-round Way—Report at the 18th National Congress of the CPC* (Beijing: People's Publishing House, 2012), 20.
7. Tianquan Cheng, and Zhi Yang, "Reflections on Several Issues Concerning the Development of Low Carbon Economy", *Economic Perspective*, Issue 9, 2012.
8. Huocan Lin, and Lei Zhu, "Continuing to Implement Sustainable Development is an Inevitable Choice", *Economic Daily*, June 2, 2012.
9. Minquan Liu, and Jiantuo Yu, "Environment and Human Development: A Literature Review", *Journal of Peking University (Philosophy and Social Sciences Edition)*, Issue 3, 2010.
10. Shouhu Du, *Environmental Economics* (Beijing: Encyclopedia of China Publishing House, 2008) 46.
11. Baoxing Qiu, "New Urbanization: From Concept to Action", *Administrative Management Reform*, Issue 11, 2012.
12. Shuhua Wang et al., "Evaluation of Suburban Economic Coordination Based on Ecological Footprint Model – Case Study on Xinle City, Hebei Province", *Geography and Geographic Information Science*, Issue 1, 2003.
13. Yun Su et al., "A Preliminary Study on the Ecological Occupation of Urban Residents' Lives – Case Studies of Beijing and Shanghai", *Resource Science*, Issue 11, 2001.
14. Hongbo Chen, and Jiahua Pan, "Progress in Theory and Practice of Ecological Civilization Construction in China", *Journal of China University of Geosciences (Social Sciences Edition)*, Issue 10, 2012.
15. Jintao Hu, "Hold high the great banner of socialism with Chinese characteristics and strive for a new victory in building a moderately prosperous society in an all-round way - Report at the 17th National Congress of the CPC", Page 20.
16. Shouhu Du, "Ecology: Cannot become a 'Short board' of Economic Development", *Sichuan Party Construction (Urban Edition)*, Issue 2, 2008.
17. Hongbo Chen, and Jiahua Pan, "Progress in Theory and Practice of Ecological Civilization Construction in China", *Journal of China University of Geosciences (Social Sciences Edition)*, Issue 10, 2012.
18. Jintao Hu, "Following the Path of Socialism with Chinese Characteristics and Striving to Build a Moderately Prosperous Society in an All-round Way - Report at the 18th National Congress of the CPC", Page 39.
19. Jinping Xi, "Opening of the 2013 Annual Conference of the Ecological Civilization Guiyang International Forum, Congratulatory Letter from Xi Jinping", *Xinhua Daily Telegraph*, July 21, 2013.
20. Hongbo Chen, and Jiahua Pan, "Progress in Theory and Practice of Ecological Civilization Construction in China", *Journal of China University of Geosciences (Social Sciences Edition)*, Issue 10, 2012.
21. Shouhu Du, "Ecology: Cannot become a 'Short board' of Economic Development", *Sichuan Party Construction (Urban Edition)*, Issue 2, 2008.
22. Shouhu Du, "Four Questions on Ecological Civilization Construction", *Open Guide*, December 8, 2007.
23. John Cobb Jr., "The Prospects for achieving ecological civilization in China are more Optimistic", *Chinese Journal of Social Sciences*, September 21, 2012.
24. Lin Wang, "Marxism has Guiding Significance for the Construction of Ecological Civilization", *China Social Science Daily*, September 21, 2012.
25. Jintao Hu, "Following the Path of Socialism with Chinese Characteristics and Striving to Build a Moderately Prosperous Society in an All-Round Way—Report at the 18th National Congress of the CPC", page 41.

26. Jinsong Zhang, "On the Construction of the Ten Major Systems of Ecological Civilization", *Administrative Forum*, Issue 3, 2013.
27. Ibid.
28. Shouhu Du, "Four Questions on Ecological Civilization Construction", *Open Guide*, December 8, 2007.
29. Shouhu Du, "Ecology: Cannot become a 'Short board' of Economic Development", *Sichuan Party Construction (Urban Edition)*, Issue 2, 2008.
30. Ibid.
31. Shouhu Du, "Four Questions on Ecological Civilization Construction", *Open Guide*, December 8, 2007.
32. Ibid.
33. Hongbo Chen, and Jiahua Pan, "Progress in Theory and Practice of Ecological Civilization Construction in China", *Journal of China University of Geosciences (Social Sciences Edition)*, Issue 10, 2012.
34. Jinping Xi, "Striving towards a New Era of Socialist Ecological Civilization", *Communist Party Member*, Issue 6, 2013.
35. Ya Li, "Ecological Responsibility of the Government in Economic Development", *Journal of the Central Party School of the Communist Party of China*, Issue 5, 2005.
36. Ibid.
37. Minquan Liu and Jiantuo Yu, "Environment and Human Development: A Literature Review", *Journal of Peking University (Philosophy and Social Sciences Edition)*, Issue 3, 2010.
38. Ibid.
39. Ibid.
40. Yi Qian, and Peng Zhang, "Research on Ecological City Construction", *Xinjiang Environmental Protection*, Issue 3, 2005.
41. "Achim Stayler's Speech at the World Expo Forum", *Wen-Hui News*, July 17, 2010.
42. Qian Li, "Incorporating the Concept of 'Low-Carbon' into Urban Development Thinking", *Economic Daily*, February 6, 2012.
43. Zhaoyi Huang, and Dongyuan Yang, "Review of Theoretical Research on Ecological Cities Domestic and Abroad", *Urban Planning*, Issue 1, 2001.
44. Baoxing Qiu, "Transforming Development Models and Building Low Carbon Cities", *China Construction Daily*, December 9, 2009.
45. Chaolin Gu, "Research Framework of Urban Planning based on Low-Carbon Concept", *Research on Urban and Regional Planning*, Issue 2, 2010.
46. Shuang Guo, "A Sample of Future Ecological Cities – Acosandi", *Building Energy Efficiency*, Issue 5, 2013.
47. Yumei Chen, "Resolving the Four Major Contradictions is the Key to Enhancing the Vitality of New City Construction", *Economic Crossroads*, Issue 12, 2011.

Chapter 3
Urban Atmospheric Environment Governance and Protection

Air quality plays a significant role in the overall urban ecological environment, heavily impacting the livelihood of its inhabitants Air pollution has become a prominent problem affecting the sustainable development of urban economy and society. With the rapid development of China's economy and the increase of urban residents' wealth, urban residents' requirements for a livable environment are increasingly enhanced and their demands for superior air quality are growing. More and more urban residents begin to pay attention to the reality that human health is threatened by various issues, such as urban visibility or haze, the destructiveness and concentration standards of PM2.5, black carbon issues, global warming and other environmental issues.

Clean air is a cornerstone of China's vision of a beautiful and ecologically mindful nation; the opportunity to breathe clean air is a fundamental aspect of a prosperous life, and a commitment from the government to its people. Thus, the urgency and importance of research on urban atmospheric environment governance and preservation in China cannot be understated.

3.1 Trends and Characteristic of Atmospheric Pollution in Chinese Cities

The swift progression of industrialization and urbanization in China since the 1990s has imposed a substantial toll on resources and environmental development, mirroring pollution characteristics seen through the industrialization process in developed nations.

S. Du and H. Du, *The Green Transformation of Urban Areas in China Under Global Warming*, https://doi.org/10.1007/978-981-95-1005-4_3

3.1.1 Changes of Urban Air Pollution in China

First, the air pollution changes from traditional soot pollution to compound air pollution including photochemical pollution.

Column 3.1 Photochemical Pollution
In 1943, Los Angeles suffered from photochemical pollution, which is different from the soot type pollution in London, England, in 1952. The so-called "photochemical" pollution is mainly caused by the photochemical reaction of nitrogen oxides emitted by vehicles under sunlight. In addition to nitrogen oxides, photochemical smog mainly contains ozone and aldehydes, as well as fine particles, which have a direct impact on the human respiratory system.

Second, the air pollution concentration has evolved from being localized to one city to being pervasive across a contiguous urban agglomeration.

With the advancement of urbanization and the continuous expansion of China's urban scale, the development of urban agglomerations and urban belts has become an important feature of urbanization. Due to the dual effects of atmospheric circulation and atmospheric chemistry, the interaction of air pollution between cities is increasingly obvious, and the impact of pollution transmission between adjacent cities is extremely prominent. In Beijing-Tianjin-Hebei, Yangtze River Delta, Pearl River Delta and other regions, the contribution rate of sulfur dioxide concentration from external sources in some cities is 30 to 40%, nitrogen oxides is 12 to 20%, and inhalable particulate matter is 16% to 26%; the change process of urban air pollution in the region shows obvious synchronization, and the frequency of heavy air pollution occurring simultaneously in a large range is increasing day by day. Heavy pollution weather generally occurs successively in cities in these regions within one day.[1]

Thirdly, primary pollutants have transformed from coarse particles to PM2.5 and ozone, indicating a transition from primary pollutants to secondary pollutants.

According to the monitoring results of the Ministry of Environmental Protection of the People's Republic of China on the air quality of 77 cities in the first quarter of 2013, the primary pollutants in cities are PM2.5 and PM10, of which the average exceeding standard rate is 49.1% and 33.6% respectively (Table 3.1)

Table 3.1 Comparison of main air pollutant concentrations in urban agglomerations of China (Year 2012)

			Unit: microgram/m^3
Region	SO_2	NO_2	Inhalable particles
Beijing Tianjin Hebei Urban Agglomeration	45	33	82
Yangtze River Delta Urban Agglomeration	33	38	89
Pearl River Delta Urban Agglomeration	26	40	58
Wuhan Urban Agglomeration	28	28	91
Chang Zhu Tan Urban Agglomeration	51	40	86
Chengdu Chongqing Urban Agglomeration	43	35	76
Ganning Urban Agglomeration	46	32	111
Urumqi	43	36	96

Column 3.2 Ozone as a Significant Contributor to Air Pollution

Apart from PM2.5, ozone is recognized as another major air pollutant.

Located in the stratosphere, ozone acts as a crucial shield against ultraviolet rays, potentially harmful to biological DNA. However, ozone on the ground will stimulate the respiratory tract. The rapid increase of ground ozone concentration in a short period of time will lead to heart attack and severe asthma. Long term exposure to high concentrations of ozone will increase the probability of death from the respiratory system by 50%. Ozone on the ground is usually formed by chemical reaction of nitrogen oxides in vehicle exhaust under sunlight.

Fourthly, the scope of pollution control has extended from industrial point sources to non-point sources like fugitive dust and mobile sources such as low-speed vehicles, and has evolved to the precursors generated by PM2.5.

Column 3.3 Secondary Pollutants

Secondary pollutants refer to new pollutants generated from the interaction or photochemical reaction of primary pollutants in the air, such as sulfuric acid mist, nitric acid mist, photochemical smoke, etc. Its general toxicity is stronger than that of primary pollutants.

The countermeasures generally adopted include technical innovation and process transformation to reduce the possibility of transformation of secondary pollutants; encourage more use of clean energy; the discharge of new pollutants shall be strictly controlled; pollution control should be carried out in a unified way across regions and even countries.

3.1.2 Situation of Urban Air Pollution in China

During the "11th Five Year Plan" period (2006—2010), China deepened the comprehensive improvement of urban atmospheric environment. The policy of "retreat from two to three" was implemented, a large number of heavily polluting enterprises were relocated and transformed, and the urban industrial layout was optimized; the transformation of urban clean energy was actively promoted, cogeneration and centralized heating was developed, and a number of small coal-fired boilers were eliminated; the Beijing-Tianjin-Hebei, Yangtze River Delta, and Pearl River Delta urban agglomerations started the oil and gas recovery and treatment of gas stations. Beijing, Shanghai, Guangzhou, Shenzhen and other cities completed 1462, 500, 514, and 256 oil and gas recovery and transformation projects respectively. The national III standard for motor vehicle pollutant emissions has been implemented all over the country, and some cities have implemented the national IV standard. The average emission intensity of motor vehicle pollutants has decreased by more than 40%. The comprehensive improvement work has achieved positive results. In 2010, the annual average concentrations of sulfur dioxide and inhalable particulate matter (PM10) in cities at prefecture level and above were 35 $\mu g/m^3$ and 81 $\mu g/m^3$, respectively, down 24.0% and 14.8% from 2005, and the concentration of nitrogen dioxide was basically stable.

However, the situation of urban air pollution in China is still very serious. On the one hand, coarse particle pollution is still the main factor of urban air pollution in China. The scope of acid rain pollution caused by sulfur dioxide continues to expand. In 2009, among 488 cities (counties) nationwide, there are 189 cities (counties) had an annual mean precipitation PH value lower than 5.0 (a relatively heavy acid rain), accounting for 38.7% of the total, and 39 cities (counties) had an annual mean precipitation PH value lower than 4.5 (a heavy acid rain), accounting for 8.0%. In 2010, the annual average concentration of sulfur dioxide in cities in key regions of China was 0.039 mg/m^3, which was 2–4 times that of developed countries. On the other hand, although the coarse particle pollution is not effectively controlled, the fine particle pollution is another prominent issue.

In September 2011, the World Health Organization released a global urban air pollution report represented by PM10, which showed that China ranked 77th among 91 countries participating in the ranking. In 31 provincial capitals and municipalities directly under the Central Government, 94% of the population is exposed to the air with an annual average concentration of more than 70 $\mu g/m^3$ of PM10, and 80% of the cities fail to meet the new ambient air quality standards of China (Table 3.2).

According to the China Climate Bulletin of 2012, PM2.5 has reached a significant level in the list of main polluting factors in most cities in China. The pollution of urban atmospheric haze and photochemical smog in the Yangtze River Delta, the Pearl River Delta, Beijing Tianjin Hebei and other regions has become increasingly prominent, with the number of annual haze days reaching more than 100, accounting for 30% to 50% of the total number of days in the year. From 2010 to 2013, urban areas in China were extensively polluted by haze for four consecutive years. The

Table 3.2 Air quality ranking of national capital cities and municipalities from 2008 to 2012

Cities	2012	2011	2010	2009	2008
Haikou	1	1	1	1	1
Kunming	2	2	2	2	2
Lasa	3	3	3	4	4
Fuzhou	4	5	6	5	3
Guangzhou	5	4	4	6	7
Nanning	6	6	5	3	5
Guiyang	7	7	8	7	6
Huhehaote	8	8	7	9	10
Shanghai	9	12	12	11	13
Chongqing	10	16	20	24	24
Changchun	11	10	10	10	9
Hangzhou	12	14	15	15	21
Hefei	13	28	22	17	31
Nanchang	14	9	9	8	8
Yinchuan	15	13	13	13	11
Shenyang	16	15	14	14	16
Changsha	17	11	11	12	12
Jinan	18	21	23	27	26
Taiyuan	19	25	24	26	20
Shijiazhuang	20	18	17	18	22
Wuhan	21	26	28	25	27
Zhengzhou	22	24	19	16	14
Ha'erbin	23	23	21	21	19
Nanjing	24	20	26	19	15
Xining	25	22	18	29	25
Tianjin	26	17	25	22	17
Xi'an	27	27	27	23	23
Chengdu	28	19	16	20	18
Wunumuqi	29	30	30	30	30
Beijing	30	29	29	28	28
Lanzhou	31	31	31	31	29

frequent occurrence of haze has become one of the major meteorological disasters and extreme weather and climate events in China.

In 2010, the annual average concentration of PM2.5 in the atmosphere of Beijing was 60–70 μ mg/m3, and that of Guangzhou was 45–50 μ g/m^3. Compared with the World Health Organization's environmental air quality guideline of 10 μ g/m^3, Beijing exceeded the standard by 6–7 times, and Guangzhou exceeded the standard by

3.5–4 times. Compared with the first phase target of 35 μg/m^3 of the World Health Organization, Beijing exceeded the standard by 0.7 ~ 1 times, while Guangzhou exceeded the standard by 0.3 ~ 0.4 times.

Since the beginning of winter in 2011, heavy fog and haze have continuously occurred in large areas of China, resulting in the closure of many traffic arteries and the cancellation of flights.

From January to March 2013, most areas in North, East and other parts of China suffered from the air pollution attack known as "the end of the air", which showed the characteristics of "wide range, long time and high concentration" (Tables 3.3, 3.4).

In Beijing, which was hit hardest by smog, heavy pollution started on January 10, 2013, and was seen from January 11 to 14. The air quality data released by the Beijing Municipal Government on January 12 showed that the concentration of PM2.5 on that day reached 886 μg per cubic meter, and the concentration of toxic haze had reached more than 35 times the health standard (25 μg per cubic meter) recognized by the World Health Organization. The international environmental protection organization Greenpeace revealed that the air quality in Beijing on Saturday and Sunday was "the worst on record". The average daily outpatient volume of children's hospitals in Beijing has been close to 10,000 in the past week, and the number of inpatients in the entire Beijing hospitals has increased by 20%, of which 30% are patients with respiratory diseases.

Table 3.3 Air quality ranking of urban areas for 1st quarter 2013

Ranking/ Type	1	2	3	4	5	6	7	8	9	10
Severe Air pollution	Shijiazhuang	Xingtai	Baoding	Handan	Tangshan	Jinan	Xi'an	Hengshui	Langfang	Wunumuqi
Good air quality	Haikou	Lasa	Zhoushan	Fuzhou	Huizhou	Xiamen	Shenzhen	Zhuhai	Jiangmen	Lishui

Table 3.4 Urban air quality ranking for March 2013

Ranking/ Type	1	2	3	4	5	6	7	8	9	10
Severe Air pollution	Tangshan	Shijiazhuang	Xi'an	Chengdu	Xingtai	Baoding	Xining	Handan	Langfang	Taiyuan
Good air quality	Haikou	Zhoushan	Lasa	Fuzhou	Huizhou	Zhuhai	Lishui	Shenzhen	Xiameng	Zhangjiakou

3.2 The Impact and Harm of Atmosperic Pollution on Urban Areas in China

3.2.1 *Severe Damage to Residents' Health*

Air pollution presents a significant threat to the health of residents. As stated in the 2010 Global Disease Burden Research Report by the American Institute of Air Pollution Impact Health, air pollution was responsible for 3.2 million deaths globally in 2010, a figure four times higher than that of a decade ago, thereby making air pollution the deadliest of the world's top ten diseases. In 2010, 1.2 million people died prematurely due to outdoor air pollution in China, accounting for almost 40% of the global total. In other words, the loss of air pollution to China is that the healthy life span of the entire population has been reduced by 25 million years. Greenpeace said that serious air pollution caused about 8500 premature deaths in Beijing, Shanghai, Guangdong and Xi'an in 2012.

3.2.2 *Economic Losses*

The substantial economic gains through development are largely offset by environmental costs including air pollution. According to a 2007 report by the World Bank, the annual economic detriment caused by air pollution to China was estimated at 152.7 billion yuan. In 2009, the losses induced solely due to air pollution reached a staggering 700 billion yuan, approximating to about 3.3% of China's GDP for that year.

3.2.3 *Deterioration of Urban Visibility*

The dense haze has significantly worsened the visibility across numerous cities. From the commencement of the winter season in 2012 until January 2013, over 20 days of haze weather were recorded in North China, Shandong, Henan, Anhui, and other regions, affecting close to 1.3 million square kilometers. The visibility in these regions was severely impacted during this period. In Hebei, northwest Shandong, east Sichuan, among other areas, the visibility was less than 500 m for between 5 to 12 days. The ensuing smog resulted in traffic congestion and regular accidents, drastically affecting the routine life and production order in the city as well as impeding the city's sustainable development.

3.2.4 Escalation of "Nitrogen Deposition"

Air pollution leads to increasingly serious "nitrogen deposition". The so-called "nitrogen deposition" refers to the emission of nitrogen into the air, which is converted into secondary pollutants such as ammonia and nitrate, and then washed into the land with rainfall and snowfall, polluting the land and entering the food chain of people, causing harm to the human body. The Agricultural Research Institute of China Agricultural University has investigated data from 270 monitoring points across the country, which shows that from 1980 to 2010, the measured nitrogen deposition from rainfall increased by 60%, that is, 8,000 g per hectare. Moreover, the composition has also changed greatly. In 2010, about one third of the nitrogen deposition composition was in the form of nitrate, and the rest was ammonium, compared with 17% in 1980.

3.2.5 Degradation of City's Livability

The concerning issue of air pollution has resulted in a decline in the quality of the city's environment, severely impacting its investment possibilities and its soft power. The pollution has driven out foreign capital and high-end talents from the city, thereby hampering the city's economic development and its potential for scientific and technological innovation.

Column 3.4 The Smog Caused a Large Number of Foreigners to Leave Beijing
"The summer of 2013 is the peak season for many people to leave Beijing, especially for families with young children who have stayed here for several years. They are reconsidering the relationship between costs and benefits, and decide to leave for health reasons." (Chad Forrest, General Manager of Huahui International Transportation Services Co., Ltd. in North China) "For our members and their families, air pollution is increasingly worrying them. Although there are various reasons for members to leave, almost every time they inevitably mentioned that air pollution is one of the reasons." (Tang Yadong, Secretary General of the European Chamber of Commerce of China) "The unprecedented level of pollution in January has become an 'outbreak point' for some families, and many people are preparing to leave." (Mr. Meng Kewen, President of American Chamber of Commerce in China).

According to a survey conducted by the American Chamber of Commerce in 2012, 36% of 224 companies in Beijing had difficulties in recruiting executives due to air quality problems, up from 19% in 2010.

3.2.6 Frequent Urban Environmental Group Events

Air pollution has increasingly become the tipping point of urban mass incidents, and environmental risks have a tendency to transform into social risks. On the one hand, China has only pursued the development of economic growth for many years, leaving many environmental hazards. On the other hand, as China has entered a special "environment sensitive period", during the "11th Five Year Plan" period, environmental protection departments alone have received nearly 300,000 complaints about environmental issues. Due to the public's lacking of understanding of the relevant information of the city, including the atmospheric environment, there is a lack of trust in enterprises and local environmental protection commitments. The superposition of various factors has led to frequent urban environmental group events, affecting the good environment for social stability and economic development.

Column 3.5 Urban PX Difficulties and Solutions

PX (p-xylene) is an important raw material for the production of plastics and other products, and petrochemical projects are now collectively referred to as PX projects.

Since the 1990s, in order to change the situation that China's crude oil production areas are mainly concentrated in the northeast, northwest and north China, and large refining and chemical enterprises are also mostly distributed in the northeast, northwest and coastal areas, China has also arranged a number of petrochemical projects in the southwest and other inland areas from the strategic perspective of energy security.

However, in recent years, there have been frequent incidents against the construction of PX plants. In 2007, the PX project in Xiamen, Fujian Province was canceled due to mass protests. In August 2011, the PX project in Dalian also triggered a public demonstration, and finally moved to Ningbo. In October 2012, Ningbo also witnessed mass incidents against the expansion of chemical plants. In 2013, Kunming and Chengdu were faced with protests from the local petrochemical projects.

The US government and industry reports believe that PX is a low toxic chemical. Only exposure to high concentrations of PX may cause eye discomfort and poor breathing. The environmental protection technology for the production, transportation and storage of PX has been quite mature. In the factory where proper environmental protection measures are taken, this substance is just an ordinary product. In the past, petrochemical projects were generally located close to rivers and seas. The fundamental reason was that they were restricted by environmental protection technology and needed to rely on flowing water to dilute pollutants. With the progress of technology, the river and sea are no longer necessary for site selection. In view of the above reasons, Houston PX Factory in the United States is only 1.2 km away from the urban area, and Yokohama PX Factory in Japan is only separated from the residential area by one road. But most Chinese people believe that PX is harmful and dangerous. The crux of all kinds of contradictions is that "officials believe that large-scale industrial projects are necessary for economic growth, while the public is worried that these projects will cause damage to the environment". The oil sector believes that the PX project is to build more oil and natural gas infrastructure to produce gasoline for increasing automobiles, and plastics and chemicals for the textile industry. However, due to the lacking of timely and accurate consensus among the government, enterprises and the public on the possible impact of the PX project on the ecological environment, the publicity and communication of the scientific demonstration of the project feasibility, and the improvement of risk prevention and control information before the launch of the project, all these factors are the important reasons for the PX dilemma.

Column 3.6 PX Project in Yunnan
It is built in Anning City near Kunming. It is a ten-million-ton fuel refinery that produces gasoline, diesel oil and aviation kerosene of the national IV standard, without PX devices and PX products. Its original intention is an important strategic project to ensure national energy security. Yunnan is at the end of the national product oil supply, and the product oil supply gap is huge. After the completion of the refinery in Anning, crude oil from the China Myanmar oil and gas pipeline can be processed on the spot, which can change the situation of oil shortage and gas shortage in Yunnan's history, and the transportation of oil from north to south.

Column 3.7 Sichuan Pengzhou Petrochemical Project
Sichuan Pengzhou Petrochemical Project is an important component of the national energy strategic layout and a basic project to adjust national energy structure. The project includes 10 million tons/year oil refining and 800,000 tons/year ethylene. The factory is located in Longfeng Town, Pengzhou City, 35 km away from downtown Chengdu. It covers an area of 4 square kilometers.

The EIA of the project was approved by the State Environmental Protection Administration. The safety assessment, geological disaster impact assessment, occupational civil health assessment and earthquake safety assessment and other special assessments and reviews have been approved by relevant Ministries and Commissions of the State. After the devastating "May 12" Wenchuan earthquake in 2008, the review of seismic safety evaluation and the review of environmental risk prevention measures were carried out. According to the review conclusion, the National Development and Reform Commission agreed to start construction.

In strict accordance with the requirements of the EIA report and the official reply, the most advanced technologies in the world are used in wastewater, waste gas, waste residue treatment, noise control and other aspects of the project. The investment in environmental protection reaches 4.19 billion yuan, accounting for 11.3% of the total investment of the project. The emissions of sulfur dioxide, nitrogen oxides and dust generated by the project are only equivalent to the annual emissions of a power plant with a 600,000 kilowatt unit operating at full load. It is equipped with an internationally advanced online monitoring system, which can monitor the compliance of wastewater and waste gas all day and all time. 126 monitoring and pumping wells are set to monitor the groundwater quality in a timely manner. Establish a four level environmental linkage monitoring system and a sound emergency prevention and control system.

Every year, 2 million tons of gasoline and 3.6 million tons of diesel will be produced according to the national IV standard by the project. Currently, there are 3.1 million motor vehicles in Chengdu, using high standard gasoline and diesel produced by the project will enhance the improvement of air quality, equivalent to reducing the emission of harmful gases in the exhaust of about 2 million motor vehicles.

3.3 The Journey of Chinese Cities in Combating Air Pollution

3.3.1 Three Stages of Urban Air Pollution Prevention and Control

In terms of urban air pollution prevention and control, China has generally experienced the following three stages:

The first stage: In 1987, China promulgated the first Law on the Prevention and Control of Air Pollution, which marked that China began to attach importance to the monitoring and prevention and control of atmospheric environmental pollution. In 1987, the atmospheric environment quality monitoring standard was promulgated for the first time, and was revised in 2000. Due to the limited types and low standards of pollutants monitored at that time, urban residents often see foggy days, while the air quality indicators are excellent. The monitoring data released by the environmental protection department is far from the actual feelings of the people.

The second stage: marked by the fact that during the "11th Five Year Plan" period (2006—2010), China began to list the reduction of the total emission of major pollutants, including sulfur dioxide, as a binding indicator. The 17th National Congress of the Communist Party of China decided to take the scientific development concept of "people-oriented, comprehensive, coordinated and sustainable development" as the guiding ideology that the Party and China must adhere to for a long time. Guided by the people-oriented scientific concept of development, the Chinese government has put forward the environmental protection goal of "letting people breathe fresh air, drink clean water and eat healthy food". The leaders of the CPC Central Committee and the State Council have repeatedly stressed that we should solve the problem that the published air quality is far from the people's perception; providing basic environmental quality including fresh air is a basic function of the government. At this stage, in order to achieve the goal of emission reduction, the state has adopted a series of policies and measures, such as preferential electricity price for desulfurization, "supporting the advanced and suppress the backwards", deadline elimination, and "regional approval limit", to increase investment in environmental protection and implement emission reduction by engineering, structure, and management. By 2010, the installed capacity of desulfurization units in China will reach 578 million kilowatts, and the desulfurization proportion of thermal power units will increase from 14% in 2005 to 86% in 2010; small thermal power plants with an installed capacity of 76.83 million kilowatts were shut down, and 120 million tons of backward iron production capacity, 72 million tons of steel production capacity and 370 million tons of cement production capacity were eliminated. During the whole "11th Five Year Plan" period, when the average annual growth rate of the national economy reached 11.2% and the total coal consumption increased by more than 1 billion tons, the total sulfur dioxide emissions decreased by 14.29% compared with 2005.

The third stage: marked by the "Ambient Air Quality Standard" (GB3095-2012) and the "12th Five Year Plan" for the Prevention and Control of Air Pollution in Key Areas issued by the Ministry of Environmental Protection and approved by the State Council in 2012. In order to adapt to the increasingly prominent situation of urban air pollution prevention, China further revised the environmental quality standard in 2012, and the Ministry of Environmental Protection issued the Ambient Air Quality Standard (GB3095-2012). The State Council also approved the "12th Five Year Plan" for the Prevention and Control of Air Pollution in Key Areas formulated by the Ministry of Environmental Protection that year. The plan proposed the goals and tasks of urban air pollution control and protection in China during the critical period of achieving the goal of building a moderately prosperous society in an all-round way. It is the guiding principle and major strategic measure for the prevention and control of urban air pollution in China. It marks the transformation of China's regional atmospheric environmental pollution prevention and control strategy and management mode, from the management of a single city in the past to the overall consideration and unified planning of the atmospheric environmental problems of China's urban agglomerations, unified monitoring, unified supervision, unified assessment and unified coordination, and the establishment of a linkage mechanism between local governments.

At this stage, the 18th National Congress of the CPC raised the construction of ecological civilization to a more prominent position, and took "blue sky, green earth, green water" as an important indicator of the construction of ecological civilization and the beauty of China, pointing out the direction for the prevention and control of urban air pollution in China.

On June 14, 2013, the State Council held an executive meeting to specially deploy the prevention and control of air pollution. The meeting pointed out that air pollution prevention is a major livelihood issue. The increasingly prominent regional complex air pollution problem in China is formed by long-term accumulation. Controlling air pollution is a complex and systematic project, which requires long-term hard and unremitting efforts.[2] In addition to putting forward suggestions on revising laws such as the Law on the Prevention and Control of Air Pollution, and combining structural adjustment and optimization, strengthening innovation drive and protecting the environment and ecology, and using hard measures to accomplish hard tasks, the meeting also proposed to reduce pollutant emissions, strictly control new energy production in industries with high energy consumption and high pollution, promote cleaner production, adjust the energy structure, strengthen energy conservation and environmental protection index constraints, and "reverse force" industrial transformation and upgrading with laws and standards, establish a regional joint prevention and control mechanism, carry out target responsibility assessment for the atmospheric environment improvement of each province (district, city), incorporate heavily polluted weather into the emergency management of local governments, mobilize the whole people to participate in environmental protection and supervision, and other ten hard measures to prevent and control atmospheric pollution.

Column 3.8 "12th Five Year Plan" for Air Pollution Control in Key Areas

Key areas include urban agglomerations and cities: Beijing Tianjin Hebei, Yangtze River Delta, Pearl River Delta, central Liaoning, Shandong, Wuhan and its surrounding areas, Chang Zhu Tan, Chengdu-Chongqing, west coast of the Straits, north central Shanxi, Shaanxi Guanzhong, Ganning, Xinjiang Urumqi and other urban agglomerations, as well as Beijing, Tianjin, Shijiazhuang, Tangshan, Baoding, Langfang, Shanghai, Nanjing, Wuxi, Changzhou, Suzhou, Nantong, Yangzhou, Zhenjiang, Taizhou, Hangzhou, Ningbo, Jiaxing Huzhou, Shaoxing, Shenyang City; Jinan, Qingdao, Zibo, Weifang, Rizhao City; Wuhan City; Changsha City; Chongqing, Chengdu; Fuzhou and Sanming City; Taiyuan City; Xi'an, Xianyang City; Lanzhou, Yinchuan City; Urumqi and other cities.

Status and pollution discharge situation: the above-mentioned key areas cover 14% of China's land area and nearly 48% of the country's population, which is a highly concentrated area of China's economic activity and pollution emissions, generate 71% of the total economy, consume 52% of coal, emit 48% of sulfur dioxide, 51% of nitrogen oxides, 42% of smoke and dust, and about 50% of volatile organic compounds. The pollutant emission intensity per unit area is 2.9 to 3.6 times the national average. It is predicted that by 2015, the GDP of key regions will increase by more than 50%, the total coal consumption will increase by more than 30%, and the car ownership (including low-speed vehicles) will increase by 50%. According to the current pollution control efforts, the new emissions of sulfur dioxide, nitrogen oxides, industrial smoke and dust, and volatile organic compounds will be 1.6 million tons, 2.5 million tons, 1 million tons, and 2.2 million tons, respectively, accounting for 15%, 22%, 17%, and 20% of the emissions in 2010.

Prevention and control objectives: by 2015, the emissions of sulfur dioxide, nitrogen oxides and industrial smoke and dust in key areas will be reduced by 12%, 13% and 10% respectively, and the prevention and control of volatile organic compounds pollution will be fully carried out; the ambient air quality has been improved. The annual average concentrations of inhalable particulates, sulfur dioxide, nitrogen dioxide and fine particulates have decreased by 10%, 10%, 7% and 5% respectively. The ozone pollution has been preliminarily controlled, and the acid rain pollution has been reduced; the average annual concentration of fine particles in Beijing Tianjin Hebei, Yangtze River Delta and Pearl River Delta decreased by 6%.

3.3.2 *The Evolution of Atmospheric Environmental Quality Standards in China*

1. In 1987, China first proposed the monitoring standard of atmospheric environment quality, and revised it in 2000. In 2012, China further revised the environmental quality standard, and the Ministry of Environmental Protection issued the Ambient Air Quality Standard (GB3095-2012). The Technical Regulations on Ambient Air Quality Index (AQI) (for trial implementation) (HJ633 ~ 2012) was issued simultaneously with the new standard.
2. Compared with the original ambient air quality standard, the revised standard will generally change the content of air quality monitoring and control in China from only coarse particles to total suspended solids including fine particles. The technical means of monitoring has changed from low level to refined, change from not publishing relevant data to publishing relevant data.

a. Change the air pollution index (API) to the "Comprehensive Air Quality Index" (AQI)

The API represents the air pollution degree with a dimension of 1 (Table 3.5).

Table 3.5 Air pollution index

<table>
<tr><th>API</th><th>Air condition</th><th>Impact to health</th><th>Measures taken</th></tr>
<tr><td>0–50</td><td>Excellent</td><td rowspan="2">Normal activity</td><td rowspan="2"></td></tr>
<tr><td>51–100</td><td>Good</td></tr>
<tr><td>101–150</td><td>Slight pollution</td><td rowspan="2">Symptoms of susceptible people are slightly aggravated, and irritation symptoms appear in healthy people</td><td rowspan="2">Patients with heart disease and respiratory disease should reduce physical exertion and outdoor activities</td></tr>
<tr><td>151–200</td><td>Minor pollution</td></tr>
<tr><td>201–250</td><td>Moderate pollution</td><td rowspan="2">Symptoms of patients with heart disease and lung disease are significantly aggravated, exercise tolerance is reduced, and symptoms are common among healthy people</td><td rowspan="2">The elderly and patients with heart and lung diseases should stay indoors and reduce physical activity</td></tr>
<tr><td>250–300</td><td>Moderately heavy pollution</td></tr>
<tr><td>> 300</td><td>Heavy pollution</td><td>The exercise tolerance of healthy people is reduced, there are obvious strong symptoms, and some diseases appear in advance</td><td>The elderly and patients should stay indoors to avoid physical exertion, and ordinary people should avoid outdoor activities</td></tr>
</table>

AQI is a dimensionless index that quantitatively describes air quality conditions. The higher the value and level of AQI, the more serious the air pollution, the greater the harm to human health (Table 3.6).

Table 3.6 Air quality index

AQI	Level	Category	Color	Health impact	Measures taken
0–50	I	Excellent	Green	Good air quality, no pollution	Normal activities
51–100	II	Good	Yellow	The air quality is acceptable, but some pollutants may have a weak impact on the health of a few sensitive people	People with abnormal sensitivity should reduce outdoor activities
101–150	III	Slight pollution	Orange	Symptoms of susceptible people are slightly aggravated, and irritation symptoms appear in healthy people	Children, the elderly and patients with heart disease and respiratory disease should reduce long time and high-intensity outdoor exercise
151–200	IV	Moderate pollution	Red	Further aggravate the symptoms of susceptible people, which may affect the heart and respiratory system of healthy people	Children, the elderly and patients with heart disease and respiratory system diseases should avoid long-term and high-intensity outdoor exercise, and ordinary people should reduce outdoor exercise appropriately
201–300	V	Heavy pollution	Purple	Symptoms of patients with heart disease and lung disease are significantly aggravated, exercise tolerance is reduced, and symptoms are common among healthy people	Children, the elderly and patients with heart disease and respiratory disease should stay indoors and stop outdoor sports. The ordinary people should reduce outdoor sports
> 300	VI	Severity pollution	Maroon	The exercise tolerance of healthy people is reduced, there are obvious strong symptoms, and some diseases appear in advance	Children, the elderly and patients should stay indoors to avoid physical exertion, and ordinary people should avoid outdoor sports

b. The classification of environmental air functional areas has been adjusted, and the third category area has been merged into the second category area.
c. The pollutant indicators monitored increased. On the basis of the past three items of sulfur dioxide, nitrogen dioxide and inhalable particles, three items of fine particles (PM2.5), ozone (O_3) and carbon monoxide (CO) have been added.
d. The air quality assessment from 12:00 on the current day to 12:00 on the next day has changed to measure the hourly and daily air quality.
e. The release frequency is higher, from once a day in the past to once an hour now.
f. The adopted standards are stricter, from only 5 levels in the past to 6 levels.
g. Added limits for PM2.5 average concentration and 8-h average concentration of ozone.
h. The concentration limits of pollutants such as PM2.5 have been tightened, and the corresponding standards have been improved.
i. The regulations on the effectiveness of monitoring data statistics have been tightened, and the requirements for effective data have been raised from 50 ~ 75% to 75 ~ 90%.
j. The analysis methods for pollution items such as sulfur dioxide, nitrogen dioxide, ozone and particulate matter have been updated, and automatic monitoring analysis methods have been added.
k. Propose the implementation period of the new standard by stages. In 2012, the new standards were implemented in Beijing-Tianjin-Hebei, Yangtze River Delta, Pearl River Delta and other key regions as well as municipalities directly under the Central Government and provincial capitals; in 2013, the new standards were implemented in 113 key cities and environmental protection model cities; in 2015, the new standards were implemented in all cities above prefecture level; and on January 1, 2016, the new standards were implemented nationwide.

3. Evaluation on the prevention and control of urban air pollution in China

   a. From the perspective of the process of controlling urban air pollution in developed countries such as the United States and the United Kingdom, it has taken at least 30 to 50 years to achieve significant results. China's population base is large and the problems encountered are much more complex; the increasingly prominent regional complex air pollution problem in the city is formed by long-term accumulation. Its governance is a complex systematic project with greater difficulty and arduousness, which requires long-term hard and unremitting efforts to achieve results.
   b. Standards and legal system construction. The western developed countries basically started to formulate their own air quality protection laws and regulations and take prevention and control measures from the 1960s to 1970s, that is, after these countries had completed the tasks of industrialization, urbanization and modernization. The United States issued the standard for total suspended solids in 1971, the standard for PM10 in 1987, and the standard for PM2.5 daily average concentration of 65 μg in 1997. In 2006, the standard was tightened to 35 μg. The whole process took 36 years. In the middle stage of industrialization, urbanization and modernization, China has put the

prevention and control of urban air pollution on the important agenda and formulated corresponding laws and regulations. In 1982, China put forward the standard of implementing total suspended particulate matter. The standard of PM10 in 1996 and the standard of PM2.5 daily average concentration of 75 μg in 2012. The whole process only took 31 years (Table 3.7).

c. China's atmospheric environmental quality standards and the types of pollutants monitored are constantly adjusted with the national economic and social development and the improvement of people's living standards. In addition to the improvement of standards, the types of pollution monitoring are also gradually increasing, and the publication of monitoring data is also being further improved.

4. Evaluation of China's atmospheric environmental quality standards

   a. Even the new improved air quality standard in China is still a relatively low standard, which only meet the lower level of international standards. For example, the limit value of PM2.5 can only be in line with the target value of the World Health Organization in the first phase, which is lower than that of developed countries such as the EU, the United States and Australia, and also lower than that of developing countries such as Thailand, India and Bangladesh (Tables 3.8, 3.9).
   b. The air quality standards implemented by a country or region should be compatible with the economic and social development level of a country or region. For example, even the standards implemented in developed countries such as the United States and the European Union are still higher than those in the first phase of the World Health Organization and lower than those in the second phase. Therefore, China's current air quality standards are in line with China's current level of economic and social development.

Table 3.7 List of time for formulating air pollution prevention laws in major industrialized countries

Country	Time of formulation and revision of the Law on the Prevention and Control of Air Pollution
United States	1963,1970, 1977
Japan	1962, 1968
France	1974
German	1974
Italy	1966
Sweden	1969, 1981
United Kingdom	1956, 1968, 1974

Source Miyamoto Kenichi (Japan), Environmental Economics, translated by Pu Yu, Shanghai Sanlian Bookstore, page 76 (2004)

Table 3.8 International comparison of air quality standards

	PM2.5		PM10	
	Annual average limit	Daily maximum limit	Annual average limit	Daily maximum limit
WHO	15μ g/m^3	35μ g/m^3	20μ g/m^3	
EU	25μ g/m^3		40μ g/m^3	
China	35μ g/m^3	75μ g/m^3		
USA	15μ g/m^3	35μ g/m^3		

Table 3.9 Comparison of primary air quality standards between the United States and China

Pollutant	USA	China
SO_2	365μ g/m^3 (0.14 ppm) The maximum concentration within 24 h can only exceed the standard once a year	24-hour average 150 μ g/m^3
Microparticle	A. 15 μ g/m^3 annual average B. 65 μ g/m^3 (0.14 ppm) maximum concentration within 24 hours, exceeding the standard at most once a year	24-hour average 75 μ g/m^3
CO	A. The maximum concentration of 10 mg/m^3 (9 ppm) within 8 hours can exceed the standard at most once a year B. The maximum concentration of 40 mg/m^3 (35 ppm) in one hour can only exceed the standard once a year	24-hour average 4 μ g/m^3 1-hour average 10 μ g/m^3
O_3	0.08 ppm 8-hours average maximum	24-hour average 200 μ g/m^3
NO_2	100 μ g/m^3 (0.05 ppm) annual average	24-hour average 80 μ g/m^3
Lead	1.5 μ g/m^3 quarterly average	

Note Ministry of environmental protection

c. There are also other views on China's air quality standards. One is that "when the United States formulates air quality standards, it is only based on scientific research conclusions about the impact of pollution on health, without considering the economic costs of these standards." Some others also believed that China's environmental protection standards, including air quality, are too low and only need to reach Grade II, which will bring the following drawbacks: first, it will urge local governments to evade their responsibility to deal with public health problems and continue to blindly pursue economic development; secondly, the pollution industries may transfer to places where the air quality is still at the first level; thirdly, the vicious circle of high law-abiding cost and low law-offending cost can continue. The maximum fine for illegal pollutant discharge by Chinese pollutant discharge enterprises is 200,000 yuan. In other countries, polluters will be fined on a daily basis, with a huge cumulative amount and no upper limit.

3.3.3 Major Challenges in Urban Atmospheric Environment Protection and Air Pollution Monitoring in China

First, the current approach to environmental management is outdated. The current urban environmental management model only considers the prevention and control of air pollution in a single city from the perspective of administrative division. The city government is responsible for the local environmental quality. The measures taken are aimed at improving the local environmental quality. Obviously, it is difficult for each city to effectively solve the increasingly serious complex and regional air pollution problem by "fighting by itself". It is urgent to explore and establish a new management model of air pollution prevention and control in regional urban agglomeration.

Second, the object of pollution control is relatively single. A comprehensive control system for multiple pollutants has not been established to improve air quality. From the perspective of pollution control factors, the focus of pollution control is mainly sulfur dioxide and industrial smoke and dust, while the control of nitrogen oxides and volatile organic compounds that have a greater impact on fine particles and ozone is weak. From the perspective of the scope of pollution control, the focus of the work is mainly on industrial large point sources, and insufficient attention is paid to the control of non-point sources such as fugitive dust and mobile sources such as low-speed vehicles.

Third, the foundation of environmental monitoring and statistics is weak. Monitoring indicators of ambient air quality are incomplete, and most cities do not carry out monitoring of ozone and fine particles. The data quality control is weak and cannot fully reflect the air pollution situation. Volatile organic compounds, fugitive dust, etc. are not included in the environmental statistical management system, and the base number is unclear, which is difficult to meet the needs of environmental management. Atmospheric environment monitoring still relies on a limited pollution measurement system. At present, only 56 cities nationwide are capable to monitor PM2.5 or ozone. Only 50 cities have PM2.5 and ozone monitoring at the same time.

Fourth, the system of regulations and standards needs to be improved. The current air pollution prevention laws and regulations lack effective measures and requirements in urban air pollution prevention, mobile source pollution control and other aspects, lack the volatile organic compounds emission standard system, the urban dust comprehensive management system needs to be improved, and the vehicle fuel standard lags far behind the motor vehicle emission standard.

Fifth, the supporting policies are insufficient. The current energy and resource prices, tax and credit policies have failed to truly reflect the social cost of pollution emissions, and the lack of corresponding incentive and restraint mechanisms has also failed to prompt enterprises to shoulder the responsibility of controlling the main body of pollution.

Sixth, investment is insufficient, and there is still a large gap between demand and supply. If the new air quality standards are implemented, it is necessary to establish and improve the pollution measurement and prediction system, adjust and optimize the ambient air quality monitoring points, and rationally arrange the national ambient air quality monitoring network. During the "12th Five Year Plan" period (2011–2015) alone, nearly 1500 monitoring points will be built, with an initial investment of more than 2 billion yuan and an annual increase of more than 100 million yuan.

3.4 PM2.5 Prevention and Control

Since 2010, haze pollution has been a widespread issue in urban areas in China. "The frequent occurrence of haze has become one of the major meteorological disasters and extreme weather and climate events in China". PM2.5 is the culprit of smog weather.

The report issued by the World Health Organization in 2013 proposed that PM2.5 is a fine particle containing toxic substances such as heavy metals produced during the burning of fossil fuels. As it can penetrate into human alveoli, stimulate respiratory tract, cause cough, asthma and respiratory tract damage, and has a causal relationship with cardiovascular and respiratory disease mortality, it is the first killer threatening human life and health. "We found that for every 10 μg of PM2.5 increased per cubic meter of air, the mortality rate increased by 20%", said Katherine Tonner of the University of London School of Health and Tropical Medicine. Therefore, in recent years, countries all over the world have included PM2.5 into the ambient air quality standards to control it as a key air pollutant. China's third revised ambient air quality standard also includes PM2.5.[3]

PM2.5 refers to particles with aerodynamic equivalent diameter less than or equal to 2.5 microns in the ambient air. The diameter of lampblack and black carbon particles in the kitchen is 0.1 ~ 1.0 μ m, which is the main source of haze. PM2.5 is divided into primary pollutants and secondary particles generated by chemical reaction in the air. Due to the complex composition of PM2.5 (more than 30,000 organic molecules alone), unclear sources, unclear source weights, and unclear key precursor pollutants and key chemical mechanisms generated by secondary generation, the prevention and control of PM2.5 is complex and difficult.

3.4.1 Differences Between Haze and Fog

Haze is a meteorological air pollution, which cannot be equated with fog. They are different in relative humidity, visibility and other aspects.

1. The difference of water content. When the moisture content is more than 90%, it is fog; less than 80% is haze, between 80 and 90% is a mixture of the two, but the main component is haze.
2. The difference of visibility. If the horizontal visibility of the target decreases to within 1 km, it is fog; those between 1 and 10 km are called fog and mist; less than 10 km and caused by dust particles are haze.
3. Difference in thickness. It is fog from tens of meters to 200 m. One kilometer to three kilometers is haze.
4. Color difference. Fog is milky white; haze is yellow and orange gray.
5. Boundary differences. The boundary of fog is very clear, and the boundary between haze and surrounding environment is not obvious.

However, with the acceleration of industrialization and urbanization in China, the distinction and boundary between fog and haze are becoming increasingly blurred. For example, many condensation nuclei formed by fog have also become harmful substances to human beings. Especially in cities where human activities are highly intensive, fog and haze often occur at the same time and are mixed together, making it difficult to distinguish them. Therefore, people increasingly confuse fog and haze, called haze.

3.4.2 Source Analysis of PM2.5

PM2.5 sources can be categorized into three groups: industrial sources, including the emissions of thermal power, steel, cement, coal-fired boilers, etc.; mobile sources, including emissions from motor vehicles, ships, aircraft, construction machinery, agricultural machinery, etc.; non-point sources, including the emission of cooking fume and decoration. The causes of PM2.5 are complex, and about 50% of PM2.5 comes from primary fine particles directly discharged from coal combustion, motor vehicles, fugitive dust, biomass combustion, etc.; about 50% are secondary fine particles formed by complex chemical reactions of gaseous pollutants such as sulfur dioxide, nitrogen oxides, volatile organic compounds and ammonia in the air (Tables 3.10, 3.11).

It can be seen from the following table that the sources of PM2.5 in the same city are different in different years and seasons (Table 3.12).

From the above analysis, it can be seen that:

1. Coal combustion is the main source of PM2.5, which is not only the main source of primary particulate matter emissions but also the source of high background values of complex pollutants.

Column 3.9 Black Carbon Pollution

A report completed by a research team composed of 31 experts from many countries

Table 3.10 PM2.5 source contribution share ratio of major cities in China

					Unit: %
Source	Hangzhou	Ningbo	Tianjin	Beijing	Chengdu
Raise dust	22.4	20.4	22.2	15.7	21.0
Coal burning soot	9.4	14.4	8.8	16.7	8.0
vehicle exhaust	17.4	15.2	21.3	5.9	13.0
Secondary sulfate	18.6	16.9	20.2	12.7	25.0
Secondary nitrate	9.6	9.8	10.1	14.7	14.0
Secondary organic carbon	/	8.8	8	/	6.0

Source Chengdu Environmental Protection Bureau

Table 3.11 Share rate of PM2.5 source contribution in Shanghai

Industries	Percentage(%)
Motor vehicles, ships, aircraft	25
Power plant boiler and industrial furnace	21
Steel industry process, petrochemical industry	15
Dust from construction sites and roads	10
Straw burning, fertilizer use, livestock and poultry breeding	4
Catering industry and civil coatings	5
Extraneous source	20

Source Interpreting the Haze Code, Liberation Daily, May 18, 2013, by Shu Jiong

after four years of research proposed that soot (i.e. black carbon) particles generated after the combustion of fossil fuels and organic fuels are the main components of urban air pollutants. In view of this conclusion, one of the purposes of the Climate and Clean Air Alliance launched by the United States in 2012 is to reduce the black carbon emissions from heavy diesel vehicles, brick making and urban waste treatment. The United States Environmental Protection Agency also increased the limits on soot emissions from power plants, diesel engines, and wood burning on the basis of 1997.

The direct use of coal as energy brings about waste of resources and environmental pollution.

The research results show that more than 100 kinds of chemical raw materials are compounded in coal, which can be extended to plastics, chemical fibers, dyes, medicine and other fields. If the price of coal is set as 1, the value added of coal chemical products with different processing depths is: coke: 1.5; asphalt: 2.0; coal tar oil: 4.0; benzene: 15.0; phenol and medium phenol: 90.0; phthalic anhydride: 100.0; plasticizer: 200.0; dye oil: 500.0; medicine: 750.0; chemical fiber: 1500.0. To use coal only as fuel will not only waste so much economic value, but also transform the compound resources into environmental toxins. Therefore, Mao Yushi believes that every ton of coal used in China in 2007 will bring 150 yuan of environmental losses, mainly including the

Table 3.12 Comparison of PM2.5 source analysis results in Chengdu

		Unit: %
Source	Winter 2011	Summer 2012
Urban dust	22.8	21.0
Secondary sulfate	26.7	25.0
Secondary nitrate	13.4	14.0
Vehicle exhaust	15.3	13.0
Soot	11.1	8.0
Cooking fume	3.7	4.0
Metallurgical dust	1.6	2.0
Secondary organic carbon	3.1	6.0
Building cement dust	0.1	3.0
Biomass burning	~	2.0
Other	2.3	2.0

Source Chengdu Environmental Protection Bureau

emission of sulfur dioxide and the pollution formed after the combustion of composite resources, but not including the factors of carbon dioxide emissions from combustion.

Source: Make Coal Really a Black Gold, Economic Reference, May 19, 1992.

2. Motor vehicles are the second largest source of PM2.5 and tend to replace coal as the first largest source.

First, the air pollution caused by motor vehicles is through their exhaust emissions, especially when the vehicle is driven at low speed due to road congestion, which is 5 to 10 times higher than that of normal driving. The second is the dust pollution caused by the rolling of wheels on the dusty hard pavement.

3. Volatile and semi volatile organic compounds (VOC) in the air are important sources of PM2.5. The sources of organic pollutants in the air include the emission of cooking fume in urban areas, and the large amount use of organic dumping in urban housing decoration.
4. Rural straw burning is also the main source of PM2.5 in the air at a certain time. For example, in the spring harvest season of 2011, the burning of straw in surrounding areas led to 4-day pollution in the central urban area of Chengdu; in the spring harvest season of 2012, the same thing happened for five days in Chengdu.
5. Due to the flow and transmission of air between regions, external sources account for a large proportion in the formation of urban PM2.5. From 2006 to March till May of 2013, the daily average concentration of inhalable particulates in the urban area of Chengdu had the highest value of 16 times of slight pollution or

more, of which 13 times were accompanied by sandstorms or strong sandstorms in the north.

3.4.3 Challenges in Urban PM2.5 Mitigation in China

Firstly, two-thirds of China's energy stems from a coal-based energy structure, led by coal power generation. China's coal consumption has escalated by more than 1 billion tons during the "11th Five Year Plan" period (2006—2010), and increased by 44% during the "12th Five Year Plan" period (2011—2015). The peak is not yet in sight.

Secondly, high-speed urbanization has led to a rapid increase in vehicles. Since 2009, China has become the world's largest auto sales market, with motor vehicles numbers in Beijing increasing from less than 3 million in 2007 to more than 5 million in 2012.

Thirdly, the diverse sources and high motility of PM2.5 mean that measures to control a single pollutant or to prevent and control a single city have little impact on PM2.5 levels.

Fourthly, the complex formation mechanism of PM2.5 and the lack of comprehensive research on the contribution of cross-regional transport of PM2.5 precursor pollutants to its formation make it difficult to assign pollution control responsibilities to different regions and to devise an effective control scheme.

3.4.4 International Approaches to PM2.5 Mitigation

In recent years, many countries in the world have incorporated PM2.5 into the ambient air quality standards to control it as a key air pollutant. Developed countries take PM2.5 as the core work of air pollution prevention and control, which covers the emission of primary and secondary particles.

1. Law goes first, which provides legal system guarantee for emission reduction. In 1955, the United States issued the first Air Pollution Control Act, and in 1963, Congress passed the Clean Air Act, which first proposed that air pollution is a cross regional national problem. In accordance with this law, the National Air Quality Standard was promulgated, and the law was amended several times in the following decades. In 1999, the United States promulgated the "Regional Haze Regulations", requiring states to formulate corresponding governance implementation plans. The states submitted the target progress and implementation strategy of regional haze pollution control in August 2006. In the 1970s, the European Union formulated the Long Range Air Pollution Transboundary Transport Protocol (CLRTP), which includes the overall goal of emission reduction and the share of each country's emission reduction. The bill covers the expansion of pollutant emission reduction types from the original sulfur dioxide and nitrogen

oxides to volatile organic compounds, ammonia and other precursors that have an important impact on the formation of PM2.5. The EU has also formulated the "European Clean Air Plan", and gradually developed from the single emission control of fixed sources and motor vehicles to the coordinated control of PM2.5 precursors. France issued an air quality order in 2010, which provides scientific and technological support and stipulates the upper limit of PM2.5 and PM10 concentrations. The order issued a series of programs aimed at reducing air pollution, such as emission reduction program, particulate matter program, carbon emission trading system, local air quality program and atmospheric protection program.

2. Setting standards forces emission reduction. In 1997, the National Environmental Protection Agency of the United States first formulated and released the ambient air quality standard for PM2.5. In 2006, it revised concentration standard of PM2.5, stipulating that the highest concentration of PM2.5 in any area and any 24-h period in the United States, whether in urban or rural areas, decreased from 65 μg per cubic meter to 35 μg, and the standard for annual average concentration was less than or equal to 15 μg per cubic meter. Germany has set emission standards and upper limits for cars, light or heavy trucks, buses, plank cars and other types of motor vehicles. Emission standards have also been set for large boilers, industrial facilities, mechanical equipment, and for small boiler equipment such as house heating equipment.

Since 1970, the United States has increased the content of strengthening the control of automobile exhaust, and in 1990, it has stipulated stricter standards for automobile exhaust emissions, new control standards have been formulated for 189 toxic pollutants.[4] According to the Clean Air Law, the air quality of the whole country is divided into three categories: not up to standard, up to standard, or insufficient data (although the data is insufficient, it can be classified as up to standard). The state and local governments where the non-conformance areas are located need to formulate an implementation plan on how to reduce pollution and meet the standards within three years.

The Air Quality Directive (2008/50/EC) issued by the European Union in 2008 stipulates that the annual average concentration limit of PM2.5 is 25 μ g/m^3. Taking the opportunity of the revision of ambient air quality standards, EU further tightened the emission standards of industrial pollutants, reduced the emissions of volatile organic compounds, odor, nitrogen oxides and particulate matter to meet the emission standards of PM2.5.

3. Establish special institutions and monitoring and evaluation system. According to the National Environmental Policy Act, the United States has established the National Environmental Protection Agency. EPA is authorized by the Act to regularly review the air quality monitoring standards. According to a number of air quality standards and policies formulated by the EPA, states must regularly submit detailed implementation plans for "meeting the standards" of air quality. If the plan is not submitted or effectively implemented, the EPA will take mandatory measures to ensure that air quality standards are met.

4. Formulate prevention and control plans and emergency measures for heavily polluted weather. In case of serious pollution, prohibit certain vehicles, or prohibit all vehicles from driving in the heavily polluted area; restrict or shut down large boilers or industrial equipment; close construction sites in the city; avoid refueling during the daytime high temperature period or delay the work requiring paint and solvent to reduce hydrocarbon emissions; industrial sector restricts or postpones some industrial activities as required by the government to reduce emissions.
5. Strengthen the effectiveness of urban planning. According to the compact urban planning, a number of living centers have been built around the city, so that traffic and exhaust emissions will not be excessively concentrated in the downtown area. "Environmental Protection Zones" have been set up in more than 40 cities in Germany. Only vehicles meeting emission standards are allowed to enter the "Environmental Protection Zones" and the speed is limited. Heavy trucks with normally high pollution discharge levels are prohibited from passing.
6. Develop public transport and reduce traffic source pollution. The intensive public transport system is closely connected with the bicycle rental system. Improve the walking environment to make it more convenient and efficient for people to walk in the city. Encourage public transportation and cycling through subsidies or publicity programs. The traffic can be effectively managed through reasonable adjustment of traffic lights and the setting of special lanes for motor vehicles. A congestion charge system will be implemented to impose a certain fee on vehicles driving in the city center during peak hours to curb unnecessary road occupation.
7. Provide air quality information to the public. In Germany, the Air Quality Monitoring Association is responsible for monitoring the concentration of pollutants in the air and providing air quality information to the public in a timely manner. The French Environment and Energy Administration will publish the air quality index map of the day and the next day on its website every day, and provide suggestions on how to improve air quality. When the pollution index exceeds the standard, the local government will immediately take emergency measures and provide health advice to the public. The government will also call for lifestyle adjustment to reduce emissions of pollutants that will lead to increased odor concentration.
8. Scientific research will provide support for urban atmospheric environment control and protection. Carry out research on the main substances, causes and formation mechanism of PM2.5, transmission and flow laws, and provide scientific basis and scientific support for targeted measures. For example, the computer model developed by the California Institute of Technology in the United States has played a huge role in controlling air pollution. According to this model, the California government has evaluated various factors that cause air pollution and conducted comprehensive treatment.
9. Taking structural adjustment of cities as the fundamental way to control urban air pollution. It includes the optimization and upgrading of economic structure, industrial structure, energy structure, transportation structure to free up environmental capacity and lay a good foundation for the improvement of urban atmospheric environment quality.

3.5 Strategies for Urban Atmospheric Improvement

The overall requirement is to effectively improve the quality of urban atmospheric environment with the fundamental starting point of protecting people's health. The general idea is to combine the adjustment and optimization of the structure, strengthen the innovation drive, control the total amount, strengthen coordination, address both the symptoms and root causes, transform the urban planning, construction and management mode, focus on the key points, take multiple measures and implement scientific policies from three aspects of production, life and ecology.

3.5.1 Countermeasures for Phased Implementation

3.5.1.1 Recent Countermeasures

1. Strengthen the sense of responsibility of local governments for local air quality, and incorporate regional air environment quality into the indicator system of the ecological red line as an important indicator for assessing government performance. Build a total amount control system, and assessment system based on urban air quality improvement. Formulate and improve the emergency management plan for urban air pollution, including production restriction for heavily polluted weather, emission restriction for heavily polluted enterprises, and traffic restriction for motor vehicles. Compulsory disclosure of environmental information of enterprises in key pollution industries. Disclosure the air quality ranking of key cities.
2. Regulate urban fugitive dust.

a. Strengthen the supervision of construction dust. Strengthen the environmental supervision and law enforcement inspection of fugitive dust during the construction of key urban projects. It is prohibited to use bagged cement, and not to mix concrete and mortar on site.
b. Road mechanical excavation and roadside demolition adopt wet method; the construction working surface shall be watered regularly to reduce dust, and the roads and vehicle entrances in the construction site shall be cleaned in time with wet method; wet method operation is adopted for muck cleaning of construction projects; the construction site must be completely enclosed and set up with a retaining wall. Open operation is strictly prohibited.
c. Reduce the road excavation area and shorten the exposure time. The excavated road shall be closed by sections and the damaged road surface shall be repaired in time. Actively promote mechanized cleaning of urban roads, increase the frequency of urban road washing and cleaning, and effectively reduce road dust load. The muck transport vehicles shall be transported in a closed manner, the

qualification management and filing system shall be implemented, the GPS positioning system shall be installed, and the muck transport vehicles in key areas and key sections shall be comprehensively monitored.

3. Accelerate the elimination of yellow label vehicles. Strictly implement the mandatory scrapping system for old motor vehicles, and eliminate yellow label vehicles within a time limit. Improve the quality of oil products.
4. Strengthen environmental supervision over the burning of straw and other organic matter. Open burning of biomass such as urban cleaning waste, garden waste and construction waste is prohibited. Comprehensive utilization measures such as straw returning to the field, straw fertilizer making, straw feed, and straw energy utilization will be promoted, and a demonstration project of straw comprehensive utilization will be established to promote the utilization of straw resources.

3.5.1.2 Medium Term Countermeasures

The medium-term countermeasure is to focus on the emission reduction of industrial pollutants and implement the main responsibility of enterprises for emission reduction and pollution control.

1. To strengthen restrictions on energy conservation and environmental protection indicators, accelerate the elimination of outdated production capacity and processes, comprehensively renovate small coal-fired boilers, and accelerate the transformation of desulfurization, denitrification, and dust removal in key industries. In 2014, to complete the task of eliminating backward production capacity in key industries such as steel, cement, electrolytic aluminum and flat glass during the "12th Five Year Plan" (2011—2015). The emission intensity of major air pollutants in key industries will drop by more than 30% by the end of 2017. Strictly control new capacity in industries with high energy consumption and high pollution. For projects that fail to pass the energy assessment and environmental impact assessment, no approval shall be given to start construction, no land, loan support, power or water supply shall be provided.
2. Strengthen the supervision of industrial pollution sources. Through online monitoring of pollution sources, regular supervision and other strengthened regulatory measures, the pollution control facilities of coal-fired power plants, industrial boilers, industrial furnaces and kilns are ensured to meet the standard steadily.
3. Improve the cleaner production level of enterprises. To promote the adoption of efficient dust removal measures in key industries such as coal-fired power plants, metallurgy, building materials, and chemicals, raise emission standards, and further reduce smoke (dust) emissions.
4. Adjust energy structure, increase the supply of clean energy such as natural gas and coal to methane.

3.5.1.3 Long-Term Countermeasures

The long-term strategy is to promote industrial upgrading, transform the development mode, and comprehensively coordinate the prevention and control of multiple pollutants.

1. Take measures to control the total amount of pollutants and coal consumption, and use strict environmental protection means to "reverse" the transmission mechanism to promote the transformation of the mode of economic development and optimize economic development.
2. Use laws and standards to "force" industrial transformation and upgrading. Formulate and revise emission standards for key industries. Reinforce penalties for environmental violations. Promote a new mechanism for energy conservation and emission reduction that combines incentives and constraints, and increase the collection of pollution charges.
3. Adopt selective incentive strategies to promote the collective action of air pollution control across urban areas. Due to the flow of the air, it is more necessary to adopt the strategy of cross regional integrated governance for the treatment of air pollution. Under the existing system, the air pollution control of a single city is often difficult to obtain the cooperation of the governments of neighboring cities, while it is impossible to change "individual behavior" into "collective action" by relying on the market alone. Through the implementation of the "selective incentive" policy, which includes social sanctions and social rewards, individuals are treated differently. Those who do not obey are excluded, and cooperative individuals are invited to participate. Such measures and means as promoting governance with awards and substituting awards for subsidies are conducive to mobilizing potential groups and local governments to participate in the collective action of air pollution control, so as to achieve the collective action from the central government to the local government in the air pollution control of trans-regional cities.
4. Establish regional air pollution joint prevention and control management mechanism. Realize regional "unified planning, unified monitoring, unified supervision, unified assessment and unified coordination". According to the social and economic development level and environmental pollution status of different cities in the region, key control areas and general control areas are divided to implement differentiated management.
5. Strengthen the construction of forest cities, filter the air with forest belts and green belts, and prevent sandstorms.

3.5.2 Key Points of Urban Air Pollution Control

Identify key areas, key industries and key pollutants for urban air quality protection based on the standards that will not endanger people's health, endanger urban environment safety and affect sustainable development of economy and society.

In addition to the key areas of pollution prevention, the key is to focus on the areas of pollution prevention, as follows:

3.5.2.1 Prevention and Control of Soot Pollution

1. Establish a prediction and early warning mechanism for total coal consumption. By improving energy efficiency, improving the energy structure, and increasing the supply of natural gas and coal to methane gas, manage to achieve the peak of total coal consumption in 2010.
2. Expand the scope of coal prohibition area. Strengthen the delineation of "standard burning areas for regulating contaminated fuels" and gradually expand the scope of standard burning areas.
3. Standardize the management of small and medium-sized boilers using waste wood, and control the smoke-free facilities within a time limit.

3.5.2.2 Control Motor Vehicle Pollution

1. Vigorously develop the urban public transport system and intercity rail transit system, implement the public transport priority strategy, improve the walking and cycling conditions of residents, and encourage the choice of green travel modes.
2. Ensure smooth traffic and ease congestion, and improve the traffic efficiency of motor vehicles. Optimize the construction of urban road network structure, stagger commute and adjust parking fees; promote urban intelligent traffic management and energy-saving driving technology.
3. Encourage the selection of energy-saving and environment-friendly vehicles, promote the use of natural gas vehicles and new energy vehicles, and gradually improve relevant infrastructure and supporting facilities; actively promote electric buses and taxis.
4. Introduce policies to regulate urban motor vehicle ownership and implement incremental control of urban motor vehicles.
5. Promote the upgrading of oil products. Strengthen the supervision and inspection of oil quality, and severely crack down on the illegal production and sale of automotive oil products that do not meet the requirements of national and local standards.
6. Strengthen environmental protection management of motor vehicles. Fully promote the management of environmental protection signs for motor vehicles; improve the environmental protection inspection and maintenance (I/M) system of motor vehicles. Accelerate the implementation of exhaust gas detection method under simple working conditions, strengthen the supervision of detection technology and data review, improve the quality control level of monitoring data of environmental protection testing institutions, and promote the standardized operation of environmental protection testing institutions.

3.5.2.3 PM2.5 Governance

1. Control man-made pollution. PM2.5 pollution is an event caused by both natural factors and human factors. Natural causes such as weather are hard for human to reach, so the control of PM2.5 pollution can only start from the control of human pollution behavior.
2. Implement joint prevention and control in regional cities, and manage them by zones and categories. According to the natural geographical characteristics of different cities, the level of social and economic development, the degree of air pollution, urban spatial distribution and the spatial transport law of pollutants in the region, the region is divided into key control areas and general control areas, and differentiated control management is implemented to formulate targeted pollution prevention measures.
3. Strengthen the control of PM2.5 precursors and promote the collaborative control of multiple pollutants. Improve the VOC pollution prevention system, and carry out thorough investigation on VOC; complete the recovery and treatment of oil and gas from urban gas stations, oil storage depots and oil tankers; vigorously reduce the emission of volatile organic compounds in petrochemical industry; actively promote the control of volatile organic compounds in organic chemical industry and other industries; strengthen the emission control of volatile organic compounds in surface coating process; promote the treatment of volatile organic compounds in solvent use process. Strictly approve the environmental protection of newly-built catering service business sites; the catering service business premises shall be equipped with efficient lampblack purification facilities, and the operation supervision shall be strengthened; strengthen the environmental supervision of open-air barbecue without lampblack purification facilities. Strengthen supervision over fireworks and firecrackers. Strictly restrict the types and time of fireworks and firecrackers. Carry out the monitoring system of volatile organic compounds and the general survey of volatile organic compounds pollution sources, establish a basic database, and carry out pilot projects to control the total emission of volatile organic compounds in key industries.
4. Control pollution from open sources and non-road mobile sources. Establish management accounts for air pollution control of non-road mobile sources such as construction machinery, agricultural machinery, industrial machinery and aircraft. Promote emission control of non-road mobile machinery. Actively carry out environmental protection treatment of construction machinery and promote the installation of post-treatment devices for air pollutants.

3.5.3 Supports from Scientific Research

In view of the current situation of "unclear situation and insufficient science and technology capacity" in urban atmospheric environment control and protection in

China, scientific research on urban air pollution prevention and control should be strengthened to provide support.

First, in view of the unique meteorological conditions and the emission of precursors in various regions, the research on the formation mechanism and source refinement of atmospheric secondary particles was carried out; according to the requirements of heavy pollution emergency decision-making, real-time or near real-time rapid analysis technology is established.

Second, in view of the newly implemented ambient air quality standards, further strengthen the scientific research on the sources and transmission laws of urban PM2.5.

Third, carry out research on emission characteristics and total amount control of volatile organic compounds in key industries.

Fourth, carry out research on the implementation of total coal volume control in cities.

Fifth, carry out research on forecasting technology of meteorological conditions that affect air quality, and carry out research on the impact of atmospheric conditions on urban air quality.

Sixth, carry out research on the damage of urban ambient air particles to people's health, and analyze the environmental quality improvement after the implementation of the new air quality standard and the resulting environmental, economic and health benefits.

3.5.4 Active and Broad Public Participation

The government, enterprises and the public are the three main bodies in the governance and protection of urban atmospheric environment. However, public awareness and participation are particularly important for urban atmospheric environment protection. This is not only because air pollution has a significant impact on public health and economic life, but also because a large number of the public can supervise legislation, enterprises and other sectors. It also lies in that non-governmental organizations can play an active role in environmental governance.

3.5.5 Publicity and Education on Environmental Protection

The code of conduct of "breathing together and striving together" should be advocated in the whole society to enhance frugal and green consumption patterns and living habits, and mobilize the whole people to participate in environmental protection and supervision.

3.6 Air Quality Protection in Major Chinese Cities

3.6.1 Beijing

First, control coal burning. Beijing proposed to reduce the city's coal consumption from 27 million tons to 15 million tons between 2010 and 2015. The main measures include moving a large number of industrial enterprises out of the city before the opening of the 2008 Olympic Games, and replacing coal with gas in the four remaining coal-fired power plants in the urban area by 2013. Beijing will actively guide the use of renewable energy to replace fossil energy.

Second, develop public transport and improve traffic congestion. In 2013, the longest subway line in the world was built in Beijing, and a large amount of investment in public transport system was subsidized to promote its development.

Third, implement the "plain afforestation project" to improve urban ambient air quality. It will take five years from 2012 to newly build 1 million mu forest area, the forest coverage in the plain area will reach more than 25%, increasing by 2.3 percentage points, and the forest coverage in the whole city will increase by 1 percentage point, turning Beijing into a "green city with thousands of acres of urban greening and surrounding".

In 2012, on the basis of completing the annual planned afforestation task of 100,000 mu and adding 1000 hectares of urban green space in the "12th Five Year Plan", Beijing implemented the plain afforestation project of 200,000 mu, with a total investment of 10 billion yuan. The 200,000 mu plain afforestation project, closely centering on the spatial layout of "two rings, three belts, nine wedges, and multiple corridors" in Beijing, focuses on afforestation and greening on both sides of the sixth ring road, 50 key villages in the urban–rural junction, as well as on both sides of key river roads, wasteland, air corridors and areas around the airport, the South to North Water Diversion Trunk Line and supporting pipe networks, in accordance with the principle of relatively concentrated and connected areas. In the selection of varieties for afforestation, attention has been paid to the characteristics of good dust retention effect, obvious carbon sequestration, more water-saving, drought resistance, cold resistance, and less susceptibility to pests and diseases.

Fourth, establish a "haze early warning" system. The signals are divided into two levels, namely yellow early warning and orange early warning. The orange early warning signal is the highest level, and its standard is: haze with visibility less than 2000 m may occur within 6 h, or haze with visibility less than 2000 m may have occurred and may continue. On January 1, 2013, 35 monitoring stations in the city started to release the concentration information of air pollutants and the air quality index in the first 24 h in real time.

Fifth, formulate and implement the Emergency Plan for Beijing's Serious Air Pollution Day: Temporary traffic control shall be implemented on vehicles with serious exhaust emissions on extremely polluted days to reduce the dust generated by construction sites and traffic. It is strictly prohibited to burn biological waste and garbage in the open air in urban suburbs. Remind the public to reduce outdoor activities and physical education classes for students, avoid large-scale outdoor competitions, take dust reduction measures at the construction site, stop earthwork at the construction site, and sprinkle water on the road to reduce dust. Government organs and institutions should stop driving 30% of official vehicles.

Sixth, formulate the Beijing Clean Air Action Plan (2011–2015), the Beijing 2012 ~ 2020 Air Pollution Control Measures, and the Notice on Tasks of the Beijing 2013 Clean Air Action Plan. Since 2013, 52 air pollution control measures have been implemented from 8 aspects, including strict control of increment, reduction of coal consumption, green transportation, dust control, industry control, increase of capacity, strengthening of law enforcement, and strengthening of security. The task has been broken down to relevant departments and units at district and county governments and municipal levels, and the annual target of average annual concentration reduction of major pollutants has been defined as 2%.

3.6.2 Shanghai

Through the promotion of four consecutive "Three-year Action Plans for Environmental Protection" since 2000, the annual investment in environmental protection has accounted for more than 3% of GDP in Shanghai. By the end of 2011, the total investment in environmental protection had reached 378 billion yuan, including 55.8 billion yuan in 2011. All the factories in the urban area have been relocated, eliminating the emission of black smoke. Many major polluters have been stopped and closed. Some industrial parks that have been dirty and disorderly for a long time have been greatly improved, and the city's air pollution prevention has achieved remarkable results. However, new environmental problems are emerging, haze and photochemical pollution are still prominent, and the type of air pollution has changed from traditional and single soot pollution to regional and complex pollution. Since the monitoring work was released on June 27, 2012 till the end of 2012, the average PM 2.5 concentration of the city was 48 $\mu g/m^3$, which was converted into an annual average concentration of 56 ~ 60 $\mu g/m^3$, exceeding the national level II standard limit. In the first quarter of 2013, severe air quality pollution has occurred many times in Shanghai.

First, improve the air quality early warning system. Since March 1, 2013, Shanghai Environmental Protection Bureau has revised the release system of air quality, and upgraded relevant websites, APP and Microblog simultaneously. The citizens can clearly see the real-time air quality status, the Bund live photos, the real-time concentration changes of pollutants and other information by logging on the home page.

Second, promote the fifth round of "Three-year (2012–2014) Action Plan" for environmental protection. The content of special atmospheric work has been specially strengthened. 53 projects have been set up with an investment of 10.3 billion yuan.

Compared with the fourth round of action plan, the projects and investment have increased by about 40%.

Third, formulate and implement the Shanghai Ambient Air Quality Compliance Plan, propose the deadline for compliance and phased objectives, and implement air pollution control in key areas according to the requirements of relevant national departments. Formulate compliance measures in terms of improving the industrial structure, strengthening pollution source control, deepening the comprehensive treatment of industrial areas, and strengthening high pollution emergency response. Through strengthening regional cooperation, promote the comprehensive control of the atmospheric environment in a coordinated and step by step manner.

3.6.3 Liaoning Blue Sky Project

Objective: By 2015, the ambient air quality of more than 70% of cities under provincial jurisdiction in the province will reach the secondary standard of the National Ambient Air Quality Standard (GB3095-2012), and the pollution of fine particles and haze will be effectively controlled. The total emission of sulfur dioxide and nitrogen oxides shall meet the national control targets.

Measures:

1. Six key measures to control air pollution were introduced, with a total investment of 7 billion yuan and 1084 projects launched.

   a. Integrated and efficient district heating. After implementation, the total number of heat sources in the district integrated efficient heating system in prefecture level cities will reach 53. The total heating area is 497 million square meters, which will reduce 156,700 tons of smoke and dust emissions, 185,700 tons of sulfur dioxide, and 68,600 tons of nitrogen oxides annually. The area of integrated efficient regional heating in the province has reached 680 million square meters, accounting for 53% of the heating area in the province.
   b. Gasification in Liaoning. Change the energy structure that has been dominated by coal for a long time and lacks high-quality energy such as natural gas. In 2011, natural gas consumption in the province accounted for only 1.8% of disposable energy, far below the national average. The goal is to cover all provincial cities except Dandong in 2013, all provincial cities and counties (cities and districts) in 2014, and more than 70% of villages and towns in 2015. The natural gas supply capacity of the province has reached 20 billion cubic meters, and the consumption has reached 18.4 billion cubic meters, replacing 24.47 million tons of standard coal, accounting for 9% of the one-time energy. By 2012, the province's main natural gas supply network had formed a gas supply capacity of 10 billion cubic meters, and the construction of a 300 km gas transmission branch line project was accelerated.

2. Strive for national policy support. In 2010, Liaoning was identified by the National Development and Reform Commission as one of the first batch of low-carbon pilot provinces in China, and the Ministry of Transport as one of the first batch of pilot provinces for the promotion and use of liquefied natural gas vehicles in China.

3.6.4 Chengdu Blue Sky Action

Chengdu is a typical city with "basin climate", and the atmospheric environment quality is genuinely not that good. It took six years from 2005 to 2011, for the number of days that the air quality exceeded the secondary standard rose from 293 to 322 days.

1. Fugitive dust. Nine dust pollution management methods and regulations, including the "Measures for the Prevention and Control of Dust Pollution in Chengdu", were introduced. Special personnel were assigned to the construction site, slag trucks were used for closed transportation, and GPS was installed for comprehensive monitoring. The "three major projects" including bare soil covering, road hardening and green belt upgrading and soil lowering will be implemented within the expressway around the city. In 2011, the utilization rate of bulk cement in the city reached 65.3%, and the production capacity ratio of pre mixed mortar reached 33%, 2.7 times higher than the national average production capacity.[5]
2. Coal pollution control. The coal-fired power plant was shut down. In April 2011, the cooling tower of Sichuan Jialing Electric Power Co., Ltd. was demolished by blasting. The city's largest gas related pollution source was shut down, reducing sulfur dioxide emissions by more than 10,000 tons annually. Previously, Chengdu Thermal Power Plant and HuaNeng Thermal Power Plant were closed. The closure of the three thermal power plants has greatly helped to improve the urban atmospheric environment. Coal burning is prohibited in the central urban area, and coal to gas project was implemented. By the end of 2011, enterprises and public institutions and large restaurants within the expressway have achieved a comprehensive coal banning, reducing coal consumption by more than 4 million tons annually.
3. Vehicle pollution control. The management of environmental labels for motor vehicles was implemented. As of November 30, 2011, 1.465 million environmental labels were issued in the city, and more than 60,000 vehicles that failed to meet the national first stage emission standards were transferred out and scrapped. Subsidies of nearly 200 million yuan were granted to owners who sold out their old cars and yellow standard cars to buy new cars. Implement traffic restrictions in areas and periods with high pollution. The restricted area is extended from the Second Ring Road to the expressway around the city. The household registration standard for new vehicles was tightened. Since July 1, 2011, the fourth phase of

the national vehicle exhaust pollutant emission standard has been implemented in stages. Chengdu comprehensively starts oil and gas recovery and treatment.

4. Treatment of cooking fume pollution in catering services. The central urban area will fully complete the governance task of catering service enterprises above certain scale that have not completed smoke management in 2010 by June 30, 2011. Jinjiang District carried out the pilot work of online lampblack monitoring. By the end of 2011, more than 90% of catering enterprises in the central urban area installed lampblack purification devices. Suburban districts (cities) and counties comprehensively promote lampblack control in catering service industry according to the standards of central urban areas.
5. Combined with the construction of national ecological county. Since 2007, Chengdu have focused on promoting the construction of provincial and national ecological counties in 14 suburban cities and counties. Focusing on the three tasks of "developing ecological economy, carrying out environmental improvement and strengthening ecological protection" in the construction of ecological county, vigorously promote the optimization and upgrading of industrial structure, transform the mode of economic development, and improve the urban and rural living environment. In 2011, Chengdu completed the construction of 1079 km of greenways, basically achieved greenway network; the opening and reconstruction of five parks were fully completed, including the famous People's Park, and the park landscape was integrated with the road and urban landscape. 6 municipal parks and 25 street greenbelts will be built.

In 2011, 9 of the 14 suburban counties in the city have met the requirements of the ecological county construction index system above the provincial level. Among them, Shuangliu, Pixian, Pujiang, Wenjiang and Qingbaijiang have become provincial ecological counties, and Xindu District has passed the acceptance or technical verification of provincial ecological counties. Shuangliu County and Wenjiang District have been officially named as National Ecological Counties by the Ministry of Environmental Protection. In December 2011, the above two counties were officially designated as National Pilot Counties for Ecological Civilization Construction by the Ministry of Environmental Protection.

6. Complete the "11th Five Year Plan" emission reduction task. During the "11th Five Year Plan" period (2006—2010), when Chengdu's GDP doubled, it cut 121,700 tons of chemical oxygen demand, down 23.65%, and 7.14 tons of sulfur dioxide, down 22.9%. During the "11th Five Year Plan" period, 2798 emission reduction projects were implemented, including 263 sulfur dioxide emission reduction projects.

3.6.5 *Joint Prevention and Control of Urban Air Pollution in Urban Agglomeration*

3.6.5.1 Beijing-Tianjin-Hebei Urban Agglomeration Jointly Harnessing Air Pollution

The Beijing-Tianjin-Hebei urban agglomeration includes Beijing, Tianjin and eight prefecture level cities in Hebei Province, including Shijiazhuang, Zhangjiakou, Chengde, Baoding, Langfang, Tangshan, Qinhuangdao and Cangzhou.

Beijing has proposed to realize the transformation from "siphon" to "overflow" in air pollution control and environmental protection. As the "12th Five Year Plan" proposed to "promote the integrated development of regional economy in the Beijing Tianjin Hebei region", it has become a national strategy to build a capital economic circle. At the same time, it has also started the process of the Beijing-Tianjin-Hebei urban agglomeration working together to prevent and control air pollution.[6] On the basis of the Beijing Olympic Games as an opportunity to start the implementation of sandstorm control and air pollution control, the Beijing-Tianjin-Hebei and surrounding air pollution prevention and control action plan has been implemented. The content includes the requirements for the reduction ratio of PM2.5, sulfur dioxide, nitrogen oxides, particulate matter and volatile organic pollutants, as well as the substantial reduction of total coal consumption.

According to the "Work Plan for Beijing's Air Pollution Control from 2010 to 2020", by 2015, the concentration of PM2.5 in the air will be 15% lower than that in 2010, and the concentration will be reduced to 60 $\mu g/m^3$; by 2020, the concentration of major pollutants in the air will be 30% lower than that in 2010, and the concentration of PM2.5 will reach 50 $\mu g/m^3$. The concentration of sulfur dioxide will be reduced to below 20 μ g/m^3, and the hours of ozone exceeding the standard will be reduced by 30%.

Since May 2013, Hebei Province has carried out the general survey of air pollution sources throughout the province so as to implement targeted supervision. In 2013, Hebei Province also carried out the key action of atmospheric environment quality to promote the adjustment of urban planning layout, industrial structure and energy structure. Control the pollution of combustion dust, industrial dust, construction dust, motor vehicle exhaust, cooking fume, accelerate the ecological environment construction in cities and surrounding areas, and implement comprehensive control of sulfur dioxide, nitrogen oxides, fine particles, volatile organic compounds and other pollutants.

The joint prevention and control of air pollution in Tianjin has been carried out in an all-round way, including promoting the optimization of industrial structure and layout, clean energy utilization, emission control of key pollutants, supervision of key environmental enterprises, and joint prevention capacity building. The government issued the "Measures of Tianjin for the Prevention and Control of Motor Vehicle Pollution", implemented the "Interim Measures of Tianjin for the Administration of Subsidies for the Early Elimination of 'Yellow Label Vehicles'", and implemented the first phase of "Yellow Label Vehicles", which is restricted by time periods and regions from July 1, 2012; 2.19 million yellow and green standard label were issued to vehicles in use, 7077 "yellow standard vehicles" were jointly examined for subsidy dismantling, and 60.885 million yuan of subsidy funds were allocated; 8170 vehicles were transferred from other provinces and cities; the "12th Five Year Plan" of Tianjin Motor Vehicle Environmental Protection Inspection Agency was prepared, and three pilot stations of simple working mode method were constructed.[7]

Shijiazhuang requires that 18 large coal burning entities in the urban area be transferred within five years, and all of them will be relocated to the industrial park or specially designated areas. By the end of June 2013, all 155 coal-fired boilers in the urban area will be dismantled. Build a low-carbon industrial system. During the "12th Five Year Plan" period, key energy users will save more than 2 million tons of standard coal. By 2015, non-fossil energy will account for 5% of disposable energy. Build a low-carbon urban transport system, improve the density of public transport network and the coverage rate of stations, and establish a low-carbon slow traffic system dominated by walking, bicycles and electric vehicles. By 2015, new energy vehicles will account for more than 90% of the public transport system.

Tangshan is an old industrial base in China, and its economic structure is biased. In the first quarter of 2013, Tangshan ranked last in the air quality report of 74 cities nationwide. Recently, the production environment of industrial enterprises in the city was examined, and 100 enterprises seriously polluting the environment were included in the first "blacklist", including steel, coking, mining, cement, paper making, plastics, electroplating and other industries, which were distributed in Luan County, Yutian, Lunan, Guye, Fengnan, Fengrun, High-tech Development Zone and other counties and districts.

In 2013, Taiyuan accelerated the construction of heat source projects to ensure full coverage of clean heating. In combination with the construction of the Central Ring Road and key urban projects, 21 urban villages were demolished and 10,000 black chimneys were pulled out, reducing the amount of coal fired in the city. In 2013, it is also planned to shut down, eliminate and relocate 100 enterprises with serious pollution, such as coal preparation plants, coal storage plants, coke delivery stations, small thermal power plants, water building materials, etc. within the scope of urban planning, and gradually withdraw the coal related industries from the main urban area.

Shanxi Province will promptly formulate the "Five Year Action Plan for Air Pollution Control", which will take PM2.5 as a binding assessment indicator and directly link it with the government performance assessment. The air pollution will be remedied by deepening the comprehensive control of air pollution in industrial enterprises, strengthening the prevention and control of motor vehicle pollution, strengthening the management of fugitive dust environment, strictly controlling the emission of air pollutants in the winter heating period, eliminating outdated production capacity, adjusting the industrial structure, strengthening the use of clean energy, properly coping with heavily polluted weather and other measures. It is stipulated that the work of taking PM2.5 as a binding assessment indicator will be leaded by the government and participated by multiple departments. The environmental protection

3.7 International Experiences in Atmospheric Control

3.7.1 With the Vigilance of the Poison Fog Incident, London Has Got Rid of the Reputation as "Fog City" for Half a Century

As early as the Industrial Revolution, there was a so-called "London smog". In the book Urban Climate published in 1818, British chemist Howard first described the cloudy air and poor visibility in London in winter. From December 5 to 8, 1952, London was shrouded in the inversion layer. It was still and windless for days. Dust, toxic gases and pollutants from coal combustion accumulated in the sky, causing heavy fog weather. The whole city was filled with a strong smell of "rotten eggs". People walked in the streets and could barely see their feet. During those days, a cattle exhibition was being held in London, 52 of 350 cattle were seriously poisoned, 14 were dying, and 1 died on the spot. Soon the citizens also felt dyspnea, eye tingling, and the number of patients with asthma, cough and other respiratory symptoms increased significantly. The death toll in the city reached 4000 from December 5 to 8. The toxic fog began to dissipate on December 9, but 8000 people still died of respiratory diseases in the following two months. Ten years later, similar incidents occurred again, causing another 1200 abnormal deaths.

After half a century of efforts, London gradually removed the name of the Fog City. The smog incident basically did not happen again, and the atmospheric environment quality has improved significantly. From 1952 to 1960, the total smoke emission in London decreased by 37%, and the sunshine duration in winter increased by 70%. By 1975, the number of foggy days in London had decreased from dozens of days a year to 15 days, and only 5 days in 1980. The main measures taken are as follow:

1. Economic transformation and structural adjustment. The year of 1956 became the watershed of London as the "Fog City". Once the British Parliament passed a large-scale discussion that year, the Clean Air Act was issued, which stipulated that all thermal power plants in London must be closed and can only be rebuilt in the Greater London Area; industrial enterprises are required to build tall chimneys and strengthen the evacuation of air pollutants; it is required to transform the traditional stoves of urban residents on a large scale, reduce the consumption of coal, and gradually realize the natural gasification of residents' lives; central heating is adopted in winter. Control the exhaust gas discharged by households and factories. Some towns are designated as "smoke and dust control areas", where only anthracite can be used. The government has invested in helping citizens to renovate their stoves, limiting some enterprises to move out of the city.
2. Legal safeguards. Following the Clean Air Act, many laws and regulations have been promulgated, such as the Law on the Control of Public Hazards, the Public Health Law, the Radioactive Substances Law, and the Regulations on the Use of

Automobiles. The Pollution Control Act, promulgated in 1974, includes protection provisions from air to soil and water. A clause on noise control has been added.

3. Improve the energy structure, replace coal with gas, and develop clean energy. With the development of the North Sea oil field, London began to replace coal with gas, which greatly reduced its dependence on coal. In 2012, the British government proposed that renewable energy should account for 15% of the energy supply by 2020. Through the green transformation of thermal power and the development of green energy such as wind energy, 40% of the electricity should come from green energy.
4. In view of the fact that traffic is becoming a new source of pollution, British Government decided to improve traffic conditions and develop public transport. With the adjustment of industrial structure and the change of energy use, coal has withdrawn from the production and life in London. Traffic emissions have replaced coal as the main source of urban air pollution. More than 58% of nitrogen oxides and 68% of PM10 come from vehicle exhaust emissions. In order to control traffic pollution, the UK further improved the Clean Air Act in 1993, adding provisions on vehicle exhaust emissions, requiring all new vehicles to be equipped with purification devices to reduce nitrogen oxide emissions.

The intensive public transport system is closely connected with the bicycle rental system. The commuter population in the city has increased, and about 727,000 people live outside London. They come to London every day by various buses.

Improve the walking environment to make it more convenient and efficient for people to walk in the city. The government requires large enterprises to encourage employees to carpool to work, take public transport or ride bicycles or walk to work.

Since 2003, the London Municipal Government has implemented the congestion charge system, imposing a certain fee on vehicles driving in the city center during peak hours to curb unnecessary road occupation. The revenue will be used to promote the development of public transport system. The "congestion charge" has been adjusted repeatedly. In 2013, it has risen to 10 pounds a day for entering the city. It effectively restricts vehicle travel. In the past, there were more than 3 million vehicles driving on the road every day, but after the congestion charge was collected, the number of vehicles dropped by 70,000 every day. The London Municipal Government also released a stricter Transport 2025 plan, which strictly restricts private cars from entering the city. It plans to reduce the flow of private cars by 9% within 20 years, and reduce the number of vehicles entering the congestion charging area by 60,000 every day, thus reducing the emission by 12%.

Promote new energy vehicles. Buyers of electric vehicles can enjoy high rebates and exemption from carbon emission taxes. London plans to build 25,000 sets of electric vehicles charging devices by 2015.

5. Strengthen urban planning, and establish multiple living centers around the city according to the compact urban planning, so that traffic and exhaust emissions will not be excessively concentrated in the downtown area. In addition, urban

expansion of green space has also played an important role in controlling air pollution.

3.7.1.1 Taking the Opportunity of Tackling Photochemical Pollution Events, Los Angeles Has Become an Important Experimental Base for the United States to Fight Against Air Pollution

In July 1943, Los Angeles was "attacked" by the "homicidal dust" haze, thousands of people had cough, tears, sneeze and other symptoms, and in severe cases, they had eye irritation, respiratory discomfort, dizziness and nausea. At first, there were rumors that this was a poison gas attack by the Japanese. Later, it was found that this kind of smoke belonged to "photochemical" smoke, which was mainly caused by the photochemical reaction of nitrogen oxides emitted by cars under sunlight. The photochemical pollution lasted until the 1970s. This kind of smog often appeared in the sky of cities, making Los Angeles one of the earliest "frog cities" in the United States. Many citizens without bad habits such as smoking suffered from serious lung disease. In September 1979, the critical "danger point" of ozone content in the urban air was shrouded in smog, and the visibility was reduced to three blocks.

Taking the opportunity of tackling photochemical pollution events, Los Angeles has become an important experimental base for the United States to fight against air pollution. By carrying out a series of "blue sky defense" to control air pollution, including scientific research, policies, laws, civic awareness and other contents, urban air quality has been greatly improved, and urban air pollution control has received good results: for most of the year, the "Hollywood" sign on the mountain can be clearly seen from downtown Los Angeles, the whole city can be clearly seen from the observatory on Mount Griffith, and the shining stars in the clean sky can also be seen at night.

1. Legal Framework Precedes Action.
   In 1970, President Nixon signed the National Environmental Policy Act, which set the goal of national environmental protection and required all government departments to consider environmental factors in their work. It became the first overall environmental policy established in the United States. After the 1950s, the United States federal government introduced a number of legislation and amendments to the problem of air pollution. In 1955, the first Air Pollution Control Law was issued, and in 1963, the Clean Air Law passed by the Congress first proposed that air pollution is a cross regional national problem. According to this law, the National Air Quality Standard was promulgated, and the Environmental Protection Agency was required to regularly review the air quality monitoring standards. In the following decades, the Act was revised several times. In 2006, the PM2.5 standard was revised, stipulating that the maximum concentration of PM2.5 in any area and any 24-h cycle in the United States, whether in urban or rural areas, decreased from 65 μg per cubic meter to 35 μg. The standard criterion for annual average concentration is less than or equal to 15 μg per cubic meter. The standard of PM10's inhalable particles is 150 μg per cubic meter in a 24-h cycle.

The 1970 edition added the content of strengthening the control of automobile exhaust; the 1990 edition stipulated stricter vehicle exhaust emission standards, and set new control standards for 189 kinds of toxic pollution. According to the "Clean Air Law", the Environmental Protection Agency classifies the national air quality into three categories: substandard, standard or insufficient data (although the data is insufficient, it can be classified as substandard). The state and local governments should work out an implementation plan on how to reduce pollution and reach the standard within three years.

In the 1990s, Los Angeles adopted a large number of local regulations and policies to control air pollution. For example, it stipulated that cars sold in this area must be clean, all cars sold after 1994 were required to be equipped with a "driving diagnosis system" to monitor the working status of motor vehicles in real time, so that cars exceeding the standard could be removed from the pollution discharge status and repaired in a timely manner. The "Pollution Prevention and Control Law", which is stricter than the federal law, has been passed to guide and urge American and foreign automobile manufacturers to improve the emission performance of automobiles. It is stipulated that by 2020, one-third of the energy of electric power enterprises in this state will come from renewable energy. It also launched a series of projects, such as the solar energy incentive plan, to encourage enterprises and households to install solar photovoltaic power generation systems and increase the use of solar energy. Guide municipal facilities to make more use of wind energy to generate electricity. Promote the electrification of transportation through tax incentive projects such as tax rebates. Encourage consumers to buy electric vehicles. As a result, Toyota Prius hybrid vehicle became the best-selling vehicle in the state in 2012, and its sales in the state accounted for more than half of the total sales in the United States.

2. Building an Institutional Framework for Targeted Urban Atmospheric Management.

   In 1970, according to the National Environmental Policy Act, the National Environmental Protection Agency was established in the United States, whose mission is to "repair the polluted natural environment, establish new rules, and guide the American people to create a cleaner environment". Before that, the government did not have a special agency responsible for dealing with threats to human health and environmental damage. In addition, the city has set up a smoke committee. The Public Affairs Bureau asked the Municipal Engineering Bureau to come up with solutions, and the health department also participated in the investigation of industrial emissions.

3. Public Participation and Collective Action Lead the Charge in Tackling Urban Air Pollution.

   Public awareness plays an important role in environmental governance. The photochemical pollution incident in Los Angeles prompted people to reflect on the environmental costs of disorderly industrial development. Marked by events such as the Silent Spring written by American biologist and environmental activist Rachel Carson in 1962 and the Declaration of the United Nations Conference on the Human Environment held in Stockholm, Sweden, in 1972, the American

people launched movements to promote environmental protection from various fields: Justice Fred Barnes of Nebraska takes the lead in cycling to work; architects discuss recycling metal pipes and soft drinks packaging to build environmentally friendly houses; university of Colorado students conducted experiments to study the flow of urban smog; a new energy vehicle was announced at a seminar held in Michigan; environmental protection organizations at all levels have been established; many large enterprises have also taken on social responsibility to add value to their image.
Various ways have been adopted, including increasing parking fees, encouraging multiple people to share a car and reducing the actual driving volume and exhausting emissions on the highway. The government also encourages people to try to use clean fuel vehicles through low interest loans and subsidies. California is the first state in the United States to install rubber sleeves on fuel pumps. The filling device in the sleeves can reduce gasoline vapor escaping into the atmosphere.

4. Development and use of new energy.
California also takes the lead in the research and development of alternative clean fuels and incentive policies. The legislation stipulates that by 2020, one-third of the energy of the state's power enterprises will come from renewable energy. A series of projects were launched, which makes California the place with the most wind and solar power installations in the world.[10]
5. Launch public awareness initiatives on environmental protection.
The Environmental Protection Agency often includes some tips to remind people to "start from me" in daily life to improve air quality. For example, in order to save electricity, the air conditioning temperature will be slightly adjusted to save energy in summer and in winter; purchase household and office equipment with "Energy Star"; carpooling, using public transport, cycling or walking where possible; in the days when the level of inhalable particles is high, reduce the number of people going out by car and reduce or stop using fireplaces; avoid using gas mowers and other garden machinery; avoid burning straw, leaves, garbage, etc.

3.7.2 Milan's Innovative Approaches to Tackle Air Pollution

Since the second half of the nineteenth century, Milan has gradually become the "economic capital" of Italy. With industrial expansion and rapid urbanization, it has become the main destination of population migration in Italy. However, in the mid-1970s, Milan began a large-scale process of urban deindustrialization, which lasted for 10 years. The urban population has migrated to the marginal areas, and the urban population has been decreasing.

Deindustrialization has not changed Milan's status as the most polluted city in Europe and Italy. The reason is that the natural geographical conditions are inadequate. The Bohe Plain where the city is located covers an area of 46,000 square kilometers. It is the largest plain in southern Europe, sandwiched between the Alps and the Yaning Mountains. Affected by the terrain, the air flow over Milan and its surrounding areas is very stable, often forming a 300-m-thick inversion layer, just like covered by a thick blanket, which is not conducive to the dissipation of the polluted air in the city.

In recent years, the major pollutants in Milan are small particles, which cause more than 550 deaths every year. The control of urban air pollution is becoming more and more difficult, and the space for further measures is becoming smaller and smaller.

In view of the above situation, Milan regards the structural adjustment of the city as the fundamental way to control urban air pollution. The main measures taken are as follow:

First, control traffic source pollution. The traffic control area shall be set up, and the vehicle congestion fee shall be charged to curb the demand for vehicles to enter the city. These two policies alone have reduced urban carbon emissions by 30 ~ 40%. In addition, regional central heating is also an important measure to reduce air pollution.

Second, find out the main substances and causes of urban air pollution, and take targeted measures. The structure of air pollution in Milan is: PM10 accounts for 22%, fugitive dust from traffic and construction accounts for 20%, secondary pollutants such as ammonium sulfate and ammonium nitrate account for 40%, industrial emissions account for 11%, and biomass (wood) combustion accounts for 7%.

Third, carry out systematic prevention and control, including ecological and environmental protection testing standards; transportation, green space management, carbon emissions, water and air quality, energy-saving and environment-friendly buildings, energy consumption, garbage disposal, etc.

Notes

1. Zhihao Ge, "The Average Annual Decrease in PM2.5 in the Yangtze River Delta Should be no Less than 6%", *News Morning News*, December 6, 2012.
2. Shujiang Liu, "Ten Hard Measures towards Mist and Haze", *Earth*, Issue 7, 2013.
3. Zhipeng Bai et al., "How to Prevent and Control PM2.5", *China Environmental News*, February 21, 2012.
4. "Virginia: Starting a Long War on Clean Air", *Green China*, Issue 2, 2013.
5. Yi Ling, "Chengdu's Air Quality Fully Meets the National Second Level Standard", *Chengdu Daily*, February 8, 2012.
6. "Joint Control of Air Pollution in Beijing-Tianjin-Hebei and its Surrounding Areas", *Beijing Daily*, May 14, 2013.
7. Ibid.
8. "Beijing, Shanghai, and Guangzhou Embark on Building a Long-Term Mechanism for Air Governance", *Economic Daily*, April 28, 2013.
9. Gaixi Zhang, "How to Join Hands for the Five Cities to Promote the 'Prohibition of Burning' Campaign", *Sichuan Daily*, May 2, 2013.
10. Yunwen Bai, and Yang Fuqiang, "Double Efforts to Make Up for Inherent Shortcomings", *China Environmental News*, May 14, 2013.

Chapter 4
Indicator System of REEFCR City

The establishment of REEFCR city is not only a systematic goal, but also a gradual process. The construction of the evaluation index system can not only evaluate the status of the establishment of REEFCR city, but also track the sustainable development of urban ecological environment and the construction process of ecological civilization. The system can monitor, evaluate, improve and manage the construction of urban ecological environment and the realization of ecological civilization, it can also orient the path of China's urban ecological environment sustainable development and ecological civilization construction to promote China's urbanization process in a more scientific, coordinated and sustainable way under the context of climate change.

4.1 Urban Ecological Environment Evaluation Focused on Resource-Efficient and Environment-Friendly

4.1.1 Overview of Urban Ecological Environment Assessment at Home and Abroad

With the rapid advancement of China's urbanization in the first decade of the twenty-first century, urban dilemmas happened in large and medium-sized cities all over the country. In particular, urban ecological degradation and environmental pollution became serious and showed an intertwined trend, changing from a single pollution to a variety of pollution chain development. The establishment of sustainable ecological evaluation system will comprehensively assess urban environmental problem and promote the construction of urban ecological civilization, which can also overcome the pitfalls of one sidedness of single resource type or pollution type. In this field,

S. Du and H. Du, *The Green Transformation of Urban Areas in China Under Global Warming*, https://doi.org/10.1007/978-981-95-1005-4_4

the United Nations Commission on Sustainable Development (CSD), the environmental sustainability index of the United States, the sustainable development index of Scotland (SISD) are representative indexes.

There are many methods and index systems of ecological environment evaluation in China, but most of them are still small-scale, and by now, there is no unified method and index system. They are generally carried out according to the actual needs, combined with the current situation of the evaluation area and under the guidance of certain principles.[1] Evaluation index system and evaluation model with urban ecosystem health as the core was developed by Guo Xiurui, Yang Jurong and Mao Xianqiang to analyze the urban ecosystem. Han Qingli, Chen Xiaodong, Chang Wenyue developed evaluation index system of sustainable development of urban ecological environment from four dimensions: natural resources, economic development, social development and ecological environment. Zhao Xiuyong and Miao Xiubo used the ecological footprint method to calculate the ecological footprint of Chinese cities, and analyzed the ecological surplus and ecological deficit of cities. Hu Xiying and Zhang Jie evaluated the spatial structure, ecological function and coordination degree of the city with nature, economy and society as three variables affecting the urban ecological environment. Based on ecology, Wang Ping and Ma Liping discussed the main body and focus of urban ecological environment system as the target and object of evaluation, they constructed the urban ecological environment evaluation index system, determined the weight of each index by analytic hierarchy process (AHP), and obtained the comprehensive evaluation results. Based on the theory of sustainable development, Liu Qingli and Chen Youfei build an evaluation index system with the goal of building an ecological city. Some studies take specific areas as the object to construct the ecological environment evaluation index system. Liu Quanyou and Zhang Suiye established a comprehensive ecological environment evaluation index system from four fields of natural resources, ecological environment, environmental pollution and social economy to evaluate the ecological environment of the border area between Shanxi, Hebei, Shandong and Henan provinces. Tan Zifang and Wei Xiaofang evaluated the basic situation of ecological environment quality in Changsha by using the urban ecological environment suitability index method. Mei Zhuohua used the composite index method to establish the ecological environment evaluation index system, and used the factor analysis method to comprehensively evaluate the ecological environment quality of Nanjing.

4.1.2 Mainstream Evaluation Methods

4.1.2.1 Delphi Method

Delphi Method was initiated by O. helm and N. Dalk in 1940s and further developed by T. J. Gordon and Rand Corporation. The investigators draw up the questionnaire and consult the members of the expert group by letter according to the established procedures. The members of the expert group gave their feedback anonymously (by letter). After several round of consultation and feedback, the opinions of the members of the expert group gradually tend to concentrate, and finally obtain the collective judgment result with high accuracy.[2]

Xie Pengfei listed the evaluation indexes proposed from the existing index system according to three dimensions of environment, economy and society, screened and eliminated the repeated, similar or inoperable indexes, and constructed the index database. They then selected 61 key indicators based on expert opinions to build a secondary indicator database, some important but difficult to quantify indicators are summarized into five "threshold conditions" for investigation. They solicited the opinions and suggestions of experts in various fields, such as expert discussion, academic discussion, questionnaire survey, then further selected an evaluation index system containing 32 indicators, and evaluated 13 eco city demonstration cases such as Caofeidian, Beichuan, Turpan and Miyun.[3]

4.1.2.2 Analytic Hierarchy Process

Analytic Hierarchy Process refers to a systematic method that takes a complex multi-objective decision-making problem as a system, decomposes the objective into multiple objectives or criteria, and then decomposes it into several levels of multiple indicators (or criteria and constraints), and calculates the hierarchical single ranking (weight) and total ranking through the fuzzy quantitative method of qualitative indicators, so as to be used as the objective (multiple indicators) and multi scheme optimization decision-making.[4]

Li Xuesong and Xia Yibing constructed the performance evaluation index system of "Resource-Efficient and Environment-Friendly" (hereafter referred to as REEF) construction through qualitative analysis, obtained the weight of each index in the index system through analytic hierarchy process. They analyzed the change trend of each index from 2006 to 2010, and made an empirical study on the performance of REEF construction in Wuhan city circle and the performance of REEF construction in cities within the city circle.[5]

4.1.2.3 Fuzzy Matter-Element Analysis

Fuzzy Matter Element Analysis is a subject between mathematics and experiment initiated by Professor Cai Wen in 1983. The key point of this new discipline is to describe things with three elements of "things, characteristics and quantity". These elements form the basic element of ordered triples, which is called matter element. It is to study matter-element and its change law, and to solve the incompatibility problem in the real world. Incompatibility is the problem that the given conditions cannot achieve the purpose. The center of these problems is how to solve these problems and find the optimal solution through the matter-element transformation of things and the structural transformation of the system. If the quantity value in the matter-element is fuzzy, it constitutes a fuzzy incompatibility problem. The matter-element analysis of this kind of problem is called "fuzzy matter-element analysis".[6]

Based on entropy Fuzzy Matter-Element Analysis, combined with Fuzzy Set Theory and the concept of European closeness, Zhu Konglai and Wang Ruyan decomposed the construction of resource-efficient and environment-friendly society into resource consumption support system, economic development support system, social development support system, ecological environment support system and scientific and technological development support system. For each supporting system, according to the principles of guidance, representativeness, integrity, relative comparability, sensitivity and priority of comprehensive indicators, pre select indicators by target analysis method and establish a pre-selected index system. For each index in the preselected index system, collect the corresponding data for quantitative judgment by means of reliability test, validity test and discrimination analysis, and eliminate the redundant and low identification indexes such as highly related to the main index information and most of the cross, so as to screen the evaluation indexes representing the essential characteristics of each system. They make an empirical analysis on the construction process of resource-efficient and environment-friendly society in Qingdao.[7]

4.1.2.4 Pressure-State-Response Model

The Pressure-State-Response Model was first proposed by Canadian statistician A. Friend, and then developed by the Organization for Economic Cooperation and Development (OECD) and the United Nations Environment Program (UNEP) in the 1980s and 1990s, which is a framework model to study environment issues.[8] Gao Cailing, Gao Ge and Zhang Xianwen established the evaluation system of Zhengzhou eco city with Pressure-State-Response Model, determined the weight of each index with the coefficient of variation method, and studied the construction status of Zhengzhou eco city and the systematic response of resource environment, ecological environment, pollution control and economic potential from 2005 to 2010.[9]

4.1.3 Two Typical Evaluation Ideas

4.1.3.1 Target Completion Oriented Evaluation System

The significant character of Target Completion Oriented Evaluation System is to proclaim a goal, for example like "Three-Step" strategy or holistic well-off society, etc. On the basis of decomposing all aspects of the goal, the corresponding secondary and tertiary indicators based on sub goals are formed to build a comprehensive and specific index evaluation system. Then calculate the weight through various evaluation methods such as principal component analysis and analytic hierarchy process, determine the threshold according to the economic principle, the law of economic development, the quantitative relationship between indicators, statistical significance and the subjectively set "threshold" level, and conduct empirical research on the evaluation object. The score obtained indicates the degree of completion of the goal, which is used for horizontal and vertical comparison.

"Building Holistic Well-Off Society" index system which was developed by National Development and Reform Commission is representative of Target Completion Oriented evaluation system. Base on the connotation of building a well-off society and principles of goals, the evaluation system covers 16 indicators of 4 parts, which includes economy, society, environment and governance. Among which, economy aspect covers 4 indicators, per capita GDP, employment proportion of non-agricultural industries, Engel coefficient, income of urban and rural residents; society aspect covers 7 indicators, Gini coefficient, coverage rate of basic social insurance, average years of education, life expectancy at birth, proportion of added value of culture, education, sports and health, crime rate and proportion of population with average daily consumption expenditure less than 5 yuan; environment aspect covers 3 indicators, energy utilization efficiency, proportion of population using improved water sources, comprehensive index of environmental pollution; and governance aspect covers 2 indicators, government transparency and governance capacity.[10]

4.1.3.2 Development Progress Oriented Evaluation System

The development progress oriented evaluation system is generally used to evaluate issues that have not clearly achieved goals and are more focused on the development process (such as sustainable development).It is difficult to determine the weight of the data in different time series due to the complexity of the data, meanwhile due to the continuity of the development process, it is also difficult to set a threshold based on the data at a certain time point, this kind of evaluation system generally uses the comprehensive index method to express the degree of development progress in direct way, which helps in three aspects: firstly, we can take a certain time point in the past as the base point, convert the current development level into the development level relative to this base point, and directly describe the development trend; secondly, the comprehensive index method generally uses dimensionless indicators, which can be compared among indicators of different units; thirdly, it can directly calculate the classification ranking list and total ranking list of various data, which is one of the most commonly used methods for horizontal comparison between similar projects.

One of the representative development progress oriented evaluation system was developed by Professor Yang Kaizhong of Peking University, named "Ecological Civilization Index" (ECI), which was calculated based on ecological footprint to form the formula of ECI:

$$ECI = \frac{\text{Regional per capita GDP}}{\text{Regional per capita Ecological Footprint}} \Big/ \frac{\text{National per capita GDP}}{\text{National per capita Ecological Footprint}} \times 100 \quad (4.1)$$

$$\text{Unit GDP Footprint (hectares/10000 yuan)} = \frac{\text{Per capita Ecological Footprint (hectare/person)}}{\text{Per capita GDP (10000/person)}} \quad (4.2)$$

Professor Yang Kaizhong's research group first calculated the ecological civilization index of China's provinces and cities in 2010. Taking into consideration that the standard deviation of the ecological civilization index of 30 provinces and cities is 47.21, the research group simply divides the national provinces and cities into four groups with 50 as a standard deviation interval: high-level group (ECI higher than 150), medium and high-level group (ECI between 100 and 150), medium and low-level group (ECI between 50 and 100) and low-level group (lower than 50). Secondly, based on the data from 2007 to 2010, the ranking change of the ecological civilization index of all provinces and cities in China is calculated. Thirdly, the research group investigates the changes and overall increase and decrease trend of unit GDP footprint in all provinces and cities. On this basis, the standard deviation and fluctuation trend of China's ECI index in 2000, 2005 and 2007–2010 are calculated. Finally, the interactive relationship between economic development and ecological footprint change in all provinces and cities is studied.[11]

4.2 Urban Ecological Environment Evaluation in Response to Climate Change: Aiming for ECO^2 Cities

4.2.1 Climate Change and ECO^2 City Construction

Important documents such as the 2003 British energy white paper "Our Energy Future: Creating a Low-Carbon Economy", the 2006 British "Economics of Climate Change: Stern Report" and the "Fourth Assessment Report of the United Nations Intergovernmental Panel on Climate Change (IPCC) in 2007" were put forward, that more and more scientific evidence shows that greenhouse gases such as CO_2 have become a direct factor of climate change. The city is the main space carrier for the formation and development of modern civilization, the main gathering place of population and industry, and the largest and most concentrated "carbon source". According to the estimation of the International Energy Agency (IEA), the energy related greenhouse gas emissions in urban areas account for 71% of the world's total emissions and will reach 76% by 2030. With the continuous growth of urban society, in the foreseeable future, following the New York metropolitan area, Tokyo metropolitan area, London metropolitan area, Paris metropolitan area and the Great Lakes metropolitan area in North America, China's Yangtze River Delta, Pearl River Delta, Beijing-Tianjin-Hebei, Chengdu Chongqing and other metropolitan areas will also rise rapidly, which may further increase the burden of urban greenhouse gas emission and form a new dual structure in carbon emission and digestion, which means cities are the main pole of carbon emissions, rather than non-urban areas as the other pole of carbon compensation. From the perspective of the relationship between human urban development and climate change, it can be considered that "it was the climate affecting the city yesterday, but it is the city affecting the climate today". Therefore, controlling urban carbon emissions and strengthening urban carbon emission reduction are of great significance to the overall pattern of global low-carbon, and also have prominent reality for a large emerging city like China. However, in the existing low-carbon city construction, due to the mismatch between the economic pattern and the carbon emission pattern, it is urgent to build a new low-carbon city with coordinated development of economy and environment.

4.2.1.1 Two Models of Low-Carbon City Development and Their Deficiencies

Although there are different definitions of low-carbon cities, the more consistent view is that "cities keep energy consumption and CO_2 emission at a low level on the premise of rapid economic development", that is, economic development is "decoupled" from energy consumption and greenhouse gas emission.[12] Research shows that since 1975, in addition to the strong decoupling achieved by the UK, major developed countries such as the United States, Germany, Canada, Australia, Italy, Spain, France and Japan have experienced strong decoupling at least once in a certain period of time, and other developed countries also show the characteristics of strong decoupling or weak decoupling.[13] As the proponent and earliest practitioner of "low-carbon economy", developed countries like European Union have led the "low-carbon revolution", including the low-carbon community construction movement in Denmark, the urban action in response to climate change in Britain, the sustainable action plan in Sweden, the low-carbon society action plan in Japan and the low-carbon city action plan in the United States (see Table 4.1), which constitute the first type of low-carbon city development model dominated by developed countries. Its main feature is to promote the innovation of low-carbon technology and low-carbon services, stimulate low-carbon fixed asset investment and infrastructure construction, and gradually form a low-carbon economic system through the low-carbon consumption of household, transportation and energy. Taking London as an example, the British government launched the low-carbon city project in 2001. After 2003, it successively issued the "London Energy Strategy", "London Planning (Revised Version)", "Climate Change Action Platform" and "Low-Carbon City" Housing Standards to cover the fields of carbon emission reduction such as "green home", low-carbon energy, transportation and waste treatment. After successfully changing the consumption concept and cultivating the low-carbon consumption market, the UK proposed to create a "low-carbon economy" in 2008. It not only issued the "Strategic Vision of Low-Carbon Industry", but also incorporated the "Carbon Budget" into the government budget framework, and announced the "UK Low-Carbon Transformation Plan" in 2009 to form a consumption driven low-carbon city development model. However, due to

Table 4.1 Low carbon policy and measures in main cities

Cities	Main policies and measures
London	(1) Improve energy efficiency of existing and newly built buildings; (2) Develop low-carbon and distributed energy supply; (3) Reduce emissions from ground transportation; (4) Build green government
New York	(1) Establishment of "energy planning department"; (2) Government funding for energy saving projects; (3) Improve energy efficiency for buildings; (4) Increase supply of clean energy; (5) Decrease greenhouse gases emission from transportation
Tokyo	(1) Help private enterprises to decrease CO_2 emission; (2) Help households to decrease CO_2 emission; (3) Decrease CO_2 emission by urban development; (4) Decrease CO_2 emission by transportation

Source: Report on Addressing Climate Change (2009)—Towards Copenhagen, Social Science Academic Press, 2009 edition, pages 225–241, by Wang Weiguang and Zheng Guoguang

the immature technology, insufficient early industrialization intervention, and the decline of residents' consumption ability and fixed asset investment ability after the global financial crisis, high technology R & D and application costs and uncertain benefits are hindering the development of low-carbon cities in developed countries. For example, the cost of CO_2 capture and storage technology (CCS) is about US $70 per ton of CO_2 capture, which can capture up to 90% of CO_2 emissions, and consume another 25% of coal to remove the original CO_2. In addition, the safety conditions of buried CO_2 are also harsh, and CCS is still a transitional solution.[14] In this sense, the low-carbon city model of developed countries is to build an international low-carbon system to realize the carbon transfer by virtue of its economic and technological advantages.

With the international climate negotiations and the extension of Global Value Chain (GVC), the manufacturing industry of low-carbon products serving low-carbon consumption in developed countries has been transferred to developing countries, and its spillover effect has triggered the development process of low-carbon cities in developing countries: the carbon regulation of international trade makes low-carbon technology introduced into the production process, and the lock-in effect and "energy hunger" promote low-carbon energy and fixed asset investment; in order to save carbon emission credits for industries and reduce the domestic environmental burden after international carbon transfer, carbon emission reduction for domestic consumption such as transportation, construction and energy has been implemented, thus forming the second type of low-carbon city development model dominated by developing countries. This production driven low-carbon city development model based on the division of labor in the global value chain is particularly prominent in China. For example, the solar energy industry in Baoding started from the manufacturing of solar silicon wafers specifically for the European and American markets. With the expansion of the solar energy industry chain upstream and downstream, it has developed into an important manufacturing base of new energy and energy equipment in the world; at the same time, relying on the solar energy manufacturing industry, Baoding will strengthen the comprehensive utilization of solar energy, so as to holistically promote the construction of low-carbon cities. Although industrialization has greatly promoted the development of low-carbon cities in China, it has gradually exposed three deficiencies: (i) Regardless of the foundation and conditions, build low-carbon cities in a tidal wave. By now, at least 100 cities in all provinces have put forward the slogan of building a "low-carbon city", trying to integrate the low-carbon planning of the three major carbon emission sources of construction, transportation and industry into the overall operation planning of the city, so as to significantly reduce the carbon emission of the whole city[15]; (ii) There is overcapacity in the low-end manufacturing and processing links of low-carbon industries, and it is a common and unreasonable phenomenon of "burning high-carbon coal to produce low-carbon energy-saving lamps"[16]; (iii) The lack of continuity and pertinence of policy support has led to insufficient support for low-carbon technologies in key areas or with great potential. On the contrary, some low-end technologies with insufficient endogenous capacity have been given living space. It is more debatable that in the rapid growth stage of low-carbon industry, is it possible to realize strong decoupling in the short term and complete the inflection point process of Environmental Kuznets curve? Compared with the consumption driven low-carbon city development model and production driven low-carbon city development model, a desirable direction is to "unify low-carbon and economy", which will realize the "linkage" development between low-carbon and economy, and improve the economy and sustainability of low-carbon cities.[17] From above perspective, the World Bank's ECO^2 urban development model provides a new example for the development of low-carbon cities in China.

4.2.1.2 ECO^2 Urban Development Model

Based on the theory of sustainable development, one of the frontier prospects for the future urban form is to build an ecological and economic city with coordinated ecology and economy. According to the estimation of the World Bank, by 2030, the urban built-up areas in developing countries will increase from 200,000 square kilometers to 600,000 square kilometers, and the global urban population will reach 5 billion. In order to cope with the trend of large-scale urbanization in developing countries in the next 30 years and the resulting pressure on economic growth and environment, the World Bank put forward the concept of Eco-Economic City (ECO^2 City) in 2008. Eco-Economic City is an economically developed and eco-friendly city. It is a new business model to promote environmental and economic synergy, interdependence and achieve sustainable urban development, which means, "through integrated urban planning and management, make full use of ecosystems, seek well-being for society and people, and protect and cultivate ecosystems for future generations"; at the same time, "creative, inclusive and sustainable economic activities can be achieved through the effective use of all tangible and intangible assets to create value and opportunities for urban residents, businesses and society".[18]

The biggest feature and advantage of ECO^2 City is to realize the coordinated development of ecology and economy through resource integration, system integration and collaborative decision-making. Among the four principles of ECO^2 City, there are two important integration forces, which endow the externality of ecological economy: (i) from the ecological perspective, integrate the city and urban environment into a complete system to include market location, resource flow, productivity layout, infrastructure construction and urban spatial form into a whole; (ii) at the economic perspective, the government and relevant stakeholders will form a coordinated system to build a three-level cooperation platform of enterprise operation, urban service and regional cooperation. Within the platform, the departments carry out internal cooperation in pursuit of sustainable operation; at the middle level of the platform, the interest classes cooperate to improve the sustainability of services; in the outer layer of the platform, a wider range of relevant stakeholders will cooperate together.[19]

4.2.1.3 ECO^2 City as Guidance to REEFCR

According to the basic concept of ECO^2 City development model, low-carbon city construction is not only the implementation of mandatory carbon emission reduction measures in various fields of urban economy and society, but also the formation of a win–win benefit mechanism for all stakeholders in urban life. This is also in line with the main principle of "one combination and two sides promotion" in the implementation of China's National Plan for Addressing Climate Change.[20] On this basis, the ecological path and economic path of low-carbon city construction were put forward, thus forming the urban low-carbon economic cycle system, as shown in Fig. 4.1.

The ecological path with energy flow as the main line (indicated by dotted line) realizes the whole process of energy planning, channel integration and carbon constraints by energy control-energy cycle-carbon emission control. Among them, carbon emissions from raw material fuel production—carbon emissions from production process—carbon emissions from consumption—carbon emissions from waste disposal in the energy cycle are particularly important. Research shows that carbon emissions are mainly concentrated in this chain. The carbon constraint on the ecological path can be measured by the carbon footprint method. At present, there are two main methods to calculate the carbon footprint at home and abroad. One is to calculate the carbon emissions in the whole life cycle of product manufacturing, use and disposal with life cycle assessment (LCA); the second is to calculate the carbon emissions from fossil fuels such as coal, oil and natural gas used in the manufacturing, use and disposal of products. In addition to the measurement of carbon emissions at the level of specific goods and services, the two important nodes of carbon emission control in low-carbon cities are communities and parks. Community is the cell of modern cities, where people live and stay, and also the end consumer market of low carbon products. Under the trend of anti-urbanization, the community also presents a

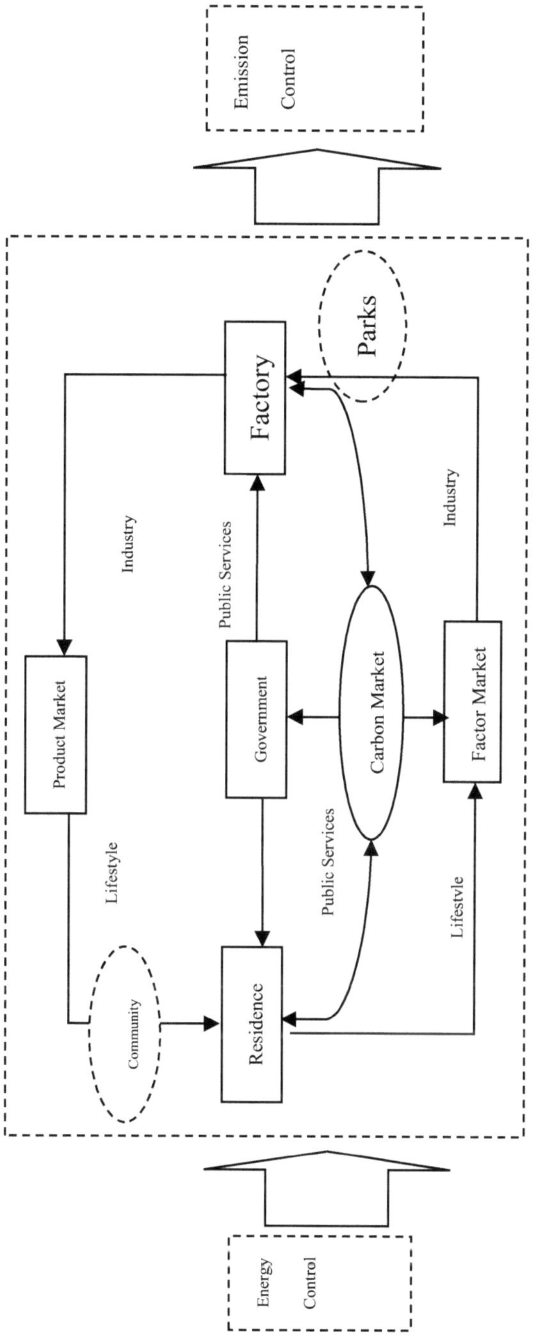

Fig. 4.1 Urban low carbon economy cycle map

energy conservation and emission reduction in areas with intensive carbon emissions such as construction, transportation and production, we can generally reduce the energy consumption intensity and carbon emission intensity of the whole city and promote the transformation of urban economic and social life from high carbon to low carbon.

Table 4.2 Typical research on evaluation of existing low-carbon cities

Type	Typical Research
Object Oriented	In "Jilin Low Carbon Development Plan" completed by the Chinese Academy of Social Sciences, a low-carbon city evaluation system including 12 indicators in four categories: low-carbon productivity, low-carbon consumption, low-carbon resources and low-carbon policies has been established
	Zhang Xueyi et al. (2010) constructed a low-carbon economy index system based on the material flow analysis method, including 13 indicators in three categories: economic development, energy consumption and natural environment
	Fu Yun et al. (2010) comprehensively considered the three aspects of economy, society and environment, described the eight major states of urban low-carbon, and used 23 specific indicators to build an index system to evaluate the urban low-carbon level from the industrial structure system, infrastructure system, consumption support system, policy system and technical support system
	Li Yunyan (2011) carried out index synthesis and integration on the basis of systematic analysis and evaluation of low-carbon construction in different aspects of the city, such as production system, transportation system, energy-saving and ecological buildings, urban air pollution control, clean energy development, etc., determined the weight of the criterion layer through fuzzy analytic hierarchy process, and obtained the comprehensive evaluation index of urban low-carbon economic development through principal component analysis
	Wang Ailan (2011) constructed a low-carbon city index system from the aspects of economic growth, urbanization rate, industrial structure, energy structure, energy utilization efficiency, transportation system, consumption mode, carbon sink forestry, institutional environment and so on
Task decomposition	Zhu Dajian (2010) advocated the concepts of "relative decoupling" (efficiency improvement under the growth of total carbon dioxide emissions) and "absolute decoupling" (stabilizing and reducing carbon dioxide emissions under the condition of economic growth), and the judgment method of "low-carbon city ecological performance = urban welfare growth (value) / resource and environment consumption (physical quantity)"

Source: Research on low-carbon economy indicators based on material flow analysis, Learning Monthly, Issue 12, 2010, by Zhang Xueyi, Wang Jianmin. Research on evaluation methods and support systems for low carbon cities, China Population, Resources and Environment, Issue 8, 2010, by Fu Yun, Liu Yijun, and Wang Yunlin. Evaluation methods and implementation approaches for low carbon cities, Macroeconomic Management, Issue 3, 2011, by Li Yunyan. Research on the construction of a comprehensive evaluation indicator system for the construction level of low carbon cities, Cities, Issue 6, 2011, by Wang Ailan

4.2.2.2 Low-Carbon Economy Practices in Wenjiang District

Wenjiang District is one of the first batch of ecological zones (counties) and construction zones (counties) in Sichuan Province, which has a deep foundation and great potential for developing low-carbon economy. In 2007, the whole district has built two national level villages and towns with beautiful environment, two provincial-level industrial ecological parks, 15 municipal ecological villages and one municipal green community, and built two provincial-level green schools, five municipal green schools and two district level green schools. In November 2007, Wenjiang District successfully passed the standard acceptance of establishing a provincial environmental protection model area, becoming the first district and county in Sichuan Province to successfully establish a provincial environmental protection model area; in 2007, the Comprehensive Improvement Project of River Water System in the Urban Area of Wenjiang District won the "China Living Environment Example Award" issued by the Ministry of Construction.

Since 2007, Wenjiang District has promoted regional economic development and energy conservation and emission reduction in a coordinated manner, and issued a series of policies and measures to support the development of low-carbon economy (Table 4.3).

4.2.2.3 Evaluation Index System of "Low-Carbon Wenjiang"

The regional development strategy of "Low-carbon Wenjiang" is closely combined with the construction of a modern economic system dominated by the service industry, the construction of a high-quality Wenjiang, the in-depth comprehensive improvement of the urban and rural environment and the establishment of provincial and national ecological demonstration areas, the development of green energy industry, energy conservation and emission reduction as a breakthrough and important starting point, the goal of "low energy consumption, low emission and low pollution", and the focus of structural adjustment and mode transformation, adhere to the principles of government promotion, planning first, market operation, public participation, demonstration driven and gradual progress, develop a low-carbon economy, promote green renewable energy industry, build a low-carbon building and transportation system, advocate a low-carbon lifestyle and build a low-carbon society.

The building of "Low-carbon Wenjiang" is both a systematic objective and a progressive process, which need to establish a multi-dimensional evaluation index system. From the macro level, the evaluation index system of "Low-carbon Wenjiang" provides a more objective, quantitative and scientific analysis and prediction means for government decision-making; from the middle level, the "Low-carbon Wenjiang" evaluation index system provides a basis for enterprises to formulate enterprise development strategies in the period of economic transformation; from the micro level, the "Low-carbon Wenjiang" evaluation index system provides a basis for guiding individuals to choose consumption and lifestyle.

Table 4.3 Main measures of "low-carbon Wenjiang"

Low-carbon City System	Formulate the opinions on "Implementing the Construction of Low-carbon Wenjiang and Building a World Garden City Demonstration Area
	Establish a leading group for building a "Low-carbon Wenjiang" and corresponding work promotion institutions
Low-carbon urban planning	Promote the "compact" urban planning and construction model
	Fully embody the mutual wedging of city and countryside in urban planning
Low-carbon industrial system	Implement the industrial development strategy
	Promote the construction of "eight functional areas" dominated by service industry
Energy saving products and technologies	Implement compulsory cleaner production audit for key enterprises in the region
	Build Wenjiang Agricultural Circular Economy Demonstration Park
	Implement centralized heating, coal liquefaction and coal gasification in science and technology park
	Prepare the regional coal pollution control plan
	LED and other energy-saving materials are widely used in municipal facilities
Green energy industry	Promote the comprehensive utilization of biomass clean energy such as biogas, straw vaporization and solidification
	Promote geothermal utilization technology and solar energy utilization technology
Low-carbon building	Bring the supervision of building energy conservation into the management procedure of project construction
	Application of new wall materials and new building energy-saving technologies
Low-carbon traffic	Develop mass rapid public transport such as subway and light rail
	Encourage and promote low emission travel modes such as walking cycling
	Encourage the use of energy-saving and environment-friendly vehicles
Low-carbon life style	Reduce the use of disposable catering and accommodation supplies
	Curb excessive packaging of goods
	Adopt energy-saving household lighting
Increase carbon sink	Develop flower industry and leisure tourism experiencing agriculture

The construction of a comprehensive evaluation index system can not only evaluate the establishment of a "Low-carbon Wenjiang" and find out the background, but also track the sustainable development of ecological environment and the construction process of ecological civilization in Wenjiang District, monitor, evaluate and improve the development of low-carbon economy in Wenjiang District, and find out the path and mode of low-carbon development in Wenjiang District, so as to be more scientific, coordinated promote the urbanization process and overall urban and rural development in Wenjiang District in a sustainable way. Therefore, the evaluation index system can be used as one of the long-term management tools for the establishment of "Low-carbon Wenjiang". It is mainly used for the comprehensive evaluation of the development level of low-carbon economy, and can be used for the dynamic tracking and comprehensive analysis of the low-carbon development progress of Wenjiang in the future, which plays a good guiding role in the development and improvement of low-carbon economy in Wenjiang District (Table 4.4).

Table 4.4 ECO^2 oriented evaluation system of low carbon city

State	Criterion	Index	Unit	Note
Ecological Path	Energy saving and emission reduction	GDP energy intensity	ton standard coal/ ten thousand yuan	Improve comprehensive energy utilization efficiency and increase the proportion of new energy utilization
		CO_2 emission per unit of GDP	ton / ten thousand yuan	
		Per capita traffic energy consumption	ton standard coal/person	
		Proportion of new energy and renewable energy in total energy	%	
Economic Path	Low carbon industry	Per capita GDP	yuan	Adjust the industrial structure, factor input structure and technological structure, promote the low-carbon of three industries, develop emerging low-carbon industries, and promote regional economic growth
		Proportion of modern service industry in GDP	%	
		Utilization rate of organic pesticides and chemical fertilizers	%	
		Growth rate of new low carbon technology investment	%	
	Low carbon lifestyle	Urbanization rate	%	In the orderly process of urbanization, build a low-carbon life composed of green environment, green buildings and green transportation

(continued)

(continued)

State	Criterion	Index	Unit	Note
		Forest coverage	%	
		Per capita green area	m^2 / person	
		New energy-saving building area ratio	%	
		Public transport travel share	%	
	Low carbon public services	Energy consumption reduction rate of public institutions	%	Reduce the carbon emissions of the government and public resources, enhance the public awareness of low-carbon environmental protection, and improve the low-carbon system
		Public awareness of low carbon	%	
		Establish carbon emission monitoring, statistics and supervision system	–	
		Public satisfaction with the environment	%	

4.3 REEFCR City Evaluation Model Establishment, Indicator Selection, and Weight Determination

4.3.1 The Basic Path of REEFCR City Evaluation

4.3.1.1 Determination of the Evaluation Index System of REEFCR City Construction Evaluation

When evaluating the construction of REEFCR cities, we must first select the evaluation indicators which are a set of index bundles with hierarchical structure composed of target layer, criterion layer and index layer. Please refer to Fig. 4.2.

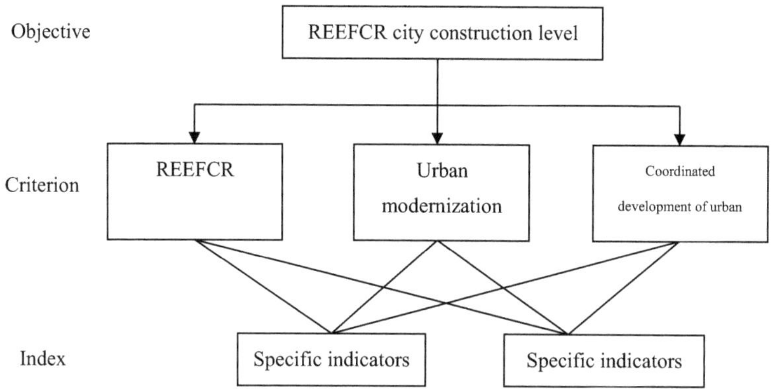

Fig. 4.2 Hierarchical structure of REEFCR city construction evaluation

4.3.1.2 Determination of the Weight of Each Evaluation Index

The commonly used methods to determine the weight are analytic hierarchy process, entropy weight method, etc. Among those methods, the more appropriate one is the analytic hierarchy process based on Delphi method.

Analytic hierarchy process uses a relative measure that can make a difference in the degree of superiority of things as an index to evaluate the degree of acceptability of things. This relative measure is called weight or priority weight. For a certain attribute, it is an index to determine the degree of superiority of things by comparing two. The larger the index value, the greater the weight, indicating the higher the degree of superiority; the smaller the index value, the smaller the weight, indicating the lower the degree of superiority. Analytic hierarchy process is applicable to the determination of the comprehensive weight of the evaluation index system with multi-level structure.[24] The key is to use a simple method to determine a set of weights used to distinguish the priority of each comparison object. Generally, the method of pairwise comparison is used to judge the superiority of the comparison object, so as to determine the weight of each single index. This paper uses analytic hierarchy process (AHP) to determine the weight of the evaluation index system of REEFCR city construction.

4.3.1.3 Unified Dimension

It is necessary to unify dimension of each indicator because different indicator has different economic meaning and unit, it can't be assigned a value directly during calculation process.

There are many methods to realize dimensional unification, of which the common ones are: straight line type, curve type and broken line type. A better method is to choose a simple and practical linear dimensionless method. Specifically, for an indicator, first collect the actual value of the indicator, then collect or calculate the standard value of the indicator (generally select the threshold or average level of the indicator as the standard value), and calculate the evaluation value according to the following formula:

$$\text{For positive indicator}:\ P_{x_i} = R_{x_i} \big/ C_{x_i} \tag{4.3}$$

$$\text{For negative indicator}:\ P_{x_i} = C_{x_i} \big/ R_{x_i} \tag{4.4}$$

4.3.1.4 Calculation of the Comprehensive Development Index of REEFCR City Construction Respectively

Calculate the comprehensive development index of REEFCR city construction by linear weighting method:

$$\begin{aligned} Eco &= \sum_{i=1}^{n} w_i e_i \\ Mor &= \sum_{i=1}^{n} w_i m_i \\ Soc &= \sum_{i=1}^{n} w_i s_i \end{aligned} \tag{4.5}$$

Among which: w_i is weighting of each system, e_i, m_i, s_i represent resource efficient, environment friendly, and climate resilient respectively. The evaluation value of development indicators after the three dimensions of "four modernizations" interaction and coordinated economic and social development are unified.

4.3.1.5 Analysis of the Construction Degree of National or Regional REEFCR City

Generally, the sum of the three benefits represents the comprehensive benefit, and the product of the three benefits represents the compound benefit. The goal of establishing the model is to obtain the maximum compound benefit on the basis of the maximum comprehensive benefit[25]:

$$H = \frac{Eco \times Mor \times Soc}{(Eco + Mor + Soc)^3} \tag{4.6}$$

At the same time, the average benefit index can also be used to replace the comprehensive benefit index for standardization:

$$H = \left| \frac{Eco \times Mor \times Soc}{\left[(Eco + Mor + Soc)/3\right]^3} \right|^k \tag{4.7}$$

Among them, k is the adjustment coefficient, and the assignment is changed due to the regional differences.

4.3.2 Basic Model of REEFCR City Evaluation

The construction of REEFCR cities not only includes the comprehensive improvement of urban ecological environment such as resource efficient, environment friendly and climate resilient, but also includes the orderly development of urban ecological civilization such as urban modernization and urban economic social subsystem coordination. Therefore, in this project, the construction of REEFCR cities is understood as three levels: resource efficient, environment friendly, climate resilient, "Four Modernizations" interaction, and coordinated economic and social development, which can be expressed as:

$$C = C(Eco, Mor, Soc) \tag{4.8}$$

C represents REEFCR city construction level, Eco represents city level in terms of resource efficient, environment friendly and climate resilient, Mor represents interaction development level of "Four Modernization", Soc represents coordinated development level of urban economic social subsystem.

Assume that the variables in above equation have the following properties: (1) they are all positive numbers, $Eco > 0,\ Mor > 0,\ Soc > 0$; (2) the first-order differential is positive and the second-order differential is negative, that is, the independent variable promotes the dependent variable, but the marginal effect decreases.

$$\begin{matrix} \frac{\partial C}{\partial Eco} > 0 & \frac{\partial^2 C}{\partial Eco^2} < 0 \\ \frac{\partial C}{\partial Mor} > 0 & \frac{\partial^2 C}{\partial Mor^2} < 0 \\ \frac{\partial C}{\partial Soc} > 0 & \frac{\partial^2 C}{\partial Soc^2} < 0 \end{matrix} \tag{4.9}$$

Assuming that Eq. 4.8 is a classical Cobb Douglas function, the total differential of Eq. (4.3) can be obtained:

$$dC = \frac{\partial C}{\partial Eco} \cdot dEco + \frac{\partial C}{\partial Mor} \cdot dMor + \frac{\partial C}{\partial Soc} \cdot dSoc \tag{4.10}$$

Multiply the left and right ends of Eq. (4.10) at the same time and make the following transformation:

$$\frac{dC}{C}=\frac{\partial C}{\partial Eco}\cdot\frac{Eco}{C}\cdot\frac{dEco}{Eco}+\frac{\partial C}{\partial Mor}\cdot\frac{Mor}{C}\cdot\frac{dMor}{Mor}+\frac{\partial C}{\partial Soc}\cdot\frac{Soc}{C}\cdot\frac{dSoc}{Soc} \tag{4.11}$$

$\frac{\partial C}{\partial Eco}\cdot\frac{Eco}{C}$, $\frac{\partial C}{\partial Mor}\cdot\frac{Mor}{C}$, $\frac{\partial C}{\partial Soc}\cdot\frac{Soc}{C}$ represent the elasticity of the three dimensions to the construction level of REEFCR cities, $\frac{dEco}{Eco}$, $\frac{dMor}{Mor}$, $\frac{dSoc}{Soc}$ represent changing rate of the three dimensions, which means the construction of REEFCR city needs to be improved from the three dimensions, and the promotion level is correlated with elasticity of the three dimensions.

4.3.3 Selection of Evaluation Indicators for REEFCR City

ECO^2-oriented REEFCR cities pay more attention to the integration, symbiosis and functional integration between economy and ecology, and their evaluation system needs to integrate multiple objectives. We constructed the evaluation index set mainly based on the "Millennium Development Goals Monitoring Indicator System" of the United Nations Development Program, "The Indicator System for Building a Moderately Prosperous Society in All Respects" of the National Development and Reform Commission, "The China ECO City Indicator System" of the China Urban Science Research Association, "The Evaluation Indicator System for Overall Urban and Rural Development" of the Development Research Center of the State Council, "the Low-Carbon Economic Development Indicator System" of the Chinese Academy of Social Sciences, and the "G20 Low Carbon Competitiveness Evaluation Index System" of the Climate Institute and the Third Generation Environmentalism (E3G).[26]

Due to the large number of original indicators in the indicator set, we use Delphi method to analyze the membership degree, sort by the frequency of experts' selection, and eliminate the indicators that are not related to the REEFCR cities. Assuming the selection frequency of the index i is M_i, the membership degree of the index is $r_i=\frac{M_i}{N}$, and the larger the value, the more important the index r_i is.

In order to further simplify the indicators and improve their evaluation ability, we have screened the indicator set twice. First, using the statistical data of China Urban Statistical Yearbook 2010 and the integrated data of CNKI China Economic and Social Development Statistical Database, this project makes correlation analysis and discrimination analysis on the indicators. Through the standardization of indicators $Z_i=\frac{X_i-\overline{X}}{S_i}$ (X_i is the original data of indicators, $\overline{X}$ is the mean value of indicators, S_i is the standard deviation of indicators, and Z_i is the standardized value), calculate the simple correlation coefficient $R_{ij}=\frac{\sum_{k=1}^{n}(Z_{ki}-\overline{Z}_i)(Z_{kj}-\overline{Z}_j)}{\sqrt{\sum_{k=1}^{n}(Z_{ki}-\overline{Z}_i)^2(Z_{kj}-\overline{Z}_j)^2}}$ and variation coefficient $V_i=\frac{S_i}{\overline{X}}$ between indicators, and eliminate the larger R_{ij} and smaller indicators V_i. Second, since the statistical data of economic and social fields are generally included in the statistical scope of the statistical system, the data can be obtained from China's urban statistical yearbooks, provincial and urban statistical yearbooks and various special statistical yearbooks. However, some data related to natural and geographical conditions are kept by the monitoring departments of the Land and Resources System and the Environmental Protection System, so it is not that accessible. Therefore, we have eliminated some indicators with insufficient data sources.

Please refer to the evaluation system of REEFCR city construction (Table 4.5).

Table 4.5 The evaluation system of REEFCR city construction

Primary indicator	Secondary indicator	Tertiary indicator	Indicator attribute
A REEFCR	A_1 RE index	A_{11} Cultivated land resource carrying capacity index	+
		A_{12} Forest resources carrying capacity index	+
		A_{13} Freshwater resources carrying capacity index	+
		A_{14} Space resources carrying capacity index	+
	A_2 EF index	A_{21} Atmospheric self-purification capacity index	+
		A_{22} Water body self-purification capacity index	+
		A_{23} Solid waste treatment capacity index	+
	A_3 CR index	A_{31} Industrial energy consumption index	–
		A_{32} Greenhouse gas emission index	–
B Urban Modernization	B_1 "Four modernizations" interaction index	B_{11} Population urbanization index	+
		B_{12} Industrialization index	+
		B_{13} Agricultural modernization index	+
		B_{14} Informatization index	+
C Coordinated economic and social development	C_1 Economic development index	C_{11} Economic advantage index	+
		C_{12} Urban rural coordination index	tend to 1

(continued)

(continued)

Primary indicator	Secondary indicator	Tertiary indicator	Indicator attribute
		C_{13} Economic vitality index	+
	C_2 Social development index	C_{21} Education index	+
		C_{22} Health index	+

4.3.4 Index Description and Methods

The REEFCR city construction evaluation index system adopts a three-tier structure, which is the primary indicator, the secondary indicator and the tertiary indicator. Among which, the primary indicator consists of 3 parts: (i) the first part is resource efficient, environment friendly, climate resilient (REEFCR) index, which is used to measure the carrying capacity of a city in terms of resources, ecological environment and combating climate change. The larger the index value, the greater the city's carrying capacity. (ii) The second part is index description of urban modernization, specifically refers to "Four Modernizations" interaction index, which measures development trends of city for a relatively long period of time in terms of industrialization, urbanization, agricultural modernization and informatization from the perspective of development economics. The larger the index value, the better the development momentum of the city. (iii) The third part is index description of coordinated economic and social development, which is to measure city development level in important fields like economy and society in different time node.

It should be noted that in the study, we uniformly adopt the evaluation index, which is mainly based on the consideration of the balance between regional differences and the consistency of evaluation standards. In such a large country as China, there are a wide range of regional economies with their own characteristics, including resource-based regions, resource-poor regions, resource-exhausted regions, developed regions and underdeveloped regions, even old, young, border and poor regions, ecologically rich regions and ecologically fragile regions, as well as various special regions, such as special economic zones and earthquake-stricken areas. Accordingly, there are many differences in the physical and geographical conditions, industrial foundation, social development, cultural attributes and other aspects of cities in the region. However, less reflection of regional differences and regional characteristics has been the deficiency of various index evaluation systems which have been widely criticized. This indicator evaluation system, which has not reflected the differences, often results in a "one size fits all" policy effect in practical application, with low operability. On the other hand, too much emphasis on regional differences and lack of unity will weaken the function of the index evaluation system to evaluate and compare at the same level. It may be a better method to study the equivalence coefficient between regional differences, but there is still no reliable method to convincingly obtain the value k or value k range.

To solve the problem, we refer to the construction idea of "Indicator System of Main Functional Areas in Yunnan Province" and adopt two methods to deal with it: (i) between the large spatial scale of the country and the small spatial scale of the city, the sub spatial scale of province is introduced. The cities within the province are relatively consistent in natural conditions, economic management, social development, cultural identity, etc., while there are wide differences among the provinces; (ii) The relative concentration degree of resources and pollution of a city in the province can be obtained by using the calculation method of similar location quotient, which can reflect the individual characteristics of resource-based cities and heavily polluted cities to a certain extent. Therefore, we make consistency comparison on the basis of eliminating regional differences, as shown in Table 4.6.

Table 4.6 Different evaluation ideas of REEFCR city construction

Evaluation of regional heterogeneity	Method	This project
Overall evaluation → Local evaluation	Independent multi region evaluation system based on Delphi method, k-value method	
Eliminate local features → Overall evaluation	"Location quotient" method	√

4.3.4.1 Index of Resource Efficient, Environment Friendly, and Climate Resilient

Resource efficient, environment friendly and climate resilient are the essential characteristics and fundamental requirements of REEFCR City. On the one hand, the city is a part of the nature after the transformation of human civilization, which constitutes an important node of resource symbiosis, environmental exchange and climate movement. Today, the city is the key link of resource circulation, environment generation and local climate formation. Since ancient times, many cases have shown that resource conditions, environmental conditions and climate conditions have a profound impact on the life cycle of urban development. On the other hand, the growth of the city itself and the economic and social life active in the city also strongly lead to the improvement of the resource, environment and climate. As an integral part of the urban ecological environment with natural characteristics, the evaluation of resource efficient, environment friendly and climate resilient is the most important evaluation content of this project, and it is also the basic characteristics of the REEFCR city construction evaluation indicators different from other urban ecological environment evaluation indicators.

The project evaluation urban ecological environment from triple aspects of resource efficient, environment friendly, and climate resilient. Although the natural resources relied on for the survival and development of cities can be summarized into eight kinds of resources: cultivated land resources, forest resources, fresh water resources, energy resources, mineral resources, grassland resources, tourism resources and space resources, in order to ensure the horizontal comparability between cities, we only choose the four major resources of cultivated land, forest, fresh water and space that reflect the natural geographical conditions. The indicators related to physical and geographical conditions in this part refer to the relevant indicators of the "Indicator System of Main Functional Areas in Yunnan Province" provided by the Yunnan training meeting on the planning of main functional areas of the National Development and Reform Commission. In terms of environment friendly, we have constructed the air self-purification capacity index, water self-purification capacity index and solid waste treatment capacity index from the perspective of waste treatment capacity, drinking water safety and air quality. In terms of climate resilient, we select the industrial energy consumption index and greenhouse gas emission index that represent the energy conservation and emission reduction capacity.

1. Calculation of specific resource carrying capacity index

$$\begin{aligned} A_{1i} &= 10 \times a\prime_{1i} + 50\, i = 1, 2, 3, 4 \\ a\prime_{1i} &= \frac{a_{1i} - \overline{a_{1i}}}{\delta a_{1i}} \\ \delta a_{1i} &= \sqrt{\frac{1}{36-1} \sum_{j=1}^{36} \left(a_{1ij} - \overline{a_{1ij}}\right)^2} \; (j \text{ means number of cities}) \\ a_{1i} &= \frac{RF_m}{NF_m} \; \mathrm{m} = \text{Cultivated land, forest, fresh water, space} \\ \overline{a}_{1i} &= \frac{1}{36} \sum_{j=1}^{36} a_{1ij} \; (j \text{ means number of cities}) \end{aligned} \tag{4.12}$$

Among which, A_{11} is cultivated land resource carrying capacity index, $a\prime_{11}$ is standardized cultivated land resource carrying capacity index, $a\prime_{11}$ is original index of urban cultivated land, $RF_{Cultivatedland}$ is density of cultivated land of the specific city, $NF_{CultivatedLand}$ is density of cultivated land of all the cities, The cultivated land density is the ratio of the effective cultivated land area to the land area of the Administrative Region, $\overline{a_{11}}$ is the average value of the original index of 36 urban cultivated land.

A_{12} is forest resource carrying capacity index, $a\prime_{12}$ is standardized forest resource carrying capacity index, a_{12} is the original index of urban forest of that specific city, RF_{Forest} is the forest density of that specific city, NF_{Forest} is the forest density of all the cities, forest density is the ratio of forest area plus green area of built-up area to land area of administrative area, $\overline{a_{12}}$ is the average value of the original index of 36 urban cultivated land.

A_{13} is the fresh water carrying capacity index, $a\prime_{13}$ is the standardized fresh water carrying capacity index, $a\prime_{13}$ is the original index of fresh water of that specific city, $RF_{Freshwatter}$ is the fresh water density of that specific city, $NF_{Freshwater}$ is the fresh water density of all the cities, fresh water density is the ratio of fresh water quantity to the territory area of the administrative region, $\overline{a_{13}}$ is the average value of original index of 36 cities.

A_{14} is the spatial resource carrying capacity index, $a\prime_{14}$ is the standardized spatial resource carrying capacity index, $a\prime_{14}$ is the original index of the urban space, RF_{Space} is the density of the city's developable space (=1- the area of the urban built-up area / the land area of the administrative region of the city), NF_{Space} is the density of all cities' developable space (=1- the area of all urban built-up areas / the land area of all urban administrative regions), and $\overline{a_{14}}$ is the average of the original indexes of 36 urban spaces.

2. Calculation of self-purification capacity index of "three wastes"

$$
\begin{aligned}
A_{2i} &= 10 \times a\prime_{2i} + 50\, i = 1, 2, 3 \\
a\prime_{2i} &= \frac{a_{2i} - \overline{a_{2i}}}{\delta a_{2i}} \\
\delta a_{2i} &= \sqrt{\frac{1}{36-1} \sum_{j=1}^{36} \left(a_{2ij} - \overline{a_{2ij}}\right)^2} \ (j \text{ means No.} j \text{ cities}) \\
a_{2i} &= \frac{RF_m}{NF_m} \ \mathrm{m} = \text{atmosphere, water and solid waste} \\
\overline{a}_{2i} &= \frac{1}{36} \sum_{j=1}^{36} a_{2ij} \ (j \text{ means No.} j \text{ cities})
\end{aligned}
\tag{4.13}
$$

Among which: A_{21} refers to the atmospheric self-purification capacity index, $a\prime_{21}$ refers to the standardized atmospheric self-purification capacity index, a_{21} refers to the original index of the city's atmosphere, $RF_{Atmosphere}$ refers to the ratio of days with grade 2 or better air quality in the city, $NF_{Atmosphere}$ refers to the ratio of days with grade 2 or better air quality in all cities, and $\overline{a_{21}}$ refers to the average value of the original index of 36 cities' atmosphere.

A_{22} is the self0purification capacity index of water body, $a\prime_{22}$ is the standardized self-purification capacity index of water body, a_{22} is the original index of the city's water body, RF_{Water} is the proportion of surface water with water quality above grade 3 in the total surface water of the city, NF_{Water} is the proportion of surface water with water quality above grade 3 in the total surface water of all cities, and $\overline{a_{22}}$ is the average value of the original index of 36 city' water bodies.

A_{23} is the solid waste treatment capacity index, $a\prime_{23}$ is the standardized solid waste treatment capacity index, a_{23} is the original index of the urban solid waste, $RF_{Solidwaste}$ is the harmless treatment rate of the urban solid waste, $NF_{Solidwaste}$ is the harmless treatment rate of all urban solid waste, and $\overline{a_{23}}$ is the average value of the original index of 36 urban solid waste.

3. Calculation of energy conservation and emission reduction capacity index

$$
\begin{aligned}
A_{3i} &= 10 \times a\prime_{3i} + 50\, i = 1, 2 \\
a\prime_{3i} &= \tfrac{a_{3i} - \overline{a_{3i}}}{\delta a_{3i}} \\
\delta a_{3i} &= \sqrt{\tfrac{1}{36-1} \sum_{j=1}^{36} \left(a_{3ij} - \overline{a_{3ij}}\right)^2} \text{ (} j \text{ means No.} j \text{ cities)} \\
a_{3i} = \tfrac{RF_m}{NF_m}\ \mathrm{m} &= \text{Energy intensity, Greenhouse gas emission intensity} \\
\overline{a}_{3i} &= \tfrac{1}{36} \sum_{j=1}^{36} a_{3ij} \text{ (} j \text{ means No.} j \text{ cities)}
\end{aligned}
\tag{4.14}
$$

Among which: A_{31} is the industrial energy consumption index, $a\prime_{31}$ is the standardized industrial energy consumption index, a_{31} is the original index of the city's energy consumption, $RF_{Energyintensity}$ is the total energy consumption per 10,000 yuan of GDP of the city, $NF_{Energyintensity}$ is the total energy consumption per 10,000 yuan of GDP of all cities, and $\overline{a_{31}}$ is the average value of the original index of 36 cities' energy consumption.

A_{32} is the greenhouse gas emission index, $a\prime_{32}$ the standardized greenhouse gas emission index, a_{32} is the original greenhouse gas emission index of the city, $RF_{GHGemissionintensity}$ is the total carbon dioxide emission per 10,000 yuan of GDP of the city, $NF_{GHGemissionintensity}$ is the total carbon dioxide emission per 10,000 yuan of GDP of all cities, and $\overline{a_{32}}$ is the average of the original greenhouse gas emission indexes of 36 cities.

4.3.4.2 "Four Modernizations" Interactive Indicators

Realizing modernization is not only a major strategic goal of China's economic and social development, but also one of the missions carried by China's urbanization itself. At this stage, the realization of modernization is mainly reflected in the "Four Modernizations" interaction of industrialization, urbanization, agricultural modernization and informatization, and the "Four Modernizations" interaction is also an important way to comprehensively promote the development of modernization at present. We have constructed four indexes of population urbanization, industrialization, agricultural modernization and informatization to represent the overall level of urban modernization development.

Calculation of "Four Modernizations" interaction index:

$$\begin{aligned}
B_{1i} &= 10 \times b\prime_{1i} + 50\, i = 1, 2 \\
b\prime_{1i} &= \tfrac{b_{1i} - \overline{b_{1i}}}{\delta b_{1i}} \\
\delta b_{1i} &= \sqrt{\tfrac{1}{36-1} \sum_{j=1}^{36} \left(b_{1ij} - \overline{b_{1ij}}\right)^2} \text{ (}j\text{ means No.}j\text{ cities)} \\
b_{1i} &= \frac{RF_m}{NF_m}\ \text{m} = \text{Population urbanization, industrialization, agriculture modernization, informatization} \\
\overline{b}_{1i} &= \tfrac{1}{36} \sum_{j=1}^{36} b_{1ij} \text{ (}j\text{ means No.}j\text{ cities)}
\end{aligned} \tag{4.15}$$

Among which: B_{11} refers to the population urbanization index, $b\prime_{11}$ refers to the standardized population urbanization index, b_{11} refers to the original index of population urbanization of the city, $RF_{Populationurbanization}$ refers to the ratio of non-agricultural population to total population of the city, $NF_{Populationurbanization}$ refers to the ratio of non-agricultural population to total population of all cities, and $\overline{b_{11}}$ refers to the average value of the original index of population urbanization of 36 cities.

B_{12} is the industrialization index, $b\prime_{12}$ is the industrialization index after standardization, b_{12} is the original index of the industrialization of the city, $RF_{Industrialization}$ is the ratio of the non-agricultural output value of the city to the total output value, $NF_{Industrialization}$ is the ratio of the non-agricultural output value of all cities to the total output value, and $\overline{b_{12}}$ is the average value of the original index of the industrialization of 36 cities.

B_{13} is the agricultural modernization index, $b\prime_{13}$ is the standardized agricultural modernization index, b_{13} is the original index of agricultural modernization of the city, $RF_{Agriculturemodernization}$ is the popularization rate of agricultural equipment in the city, $NF_{Agriculturemodernization}$ is the popularization rate of agricultural equipment in all cities, and $\overline{b_{13}}$ is the average value of the original index of agricultural modernization in 36 cities.

B_{14} is the informatization index, $b\prime_{14}$ is the standardized informatization index, b_{14} is the original informatization index of the city, $RF_{Informatization}$ is the per capita R&D cost of the city, $NF_{Informatization}$ is the per capita R&D cost of all cities, and $\overline{b_{14}}$ is the average value of the original informatization index of 36 cities.

4.3.4.3 Indicators of Coordinated Economic and Social Development

Coordinated economic and social development is the main content and important guarantee of urban ecological civilization construction. The construction of urban ecological civilization requires the transformation of urban economic function from production to life, and the transformation of urban social function from management to service. Therefore, cities that adapt to the ecological civilization model must be cities with coordinated economic and social development. In terms of economic development, we use economic advantage index, urban–rural coordination index and economic vitality index to evaluate. In terms of social development, we use education index and health index to evaluate.

1. Calculation of economic development index.

$$C_{1i} = 10 \times c\prime_{1i} + 50\, i = 1, 2, 3$$
$$c\prime_{1i} = \frac{c_{1i} - \overline{c_{1i}}}{\delta c_{1i}}$$
$$\delta c_{1i} = \sqrt{\frac{1}{36-1}\sum_{j=1}^{36}\left(c_{1ij} - \overline{c_{1ij}}\right)^2} \; (j \text{ means No.} j \text{ cities}) \tag{4.16}$$
$$c_{1i} = \frac{RF_m}{NF_m}\ \mathrm{m} = \text{Economic advantages, Urban Rural Coordination, Economic vitality}$$
$$\overline{c}_{1i} = \frac{1}{36}\sum_{j=1}^{36} c_{1ij} \; (j \text{ means No.} j \text{ cities})$$

Among which: C_{11} is the economic advantage index, $c\prime_{11}$ is the standardized economic advantage index, c_{11} is the original index of the city's economic advantage, $RF_{Economicadvantages}$ is the per capita GDP of the city, $NF_{Economicadvantages}$ is the per capita GDP of all cities, and $\overline{c_{11}}$ is the average value of the original index of 36 cities' economic advantages.

C_{12} is the urban–rural coordination index, $c\prime_{12}$ is the standardized urban–rural coordination index, c_{12} is the original urban–rural coordination index of the city, $RF_{Urbanruralcoordination}$ is the urban–rural residents' income ratio of the city, $NF_{Urbanruralcoordination}$ is the urban–rural residents' income ratio of all cities, and $\overline{c_{12}}$ is the average of the original urban–rural coordination index of 36 cities.

C_{13} is the economic vitality index, $c\prime_{13}$ is the standardized economic vitality index, c_{13} is the original index of the economic vitality of the city, $RF_{Economicvitality}$ is the proportion of the foreign capital economy in the GDP of the city, $NF_{Economicvitality}$ is the proportion of the foreign capital economy in the GDP of all cities, and $\overline{c_{13}}$ is the average value of the original index of the economic vitality of 36 cities.

2. Calculation of social development index.

$$C_{2i} = 10 \times c'_{2i} + 50\, i = 1, 2$$
$$c'_{2i} = \frac{c_{2i} - \overline{c_{2i}}}{\delta c_{2i}}$$
$$\delta c_{2i} = \sqrt{\frac{1}{36-1}\sum_{j=1}^{36}\left(c_{2ij} - \overline{c_{2ij}}\right)^2} \; (j \text{ means No.} j \text{ cities}) \tag{4.17}$$
$$c_{2i} = \frac{RF_m}{NF_m}\ \mathrm{m} = \text{Education, health}$$
$$\overline{c}_{2i} = \frac{1}{36}\sum_{j=1}^{36} c_{2ij} \; (j \text{ means No.} j \text{ cities})$$

Among which: C_{21} is the education index, $c\prime_{21}$ is the standardized education index, c_{21} is the original index of the city's education, $RF_{Education}$ is the high school gross enrollment rate of the city, $NF_{Education}$ is the high school gross enrollment rate of all cities, and $\overline{c_{21}}$ is the average value of the original index of 36 cities' education.

C_{22} is the health index, $c\prime_{22}$ is the standardized health index, c_{22} is the original index of the city's health, RF_{Health} is the per capita life expectancy of the city, NF_{Health} is the per capita life expectancy of all cities, and $\overline{c_{22}}$ is the average value of the original index of 36 cities' health.

4.3.5 *Weight Determination*

4.3.5.1 Analytic Hierarchy Process for Weight Determination (AHP)

According to the basic idea of APH, the index system is divided into three levels, namely, target level, criterion level and index level. To compare the influence of No. N index of b_1 、 $b_2......b_n$ on F factor, we usually use the method of comparing two indexes to express the ratio of a_{ij} the influence of the F index and the pair b_i and b_j. . AHP uses Sadi scale (that is, the ratio scale whose standard value is limited to the range of 1 ~ 9, and the specific scale evaluation standard is shown in the table) to determine the value of a_{ij}. In order to ensure the scientific rationality of the evaluation of a_{ij}, Delphi method is usually used to assign the value of a_{ij}, that is, set up a questionnaire, invite experts in relevant fields, ask them to give a_{ij} the value of the impact between the two indicators of the index system on the evaluation objectives, and give their trust coefficient according to the knowledge, qualifications and industry experience of each expert and scholar, and then the final value is obtained by weighted summary (see Table 4.7).[27]

Combine all the values a_{ij} given by the experts and arrange them in a matrix form, namely: $A = (a_{ij})_{n\times n}$

$$(a_{ij})_{n\times n} = \begin{bmatrix} a_1/a_1 & a_1/a_2 & \cdots & a_1/a_n \\ a_2/a_1 & a_2/a_2 & \cdots & a_2/a_n \\ \cdots\cdots & \cdots\cdots & \cdots\cdots & \cdots\cdots \\ a_n/a_1 & a_n/a_2 & \cdots & a_n/a_n \end{bmatrix} \tag{4.18}$$

Among which: $a_{ij} > 0$, $a_{ij} = 1/a_{ji}$, and $a_{ii} = 1$, a matrix that satisfies this condition is called a judgment matrix or a contrast matrix.

After n indicators of $a_1, a_2, a_3 \cdots\cdots a_n$ have been determined and a judgment matrix is established, the indicator weight needs to be determined on this basis. By using the square root method to find the maximum eigenvalue of the judgment matrix, and then to find n indicators of $a_1, a_2, a_3 \cdots\cdots a_n$ in the corresponding eigenvector,

Table 4.7 Sadi scale

Scale a_{ij}	Meaning
1	b_i compared with b_j, it is of equal importance
3	b_i compared with b_j, one factor is slightly more important than another
5	b_i compared with b_j, one factor is obviously more important than another
7	b_i compared with b_j, one factor is more important than another
9	b_i compared with b_j, one factor is much more important than another
2、4、6、8	Intermediate value of the above two adjacent judgments
Reciprocal	b_i and b_j are reciprocal to each other, that is $a_{ij} = 1/a_{ji}$

the relative weight of this indicator in $w_1, w_2, w_3 \cdots\cdots w_n$. Specific steps are as follows:

1. Calculate the geometric mean of all elements in each row of the judgment matrix

$$\overline{w}_i = \sqrt[n]{\prod_{j=1}^{n} a_{ij}}\ j = 1, 2, 3 \cdots\cdots n \tag{4.19}$$

2. Normalize the geometric mean of all elements in each row, i.e. calculate:

$$w_i = \overline{w}_i \Big/ \sum_{i=1}^{n} \overline{w}_i\ (i = 1, 2, 3 \cdots\cdots n) \tag{4.20}$$

The column matrix (w_i) is thus established, and at the same time, for the convenience of calculation, let $\left(v_j\right)^T = (w_i)$, namely:

$$\overline{w} = (w_i) = \begin{bmatrix} w_1 \\ w_2 \\ w_3 \\ w_4 \end{bmatrix} = (v_1, v_2, v_3, v_4)^T = \left(v_j\right)^T = \overline{v} \tag{4.21}$$

According to the above calculation method, the risk weight of each early warning indicator relative to its level can be obtained.[28]

However, the judgment matrix is obtained through a pairwise comparison of two factors, and in many such comparisons, some inconsistent conclusions may often be obtained. For example, when the importance of factors i, j, k is very close, experts may draw contradictory conclusions such as i is more important than j, j is more important than k, and k is more important than i when comparing indicators pairwise, which is especially likely to happen when there are a large number of indicators. At the same time, since 1 to 9 are used in the Sadie scale table to calibrate the influence degree of the given two indicators on a certain factor, it may cause the reciprocal of some calibration numbers to be cyclic decimals, and the method of rounding is adopted in the calculation process. The condition that will be destroyed $a_{ji} = 1/a_{ij}$, resulting in the satisfaction of the condition of the consistency of the judgment matrix: there is a unique non-zero Eigen root $\lambda_{\max} = n$ failure.

Among which:

$$\lambda_{\max} = \frac{1}{n} \sum_{i=1}^{n} \frac{\sum_{j=1}^{n} \left(a_{ij} \times v_j\right)}{w_i} \tag{4.22}$$

Therefore, the judgment matrix also needs to be checked for consistency.

AHP achieves this purpose mainly by adopting the random consistency ratio, and the test formula is:

Table 4.8 Modified value degrees of freedom index RI

Dimension	1	2	3	4		5	6	7	8	9
RI	0.00	0.00	0.58	0.90		1.12	1.24	1.32	1.41	1.45

$$CR = CI/RI \tag{4.23}$$

Among them: CI is the consistency index, and $CI = \frac{\lambda_{\max}-n}{n-1}$, n is the order of the judgment matrix, $\lambda_{\max}$ is the maximum eigenvalue of the judgment matrix, RI is the scalar value, also called the correction value freedom metric index, as shown in Table 4.8:

The larger the value CR is, the worse the consistency is. Otherwise, the better the consistency. When $\lambda_{\max} = n$, $CR = 0$, are completely consistent. It is generally believed that as long as $CR \leq 0.1$, the judgment matrix is considered consistent. Otherwise, it is necessary to re-comparison until the test is passed.[29]

4.3.5.2 The Weight of the REEFCR Urban Construction Evaluation Index System

According to the above theoretical method, we use Yaahp6.0 software to determine the weight of each index of the REEFCR city evaluation index system as follows (see Table 4.9).

4.4 REEFCR Cities Evaluation in China

4.4.1 Data Source and Processing

According to the "REEFCR" city evaluation index system, and on the basis of data availability, we selected 31 provincial capital cities and 5 cities under separate state planning that enjoy provincial-level economic management authority in Shenzhen, Qingdao, Dalian, Xiamen, and Ningbo as evaluation object. Relevant data mainly come from "China Urban Statistical Yearbook" and "China Environmental Statistical Yearbook" from 2000 to 2012, and some of them come from "60 Years of New China Statistical Data Compilation", CNKI China Economic and Social Development Statistical Database, Guotai Junan "Regional and Cities" database, statistical yearbook of relevant cities, etc.

Because the units of the data are inconsistent, in order to be able to compare, the threshold method and the average method are generally used to perform dimensionless processing on the data. For example, the selection of the threshold mainly refers to the authoritative and real-time government-related plans and the to-be-achieved

Table 4.9 Weights of REEFCR city

First-level indicator	Second-level indicator	Third-level indicator	Weights
REEFCR	Resource efficient index	Cultivated land resource carrying capacity index	0.0536
		Forest resources carrying capacity index	0.0378
		Freshwater resources carrying capacity index	0.0478
		Space resource carrying capacity index	0.0527
	Environment friendly index	Atmospheric self-purification ability index	0.0527
		Water body self-purification ability index	0.0493
		Solid waste treatment capability index	0.0412
	Climate resilient index	Industrial energy consumption index	0.0631
		GHG emission index	0.0616
Urban modernization	"Four Modernizations" interaction index	Population urbanization index	0.0647
		Industrialization index	0.0631
		Agricultural modernization index	0.0488
		Informatization index	0.0550
Coordinated development of economy and society	Economic development index	Economic advantage index	0.0746
		Urban and rural coordination index	0.0613
		Economic vitality index	0.0600
	Social development index	Education index	0.0557
		Health index	0.0531

goals proposed in the documents, such as the national economic and social development "12th Five-Year Plan" and various "12th Five-Year Plan" special plans, and the statistical goals of a well-off society. For other index data, the dimensionless processing is carried out according to the average method. The threshold method indicates the degree to which each indicator achieves the ultimate goal; the average method indicates the "leading" or "lagging" degree of each indicator value relative to the average level. Since this project has indexed the specific indicators, the data has been dimensionless in the process of standardization. The process of indexation is a new distribution situation formed by applying the "penalty" of the standard deviation according to the distribution of the data itself, and the ranking order is obtained on this basis.

4.4.2 REEFCR City Comprehensive Evaluation Results

4.4.2.1 The Overall Situation of REEFCR City Urban Construction

According to the weights of each index determined by the AHP, this project synthesizes the REEFCR urban construction level value. As shown in Table 4.10, in 1999, the REEFCR city index was only 24.8657. Since the beginning of the new century, with the advent of the rapid urbanization stage, the city's ability to allocate resources and cope with the environment has gradually increased, and economic development has accelerated. Concentration, internal subsystems are more coordinated, and the construction level of REEFCR cities has gradually improved. By 2011, the REEFCR city index reached 81.5028, an increase of 2.28 times. According to the quantitative relationship of the three dimension indices, the level of urban ecological environment construction such as resource efficient, environment friendly, and climate resilient has increased by 1.52 times; the level of urban modernization promoted by the interaction of the "Four Modernizations" increased by 4.35 times, and the coordinated development level of urban economy and society increased by 2.90 times, which shows that the progress of these three dimensions has jointly promoted the improvement of the construction level of REEFCR cities in China. The role of REEFCR urban construction is becoming more and more significant.

4.4.2.2 The Spatial Pattern of REEFCR Urban Construction

Further investigation of the achievements of 31 provincial capital cities and Shenzhen, Qingdao, Dalian, Xiamen and Ningbo in the construction of REEFCR city in 2011 that enjoy provincial-level economic management authority, we can obtain the following REEFCR cities' comprehensive evaluation results, which are shown in Table 4.11.

From the evaluation results of the REEFCR city in 2011, it can be seen that Shanghai, Beijing and Shenzhen ranked in the top three with scores of 95.643, 94.592 and 91.375 respectively; Guiyang, Yinchuan and Xining ranked the last three with scores of only 63.582, 60.429 and 58.542. We simply divide the 36 cities into four groups with 10 as an interval:

High-level group (score higher than 90): 4 cities are in the high-level group, namely Shanghai, Beijing, Shenzhen, and Tianjin. These cities are all concentrated in the most economically developed eastern coastal area of China, and are the central cities of the Yangtze River Delta Economic Zone, the Pearl River Delta Economic Zone, and the Beijing-Tianjin-Hebei Economic Zone. Whether the resource allocation ability, environmental governance ability, risk resistance ability, or industrial

Table 4.10 1999 to 2011 REEFCR urban construction index and composition

Year	REEFCR index	Urban modernization index	Urban economic and social coordinated development index	REEFCR city index
1999	14.8818	3.5281	6.4558	24.8657
2000	16.0724	4.3573	7.2305	27.6602
2001	17.3582	4.6659	8.1982	30.2222
2002	18.7468	5.3658	9.0700	33.1826
2003	20.2466	6.7706	10.1583	37.1756
2004	21.8663	7.0962	11.3774	40.3399
2005	23.6156	8.1607	12.7426	44.5189
2006	26.5049	9.3848	14.2718	50.1614
2007	27.9452	11.7925	16.4844	56.2221
2008	29.5489	12.4113	17.9025	59.8627
2009	32.1288	14.2730	20.0508	66.4526
2010	34.6991	16.4140	23.4569	74.5699
2011	37.4750	18.8761	25.1517	81.5028

Table 4.11 REEFCR city comprehensive evaluation results

Sort	Score	Sort	Score
Shanghai	95.643	Ha'erbin	78.164
Beijing	94.592	Shijiazhuang	77.393
Shenzhen	91.375	Changchun	76.549
Tianjin	90.590	Changsha	74.386
Guangzhou	89.152	Fuzhou	74.118
Nanjing	88.347	Nanchang	73.875
Hangzhou	88.105	Taiyuan	73.326
Xiamen	86.332	Huhehaote	72.658
Ningbo	84.892	Nanning	71.456
Dalian	83.386	Lanzhou	70.116
Qingdao	82.592	Hefei	69.840
Xi'an	81.994	Wulumuqi	69.285
Chongqing	81.756	Kunming	68.465
Chengdu	80.065	Haikou	67.954
Wuhan	80.003	Lasa	63.963
Jinan	79.874	Guiyang	63.582
Shenyang	79.356	Yinchuan	60.429
Zhengzhou	78.942	Xining	58.542

structure, technological innovation, urban management, and social development, it is at the leading level in the country, which has laid a solid foundation for the construction of REEFCR city. Among them, Shanghai and Beijing are far ahead in the construction of REEFCR city, and Tianjin has entered the high-level group due to its vigorous promotion of ecological economic city construction in recent years.

Middle and high-level group (scores between 80 and 90): A total of 11 cities are in this range, namely Guangzhou, Nanjing, Hangzhou, Xiamen, Ningbo, Dalian, Qingdao, Xi'an, Chongqing, Chengdu, Wuhan. Seven of these cities are in the eastern region, one is in the central region, and three are in the western region. Except for Guangzhou, which is a first-tier city, all other cities are traditional second-tier cities. Since these cities are the provincial capitals or economic center cities of the province, and some of them are regional central cities, they have gathered more manpower, material resources and financial resources for the construction of REEFCR city, and are the main force of the construction of innovative REEFCR city.

Middle and low-level group (scores between 70 and 80): a total of 13 cities are between this level, including Jinan, Shenyang, Harbin, Shijiazhuang, Changchun, Fuzhou, Nanchang in eastern coastal area, and including Zhengzhou, Changsha, Taiyuan in the central region, and Hohhot, Nanning, and Lanzhou in the western region. Stimulated by major regional policies such as the National Comprehensive and Supporting Reform Pilot Zone for the Construction of a Resource-conserving and Environment-friendly Society, the Revitalization of Northeast Old Industrial Bases, the Central Plains City Cluster, the Economic Zone on the West Coast of the Straits, the Beibu Gulf Economic Zone, and the Lanzhou New District, in recent years, these cities had very rapid economic development, and the construction of REEFCR city is accelerated, but in general, they are still at the low-medium level among the 36 cities.

Low-level group (score below 70): a total of 8 cities are below 70, the lowest level among the 36 cities, namely Hefei, Urumqi, Kunming, Haikou, Lhasa, Guiyang, Yinchuan, Xining. Although these cities have comparative advantages in urban ecological environment, they are at a low level in the construction of REEFCR city due to various factors such as insufficient urban economic development and lagging social development.

Notes

1. Rongxing Song, and Haitao Sun, "Research on Sustainable Development Capability of Urban Ecological Environment", *Research on Financial Issues*, Issue 7, 2007.
2. Xiumei Zhang et al., "Review of Network Information Resource Evaluation", *Library Science Research*, Issue 12, 2013.
3. Pengfei Xie, "Sustainable City Indicator System Construction and Sustainable City Demonstration Evaluation", *Urban Development Research*, Issue 7, 2010.
4. Jing Zhao, *Mathematical Modeling and Experiments* (Beijing: Higher Education Press, 2000), 39.

5. Songxue Li, and Yibing Xia, "Performance Evaluation of "REEF" City Construction in Wuhan Urban Circle Based on Analytic Hierarchy Process", *Yangtze River Basin Resources and Environment*, Issue 7, 2012.
6. Bin Zhang et al., *Fuzzy Matter Element Analysis* (Beijing: Petroleum Industry Press, 1997).
7. Konglai Zhu, and Ruyan Wang, "Research on Comprehensive Evaluation of REEF Society", *China Population, Resources and Environment*, Issue 12, 2011.
8. Zan Zhao, "Analysis of the Impact Mechanism of Tourism Development on Ethnic Traditional Culture Based on the PSR Model Framework", *Chinese Journal of Agriculture*, Issue 9, 2010.
9. Cailing Gao et al., "Evaluation of Sustainable City Construction in Zhengzhou Based on PSR Model", *Regional Research and Development*, Issue 4, 2013.
10. Shantong Li et al., "The Goal and Indicator System for Comprehensively Building a Moderately Prosperous Society", *Survey and Research Report,* No. 20, 2004.
11. Kaizhong Yang, "Which Province Has a More Civilized Ecology - Ranking of Ecological Civilization Levels in Various Provinces, Districts, and Cities in China", *China Economic Weekly*, Issue 12, 2011.
12. Zhangping Xin, and Yintai Zhang, "Low-Carbon Economy and Low Carbon Cities", *Urban Development Research*, Issue 4, 2008.
13. Guiyang Zhuang, "Low-Carbon Economy Leads the Development Direction of the World Economy", *World Environment*, Issue 2, 2008.
14. "CCS: Accelerator Towards a Low-Carbon Era, but Who's Gonna Pay for It", *Science and Technology Daily*, September 6, 2009.
15. "Hundreds of Cities are Vying to Label Themselves as 'Low-Carbon', and a New Round of 'Urban Construction Impatience' Needs to be Vigilant", *Xinhua Current Affairs*, December 3, 2010.
16. Jun Bi, "Low Carbon Cities Cannot be Built on High Carbon Development", *People's Daily*, October 12, 2011.
17. Jiahua Pan, "Economy Needs Low Carbon, Low Carbon Needs Economy", *Journal of Huazhong University of Science and Technology (Social Science Edition)*, Issue 2, 2011.
18. Hiroaki Suzuki et al., *ECO^2 Cities: Ecological Cities as Economic Cities* (New York: World Bank Publications, 2010).
19. Ibid.
20. Kai Ma, "Global Warming is a Common Challenge Facing Humanity", *Green Leaf*, Issue 8, 2007.
21. Binbin Wang, and Shouhu Du, "ECO^2: The Third Mode of Low-Carbon City", *Journal of Sichuan Normal University (Social Science Edition)*, Issue 6, 2012.
22. Edward L Glaeser, "The Greenness of Cities: Carbon Dioxide Emissions and Urban Development", *Journal of Urban Economics*, 2010.
23. Chris Goodall, *How to Live a Low-Carbon Life: The Individual's Guide to Stopping Climate Change* (London: Earthscan, 2010).
24. Jianping Xu, *Application of Mathematical Models in Geographic Information Systems* (Beijing: Higher Education Press, 2002) 87.
25. Ibid.
26. Binbin Wang, and Shouhu Du, "ECO^2: The Third Mode of Low-Carbon City", *Journal of Sichuan Normal University (Social Science Edition)*, Issue 6, 2012.
27. Jiangbo Qin, and Hongqi Wang, "Construction of a Performance Evaluation Model for Bank Credit Risk Management Based on AHP Method", *Financial Theory and Practice*, Issue 1, 2009.
28. Rongwei Song, "Discussion on the Construction of Credit Risk Early Warning Indicator System by Commercial Banks", *Journal of Sichuan Normal University (Social Science Edition)*, Issue. 5, 2007.
29. Ibid.

Chapter 5
Domestic Practices of REEFCR City Development

As the main settlement of human beings and the main place of wealth creation, City is the center of politics, economy, society and culture, and it is also the engine of coordinating urban and rural development. The construction of urban ecological civilization is the key and main body of national and regional ecological civilization construction, and the sustainable development of cities is the focus and foundation of national and regional sustainable development.

The sustainable development of urban ecology in China is facing severe challenges. Not only is that China's urban ecological sustainable development started relatively late, but China is facing different tasks and challenges from developed countries in the process of transitioning from a planned economy to a market economy. It is important to learn from the successful experience of developed countries and summarize own development experience. Facing the huge pressure of resource, environment and climate change, the traditional urban development model of extensional growth has been difficult to adapt to the development requirements under the new situation. In the future, Chinese cities need to actively practice and explore a new urban development path that is resource-efficient, environment-friendly, and climate-resilient.

According to the actual situation of China's current economic and social development, the program chooses cities with different resource endowments, environmental capacities, and levels of economic development to study, focusing on the main practices of cities in different regions and with their own characteristics in the construction of REEFCR city. The program also sorts out and evaluates, analyzes the existing problems and causes, and reveals the characteristics of different urban development and the experience of typical urban ecological sustainable development.

S. Du and H. Du, *The Green Transformation of Urban Areas in China Under Global Warming*, https://doi.org/10.1007/978-981-95-1005-4_5

5.1 Disaster Prevention and Reduction—Ningbo Practice

Low-carbon economy provides economic, technological and institutional support for sustainable urban development. The development of low-carbon economy is an opportunity for countries and regions to enhance their competitiveness in future development. Developing a low-carbon economy is not only China's international responsibility to combat climate change, but also an inherent requirement to ensure China's energy security, optimize economic structure, transform development mode, and achieve sustainable development. Developing a low-carbon economy is also the best path for Ningbo to achieve double growth in both the speed of economic development and the quality of development.

Since December 2009, Ningbo City has cooperated with the World Bank to carry out a study on the subject of "Construction of a Disaster Prevention and Reduction System in Ningbo City to Address Climate Change". The study took Ningbo as a case city to seek new methods and new paths to build a climate resilient city and to improve the disaster reduction and prevention system. Coping with climate change involves all aspects of the ecological environment, resources and energy, domestic and foreign affairs, national security, economic and social issues, and is a major challenge facing the world. To comprehensively improve the ability to deal with climate change, it is necessary to continuously improve the level of ecological and environmental protection, and build a disaster prevention and mitigation system for climate-adapted cities on the basis of the scientific development concept, so as to comprehensively improve the ability of the whole society to prevent and reduce disasters. As a coastal port city, Ningbo has a developed economy and a fast process of industrialization and urbanization. However, it has a large population, few resources and a relatively weak ecological environment. "Low-carbon Ningbo" is imperative.

5.1.1 Urban Vulnerability and Climate Change in Ningbo

Ningbo City is located in the middle of China's coastline and on the south wing of the Yangtze River Delta. It is one of the most famous coastal port cities in China. Ningbo has jurisdiction over 11 counties, county-level cities and municipal districts, including Cixi, Yuyao, Fenghua, Xiangshan, Ninghai, etc. The total area is 9365 square kilometers, of which the urban area is 1033 square kilometers. By the end of 2008, the fixed population was 9 million.

Ningbo has a long coastline, zigzag harbors, and dotted islands. The total sea area of the city is 9758 square kilometers, and the total coastline is 1562 km, including 788 km of mainland coastline and 774 km of island coastline.

As the main stream of Ningbo, the Yongjiang River is one of the eight major river systems in Zhejiang Province. The Yongjiang River Basin has a lot of rainwater and abundant water resources. The average annual precipitation is 1300 mm—1400 mm, and the precipitation from May to September in the main flood season accounts for 60% of the whole year.

Natural disasters in Ningbo are mainly caused by some severe weather (typhoons, droughts, etc.), such as floods, landslides and seawater erosion. The impact period of typhoons is mainly concentrated from July to September each year, with an annual average of 2.8 times. Super typhoons (with an average rainfall greater than or equal to 200 mm) occur every few years, causing serious damage to Ningbo. Since 1953, a total of four super typhoons have landed in Ningbo, and the storms have caused huge losses to Ningbo. For example, the No. 5612 strong typhoon has seriously affected Xiangshan County, and the cumulative damage caused by the No. 9711 typhoon has exceeded 4.5 billion Yuan. The average annual number of storms is 2 to 5, mainly concentrated in the rainy season from June to early July and the typhoon period from August to September, with the highest frequency of outbreaks in September. From the perspective of spatial distribution, Ninghai County has more storms than other counties and urban areas. Heavy rains often cause floods, such as the July 30, 1988 flood that killed more than 100 people. Drought usually occurs from August to September after the rainy season, especially in Ninghai, Xiangshan and other counties and mountainous areas. Drought occurs every 2 to 3 years, while in other areas, it usually occurs once every 4 to 5 years.

In recent years, with the increasing impact of global warming and the accelerated social and economic development, the occurrence of sea disasters such as storm surges, tides, red tides, etc., has affected all aspects of Ningbo. According to a study by the Organization for World Economic Cooperation and Development, Ningbo is one of the top 20 port cities in the world in terms of vulnerability and high risk of being affected by extreme climates. The rapidly increasing risk in Ningbo and the other cities analyzed is driven by population growth and urbanization.

The results of climate change caused by human activities are mainly measured by the natural disasters caused. The impact of human activities on climate change is analyzed from the urbanization and industrialization of Ningbo city; at the same time, how climate change affects urban vulnerability is analyzed from the poor population most vulnerable to climate change; government behavior is used to analyze the city's enhanced response to climate change. The relationship between climate change and cities and their vulnerabilities is shown in Fig. 5.1.

Cities and Climate Change focuses on analyzing human-induced climate change or so-called Anthropogenic Global Warming (AGW), which in turn can trigger natural disasters that affect human activities. Of course, its impact has both positive and negative effects. According to big data and the actual situation, the impact of climate change on human activities is mostly negative. For more than 100 years since the Industrial Revolution, climate change has been mainly caused by the impact of human activities—the massive burning of fossil fuels has triggered the greenhouse effect and accelerated global warming; the development and use of land by humans has changed the state of the land and vegetation on the earth surface, which has a significant impact on the entire climate system. From this point of view, climate change has and will continue to have a wider and deeper impact on the global ecological environment, further threatening ecological security.

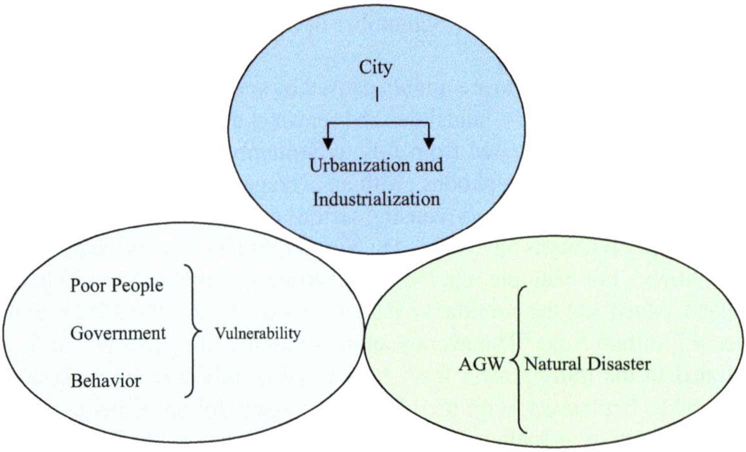

Fig. 5.1 Climate Change, Vulnerability of Cities

From the urban level analysis, human activities that lead to climate change are mainly urbanization and industrialization. During the "11th Five-Year Plan" period (2006—2010), Ningbo's urbanization has reached 65%, and the urbanization rate is expected to reach 70% during the "12th Five-Year Plan" period (2011—2015); Ningbo's heavy chemical industry structure features are very obvious, including power, petrochemical, steel, paper and other industries. They are all industries with high energy consumption and high carbon emissions. The rapid urbanization process of Ningbo City and the characteristics of heavy chemical industry structure make the development of a low-carbon economy in Ningbo a long way to go. The aggravation of climate change in Ningbo can be seen from the ambient air quality rate and acid rain rate. The urban ambient air quality rate dropped from 97% in 2001 to 89.7% in 2009. From 2001 to the present, the acid rain rate has risen from 73.1 to 97.2%, and almost all major areas in the city are areas with heavy acid rain. In the 10 years from 1991 to 2000, there were only 11 days of haze weather in Ningbo urban area. In 2001, dates of haze reached 10 days, every year after that it was more than 20 days, and in 2009 it reached 30 days.[1]

The urban vulnerability of Ningbo under climate change also includes the sensitivity before the disaster, the coping ability during the disaster and the resilience after the disaster.

Sensitivity before disasters: it mainly includes the degree of response of climate resources, water resources, land resources and biological resources to climate change and disasters.[2] Taking climate resources as an example, Ningbo's climate shows a warming trend. Although the precipitation did not change in trend, the number of precipitation days obviously showed a decreasing trend, which mainly due to the decrease in the number of light rain days, while the number of precipitation days above moderate rain showed a slow increase trend, indicating that the probability of heavy precipitation in Ningbo is increasing. At the same time, the annual average wind speed in Ningbo showed a decreasing trend, and the strong winds above level 8 also showed a decreasing trend, but the number of typhoons affecting Ningbo showed a slow increase. In addition, the foggy weather in Ningbo has decreased, the hazy weather has increased, and the number of snowfall days has decreased significantly. Global warming will make it more difficult to dispatch water, electricity and other energy and resources in Ningbo.[3] Therefore, although the sensitivity before disasters occurs in the vulnerability of Ningbo City caused by climate change is good or bad, most of them are negative impact.

Ability to cope with disasters: Ningbo City has encountered many natural disasters caused by extreme weather conditions such as drought, typhoon, snow disaster, and freezing in recent years. Although it is impossible to reverse and change the occurrence of natural disasters, it is feasible to actively and properly respond to the occurrence of disasters and increase the urban disaster response capacity. For the government, there are various contingency plans for dealing with natural disasters and emergencies; when disasters occur, government departments at all levels can quickly organize the masses to fight against disasters. The Ningbo Municipal Government can establish a set of operational, flexible and effective response and prevention mechanisms, and should gradually shift from a passive emergency response mechanism to an active prevention mechanism to enhance the orderliness and effectiveness of natural disaster prevention management.

Resilience after disasters: resilience after disasters also requires government departments to establish and improve a disaster prevention management system with smooth information, quick response, strong command, clear responsibility, legal operation, and low cost. It can change the passive response mode through the early warning analysis of natural disasters. There are two main natural disasters that occur most frequently in Ningbo: one is typhoon in summer and autumn, and the other is road freezing in winter. For typhoon prevention, Ningbo City's already has the "Ningbo City Emergency Plan for Typhoon Prevention", and there is a complete set of preventive measures. For extreme climates such as freezing, the Ningbo Municipal Government has issued the "Ningbo Meteorological Disaster Prevention Regulations" to strengthen the city's meteorological disaster prevention work, avoid and reduce the loss of meteorological disasters, and ensure economic and social development and the safety of people's lives and properties. Therefore, it is necessary to improve the system construction through laws and regulations, so that the city can resume production and life as soon as possible after the disaster.

5.1.2 Urban Vulnerability and Geological Disasters in Ningbo

5.1.2.1 Sudden Geological Disasters in Ningbo

In 2010, Ningbo had a total of 252 sudden geological disaster points (119 collapses, 87 landslides, 45 debris flows, and 1 ground subsidence), of which 153 threatened permanent residents, 1653 households with threatened permanent residents, and 4869 people were living in danger.[4] The geological disaster points are mainly distributed in the hilly and mountainous areas in the south and northwest of Ningbo City. Among them, there are 60 in Yuyao City, accounting for 23.8% of the total number of potential geological hazards, 56 in Ninghai County, accounting for 22.2%, and 25, 33, 23, and 17 in Cixi City, Fenghua City, Yinzhou District, and Xiangshan County, accounting for 13.8%, 17.1%, 9.1% and 6.7% of the city's total, respectively. There are less than 10 potential geological hazards in Zhenhai, Beilun, Dongqian Lake, Daxie and Jiangbei districts, a total of 28, accounting for 11.1% of the total number of hidden danger points in the city. The scale of disasters is mainly small, of which 2 are large, 24 are medium and 226 are small. Most of the hidden dangers of geological disasters are caused by the destruction of the stability of the mountains caused by cutting slopes, building roads, and building houses. In 2010, 13 geological disasters occurred in Ningbo, including 7 collapses and 6 landslides. The scale of the disasters was small, and no casualties and property losses were caused. In the nationwide emergency action to re-investigate the hidden dangers of geological disasters during the flood season, Ningbo City confirmed 61 newly discovered hidden dangers of geological disasters after investigation.

5.1.2.2 Disaster Mitigation and Prevention of Geological Disasters in Ningbo

Early Warning Mechanism of Geological Disasters

Firstly, professional monitoring instruments such as automatic displacement alarms were installed in high-prone areas of geological disasters and major hidden dangers. In 2012, five automatic meteorological observation stations were built to explore the establishment of quantitative monitoring and early warning of changes in rainfall and geological disasters, so as to improve the initiative and effectiveness of disaster prevention and relief. It is important to continue to improve the meteorological forecast (alert) of sudden geological disasters in the flood season, strengthen the analysis of geological conditions and rain conditions, further improve the forecast (warning) system, and improve the timeliness and accuracy of short-term and near-disaster forecasts. The second is to formulate and improve the meteorological warning and forecast work plan for sudden geological disasters, strengthen the release of geological disaster forecast (warning) information, and make full use of TV, radio, internet and other carriers or mobile phone text messages to timely and effectively send information to disaster prevention related personnel. Third, all localities should revise and improve emergency plans for sudden geological disasters. The people's governments of townships (towns) located in geological disaster-prone areas should formulate and complete emergency plans for sudden geological disasters, and organize emergency drills on a regular basis.

Construction of Mechanisms for Preventing and Controlling Geological Disasters

As a lifeline project, the prevention and control of geological disasters is an important part of the government's performance of social management. It is necessary to implement the national and Zhejiang provincial regulations on the prevention and control of geological disasters and the "Opinions on Further Strengthening the Work on the Prevention of Geological Disasters". Governments at all levels should effectively strengthen leadership. The main leaders of the government are responsible for the prevention and control of geological disasters. All localities should implement the inclusion of geological disaster prevention and control funds into the financial budget of the same level, and effectively manage and make good use of the special funds. At the city and county levels, a geological disaster prevention leading group with government leaders as the team leaders and relevant departments as members should be established to clarify responsibilities. Through the joint meeting system platform, a work pattern in which the government has unified leadership, departments are responsible for their respective responsibilities, disaster management is managed at different levels, and disaster prevention information shared is formed. Counties (cities) and districts with heavy tasks of geological disaster prevention and control shall establish special geological environmental management agencies or geological environmental monitoring stations.[5]

5.1.3 Disaster Reduction and Prevention System of Ningbo City

5.1.3.1 Ningbo City's Basic Ideas for Coping with Climate Change

A resilient city is one that understands the hazards it faces and controls its development, while systematically adapting to the impacts of climate change through disaster risk management and follow-up activities. Ningbo aims to improve the city's ability to adapt to climate change by reducing the city's vulnerability to current natural disasters and the impacts of expected climate change.

1. Climate resilient cities construction.

The Ningbo Climate Resilient Cities project aims to build the city's capacity to prepare for and reduce the expected impacts of existing natural disasters and climate change, prepare local response action plans to shape future planned actions and incorporate research findings into the existing planning process, such as the "12th Five-Year Plan". The Climate Change Resilient Cities Framework advocates mainstreaming climate change and disaster risk management into urban planning and management. Given the clear evidence of climate change and its impact on the poorest communities, integrating climate change issues into development planning is a high priority. The linkages between climate change and disaster risk and poverty underscore the need to strengthen social, economic and environmental resilience, especially in cities with high density of assets and populations. City governor need specific local driving strategies to help them identify, reduce, manage and respond to risks through planning. The purpose of such proactive planning is to significantly reduce its vulnerability and manage the potential impacts of climate change and related natural disasters.

2. Climate change adaptable urban disaster reduction and prevention system building.
   Ningbo Municipal Government attaches great importance to the development of a disaster prevention and reduction system. In order to fight against natural disasters, a lot of financial and material resources have been invested in the construction of high-standard seawalls, flood control, comprehensive management of small watersheds and urban disaster emergency response systems in the past few years. After years of hard work, almost all seawalls built have reached the once-in-50-year standard. According to the actual situation, Ningbo has successively issued local regulations such as "Ningbo Flood Control Regulations", "Ningbo City Emergency Plan for Typhoon Prevention", "Ningbo City's Management Measures for Mitigating Disaster Prevention" and "Ningbo City Meteorological Disaster Warning Signal Release and Dissemination Measures". The "Plan for the Construction of Emergency Response System for Public Emergencies in Ningbo during the '12th Five-Year Plan Period'", which includes various disaster monitoring and early warning systems including natural disasters, emergency command systems, emergency teams, material support, education, training and drills, etc. Of course, with the rapid economic development, urban scale is constantly increasing, and more and more new disasters and secondary disasters occur frequently. Ningbo needs to study and establish a more macroscopic regional construction for disaster prevention and mitigation systems to promote sustainable urban development.

5.1.3.2 The Construction Path of Ningbo City Disaster Reduction and Prevention System Under Climate Change

1. Building a city that is adaptable to climate change.
   First, we must clarify the global, national and local climate characteristics and climate change trends, especially extreme climate phenomena, and clarify the

relationship between human economic and social systems and climate change, mitigation of climate change from the perspective of human economic and social activities. Therefore, it is necessary to strengthen the formulation and construction of special plans for climate change, and make full use of the outline and leading role of the plans to coordinate the actions of various departments (regions) to address climate change. On the basis of planning, strengthen climate change legislation at the national level, regulate the economic and social activities of the whole society with laws, clarify their respective responsibilities and obligations, and effectively achieve climate security that is conducive to the sustainable development of mankind. Second, we must give full play to the supporting role of science and technology on climate change. Through the use of science and technology to improve the study of climate change, climate change trend prediction, climate change impact analysis, improve the predictability of climate change, and enhance the pertinence, effectiveness and scientific aspect of climate change response, so as to reduce existing or possible negative impact on human economy and society. Finally, it is necessary to improve the disaster prevention and mitigation capabilities of climate change-adapted cities. The ability to respond to climate change and prevent extreme climate disasters is an important aspect that reflects the level of harmonious society construction and China's comprehensive national strength in the next 20 years. Climate change and disaster prevention and mitigation should be incorporated into the national security system, and the entire society should be mobilized to jointly enhance disaster prevention. Disaster reduction, the ability to resist extreme meteorological disasters, reduce the risk of climate change, and improve the ability of agricultural production, water resources security, public health and other fields to adapt to climate change.

2. Building a disaster reduction and prevention system for climate change-adapted cities.

   First, improve the pre-disaster adaptability of cities to climate change and natural disasters. Strengthen the short-term and medium-term forecasts and refined forecasts of extreme climate change and major climatic phenomena and their impacts, improve the accuracy and timeliness of major meteorological disaster forecasts, and form a nationwide, multi-level, and rationally distributed meteorological monitoring and forecasting network to achieve disaster early warning analysis and risk analysis of climate events. Second, strengthen the ability of cities to cope with climate change and natural disasters during the process of disasters. Establish different levels of natural disaster emergency response systems, establish a vertical organization and command system for hierarchical response and territorial management, build a horizontal departmental collaboration and linkage system for information sharing, division of labor and collaboration, and establish a disaster emergency response system for the government, enterprises, and the masses. Thirdly, accelerate the resilience of cities to climate change and natural disasters. To give full play to the important role of the government in post-disaster reconstruction, the government should effectively do a good job in post-disaster reconstruction and recovery in terms of organizational leadership, safeguard measures, responsibility implementation, and policy measures. The government strengthens the management of funds and materials, strengthens supervision and inspection, and coordinates the relationship between post-disaster reconstruction and daily work, so as to ensure that post-disaster recovery and reconstruction work is progressing steadily.[6]

5.2 Low Carbon Shanghai Expo—Shanghai Practice

Shanghai is not only China's largest economic center city, but also an important international port city. The city's GDP has maintained a growth rate of over 10% for eleven consecutive years. On this basis, Shanghai has set its medium and long-term strategic goal of building a socialist modern international metropolis with a modern service industry and advanced manufacturing industry as an international financial center and an international shipping center by 2020. From the perspective of Shanghai's own resource endowment—the scarcity of resources and energy and the state of urban construction—the contradiction between more people and less land, ecological environment carrying capacity and urban development, to achieve the goal of building an international metropolis, the road of green, low-carbon and sustainable urban construction must be taken. The goal of building an international metropolis must also be achieved by comprehensively improving Shanghai's urban ecological environment indicators.

5.2.1 Low-Carbon World Expo—The Banner of Shanghai's REEFCR City Construction

The 41st World Expo lasted 184 days from May 1, 2010 to October 31, 2010, and was held on both sides of the Huangpu River in the center of Shanghai, in the Binjiang area between Nanpu Bridge and Lupu Bridge. The Shanghai World Expo has a venue area of 5.28 square kilometers, and a total of 240 countries and regions from around the world participated, creating the largest record in the history of the World Expo. Under the theme of "Better City, Better Life", the Shanghai World Expo showcases the city's civilization achievements and exchanges the city's development concept through the four pavilions on one axis, the theme pavilion, the national pavilion, the local pavilion, the enterprise pavilion, the organization pavilion, and urban practice area, which fully demonstrates that the Shanghai World Expo is a green World Expo, a banner of Shanghai's REEFCR city construction, and guides the low-carbon sustainable development of the city. As shown in Fig. 5.2.

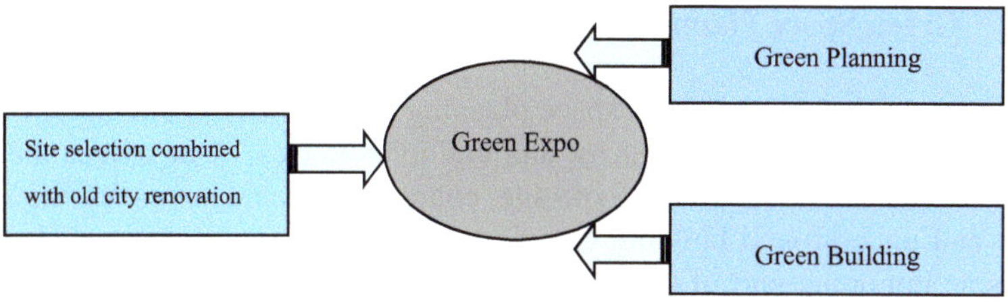

Fig. 5.2 Low-carbon world expo—the banner of Shanghai's REEFCR City

5.2.1.1 Site Selection

The site selection of the Shanghai World Expo Park is combined with the renovation of the old urban area of Shanghai, from the previously considered suburban green area to the industrial area on both sides of the Huangpu River. Such site selection is a careful consideration. From the factors considered in the site selection of the Expo site, the site selection of the eligible venues must firstly have a vast land scale, which is sufficient to hold such an exhibition of world civilization; secondly, it is necessary to have a relatively complete supporting infrastructure construction and convenient transportation conditions, which can reduce the waste of resources caused by repeated investment; thirdly, it is necessary to have a good natural environment, humanistic environment and landscape environment. The World Expo is an international display of civilization, and such a good environment is also manifestation of the World Expo; last but not least, the site should be located in the key development or reconstruction area of the city. Only in this way can the relevant facilities be fully utilized after the World Expo and the close integration of urban planning and urban development can be achieved.

As a natural port running through downtown Shanghai, the riverside area on both sides of the Huangpu River not only has a long history, profound cultural heritage, unique natural landscapes, and complete urban hardware facilities, which was in line with the concept of site selection, but also under the goal and the concept of sustainable urban development, the industrialized products of the cities on both sides of the Huangpu River during the start-up period need to be renovated and updated in a timely manner. Selecting the site of the Expo Park on the Huangpu River can not only make full use of the river, but also transform the waterfront area to achieve a win–win situation between the construction of the World Expo Park and the transformation of the Huangpu River Industrial Belt. The Shanghai World Expo has realized the five goals of the Huangpu River development: ecological priority, remodeling functions, public river banks, restoration of style and urban landscape, and promoted the transformation of the Huangpu River from the original urban industrial ecological coastline to the urban public open space. The site fully demonstrates the green environmental protection concept of Shanghai World Expo, and maximizes the utilization of resources under the premise of equal emphasis on governance and development.

5.2.1.2 Green Space Planning

The Shanghai World Expo green space planning has formed the structural concept of "one axis, two belts, five gardens, and multiple wedges". One axis is the Expo axis, as the main entrance of the Expo site, connecting the main venues, the above-ground and underground building complexes of the rail transit station. The green slope is an important part of the Expo axis, using a large area of grass, with linear low shrubs and plants, to create a feeling of being close to nature, fresh and pleasant. The two belts are the green belts along both banks of the Huangpu River, which integrate functions such as landscape, protection, flood control, and ecology, and are an important guarantee for a green World Expo. The five parks are the Expo Park, Bailianjing Park, Houtan Wetland Park, Jiangnan Park and Qiuxin Park built along the banks of the Huangpu River. The Expo Park is a large-scale waterfront green space in the central city, the Bailianjing Park is an important part of the urban green ecological corridor, and the Houtan Wetland Park is a belt-shaped artificial wetland system with water purification functions that can replicate the ecological purification model of the water system, Jiangnan Park and Qiuxin Park in the waterfront area are integrated of water resources, water landscape and natural landscape, and the integration with other structural concepts provides the sustainable development of Shanghai and the REEFCR city construction sufficient ecological security support. Multi-wedge is a vertically distributed wedge-shaped green space structure composed of various green spaces. It includes protective green space, buffer green space, supporting green space and road greening in the park. Under such a concept of the Expo green space planning structure, the green space covers an area of more than 1 million square meters, accounting for 30% of the Expo site. It fully explains the ecological, environmental protection and green Expo concept that Shanghai Expo upholds.

5.2.1.3 Green Building

Green building is a building that maximizes energy saving, land saving, water saving and material saving in the whole life cycle of the building, so as to achieve the optimal utilization of resources and the lowest pollution of the environment, that is, a building that coexists in harmony with nature. In the Expo area, more than 90% of the venues use environmentally friendly and recyclable green buildings materials, try not to use marble, granite and other building materials with poor thermal insulation and energy saving, and strictly follow the national energy-saving regulations. Control energy consumption, water consumption, indoor air quality, use of renewable materials. The rattan material of the Spanish Pavilion, the bamboo material of the Norwegian Pavilion, the natural ventilation design of the World Expo Performing Arts Center, the solar photovoltaic building integration technology of the theme pavilion, the flat greening of the north and south squares of more than 30,000 square meters, The 7000-square-meter vertical greening and the wheat-straw compressed wall and soil materials of the Vanke Enterprise Pavilion are all full manifestations of the green building concept in the World Expo. In the urban best practice area, new energy (photovoltaic power generation, wind power generation, river water source heat pump, LED semiconductor lighting, etc.), intelligent technology (river water source cooling system, ground source system, rainwater collection system, ice storage system, etc.) applied to the specific design and operation of the pavilion.

5.2.2 Shanghai's REEFCR City Construction Principles Under the Low-Carbon World Expo

5.2.2.1 Principle of Economic Development

Urban construction should pursue economic and social development. Of course, such development should be based on the unification of economic, social and environmental benefits. In the construction of a REEFCR city, Shanghai highlights resource conservation, environmental protection, and climate safety, which in turn lays an external foundation for the city's long-term economic development. At the same time, only with good economic development can we provide effective prevention and control measures and standardized management for resource conservation, environmental protection, and climate security. In a word, pursuing rapid economic growth with long-term development as the goal without sacrificing the environment is not only the ultimate goal of Shanghai's REEFCR city construction, but also a necessary way to advance towards the goal of an international metropolis. The level of economic development and the quality of development are the criteria to measure the current situation and prospects of urban construction and development. On the road of green, low-carbon and environmentally friendly urban construction, Shanghai will comprehensively improve the level of the city through the development of the urban economy.

5.2.2.2 People-Oriented Principle

Urban construction is not only a demonstration of the country's economic strength, but also should be put into practice. From the perspective of people's needs, we should build a city that people need. Because the city is a complex of people, without people, the city will also lose the soil for survival. At the same time, with the acceleration of China's urbanization, cities will become the basic areas where the future population will live. The accompanying emergence of "urban diseases" such as high pollution, high consumption, high waste, low ecological benefits, low economic benefits, and low social benefits has caused us to think deeply about how to improve the quality of life and happiness of residents. People-oriented means that urban construction is required to conform to human nature without sacrificing people's survival and development needs. In general, it is necessary to protect the ecological environment and preserve the original historical and cultural environment, as well as to provide sound infrastructure construction, a sound employment mechanism, and so on. The theme of Shanghai World Expo "Better City, Better Life" fully reflects the people-oriented principle. In the Action Plan to Welcome World Expo Civilization, the principle of people-oriented is explained from two aspects: for the people and from the people, that is, the people will actively and extensively participate in promoting the realization of the overall people's interests. During the planning and holding process of the World Expo, not only the site selection, green planning, green buildings, the display of outstanding urban achievements in the best practice area, but also the corresponding supporting measures and services provided to visitors and the follow-up use after the World Expo, which fully demonstrates that people's interests are put in the first place, and from the perspective of people to seek maximized economic utility. All of this benefits from the fact that people are the main body of urban construction and the owner of the achievements of urban construction. Only by focusing on people can we keep up with the constantly improving needs of people, so that cities can achieve rapid development while meeting people's needs.

5.2.2.3 Principles of Ecological Environment Protection

Urban construction should pay equal attention to development and protection. Through the protection of the ecological environment, the existing environmental problems should be treated, and the emergence of new environmental problems should be prevented, so as to achieve the sustainable development of the city and let the city's economy and environment develop in a healthy and harmonious manner. A number of large cities that have risen under the growth model of extensive economy are facing resource and environmental problems brought about by early development, and must seek new green development through the protection of the ecological environment. As an early developed city in China and the largest economic center city at present, Shanghai seeks development under the current wave of low-carbon economy. Shanghai is not only faced with scarce natural resources like land, coal-dominated energy structure, and uneven population quality, but also suffers from the threat of reduced ecological environment quality such as coal-based pollution, water pollution, and domestic waste pollution. Under the trend of global warming, it is inevitable to take the road of low-carbon economy. A low-carbon economy is an economic development model that achieves a win–win situation for economic and social development and ecological and environmental protection by reducing the consumption of high-carbon energy such as coal and oil, in order to achieve less emissions of greenhouse gases. Urban construction is the carrier of realizing a low-carbon economy. Low-carbon energy systems, low-carbon technologies, and low-carbon industrial systems will all be reflected in the construction of REEFCR city. Taking Shanghai World Expo as an example, it is the best practitioner of energy conservation, emission reduction and low carbon. Whether it is the construction of Shanghai World Expo infrastructure and supporting facilities, or the display of outstanding achievements in the construction of human cities in the Shanghai World

Expo area, it is the practice of new energy utilization, environmental protection technology innovation, and green building concepts. In the construction of the REEFCR city, Shanghai must firmly abide by the principle of ecological environment protection, and take the road of urban ecological construction in which population, society, economy, resources and the environment are in harmony.

5.2.2.4 Principles of Scientific and Technological Innovation

The development of science and technology is the direct driving force of economic growth. The application of high technology is a powerful means to reduce consumption, improve utilization and ensure quality. The road of Shanghai's REEFCR urban construction should adhere to the timely transformation of industrial structure and economic structure, the rational management of urban planning and urban construction, and the timely implementation of environmental governance and ecological protection. The knowledge innovation, technological innovation and management innovation in scientific and technological innovation provide a solid guarantee for the realization of these goals. The Shanghai World Expo is a grand event where human scientific and technological achievements are gathered and displayed. While pursuing high-speed urban construction, ensuring high-standard construction quality is inseparable from the application and innovation of high-tech. Shanghai is pursuing the development goal of an international metropolis. In the current REEFCR city construction, Shanghai should increase investment in scientific and technological research and development and innovation. Through the improvement of science and technology, Shanghai will achieve better and faster development.

5.2.3 The Focus of Shanghai's REEFCR City Construction under the Low-Carbon World Expo

Under the increasingly severe challenges of climate change and the increasingly scarce energy supply, energy-saving and low-carbon development has become the mainstream development direction of various countries. How to transform the mode of economic development from extensive to intensive, how to adjust the economic and industrial structure to a service-oriented, innovative and knowledge-based tertiary industry, and how to improve the utilization of new energy and renewable resources in the economic development structure, become the focus of national development today and for a long time to come. As the basic carrier of the integration of economic development, social life and ecological environment, the urban development of Shanghai has a greater mission and practical significance when facing the current tasks of energy conservation, emission reduction and low-carbon development. During the

"12th Five-Year Plan" period (2011–2015), Shanghai has promoted energy conservation, emission reduction and low-carbon development, and released the "12th Five-Year Plan" for Shanghai's energy conservation and climate change response, striving to achieve zero growth in the total consumption of traditional fossil energy by 2020. The goal of reducing carbon dioxide emissions from GDP by 40% to 50% compared to 2005. Shanghai should focus on the following aspects in coping with climate change and building REEFCR city.

5.2.3.1 Research and Development of New Energy

Actively develop new energy utilization technology, energy-saving and low-carbon technology, and change the traditional energy consumption structure dominated by coal power, thermal power generation and petrochemical. Through the full utilization and recycling of energy, it can reduce environmental pollution and ecological damage, realize the natural utilization of resources and the recycling and self-cleaning of the ecosystem.

5.2.3.2 Green Buildings Construction

Vigorously develop green buildings, adopt recyclable and degradable building materials with low pollution and low energy consumption, and scientific and reasonable building planning to rationally utilize various ecological energy sources, thereby maximizing the use of resources and reducing construction waste. According to Table 5.1, from 2005 to 2011, the amount of garbage generated in Shanghai cities showed an increasing trend in general, with the fastest growth in 2011, and the amount of garbage generated was 1.47 times that of 2005. The sharp increase in waste generation in 2011 was due to the increase in construction waste. As can be seen from Fig. 5.3, the construction waste in 2011 increased by 184 percentage points compared with the average of the previous six years.

Table 5.1 Environmental situation in Shanghai

							Unit: 10,000 ton
Year	2005	2006	2007	2008	2009	2010	2011
Garbage Generated(tons)	777	805	852	841	870	890	1142

Source According to the 2012 Shanghai Statistical Yearbook

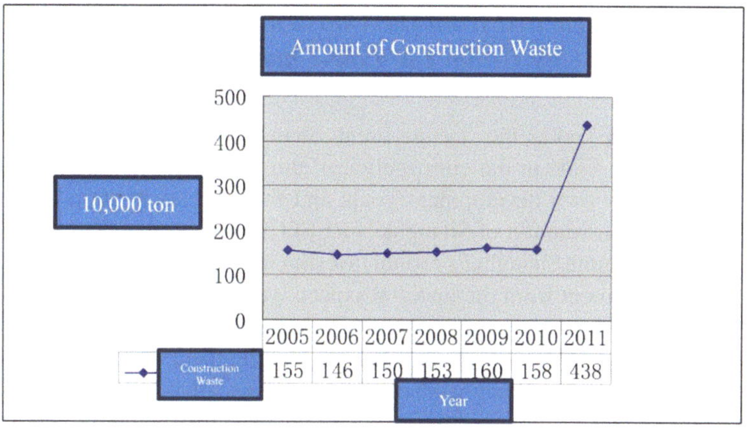

Fig. 5.3 Shanghai urban construction waste generation (*Source* According to the 2012 Shanghai statistical yearbook)

5.2.3.3 Coordinated Development of the New City and the Renovation of the Old City

Actively combine the development of the new city with the renovation of the old city, not only pay attention to the existing environmental and ecological problems of the old city, but also use the old city as a lesson to find an entry point for the perfect connection between the environment and architecture in the construction of the new city, so that the construction of the new city and the renovation of the old city should be carried out at the same time, to create a city image with clarity and development coexisting on the whole.

5.2.3.4 Environmental Protection Concept Promotion

We should not only apply the concept of green environmental protection to urban planning, but also integrate it into the main body of urban life—the life and consumption of residents. From the perspective of demand stimulating consumption, if there is no demand, there will be no supply. If the people living in it have strong consciousness of environmental protection and are active propagandists and practitioners of environmental protection, then the behaviors in the market at the cost of harming the ecological environment will be abandoned, and the cities they live in will become better, and their lives will be happier.

5.2.4 *Lessons Learned from the Construction of Shanghai's REEFCR City Under the Low-Carbon World Expo*

Taking the World Expo as the starting point, Shanghai has shown a good demonstration and leading role in the construction of the REEFCR city. However, in the face of Shanghai's own development goals and the current situation of resource bottlenecks, the construction of Shanghai's REEFCR city needs certain mechanism guarantees. To promote Shanghai's capital investment in the construction of the urban ecological environment from the material aspect, we must also increase the promotion of the mindset of environmental protection, low carbon, green and livable city from the consciousness level to guide the green development action. In general, the REEFCR construction of Shanghai needs to achieve sustainable urban development with government orientation, public participation, scientific planning, and rational construction.

5.2.4.1 Government Orientation

The government needs to provide guarantees for the construction of REEFCR cities in terms of systems and funds. On the one hand, the system is inclined, which guides the construction of REEFCR cities. It can also be seen from the above that the Shanghai Municipal Government has established a series of rules and regulations in response to some urban construction problems and development needs under the background of national policies and its own characteristics. On the other hand, for capital investment, the Shanghai government has increased capital investment in ecological environment construction, not only to control existing ecological environment problems, but also to give priority to urban planning and construction projects that meet environmental protection standards. Government orientation is the strong external environmental support for the construction of Shanghai's REEFCR city. Under the positive orientation of the government, it will guide the sustainable development of Shanghai.

5.2.4.2 Public Participation

On the one hand, the government should strengthen the publicity of ecological environmental protection awareness, enhance people's environmental protection consciousness from the awareness level, and practice this concept from the small things around them; on the one hand, it is necessary to formulate corresponding rules and regulations to give negative reinforcement to behaviors that do not conform to the corresponding environmental protection, so as to prevent such behaviors from recurring. Encouraging and advocating public participation can not only make the needs of the public more practical, but also through the improvement of the public's self-awareness of environmental protection, social supervision and extraction of opinions on some behaviors that seriously affect the ecological environment in Shanghai's urban construction, so as to allow urban construction walk along the right path.

5.2.4.3 Scientific Planning

Scientific planning is the premise of rational construction. Without a scientific planning, the rationality of construction is just out of reach. When scientific planning rises to a strategic level, the government needs to participate and supervise the whole process. It is necessary to carefully approve urban planning projects. Reject projects that do not meet the unification of ecological and environmental benefits and social and economic benefits. It is also necessary to actively participate in the planning of relevant urban areas, and use the existing high-tech planning talents to provide talent support and technical guarantee for scientific planning. In the current urban planning of Shanghai, it is necessary to actively promote the construction of an international central business district in the Expo area, speed up the construction of the Disney project, promote the construction of the Hongqiao Business District—a gathering place for business development, and promote the construction of suburban new towns.

5.2.4.4 Rational Construction

As a historical old city with early development, Shanghai not only has early buildings with strong historical and cultural colors and ancient buildings left, but also has unreasonable urban construction in the early urbanization stage. In the current urban construction, it is necessary to match the future urban development with the current construction status and style, which not only requires a reasonable urban planning, but also puts the actual construction status of the urban planning in the first place. From the perspective of reasonable construction, such a supervision mechanism controlled by the government and public participation is required to make timely adjustments to the construction situation that is unreasonable and violates the relevant laws and regulations on ecological and environmental protection, so as to ensure the implementation of scientific planning to benefit the public.

From above guidance of the principles of people-oriented, ecological environment protection, scientific and technological innovation and economic development, Shanghai needs to rely on the mechanism of government guidance, public participation, scientific planning and reasonable construction to focus on the research and development of new energy, develop green buildings, coordinate the development of new cities and the transformation of old cities, and publicize the concept of environmental protection, so as to better build a REEFCR city and promote the green and sustainable development of the city, As shown in Fig. 5.4.

The Shanghai World Expo is a green world expo, which fully reflects the harmony between people and the natural environment and between people. It also fully demonstrates the innovative urban construction concept and sustainable urban planning

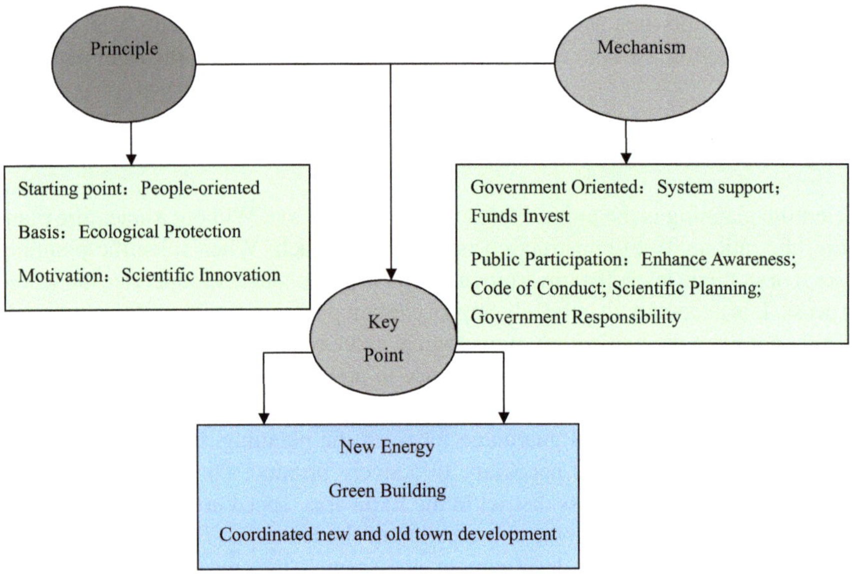

Fig. 5.4 REEFCR city construction in Shanghai

scheme. It is a practice of low-carbon, green, environmental protection and sustainable REEFCR urban construction. No matter from Shanghai's own demand for sustainable development, the trend of rapid urbanization, or the goal of an international metropolis, Shanghai's REEFCR city construction will play an increasingly important role. Under the theme of "Better City, Better Life", the Shanghai World Expo is a good starting point for the construction of Shanghai's REEFCR city. The post-World Expo era will surely bring a new round of economic development, social harmony, and ecological civilization to Shanghai.

5.3 "China Electricity Valley"—Baoding Practice

In the context of global warming, the development of a low-carbon economy has become the consensus of the international community. As early as 2006, Baoding City clearly put forward the strategic concept of building "Baoding—China Electricity Valley", and started to focus on the development of low-carbon economy. Relying on the foundation of new energy and energy equipment industry in Baoding National High-Tech Zone, cultivate six major industrial systems of wind power, photovoltaic, biomass power generation, power saving, power storage, power transmission and transformation, so as to build Baoding into a new energy with international influence Industry Base. At the beginning of 2008, with its leading advantages in the development and application of new energy industry, Baoding was listed as the first batch of "Low-Carbon City Project Pilot Cities" by the World Wide Fund for Nature. In August 2010, Baoding, together with eight cities including Tianjin, Chongqing, Shenzhen, Xiamen, Hangzhou, Nanchang and Guiyang, became China's first pilot cities to develop low-carbon industries and build low-carbon cities.

Baoding is a typical inland medium-sized city with a large population density and sufficient cheap labor, but its resources are relatively poor, and its development lags behind the eastern region. It has a good location advantage and is adjacent to China's capital city. It is an important city in the Bohai Rim Economic Circle, located in Beijing, Tianjin and Tang Industrial Zone. Due to the advanced geographic location, Baoding can benefit from big cities in terms of technology, investment, talents and other factors. Baoding's ecological environment is relatively weak, and at the same time it shoulders the major mission of protecting Baiyangdian Lake and maintaining the ecological environment of the Beijing-Tianjin area. Therefore, in the process of accelerating urbanization and industrialization, it is required to combine urban construction and ecological protection, and completely abandon the traditional and extensive type of production and lifestyle. In this context, Baoding's low-carbon city path is closely aligned with the national development requirements. Baoding's path of "Developing New Energy Industry, Building China's Electric Valley, and Building a Low-Carbon REEFCR City" is walking towards a scientific and sustainable development.

5.3.1 Baoding's Low Carbon Economic Development Road

The main focus of Baoding's low-carbon economic development road is to develop new energy industry and apply new energy technology achievements to urban life, so as to truly build a low-carbon city in an all-round way. When it was identified as the first batch of "Pilot Cities for Low-Carbon City Projects", Baoding seized the opportunity to formulate the first Low Carbon City Development Plan in China, and then issued the Opinions on Building a Low-carbon City, which clarified as "one concept", "three main tasks" and "five key projects" of building a low-carbon city in Baoding.

5.3.1.1 "One Concept"

To explore an ecological and civilized development road that conforms to Baoding's development reality, energy conservation, environmental protection and green low-carbon, with the urban economy dominated by low-carbon industry, citizens taking low-carbon life as the concept and behavior characteristics, and the government taking low-carbon society as the construction blueprint.

5.3.1.2 "Three Main Tasks"

Firstly, develop low-carbon economy and cultivate low-carbon industries. Accelerate the development of new energy and energy equipment manufacturing industry, further improve the six industrial systems, create "China's Electric Valley", and build an industrial support system for low-carbon cities. Secondly, establish a low-carbon concept and build a low-carbon society. By carrying out various social activities, to establish a low-carbon awareness and concept among departments at all levels and the general public, and promote low-carbon lifestyles and urban construction. Thirdly, strengthen low-carbon management and strengthen energy conservation and emission reduction. Energy conservation and emission reduction in industrial enterprises, in buildings, in urban transportation and in commercial circulation, as well as rural energy conservation needs to be enhanced.

5.3.1.3 "Five Key Projects"

Firstly, the construction project of "China Electric Valley": strive to achieve the output value of new energy and energy equipment industry of 150 billion yuan by 2015, making Baoding one of the leading cities in the development of China's new energy industry. Secondly, the construction project of "Solar City": strive to achieve 90% of solar lighting in urban courtyards and public places through five years of construction, and basically achieve the integration of solar facilities in new buildings. Thirdly, urban ecological environment construction project: implement the "Blue Sky Action", plan to ban all 1100 decentralized coal-fired boilers in the urban area in three years, and implement the "Green Water Plan" focusing on urban sewage treatment plants and large water system construction. Accelerate the construction of urban water system to build "Two Rings, Four Corridors, Five Lakes and Ten Parks". At the same time, "Green Shade Action" and "Forest with Carbon Plan" which focusing on urban greening will be implement and strive to achieve 13.5 square meters of green space per capita, 43% green coverage and 40% green space coverage by 2015, manage to become a National Garden City and a National Forest City. Fourthly, the demonstration project of low-carbon communities: by 2015, the scale of low-carbon community construction will reach 50% of the existing communities. Fifthly, the low-carbon urban transportation system integration project: carry out the low-carbon transportation integration scheme design, vigorously advocate low-carbon travel, control the development of high fuel consumption and high pollution automobile, encourage the production and use of energy-saving and environment-friendly vehicles, new energy vehicles and electric vehicles, and accelerate the construction of natural gas booster stations and electric vehicle charging stations. By 2015, a bus rapid transit system will be established and a fast public transport network will be built within the urban area and between the urban area and the satellite city.[7]

5.3.2 *The Construction Effort of "China Electric Valley" in Baoding*

In the process of building "China Electric Valley", Baoding City will combine the utilization of new energy with urban infrastructure construction, which better reflects the requirements of developing a low-carbon economy, and creates a new business card for Baoding—"Solar City".

In 2007, Baoding City launched a project called "Solar City" to widely promote the application of photovoltaic LEDs and photothermal products throughout the city to build Baoding into a leading city in the development and application of China's new energy industry. The project will be like "sunshine" to illuminate Baoding, warm Baoding, integrate into Baoding life, and promote Baoding Development. In 2012, the blue solar photovoltaic panels have spread all over the streets and alleys of Baoding City, and even the corners of large and small tourist attractions, squares, campuses, institutions and communities in Baoding City. The completed solar energy application project can save 21 million kilowatt hours of electricity and reduce 17 thousand tons of sulfur dioxide emission every year. It can save energy and reduce harmful gas emissions and protect the urban ecological environment. As a result, Baoding has also been named as the first demonstration city with comprehensive solar energy application specifications in China, and has been rated as "China's top 20 cities for energy conservation and emission reduction".

It can be seen from below charts that Baoding is striving to achieve "resource conservation" in general. From the comparative analysis of energy consumption in Baoding, we can see that the energy saving effect of Baoding is obviously better than that of Hebei Province, but far behind that of Beijing. At the same time, the energy saving ability is not stable enough, especially the energy consumption per unit of industrial added value. As a result, Baoding must make more efforts to control energy consumption and save resources in the transformation of the new development model of the secondary industry; at the same time, when building a low-carbon city to develop a low-carbon economy, Baoding should firmly grasp the source of energy, and explore a better way to build a low-carbon economy (Figs. 5.5, 5.6, 5.7).

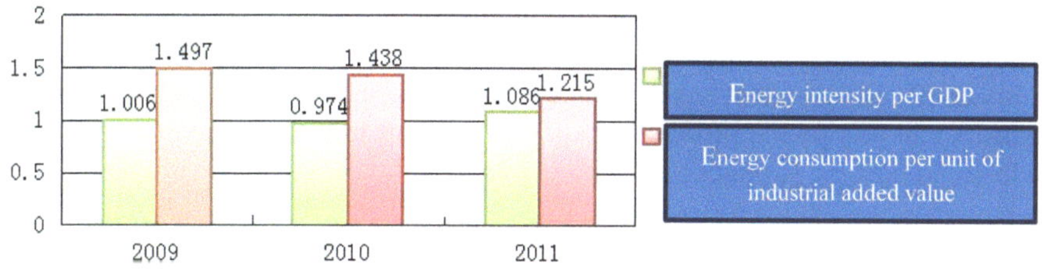

Fig. 5.5 Analysis of energy consumption in baoding from 2009 to 2011

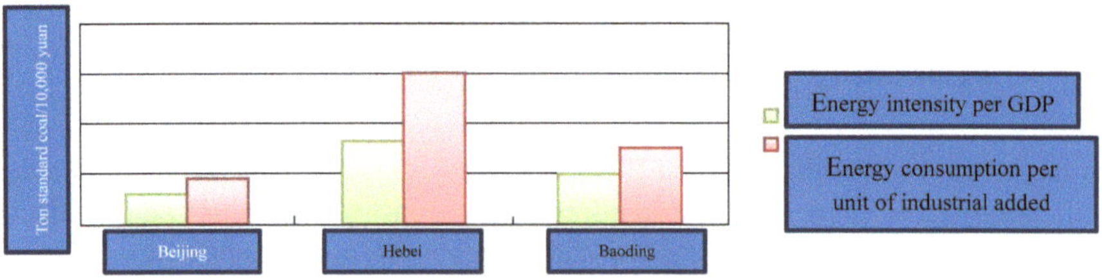

Fig. 5.6 Comparison of absolute energy consumption among Beijing, Hebei and Baoding

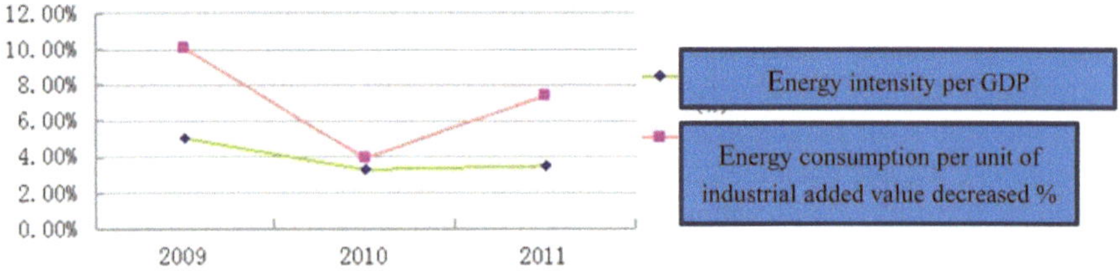

Fig. 5.7 Relative analysis of energy consumption in Baoding from 2009 to 2011 (*Source* statistical bulletin of national economic and social development of Baoding City in relevant years)

5.3.3 Development of New Energy Industry: Leading Enterprises-Driven Overall Development

As an emerging industry derived from the discovery and application of new energy, the development of new energy industry has become an irresistible trend. To build a low-carbon city, it is necessary to make a fundamental structural adjustment in the use of energy, and actively promote the comprehensive development and utilization of solar energy, natural gas, geothermal energy, biogas and other clean energy in the production and living fields. As the fastest growing and most powerful supporting industry in Baoding's economic development, the new energy industry is now an extremely important growth point in the process of Baoding's economic development. It plays a leading role in the implementation of low carbon economy in Baoding and is the first way to achieve low-carbon economy in Baoding. The development of new energy industry in Baoding City has an obvious feature, which is to focus on cultivating leading enterprises in each new energy industry, so that each new energy industry can rely on the powerful leading enterprises to develop, so as to drive the industry to become stronger.

1. In the wind power industry, AVIC Huiteng Wind Power Equipment Co., Ltd., as a leading enterprise in the industry, is the only enterprise in China that can independently research and develop wind power blades. Due to its development, China Electric Valley has formed the most complete wind power machine, wind power component R&D and manufacturing industry cluster in China, leading the development of China's wind power industry in the fields of technology

research and development, talent training, equipment testing and certification, and standard formulation.

2. In terms of solar energy industry, Tianwei Yingli Co., Ltd. is the only domestic manufacturer of polycrystalline silicon solar cells with a full industrial chain, with an annual output of 600 MW of solar cells and modules, accounting for about 1/10 of the world's output. Under its strong driving force, China's PV industry in Electric Valley has formed a group of enterprises, including photovoltaic organization and production, photovoltaic system control and inverter device production, photothermal product manufacturing, photovoltaic power station system design, construction, operation, and photovoltaic LED lighting device production. The industry chain involves photovoltaic, photovoltaic products, R&D, manufacturing and application. In terms of urban construction application, solar photovoltaic lighting is widely used in urban roads, squares, offices, courtyards, parks and other places. At present, about 10,000 solar lamps installed and used can save 18.3 million kilowatt hours of electricity a year.
3. In terms of power transmission and transformation and energy conservation industry, China Electric Valley has cultivated a number of major original independent innovation projects in the field of power conservation. It has a number of major independent innovation technologies in the three major links of power transmission, distribution and utilization, including large power grid stability system control technology, large motor cascade speed regulation power saving technology, composite optical cable technology, etc., which can greatly improve the power saving efficiency.[8] Baoding Tianwei Group, as the largest power transmission and transformation manufacturing base in China with complete industrial chain and complete independent intellectual property rights, has ranked first in the world in terms of transformer output for three consecutive years.
4. In terms of photovoltaic industry, Yingli Group is the leading company in Baoding High tech Zone, which on one hand maintains the large-scale expansion of photovoltaic modules, on the other hand, accelerates the construction of industrial system, and has entered the substantial project operation stage in terms of high-purity silicon production, localization of supporting products, etc. At present, Baoding High-tech Zone has a polysilicon production capacity of 3000 tons, and a capacity of 600 megawatts for ingots, silicon wafers, batteries and modules. A complete industrial chain for research, development, manufacturing and application of solar photovoltaic products has been formed, and an international solar photovoltaic industrial system is developing.[9]
5. In the energy storage equipment industry, Fengfan Group, famous for its branding "good horse with good saddle, good car with Fengfan", is the largest enterprise with the strongest technical strength and the highest market share in China's leading-acid battery industry. Fengfan battery is matched with more than 40 mainstream models at home and abroad. More than 70% of medium and high-end cars produced in China are equipped with Fengfan battery.[10]

Baoding has cultivated six industrial systems to build "China's Electricity Valley", namely, photovoltaic, wind power, biomass power generation, power saving, power storage, power transmission and transformation. During the "12th Five Year Plan" period (2011—2015), one of the focuses of new energy development and utilization is the utilization of clean energy such as solar photovoltaic power generation and wind power generation. China is a large producer of photovoltaic solar energy, and the photovoltaic industry is also one of the new energy industries in China with international influence.

Baoding's biggest advantage in building a "China Electric Valley" lies in Baoding National High Tech Zone, which is known as the "Cradle of China's Electric Valley Miracle". Baoding National High Tech Zone was established in 1992. Combining its own regional advantages and industrial characteristics, it chose a development path with new energy industry as the main direction, and was rated as the "Economic Park with the Most Investment Potential in China" in 2010. At present, it is the only "National New Energy and Energy Equipment Industry Base" and "National Science and Technology Trade Promotion Export Innovation Base (new energy)" in China. The new energy and energy equipment industry represented by wind energy and solar energy has a strong industrial foundation. The development goal of Baoding High Tech Zone in the new era is "China Smart Power Valley, North Low Carbon New City", which emphasizes to build a new science and technology city with international influence under the guidance of low carbon concept, supported by characteristic industries, and driven by scientific and technological innovation. It can be seen that the development of "China Electric Valley" is inseparable from the development of "Baoding High Tech Zone". The following are a number of "first" glories based on the strategy of Baoding High Tech Zone and China Electric Valley: China's first large-scale solar cell manufacturer with a full industrial chain; China's first high-power wind turbine blade research and development center; China's first large-scale wind turbine machine exported to the United States; China's first large wind turbine transmission detection platform; China's first diameter Φ 320 mm germanium single crystal rod; the first solar photovoltaic building in China.

In recent years, the development of Baoding's "China Electric Valley" has shown great vitality. It has been successively named as the National Renewable Energy Industrialization Base, the National New Energy Hi Tech Industry Base, the National Torch Plan New Energy and Energy Equipment Industry Base, the New Energy Hi Tech Export Innovation Base, and the National New Industrialization Demonstration Base, all above forming a good national policy platform and establishing an important leading position in the low-carbon industry. Now it is marching towards the goal of building World-Class Park.

5.4 Trial on Building Resource-Efficient, Environment-Friendly City—Wuhan Practice

Wuhan City Circle refers to the city circle with Wuhan as the center, including Xianning, Huangshi, Huanggang, Xiantao, Tianmen, Ezhou, Qianjiang and Xiaogan. Therefore, it is also called "1 + 8" city circle. Wuhan city circle, which covers half of Hubei Province's population and two-thirds of its GDP, is an important indicator of Hubei's economic development; at the same time, "Wuhan City Circle", as the first of the four major urban circles in central China, plays a pivotal role in China's "Rise of Central China" strategy. With the continuous progress of urbanization and the deepening of industrialization, urban development and industrial production are increasingly demanding and damaging the nature. The resource and environment situation in the urban circle is not optimistic. The traditional development mode has become an obstacle to the sustainable development of the urban economy. Only by accelerating the transformation of the economic development mode, saving resources, protecting the environment, and maintaining the ecological balance can Wuhan's urban economy develop well and rapidly.

In December 2007, Wuhan City Circle was approved to be a comprehensive supporting reform pilot area for building a national resource-efficient and environment-friendly city (hereinafter referred to as "REEF" city). The construction of "REEF" city has pointed out the general direction for the development of Wuhan City Circle, that is, starting from the actual situation of the region, combining the requirements of resource-efficient and environment-friendly society construction, changing the mode of economic development, speeding up industrial upgrading, comprehensively promoting the reform of economy, science and technology, transportation and other fields, and ultimately driving the development of the central region. Fully understand and analyze the characteristics of the "REEF" city, Wuhan City Circle has launched the construction of the REEFCR city based on the construction of "REEF" city by focusing on the three key points of resources, environment and ecology. With the implementation of a number of major projects, the city circle has made remarkable achievements in ecological construction, environmental protection, resource conservation, etc.

5.4.1 Major Achievements of National Pilot Cities for Water Ecosystem Protection and Restoration

In 2005, Wuhan was approved by the Ministry of Water Resources as one of the first pilot cities for water ecosystem protection and restoration in China. In order to coordinate the restoration and construction of the water ecosystem, Wuhan has successively issued several local regulations and normative documents. During the "12th Five Year Plan" period (2011—2015), according to the completed "12th Five Year Plan Draft of Wuhan Environmental Protection", Wuhan plans to focus on the implementation of eight major environmental protection projects, including water environment protection, at a rate of 3% (the proportion of GDP) of the environmental protection investment index each year. The total investment will be four times that during the "10th Five Year Plan" period. It has provided support for the comprehensive construction of Wuhan "1 + 8" Urban Circle Comprehensive Supporting Reform Pilot Zone for a resource-saving and environment-friendly society approved by the State Council.

5.4.1.1 Sewage Treatment—"Clean Water Entering the Lake" Project

The project of "Clean Water Entering the Lake" started in April 2006, which is an emergency protection measure taken by Wuhan to prevent industrial wastewater and domestic sewage from being directly discharged into the lake. Wuhan first defined the "three lines" according to the regional topography of 40 lakes in the central area of Wuhan and the basic situation of land use around the lakes, that is, the "blue line" determined according to the highest control water level of the lakes, the "green line" determined according to the green land and its control range, and the "gray line" defining the normal land and controllable land. The definition of these three lines has laid a foundation for the subsequent lake protection work. On the basis of the "third lines", the main work of the second phase of the project is to formally implement sewage interception. The key of sewage interception is "pollution control", and the key of "pollution control" is the construction of sewage treatment infrastructure. In terms of sewage treatment, Wuhan City adopts the way of centralized treatment as the main and decentralized treatment as the auxiliary. On the one hand, it continuously improves the construction of pipe networks and strengthens the pollution control of main pipe networks in the city; on the other hand, for the outlets that cannot achieve centralized treatment, Wuhan City conducts differentiated and decentralized treatment according to the discharge volume and water quality characteristics of sewage from different outlets, ensuring the overall effect of sewage interception in the city.

According to the data in Table 5.2 and Fig. 5.8, from the perspective of absolute value, the sewage treatment plants in Wuhan increased from 2005 to 2010, and the total annual sewage treatment capacity also doubled. The average sewage treatment capacity of each sewage treatment plant in 2010 was 54 million tons, more than twice that of 2005. It can be seen that the sewage treatment level in Wuhan has improved in terms of quantity.

From Fig. 5.9, we can draw the following conclusions: from 2005 to 2010, the sewage treatment rate in Wuhan has steadily improved. The sewage treatment rate in 2010 is three times that of 2005, reaching a high level of 80.03%. From Table 5.3, it can be clearly seen that the total sewage discharge in Wuhan from 2005 to 2010 has basically remained stable. Due to technological progress, management improvement and other reasons, the sewage treatment rate has increased, the sewage treatment volume has increased year by year, and the water pollution control has achieved remarkable results.

Table 5.2 Analysis of wastewater treatment capacity in Wuhan (2005–2010)

Year	Sewage treatment plant	Treatment volume (100 million tons)	Average treatment capacity (100 million tons)
2005	7	1.79	0.26
2006	8	2.98	0.37
2007	10	3.10	0.31
2008	10	4.57	0.46
2009	10	5.26	0.53
2010	10	5.37	0.54

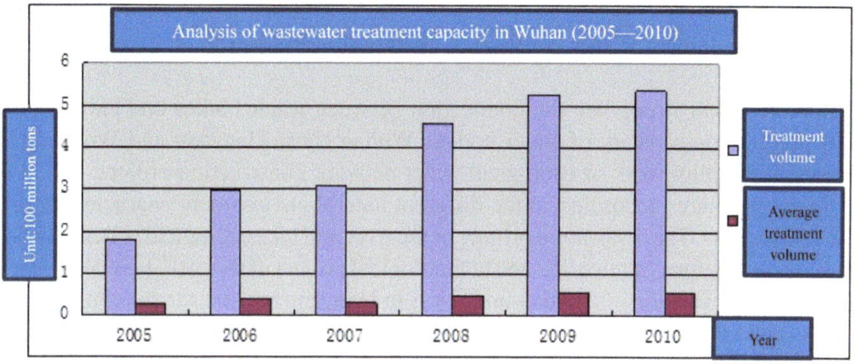

Fig. 5.8 Analysis of wastewater treatment capacity in Wuhan (2005–2010) (*Source* According to the 2005–2010 Wuhan Water Environment Status Bulletin)

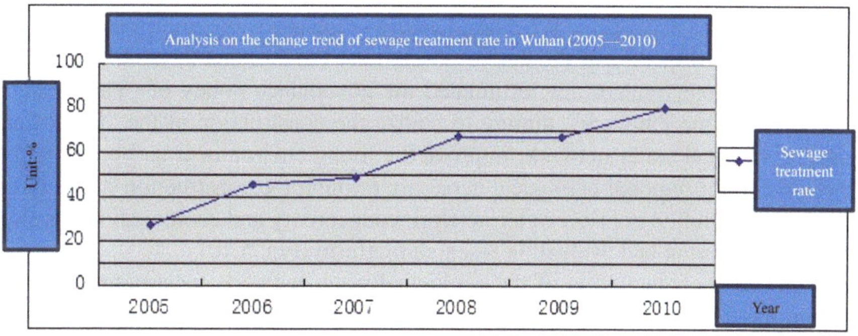

Fig. 5.9 Analysis on the change trend of sewage treatment rate in Wuhan (2005–2010) (*Source* According to the 2005–2010 Wuhan water environment status bulletin)

Table 5.3 Analysis of sewage treatment rate in Wuhan (2005–2010)

Year	Total sewage discharge (100 million tons)	Sewage treatment volume (100 million tons)	Sewage treatment rate (%)
2005	6.57	1.79	27.25
2006	6.57	2.98	45.36
2007	6.37	3.10	48.67
2008	7.89	4.57	67.21
2009	7.84	5.26	67.09
2010	6.71	5.37	80.03

5.4.1.2 Ecological Water Network Construction Project

The project will strengthen the connection between water bodies and enhance the self-purification capacity of water bodies. Wuhan chose Hanyang and Wuchang to carry out the pilot work of ecological water network construction project, and took different measures according to the different natural environment characteristics of the two regions. The restoration project of the river and lake ecological water network in Hanyang region is a scientific and technological project of the "10th Five Year Plan" in China. It covers the main lakes and rivers in Hanyang and the surrounding waters. The project emphasizes the connection of Longyang Lake and North South Taizi Lake, and the restoration of the connection between rivers and lakes. Through the restoration of the connection of various water bodies, they can be interconnected to form a dynamic water network, so as to accelerate the virtuous cycle of water bodies and strengthen the self-purification ability of water bodies. The construction of the ecological water network in Wuchang District emphasizes the improvement of the water ecological quality of the whole "Great East Lake" water system. In order to achieve this goal, Wuhan has formulated the governance policy of "Three Major Projects and One Platform", aiming to realize the construction of the "Great East Lake" ecological water network, improve the living environment and promote the development of regional ecological economy through the construction of the three projects of pollution control, water network connectivity and ecological restoration and the monitoring and evaluation research platform (Fig. 5.10).

With the implementation of the ecological water network construction project, Wuhan has achieved the governance goal of "turning stagnant water into active water", connected all water systems in Wuhan, gradually formed a perfect ecological water network, enhanced the exchange ability of water bodies, significantly improved the restoration function of the water ecological environment, and finally improved the water ecological quality of the main lakes and rivers in Hanyang and the surrounding waters, as well as the entire "Great East Lake" water system. Through the project of "Clean Water Flowing into the Lake", Wuhan has established ecological sewage treatment facilities, increased the efforts of manual pollution control, successfully reduced the discharge of industrial wastewater and domestic sewage from the source, and improved the water quality of rivers and lakes within the territory.

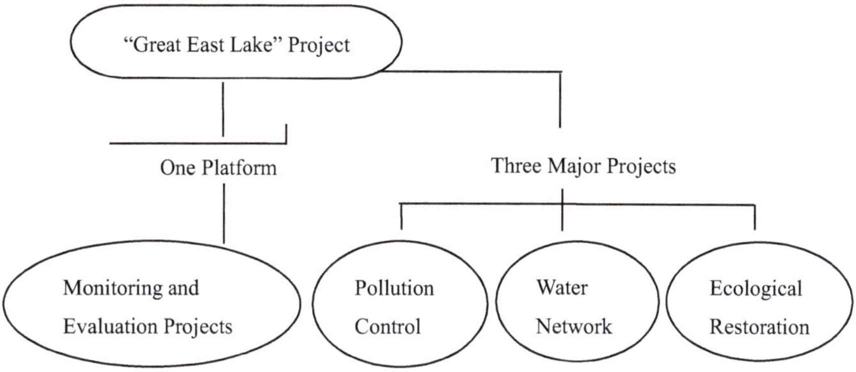

Fig. 5.10 "Great East Lake" project

We collected the data on water quality of rivers and lakes in Wuhan Water Environment Status Bulletin from 2005 to 2010, and drew the following figure:

From Figs. 5.11 and 5.12, we can see that the water quality of most rivers and lakes in Wuhan is classified as Class II or Class III. Since Wuhan was approved by the Ministry of Water Resources as one of the first pilot cities for water ecosystem protection and restoration in China in 2005, the water quality of rivers and lakes in Wuhan has improved obviously; since 2007, due to the construction of the "REEF" society, the government's financial support for water ecological governance has been further increased. Two sewage treatment plants have been built to improve the overall sewage treatment capacity. In addition to Wuhan's years of experience in water control, the water quality of rivers has generally improved, and the water quality of lakes has also been steadily and continuously improved. It can be seen that the water quality of rivers and lakes in Wuhan has been greatly improved after five years of water ecological treatment.

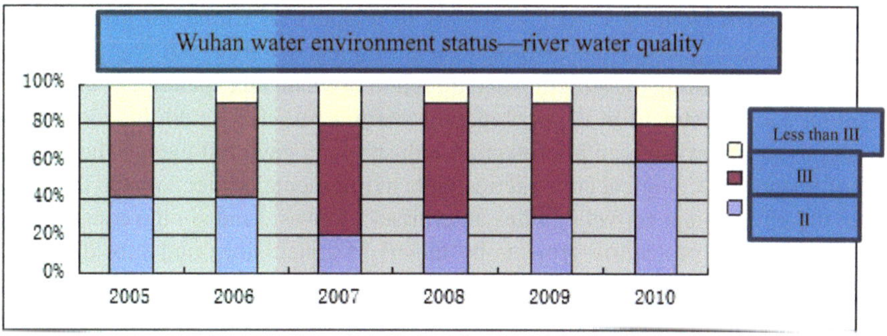

Fig. 5.11 Analysis on water quality changes of rivers in Wuhan City (2005–2010) (*Source* According to the 2005–2010 Wuhan Water Environment Status Bulletin)

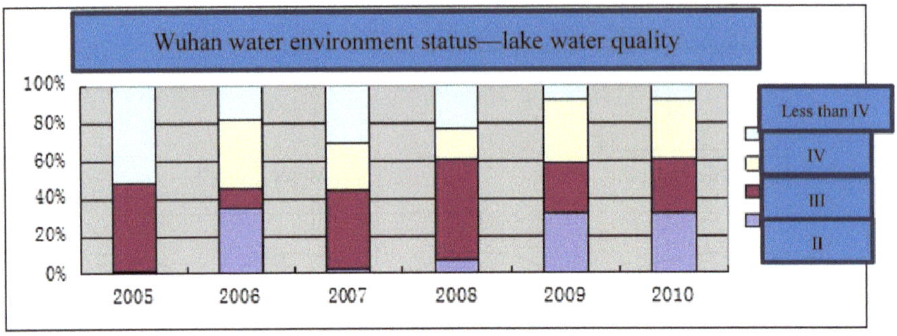

Fig. 5.12 Analysis of lake water quality change in Wuhan City (2005–2010) (*Source* According to the 2005–2010 Wuhan Water Environment Status Bulletin)

5.4.2 *Practices and Experiences of Pilot Cities for Water Ecosystem Protection and Restoration*

In September 2008, the People's Government of Hubei Province officially adopted the Outline of the Ecological Environment Planning for the Construction of the "REEF" Society in Wuhan City Circle. Wuhan seized the opportunity and took a series of measures to improve the development of environmental protection industries, actively raised funds for the ecological construction of the city circle, mobilized the power of the government, society and market, and made efforts to promote the diversification of investment subjects and investment channels, also encourage all sectors of society to invest in the construction of the ecological environment of the city circle. The following are the main practices and experiences:

5.4.2.1 Government Investment Increasement

In the process of building a "REEF" society in Wuhan City Circle, the government, on the one hand, carried out a reform on ecological security and environmental protection by adjusting the structure and direction of financial expenditure, increased attention and investment in the ecological environment, stimulated the continuous development of environmental protection industry, and gave full play to the special role of finance in ecological construction and environmental protection. On the other hand, the government actively guides enterprises to invest funds in the construction of environmental protection projects by means of concessions and subsidies, and develops a performance evaluation mechanism to give greater preferential treatment to environmental protection project investment. In addition, governments at all levels in the city circle must also pay close attention to the financial budget, incorporate the environmental protection budget into their own financial budget, and make strict regulations on the proportion and annual growth rate of the environmental protection budget.

5.4.2.2 Establishment of Ecological Environment Protection Fund and Special Fund for Development of Environmental Protection Industry in Urban Agglomeration

Since the beginning of the construction of the "REEF" society, Wuhan City Circle has planned to establish the Wuhan City Circle Ecological Environment Protection Foundation. The main task of the Foundation is to widely accept donations of various tangible assets and intangible assets from various regions, and provide financial, material and technical support for the ecological construction and environmental protection of Wuhan City Circle. The special fund for the development of environmental protection industry set up by the People's Government of Hubei Province, which is based on the provincial financial budget arrangement. The fund is mainly used to support the ecological construction and environmental protection industry development of Wuhan Urban Circle, and ensure the smooth implementation of the experiment of "REEF" society. In addition, the city circle also raises funds by issuing special water environment governance bonds. The issuance of special governance bonds for water environment is another innovative measure of Wuhan City Circle to improve water environment and raise environmental protection funds. This measure attempts to raise funds for water pollution control by issuing bonds. It focuses on the prevention and control of water pollution of rivers and lakes in the urban circle, the restoration of urban wetland ecosystems, and the promotion and application of ecological and environmental protection technologies.

5.4.2.3 Pilot Reform of Environmental Taxes and Fees

In order to take the lead in eliminating the impact of tax policies that are not conducive to environmental protection and ecological construction, improve the green degree of national tax revenue, and regulate and guide the production behavior of operators and the consumption behavior of consumers from the perspective of taxation, Wuhan Metropolitan Area has applied to the relevant national departments for the reform of the environmental tax collection system. The first specific content of the environmental tax system reform of the tax is to carry out the value-added tax reform, and implement the tax preference on value-added tax for certified energy saving and environmental protection product manufacturers and enterprises that effectively develop and utilize renewable energy, actively promote the circular economy and achieve "zero emissions". Secondly, reinvestment tax rebate is implemented for environmental protection and energy conservation enterprises, especially for large energy conservation and environmental protection enterprises. After the enterprise's tax is truthful and paid to the treasury on schedule, the local finance will subsidize and return the part of annual revenue growth to the enterprise.

5.4.2.4 Water Control According to Law

Before the formal commencement of water ecosystem protection and restoration, Wuhan formulated the Wuhan Water Ecosystem Protection and Restoration Plan, which defined the basic direction of the project, and on this basis, prepared the Wuhan Water Ecosystem Protection and Restoration Pilot Work Implementation Plan, which provides a specific implementation plan for the implementation of the project. The formulation of the Plan and the Implementation Plan is the policy basis for water ecological protection and restoration. In addition, Wuhan has also started the construction of relevant laws and regulations, and has successively issued a number of local regulations and a series of relevant normative documents, such as Wuhan Lake Protection Regulations, Wuhan Urban Drainage Regulations, Wuhan Water and Soil Conservation Regulations, which provide legal protection for the work.

5.5 Low Carbon Consumption Model—Nanchang Practice

Since the twenty-first century, Nanchang has been committed to build a green development path, from the concept of "not only golden mountains and silver mountains, but also green water and green mountains", to the in-depth implementation of the concept of "Ecological City" and "Green Development", to the strategic practice of Poyang Lake Ecological Economic Zone. In order to implement the sustainable development strategy, transform the economic development mode and improve the industrial information structure, Nanchang has formulated the development goal of "Building a Low-Carbon City and Achieving Green Rise". After that, Nanchang became the only central provincial capital city in China to develop a low-carbon economy pilot. Nanchang City conducts urban low-carbon operation under the leadership of the government, implements a sustainable urban low-carbon consumption mode, and realizes the urban low-carbon consumption mode and green lifestyle by building a green transportation system, developing green buildings, changing residents' lifestyle, etc.

5.5.1 Current Situation of Ecological Environment in Nanchang

5.5.1.1 Abundant Natural Resources

Nanchang, known as "seven gates, nine states and eighteen slopes, and three lakes and nine waterway connecting Jiangxi and Poyang", is a modern city integrating modern and ancient times. Nanchang is developed by water and thrives on the edge of water. It has the natural terrain of "West Mountain and East Water", and is a veritable oriental water city with extremely rich water resources. Nanchang is dotted with rivers, lakes and ponds. With Poyang Lake as the center, there are hundreds of lakes of different sizes, such as Qingshan Lake, Jinxi Lake, Qinglan Lake and Yao Lake. In the northeast of the urban area, there are Aixi Lake, Qingshan Lake and Xianshi Lake. The city has four scenic lakes in the east, west, south and north. Nanchang has 210,400 hectares of arable land. The effective irrigation area is 189,800 hectares, accounting for 90.2%. In the effective irrigation area, the area of harvest during droughts and floods is 155,700 hectares, accounting for 82.0% (Tables 5.4, 5.5, 5.6, 5.7).

Nanchang has 132,000 hectares of forest land, 17.1% forest coverage, and 2.2 million cubic meters of standing trees. There are 413 kinds of main trees, including pine, fir and camphor. Gingko, metasequoia, known as living fossil, and kiwi, known as the king of fruits are also scattered. Timber forest and firewood forest are in the majority, accounting for 39% and 31.8% of the forest land area respectively; the proportion of protective forest and special forest is relatively small, accounting for 20.9% and 4.5% of the forest land area respectively.

Table 5.4 Water area of Nanchang city

Total area(km^2)	Water area(km^2)	Percentage(%)
7402.36	2204.37	29.78

Table 5.5 Water volume of Nanchang city

Annual average water yield(100 million cubic meters)	Surface water resources(100 million cubic meters)	Surface runoff(100 million cubic meters)	Reduction water volume(100 million cubic meters)	Groundwater resources(100 million cubic meters)
66.25	61.53	51.42	4.07	14.97

Table 5.6 Nanchang water resources

Water resource reserves(10,000 kilowatts)	Resources available for development(10,000 kilowatts)	Percentage(%)
7.27	3.45	33.7

Table 5.7 Proportion of forest land in Nanchang

Forest area (10,000 hectares)	Forest coverage(%)	Volume of standing trees (10,000 m3)	Proportion of timber forest(%)
3.2	17.1	220	39
Proportion of fuel forest(%)	Proportion of shelter forest(%)	Proportion of special forests(%)	
31.8	20.9	4.5	

Nanchang has a wide variety of wild animals and plants. There are more than 480 kinds of wild animals, including more than 20 national protected birds and 12 rare birds (Fig. 5.13).

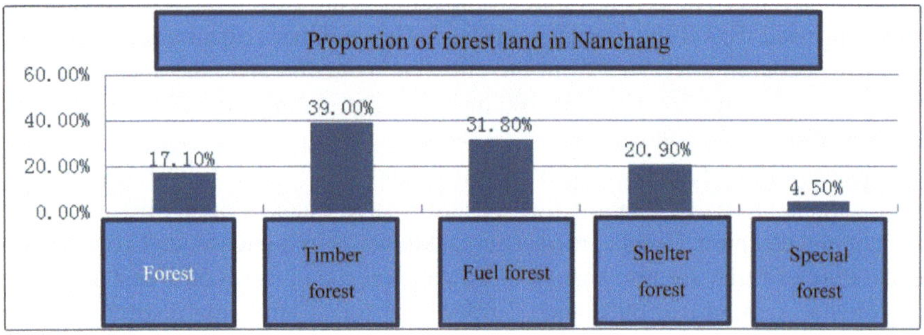

Fig. 5.13 Histogram of specific gravity of forest land in Nanchang City

5.5.1.2 Good Climatic Conditions

Nanchang has a subtropical humid monsoon climate, with a mild climate and ample sunshine. The midsummer and winter of a year are long, and the spring and autumn seasons are short. It is a typical "hot summer and cold winter" city, so people usually called Nanchang a stove in summer. The annual sunshine duration is 1723 ~ 1820 h, and the sunshine rate is 40%. The annual average temperature is 17°C ~ 17.7°C, the extreme maximum temperature is 40.9°C, and the extreme minimum temperature is -15.2°C. The annual rainfall is 1600 mm ~ 1700 mm, the precipitation days are 147 ~ 157 days, the annual average rainstorm days are 5.6 days, and the annual average relative humidity is 78.5%. The annual average wind speed is 2.3 m/s. The annual frost-free period is 251 ~ 272 days. The wind tends to be northerly in winter and southerly in summer. This climate is suitable for the growth of plants and flowers. It is an ideal area for building a "garden city" and also lays a foundation for building a low-carbon city.

5.5.2 Low Carbon Urban Lifestyle in Nanchang Guided by the Government

The process of environmental protection in China has proved that the government plays a leading role in environmental protection, and government leadership is the key to achieve a low-carbon model of urban development.

5.5.2.1 Necessity of Developing Low-Carbon Urban Lifestyle in Nanchang

First of all, the relatively serious urban pollution, unbalanced urban and rural development, uncoordinated urban and regional development and other problems show that low carbon urban life is imperative in Nanchang. The problems in urban ecological environment construction include transportation, buildings, residents' lifestyle, etc. can only be solved by carrying out low carbon construction through implementation of the sustainable development strategy, implementation of the scientific concept of development, and eventually achieving dual development of economy and environment.

Secondly, Nanchang is facing a major strategic opportunity brought about by the new round of national economic development strategy transformation and adjustment. Whether Nanchang can accurately grasp the requirements of national economic development, seize the first opportunity, create a new life model in Nanchang, and achieve a win–win situation in economy and quality depends to a large extent on whether Nanchang can actively develop low-carbon urban lifestyle and low-carbon economy.

Thirdly, as a relatively developed region in the central region, Nanchang has become the only capital city in the central region to develop a low-carbon economy pilot. Whether Nanchang can actively develop low-carbon urban life, actively implement low-carbon policies, and actively develop low-carbon economy, it will have a great impact on the development of low-carbon economy in other regions and cities in the central region.

5.5.2.2 Basic Principles, Objectives and Main Tasks

The basic principle of Nanchang's low-carbon development can be summarized as follows: adhere to "two promotions" and "equal emphasis on three". On the one hand, it is emphasized that low carbon development and economic development should promote each other, while taking into account the coordination and interaction with energy conservation and emission reduction, circular economy, and ecological environment policies. On the other hand, Nanchang also proposed that the low carbon of traditional industries should pay equal attention to the pillar of low carbon industries, emphasizing innovation in science and technology and systems, and at the same time improving the share of low carbon products in the external market and the demonstration application to the domestic market.

The goal of Nanchang's low carbon pilot project is to effectively control the city's carbon dioxide emission intensity, improve the quality of economic development, further optimize the industrial structure, economic structure and energy structure, establish and improve the low carbon development laws and regulations guarantee system, policy support system, technology innovation system, incentive and restraint mechanism, to form a low-carbon city development model with Nanchang characteristics and citizens with high low-carbon awareness, and build a national low-carbon development demonstration city.[11]

The main tasks of Nanchang to develop low-carbon are as follows: to build a low-carbon society and advocate low-carbon life; develop low-carbon transportation; innovate the system and mechanism and establish a low-carbon technology support system; adjust the industrial structure and change the mode of economic development; optimize the energy structure and increase the proportion of low-carbon energy; promote energy conservation and consumption reduction, and improve energy utilization efficiency; develop ecological agriculture and increase forestry carbon sink.

5.5.2.3 Main Practices and Results

1. Improve low carbon awareness. By making full use of newspapers, radio, television, the Internet and other social channels to carry out low-carbon publicity, so that governments, enterprises and citizens at all levels in Nanchang can clearly understand their responsibilities and obligations, which popularize the concept of low-carbon in the whole society, improve public awareness of the importance and urgency of carrying out low-carbon city pilot projects, and establish social public ethics for low-carbon production, low-carbon consumption and low-carbon life. It helps to achieve the object of "government guidance, increased investment, public participation and coordinated development".
2. Optimize urban planning. Optimize urban planning according to the low carbon concept, adhere to the way of promoting urban scale in clusters, and adhere to the cluster multi-functional urban complex such as employment and life as the main carrier of urban development. It is planned to build a low-carbon greenway network, build an "urban pastoral context" of "full connectivity", and achieve a natural low-carbon landscape of "showing mountains and dew". By emphasizing the layout of low carbon facilities such as solar roofs, solar street lamps, three-dimensional gardens, electric car stations, green buildings, garbage classification, etc., a visual low carbon city will be built.
3. Develop low-carbon transportation. The national IV emission standards shall be strictly implemented for motor vehicles, and the Euro IV emission standards shall be implemented for new public vehicles. To expand the traffic restrictions on highly polluting motor vehicles in urban areas, and encourage the early elimination of highly polluting motor vehicles in the main urban areas. Strengthen the management of motor vehicles, encourage the purchase of environment-friendly and energy-saving vehicles such as small emissions and new energy, develop low emission and low energy consumption vehicles, and promote the use of electric vehicles. Combined with parking lot and gas station, build charging facility system. Promote the use of energy-saving and new energy vehicles in buses, taxis and official vehicles. Accelerate the construction of subway, complete the construction of subway lines 1 and 2 in 2016, and complete the construction of

subway line 3 in 2020, forming a rail transit skeleton network composed of lines 1, 2 and 3. Accelerate the modernization of water transport. Seizing the opportunity of the construction of the National Golden Waterway and Poyang Lake Ecological Economic Zone, we will actively promote the construction of Nanchang Port. By 2015, 14 of 1000 to 2000 ton berths and 8 of 500 to 1000 ton berths will be built. The annual throughput capacity of the port will be 7.35 million tons, and the annual throughput capacity of containers will be 160,000 TEUs. Build an intelligent transportation network. We will promote the integration of public transportation in four counties and five districts, speed up the construction of unblocked projects, develop intelligent transportation systems, comprehensively promote the dynamic management of urban transportation informatization, and promote the seamless connection of multiple transportation modes. We will give priority to public transport, formulate and accelerate the implementation of bus lane planning, and establish a bus rapid transit system. Develop a "free bicycle" service system. We will study measures to improve the level of roadside parking fees in central urban areas, collect congestion fees on important roads, and limit the travel of traditional energy private cars during peak periods. We will implement the "free bicycle" action step by step in a planned way to facilitate citizens to transfer to public transport, implement a point incentive system, and encourage citizens to travel low-carbon. Public bicycles not only improve the utilization rate of road resources, relieve urban traffic pressure, save energy consumption, facilitate the travel of citizens, but also lead the lifestyle of "low-carbon travel, green life".
4. Advocate low-carbon life. The government takes the lead in setting an example, guiding the whole society to establish a correct concept of low-carbon consumption, advocating a frugal and rational low-carbon life, so that the public can start from their own living habits, control or pay attention to their personal carbon footprint, oppose and limit high carbon consumption, and make low-carbon life gradually become a conscious action of citizens. Actively guide green consumption concepts such as reasonable shopping, moderate consumption and simple life to become social fashion. Build a low-carbon living index, evaluate the low-carbon living standard, improve supporting facilities, and guide the transformation of residents' lives to a low-carbon way. Accelerate the application and promotion of biogas in rural areas, build large and medium-sized biogas projects, develop straw gasification and solidification, accelerate the upgrading of firewood saving stoves, energy-saving stoves and coal saving stoves, and promote the low-carbon life of farmers. Support various service organizations, industry associations, societies and other non-profit organizations to provide targeted low-carbon guidance and services to the whole society, change traditional concepts, and promote low-carbon and green consumption, and form a healthy and civilized low-carbon lifestyle in the whole society.

In a word, Nanchang, as the only pilot city of low carbon in central China, conducts low-carbon urban operation under the leadership of the government, actively explores low-carbon development models that meet the characteristics of its own city, actively explores systems and mechanisms conducive to energy conservation, emission reduction and the development of low-carbon industries, actively advocates low-carbon green lifestyles and consumption models, innovates low-carbon technologies, changes lifestyles, and minimizes urban greenhouse gas emissions. Nanchang city striving to achieve sustainable low-carbon urban consumption mode and low-carbon lifestyle as soon as possible, and make contributions to address global climate challenges.[12]

5.6 Green Olympics—Beijing Practice

As one of the four ancient capitals in China, Beijing has a history of more than 3000 years as city and more than 850 years as capital. Beijing plays an important role in China's economic rise and development. With the accelerating trend of urbanization, the contradiction between the development and the environment that cities are facing is also growing. Beijing stands at the forefront of China's economic development, innovates the urban development mode, and takes action to create a connotative and intensive model of sustainable development under the constraints of resource and energy shortage and small environmental capacity. Whether it is from the successful bid of Beijing for the Olympic Games to actively strive to achieve the Olympic commitments from energy to transportation, from environmental quality to the improvement of people's food and clothing, or the practice of green Olympics during the Olympic Games, or the first to form a new pattern of scientific development and create an advanced demonstration area of green development with clean production and beautiful environment, the goal of initially forming a green city where people and nature coexist harmoniously is to build a REEFCR city with resource conservation, environmental friendliness and climate security in response to climate change.

5.6.1 The Situation of Beijing Urban Ecological Environment

Since the success of Beijing's bid for the Olympic Games in 2001, Beijing has been in the forefront of environmental governance and protection, accelerating the development of new energy industries, eliminating industries with high pollution, high consumption and high emissions, promoting pollution prevention and ecological construction, and taking the 2008 "Green Olympics" as an opportunity, integrating green ideas into all aspects of residents' lives. At the same time, as one of the development directions after the Olympic Games, the concept of "Green Beijing" has also become the development strategy of Beijing. Under the guidance of this strategy, Beijing's economic development, urban planning, environmental governance and ecological construction are also making progress together in synergy. According to the Technical Specifications for Ecological Environment Assessment (Trial), the ecological environment quality index of Beijing reached 66.1 in 2010, indicating good ecological quality.

5.6.1.1 Continuous Decline of Major Pollutants Discharge

During the "12th Five Year Plan" period, the emission of major pollutants in Beijing decreased by 39.73%, significantly exceeding the national target of 19.33%, ranking the first in the country. Figure 5.14 lists the emissions of sulfur dioxide, smoke, dust and chemical oxygen demand in the four years from 2007 to 2010. It can be seen that the emissions of major pollutants in Beijing generally show a downward trend, with sulfur dioxide emissions falling the fastest. The reduction in 2010 compared with 2007 was about 31.2 percentage points.

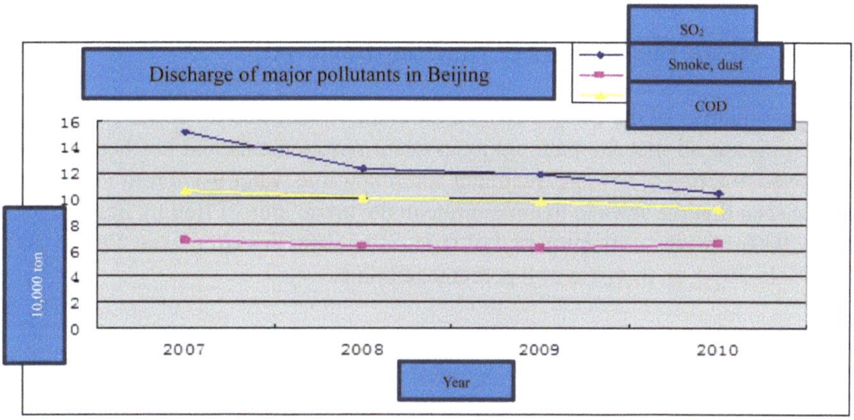

Fig. 5.14 Changes in the discharge of major pollutants in Beijing (*Source* According to the 2007–2010 Beijing Environmental Status Bulletin)

5.6.1.2 Steady Improvement of Air Quality

In 2010, the number of days with air quality above Grade II (including Grade II) in Beijing accounted for 78.4% of the total number of days in the year, the best level since 12 consecutive years of improvement. Figure 5.15 clearly shows the changes in the number of days with air quality of Grade II and better than Grade II in Beijing since 2001. In 2011, the air quality in Beijing was better than that in Grade II (including Grade II) for 286 days, 54.6 percentage points higher than that in 2001, including 74 days in Grade I, and an increase of 57.4 percentage points over that in 2009.

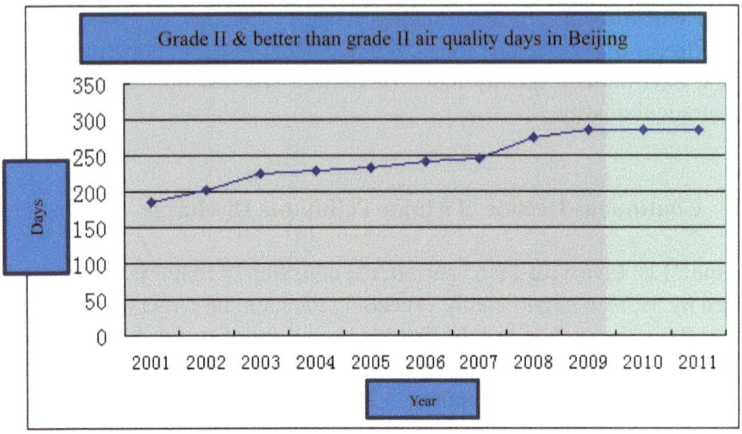

Fig. 5.15 Change trend of grade II and better than grade II air quality days in Beijing (*Source* According to the 2007–2010 Beijing Environmental Status Bulletin)

5.6.1.3 Steady Improvement of Water Environment

The water quality of the exit sections of the Juma River, Juhe River and North Canal in Beijing has all met the national assessment requirements and has been steadily improved in terms of sewage treatment and renewable water use. From Fig. 5.16, it can be seen that the sewage treatment rate in the urban area of Beijing has remained above 93%, and the utilization rate of renewable water has risen from 57% in 2008 to 65% in 2010, an increase of 8 percentage points.

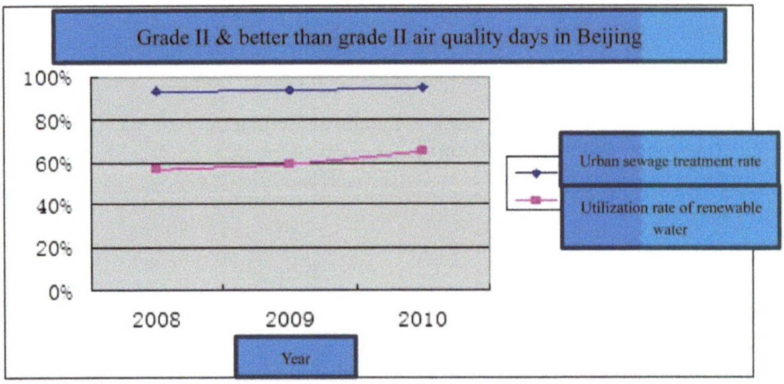

Fig. 5.16 Sewage treatment rate and reclaimed water utilization rate in Beijing (*Source* According to the 2007–2010 Beijing Environmental Status Bulletin)

5.6.1.4 Steady Improvement of Green Construction

In 2010, the city basically formed three ecological barriers, namely mountain area, plain area and green isolated mountain area. The afforestation area of 10,700 hectares and the urban green area of 617.5 hectares were increased, and the urban green coverage rate was increased from 42 to 45%, making Beijing a natural landscape surrounded by forests in the urban area and green sea and countryside in the suburb. As shown in Fig. 5.17, Beijing's urban greening, forest greening and forest area have been steadily strengthened.

Taking on the achievements made in environmental construction during the "11th Five Year Plan" period (2006–2010), Beijing has formulated the "Environmental Protection and Ecological Construction Plan of Beijing during the '12th Five Year Plan' Period" and the "Green Beijing Development and Construction Plan during the '12th Five Year Plan' Period" in accordance with the requirements of building a "Humanistic Beijing, Scientific and Technological Beijing, Green Beijing" and a World City with Chinese characteristics. In the "Environmental Protection and Ecological Construction of Beijing during the '12th Five Year Plan' Period", it is proposed to accelerate the adjustment of the economic and energy structure, optimize the urban layout focusing on improving the ecological environment, strengthen the construction of urban infrastructure, and accelerate the prevention and control of environmental pollution, so as to realize the urban function positioning of livable cities and ecological cities, and achieve the harmony and unity of economy, society and nature; in the "Green Beijing Development and Construction Plan of Beijing during the '12th Five Year Plan', it is proposed to build a green Beijing from the three systems of green production, green consumption and ecological environment by comprehensively considering such factors as urban function layout, facility construction management and production and living behavior.

From the opening year of the "12th Five Year Plan" (2011), it can be clearly seen that the quality of ecological environment construction in Beijing is gradually improving, and the ecological quality index of Beijing is 66.4. The emission

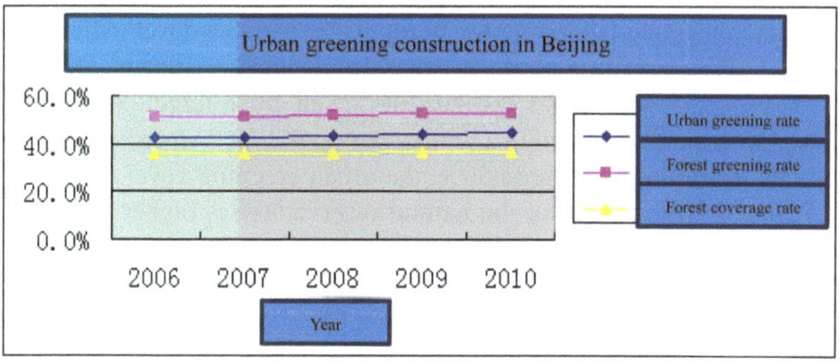

Fig. 5.17 Greening construction in Beijing (*Source* According to the 2007–2010 Beijing Environmental Status Bulletin)

of major pollutants, mainly sulfur dioxide, carbon oxide, chemical oxygen demand and ammonia nitrogen, continued decrease which led the national level; the Environmental Quality Assessment Method for Surface Water has been implemented. The sewage treatment rate has reached 82%, and the use of reclaimed water accounts for 19% of the total water use in the city; the city added 13.2 million hectares of green land, with the greening rate of 54%, the forest coverage rate of 37.6%, and the urban green coverage rate of 45.6%.

5.6.2 Sustainable Development of Beijing Green Olympics

As the engine of economic growth, the sustainability of urban development determines the height of city development. In the face of the seriousness of climate change and the urgency of development, sustainable development has been placed on an important agenda. By integrating the four aspects of resources, environment, economy and society, urban sustainable development can be defined as paying attention to the balance of resource development and utilization within the allowable range of environmental capacity, in order to obtain the maximum economic output with the minimum environmental cost, and pursue the harmony and unity of economy, society and environment.

5.6.2.1 Sustainable Exploration Before the Olympic Games

Whether it is the special requirements of the Olympic Charter for the environmental protection of the cities bidding for the Olympic Games or the pressure from the contradiction between the rapid economic development and the sharp deterioration of the environment, it is an accidental necessity for Beijing to take the road of sustainable urban construction. The preparation for the Olympic Games is also for the shaping and inheritance of Beijing's new image. Before the Olympic Games, Beijing allocated 12.2 billion US dollars and completed 20 major environmental governance projects, opening a good beginning for Beijing's sustainable development.

Thanks to the joint efforts of the Beijing Municipal Government, social organizations and citizens, Beijing has exceeded its seven green target commitments for hosting the Olympic Games within a limited period of time. Among them, the forest greening rate in Beijing is close to 50%, the urban greening coverage rate is more than 40%, and the proportion of the natural reserve area is higher than 8% of the city's area. Three green ecological barriers consisting of mountain green screen, plain green network and urban green landscape are basically formed, as shown in Table 5.8. These not only indicate that Beijing has actively implemented the environmental commitment of the original application for hosting the Olympic Games and has the realistic qualification to host the Olympic Games, but also indicate that the ecological environment of Beijing has changed to a benign development, and that Beijing has seized the opportunity of bidding for the Olympic Games and taken

Table 5.8 Implementation of seven greening indicators in 2007

No	Committed indicators	Implementation (By the end of 2007)
1	The greening rate of urban trees shall reach 50%	51.6%
2	The greening rate of trees in mountainous areas shall reach 70%	70.49%
3	The urban greening coverage shall reach 40%	43%
4	The city should form three green ecological barriers consisting of mountainous areas, plains and urban green isolation areas	In place
5	12,000 hectares of green isolation belt should be built in the urban area	12,600 hectares built
6	The area of urban nature reserves shall not be less than 8% of the total land area of the city	8.18%
7	23,000 hectares of green belt should be formed on both sides of the "five rivers and ten roads"	25,000 hectares built

it as an opportunity to promote environmental protection by building an ecological city and hosting a green Olympics.

5.6.2.2 Sustainable Exploration During the Olympic Games

After a series of preparatory work for the Olympic Games for seven years, "green" has not only been integrated into mindset of all residents in Beijing at the conceptual level, but also demonstrated to the whole country a model of healthy and sustainable urban development with data and results at the operational level. In response to the theme of "changing traditional concepts and promoting low-carbon economy" on the World Environment Day in 2008, China proposed the theme of "Green Olympics and Environment-Friendly Society" in combination with the opportunity of hosting the Olympic Games, thus making the concept of creating an ecological environment conducive to living and development through human behavior deeply rooted in people's minds. At the same time, during the 17 days Olympic Games, this green spirit was displayed and continued, thus showing the world an Olympic pageant with appropriate sports, culture and environment. According to the United Nations Environment Program, Beijing has achieved and exceeded its commitment to the Green Olympics through effective environmental improvement and protection measures, and greatly improved the environmental protection standards for holding large-scale events.

During the Olympic Games, especially under the special circumstances of large flow of people and large consumption of materials, the air quality in Beijing did not deteriorate, but reached the standard every day, with the concentration of major pollutants dropping by about 50%. For the whole year of 2008, the number of days with air quality above Grade II in Beijing, including Grade II, accounted for 74.9%

of the whole year. This is mainly due to the application of clean energy and clean technology, as well as the enhancement of the city's environmental awareness.

Guided by the scientific and technological Olympics and driven by the humanistic Olympics, the Green Olympics has been fully reflected in energy conservation and emission reduction. First of all, when carrying out frequent activities such as the transportation of Olympic equipment and the movement of staff in the venues, we used nonpolluting, high-performance and low energy consumption electric vehicles as the transportation mode, thus creating the first "zero emission" in the Olympic Games. Secondly, as the independent innovation and R&D achievements of China's "863 Plan", 500 new energy vehicles including pure electric buses, hybrid cars, fuel cell cars, fuel cell city buses and all kinds of pure electric sports cars were put into use during the Olympic Games and the Paralympic Games. And for many tourists, Beijing has set up a special Olympic electric bus to pick them up and send them off. In addition, large Olympic venues and supporting facilities use new energy to save energy and reduce consumption. Whether one fifth of the electricity in major Olympic venues, such as the Bird's Nest and the Water Cube, depends on wind power generation, or relies on the solar grid connected photovoltaic power system built in Beijing to achieve the lighting of lawn lamps and street lamps in 90% of Olympic venues, it is through the effective use of new energy to achieve environmental protection and low-carbon during the Olympic Games.

5.6.2.3 Sustainable Exploration After the Olympic Games

The Olympic Games has left important green "legacies" for Beijing. For these legacies, Beijing has not only standardized their management, but also considered their subsequent use in the early preparation work, so as to achieve environmental protection effects such as no waste of resources and recycling of facilities. After the Olympic Games, Beijing continues the exploration of urban sustainable development by inheriting the spirit of green Olympics, continuing to adjust the industrial and energy structure, promoting new energy and new technology, and putting forward new ideas of Green Beijing based on the spirit of Green Olympics, so that Beijing can achieve better and faster sustainable development.

In order to continue the spirit of Beijing's green Olympics, the new concept of Green Beijing was put forward at the right time, so that the connection between the green construction during the Olympic Games and the green exploration after the Olympic Games was completed seamlessly. Green Beijing requires Beijing to pay attention to the environmental and ecological sustainability of all aspects of the city in the process of urban planning and development, and pursue the shaping of a new image of Beijing at a higher level that is more coordinated and unified in economy, society and environment. In addition, the Beijing spirit of "Patriotism, Innovation, Inclusiveness and Virtue" was put forward in 2011. As the summary of the spiritual wealth formed by the Beijing people in the long-term development practice, the Beijing Spirit provides support for the future construction and development of Beijing. Whether it is the Green Olympics, or the Green Beijing, or the

Beijing Spirit, it is the performance that Beijing constantly updates its ideology in the process of urban construction, determines the efficiency of action from the height of thought, reflects the spiritual pursuit of the Beijing people, and through such spiritual transmission, it constantly walks in the forefront of urban construction and development.

5.6.3 Green Beijing—Prospect of a World City with Chinese Characteristics: "Harmonious Coexistence of Human and Nature"

Throughout the history of Beijing's urban development, from Green Olympics to Green Beijing, and from Olympic Cities to World Cities, Beijing has integrated the construction of a World City with Chinese characteristics into the Beijing Urban Grand Plan, which is the only way to conform to the trend of development, seize development opportunities, and seek higher level of development. Under the concept of Green Olympics, the green spirit of Beijing Olympic Games has radiated to every corner of this historic city that is good at inheriting excellent culture and has put forward a new concept of Green Beijing on the basis of inheriting and carrying forward. As the three development directions after the Beijing Olympic Games, "Green Beijing, Humanistic Beijing, Science and Technology Beijing" is the tireless spirit of Beijing in pursuing urban sustainable development in the context of new environmental issues, human settlement requirements and economic growth. The "Green Beijing, Humanistic Beijing, Science and Technology Beijing" concept promote each other and seek development in balance, and are committed to the ambitious goal of building a world city with Chinese characteristics. From the past tense of the Green Olympics to the present tense of Green Beijing, we can see the future tense of Beijing as a world city. How to build a world city with Chinese characteristics? At the national level, the rise of Hong Kong, Shanghai and Beijing will drive the development of the Pearl River Delta, Yangtze River Delta and Bohai Rim metropolitan areas, thus promoting the formation of China's world urban regional system. From the perspective of its own construction, Beijing will continue to implement the transformation of the mode of economic development, promote the obvious improvement of economic strength, the continuous optimization of urban functions, a more harmonious social environment, and the continuous improvement of citizens' well-being, so as to build itself into a center of international economic and trade activities and transactions, a gathering place of high-end talents, a place of high-tech research and development, and a harmonious and livable city.

Green Beijing is the development direction of building a World City with Chinese characteristics. The Overall Plan of Beijing (2004–2020) divides Beijing's urban development goals into three stages according to the urban positioning of "National Capital, World City, Cultural City and Livable City". They are: the first stage of building the basic framework of a modern international city from 2004 to 2008;

the second stage of striving to establish the status of a modern international city with distinctive characteristics from 2009 to 2020; from 2021 to 2050, the city will be built into the third stage of the World City, with an overall coordinated and sustainable development of economy, society and ecology. At the same time, the planning objectives are clearly put forward in terms of population size, spatial layout, urban structure, traffic planning, urban environment, urban greening, urban safety, old town protection and infrastructure. For example, in terms of urban environment, it is proposed to protect the ecological environment and achieve the goal of building an ecological city by 2020 by clearly defining prohibited construction areas, restricted construction areas and adaptive construction areas, and rationally using land. In terms of environmental greening, it is proposed that through the green transformation of economic development, the city's forest coverage rate will reach 55% by 2020, and the urban green space rate will reach 44% to 48%. It can be seen that the process of urban construction in Beijing is a dynamic and sustainable development process, in which Beijing is purposeful and constantly improving the next goal based on the completion of the previous goal.

The Green Beijing Action Plan (2010 ~ 2012) sets out the short-term goal of building a Green Beijing in 2012 by building three systems of green production, green consumption and ecological environment through implementing nine major projects, namely: clean energy utilization projects, green building promotion projects, green transportation and travel projects, energy conservation and environmental protection new technologies and new products promotion projects, waste gas resources comprehensive utilization projects, air pollution comprehensive prevention and control projects, recycling water resources utilization project, the urban and rural greening and beautification project and the green model building project, which will improve the ten mechanisms of organization and leadership, legal guidance, standard access, price micro control, finance, taxation, science and technology support, market service, evaluation and assessment, coordination and cooperation, and social participation, so as to lay a solid foundation for building Beijing into a green, sustainable, modern World City. In addition, an indicator system for the construction of Green Beijing is proposed, in which the ecological environment indicator system is composed of five indicators, namely, the proportion of days with air quality of Grade II and better than Grade II in the whole year, the decline rate of COD emissions, the decline rate of SO_2 emissions, the greening rate of trees, and the per capita public green area. Although the Green Beijing Action Plan is only a planning guide for two years, it plays an important role in guiding and encouraging the construction of a world city with Chinese characteristics by consolidating the green achievements of the Green Olympics, carrying forward the green spirit of building a sustainable city in Beijing.

To build Beijing into a world city with Chinese characteristics, the most important thing is to improve the quality of urban development, improve urban functions and improve the living standard of citizens. Adhering to such ideas and efforts, Beijing is one of the only two cities to achieve emission reduction targets among many cities in China in the energy conservation and emission reduction in 2011, and has initially built a unique park system in Beijing, committed to building a green layout of "two rings, three belts, nine wedges, and multiple corridors". In addition, in the face of the congenital restrictions such as the lack of land and green space in Beijing's urban area, a variety of greening methods have been implemented, which makes it possible to "see the seam and insert green, penetrate the wall for green, vertically hang green, and green the roof". This not only saves space and water resources, but also improves the overall green range and level of Beijing, creating a beautiful picture of people living in harmony with nature. At the same time, the three major concepts of "humanistic Beijing, scientific and technological Beijing and green Beijing" also put forward the development path of building a world city with Chinese characteristics from three directions. In the process of building a World City with Chinese characteristics in the future, we need to devote ourselves to the construction of a city where people and nature coexist harmoniously, such as a bluer sky, clearer water, greener space, more high-tech, more talents, a larger international stage, and a more livable environment.

5.7 Low Carbon Energy, Industry and Lifestyle—Guangyuan Practice

5.7.1 Overview of Guangyuan City

Guangyuan City is located at 104° 36 ' ~ 106° 45'E in the east diameter and 31° 31' ~ 32° 57'N in the north latitude. It is the junction of the northern mountains around the Sichuan Basin, the upper reaches of the Jialing River and Sichuan, Shaanxi and Gansu provinces. It was formerly called Lizhou. In 1985, Guangyuan was established as a prefecture level city under the jurisdiction of Sichuan province, governing Lizhou, Yuanba, Chaotian three districts and Cangxi, Wangcang, Jiange and Qingchuan four counties, covering an area of 16,300 square kilometers and an urban area of 38.13 square kilometers. Guangyuan is an important ecological barrier in the upper reaches of the Yangtze River and a key area for national ecological construction.

In 2008, 7 counties and districts in Guangyuan were stricken by the devastating 5.12 Wenchuan earthquake. Qingchuan County became a severely affected county, according to statistics, the direct economic loss exceeded 120 billion yuan. The gross domestic product (GDP) of Guangyuan in that year was 23.356 billion yuan, an increase of 3.3% over the previous year at comparable prices (the same below), and the growth rate was 11 percentage points lower than that of the previous year.

In post disaster reconstruction, Guangyuan City adheres to the principle of "planning first, people's livelihood first, scientific reconstruction, low carbon development, and reconstruction of spiritual and material homes at the same time", formulates the development goal of "low carbon Guangyuan", and actively carries out post disaster reconstruction. In December 2008, Guangyuan municipality analyzed the resource transformation strategy and proposed the concept of "low-carbon reconstruction of resource-based disaster-stricken areas". In May 2009, Guangyuan clearly proposed "take the road of low-carbon economy and strive to promote the sustainable development of Guangyuan". So far, Guangyuan has begun to vigorously implement the strategy of resource transformation, giving full play to the advantages of clean energy such as natural gas, hydropower, wind energy and geothermal, practically promoting low-carbon economic structure and industrial operation, realizing the healthy, coordinated and sustainable development of economic society and population, environmental resources, marking the official launch of the post disaster construction of "Low-Carbon Guangyuan".

5.7.2 *Low-Carbon Guangyuan Model of "Linkage of Three Modernizations"*

In June 2009, Guangyuan issued the Opinions on Promoting Clean Energy and Building Circular Economy Industrial Parks to Achieve Low Carbon Development, which guided Guangyuan to actively explore the basic mode of "three modernizations" of low-carbon economy development, namely, "low-carbon energy, low-carbon industry, and low-carbon life".[13]

5.7.2.1 Low-Carbon Energy

In view of different energy sources, the amount of carbon emissions varies greatly (Table 5.9). Guangyuan actively adjusts its energy structure and reduces carbon emissions from energy consumption through projects such as "gasification Guangyuan", new energy development, hydropower development and rural biogas projects.

1. Gasification Guangyuan
   The project is a major livelihood project to implement the resource transformation strategy, rely on the natural gas resource advantages of Guangyuan City, and promote low-carbon development. It is also a key civil natural gas project that Petro China supports the construction of old areas and boosts post disaster reconstruction. The project covers an area of 338 mu, with a total investment of 1.6 billion yuan. It is proposed to build two sets of 240,000 t/y natural gas comprehensive utilization devices and auxiliary facilities, with a daily treatment of 2 million cubic meters of natural gas and an annual output of 480,000 tons of LNG. At the same time, a gas transmission pipeline from the terminal station in

Table 5.9 Reference coefficient of carbon emission of various energy sources

Energy source		Potential emission coefficient	Carbon oxidation rate
solid fuel	anthracite	101.59	0.918
	bituminous coal	95.53	0.915
	lignite	103.97	0.933
	coking coal	91.09	0.980
	briquette	123.31	0.900
	coke	107.94	0.928
liquid fuel	crude oil	73.69	0.979
	fuel oil	77.40	0.985
	gasoline	69.36	0.980
	diesel oil	74.02	0.983
	jet kerosene	71.57	0.981
	NGL	63.12	0.989
	petrochemical feedstock	73.40	0.982
gaseous fuel	natural gas	56.22	0.990

Source The data is weighted according to the data of the Global Climate Fund, the Chinese Academy of Engineering and the United States Department of Energy

Panlong Town, Lizhou District to Huilonghe Industrial Park and 45 LNG filling stations will be built. After the completion of the project, the annual output value will be 2 billion yuan, the annual profits and taxes will be 320 million yuan, 4500 people will be employed, the fuel cost for LNG passenger and cargo vehicles will be reduced by more than 25%, and sulfur dioxide will be reduced by 99%, nitrogen dioxide by 80%, carbon monoxide by 94% and carbon dioxide by 25%.[14]

At present, Jiulongshan gas field purification plant, Yuanba gas field purification plant, oil sand comprehensive utilization and other projects have been completed or under construction, forming a natural gas production capacity of 3 million cubic meters per day, with 31,000 new natural gas users, 209.89 million cubic meters of civil and industrial gas, and 75% of urban gasification rate. 47 boilers have been converted from coal to gas; two CNG filling stations will be built, with the use of more than 3000 CNG vehicles and two liquid light hydrocarbon filling stations. It is planned that by the end of the "12th Five Year Plan", 96,200 new natural gas users will be developed, and the city's urban gasification rate will exceed 80%; 11 new CNG gas stations will be built, bringing the total number of CNG gas stations to 17 and 20 new LNG gas stations; 8300 CNG vehicles, 7000 LNG vehicles and 15,300 natural gas clean energy vehicles were newly developed; five small enterprises have completed 2780 households of coal to gas, totaling 5166 households. Cangxi Natural Gas Industrial Park (10.9 km^2) and Lizhou Natural Gas Supporting Industrial Park (2.2 km^2) will be built.[15]

2. New energy
   Guangyuan firmly grasped the advantages of abundant reserves of hydropower, solar, wind, geothermal and other emerging energies to develop new energy and reduce carbon emissions. By the end of 2012, Chaotianfangdiping Wind Power Project (100,000 KW) had been completed; Tingkouzi Water Conservancy Project (1.1 million kW), biogas hydropower station (60,000 kW), four cascade power stations (38,000 kW) in the Dongjiang River Basin, Cangxi Navigation Power Complex (66,000 kW) and Qingjiang River Basin Water Conservancy Project (26,000 kW) are under construction; Lizhou District wind power project (100,000 kW) has been officially signed. Geothermal energy projects, such as geothermal agriculture, geothermal flower garden and geothermal hot spring tourism, were launched in an all-round way. Getianci Hot Spring was completed and put into use, and the preliminary work of Chaotian Kaidi Biomass Project was orderly promoted. It has applied for and reviewed the "Selection and Pilot Project of Elegant Varieties of Jatropha Curcas", implemented the national science and technology project of "Popularization and Demonstration of Planting Technology of Improved Varieties (Bodhi) of Impatient Seeds", developed 20,000 mu of Jatropha curcas forests in the city, and built 1000 mu of demonstration forests of improved varieties of Impatient Seeds.[16]
3. Rural biogas
   Guangyuan City takes the opportunity of post disaster reconstruction and new rural construction to vigorously promote rural biogas construction. 22,000 rural household biogas digesters, 24 biogas projects, and 58 purification biogas digesters (4225 m^3) for large and medium-sized biogas projects of breeding farms (3620 m^3); develop 212,700 rural households for comprehensive utilization of biogas; 340,200 mu of biogas liquid seed soaking was promoted, and 9,556 households were built as ecological homes; 70 biogas service outlets were built, and the rural biogas penetration rate reached 47%. In 2012, Guangyuan City built 20,000 rural household biogas digesters, 3,000 cubic meters of biogas digesters for domestic sewage purification and 2 biogas digesters for aquaculture (1000 cubic meters); popularize glass fiber reinforced plastic arched biogas digesters to make the coverage area of this technology reach more than 50%; Promote the use of 20,000 sets of biogas pumping units; 3 county-level biogas service stations and 57 rural biogas service outlets will be built; continue to carry out comprehensive utilization of biogas, and add 150,000 households for comprehensive utilization; we will promote biogas seed soaking of 20,000 hectares, and increase 6,000 households in the ecological home model; reduce carbon emissions by more than 1 million tons.

5.7.2.2 Industrial Low Carbonization

Guangyuan seized the opportunity of low carbon development after the disaster, took reasonable planning of industrial layout as the premise, and reduced carbon emissions by adjusting the industrial structure; promote low-carbon and clean production technologies and develop low-carbon industries by building low-carbon industrial parks; develop circular economy and realize low-carbon agriculture by introducing comprehensive utilization of biological and biogas power generation technology; develop low-carbon tourism by carrying out low-carbon publicity, holding low-carbon activities. After several years of construction, Guangyuan has basically formed an industrial development trend of low emissions, less pollution and high efficiency, creating a low-carbon industrial model of Guangyuan (Fig. 5.18).[17]

Industrial Structure Adjustment

In terms of industry, the city has basically formed five industrial sectors: energy, agricultural and sideline products processing, building materials, electronic machinery and metals, among which the energy, agricultural and sideline products processing sector has been adjusted to the leading sector of Guangyuan industry. In terms of agriculture, Guangyuan actively promoted the transfer of "grain pig type" to "multi economy type", "quantity type" to "quality type", "traditional type" to "science and technology type", and "small farmer type" to "scale model". In terms of overall layout, it formed leading industries and characteristic industries with prominent scale, initially formed six industrial demonstration belts, and greatly optimized the agricultural industrial structure. In terms of modern service industry, Guangyuan City focuses on commercial logistics and tourism, and pays close attention to the development of modern service industry. At present, the development of modern service industry is accelerating, the transformation of convention and exhibition center, the old city central business district and the building of characteristic blocks of Guyan Road are accelerating, logistics distribution, information services, convention and exhibition economy and community services are developing rapidly, and the tourism market has begun to take shape.

Low-Carbon Industry

In accordance with the idea of low carbon reconstruction and low carbon development, Guangyuan City starts from building low carbon industrial parks and promoting the application of new technologies to develop low carbon industries. First, in terms of low-carbon park construction, Guangyuan follows the principle of intensive land use and enterprise interaction to achieve low-carbon park design; through the selection and promotion of cleaner production technology by enterprises, the low-carbon of the park units can be achieved. New energy enterprises such as solar energy in the park, high energy consuming enterprises such as electrolytic aluminum and cement plants, high-tech enterprises such as phase-controlled radar and LED, and logistics enterprises, all these enterprises rely on each other, complement each other through resources, promote each other, and develop together to achieve low emissions, low energy consumption, and high output. By 2015, the sales revenue of Guangyuan

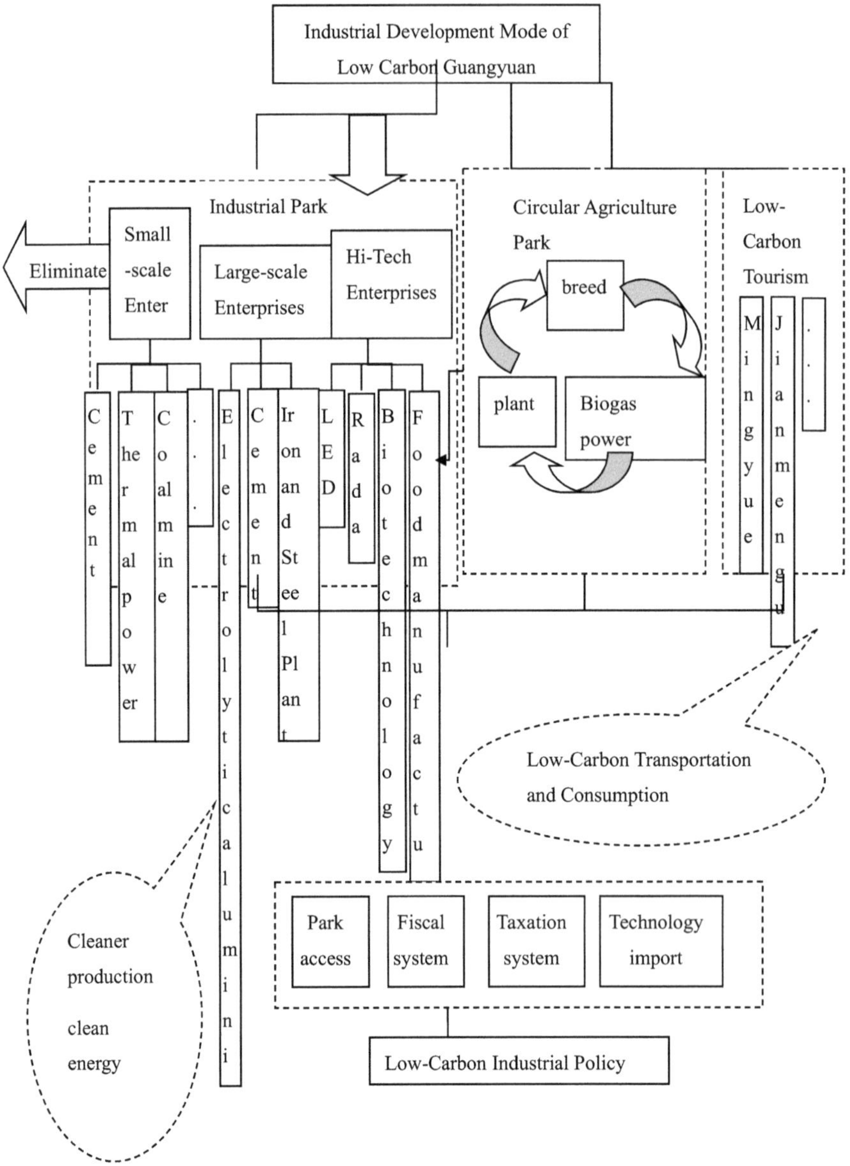

Fig. 5.18 Low carbon Guangyuan industrial development mode

Low Carbon Industrial Park will reach 55 billion yuan, accounting for 60% of all industrial parks; among them, one park with sales revenue of more than 20 billion yuan, one park with sales revenue of more than 10 billion yuan, and three parks with sales revenue of more than 5 billion yuan will be built. Second, on the promotion of low-carbon technologies, Guangyuan actively promotes enterprises to apply low-carbon technologies and eliminate backward production capacity. During the "11th Five Year Plan" period (2006—2010), Guangyuan closed 12 small coal mines, eliminated more than 70 production lines and equipment from 23 enterprises, and saved 189,000 tons of standard coal. Support enterprises to improve technology and promote cleaner production. At present, 10 enterprises that have passed the cleaner production audit and acceptance have implemented 54 low-cost schemes, achieving economic benefits of 1.16 million yuan, saving 12,000 tons of water, saving 2.2 million hours of electricity, saving about 1,000 tons of standard coal, and making an important contribution to the city's GDP energy consumption reduction of 20.11%.

Low-Carbon Agriculture

Guangyuan adheres to the interaction between agricultural parks and new village construction, and the interaction between leading enterprises and farmers; develop biotechnology and solar energy technology, and develop the circular economy of breeding industry. By now Guangyuan has built 41 comprehensive modern agricultural parks, promoted 112 new technologies such as biological prevention and control, established 150 rural professional cooperatives, and introduced 81 leading enterprises. Among them, Longtan Modern Agriculture Comprehensive Demonstration Zone has made great efforts to develop breeding industry, characteristic planting industry and eco-tourism, and has initially formed a "pig biogas fruit" circular agriculture model and an "orchard + farmhouse" leisure tourism model.

Low-Carbon Tourism

Guangyuan vigorously promotes low-carbon tourism based on its own tourism resources. At present, the city has successfully created 11 national 4A level tourist attractions and 3 national 3A level tourist attractions, with remarkable achievements in low-carbon tourism. First, the construction of scenic spots highlights the concept of low-carbon tourism. In the process of scenic area construction, Guangyuan City has added low carbon indicators and implemented the concept of low carbon from all aspects of project planning, approval, bidding and construction. Donghekou Earthquake Heritage Park widely uses stone, wood, vines and other building materials. Dachao Posthouse uses building heating, the use of solar energy lamps in the landscape of Huangze Temple, and promote energy-saving lamps in various scenic spots. Second, the operation of the scenic spot implements the low-carbon concept. Guangyuan City, based on the characteristics of tourism resources, reasonably introduces tourism products, plans tourism routes for tourists, and realizes low-carbon travel; all scenic spots carry out water and electricity conservation activities, implement projects such as reduction, reuse, recycling and alternative use, reduce tourism waste, and achieve low-carbon tourism; all tourism enterprises reduce the carbon emissions of enterprise operation and achieve low-carbon operation by purchasing new power tourism vehicles. Jianmenguan Scenic Area has launched a low-carbon tourism plan according to its own characteristics: since April 2010, 2 yuan has been spent on each Jianmenguan tourism ticket to support low-carbon development, and the funds raised will be used for carbon sequestration afforestation to offset some of the carbon dioxide generated in tourism activities.

5.7.2.3 Low-Carbon Life

Low-Carbon Governance

Low carbon governance is a demonstration project for the construction of "low carbon Guangyuan". Guangyuan municipal governments at all levels give priority to the procurement of green products, and include the government's procurement of low-carbon products in the assessment indicators; in the process of work, the government at all levels improve the information sharing platform, promote paperless office, reduce administrative costs, and improve work efficiency; strengthen daily management of official vehicles, implement rated standards, and reduce energy consumption of official vehicles; through low-carbon governance projects, effectively reduce the carbon emissions of government operations, and guide enterprises and the public to participate in low-carbon consumption and low-carbon life.

Low-Carbon City Planning

In the process of urban planning, Guangyuan implements the "green wedge embedded" regional public transport-oriented space to build a spatial pattern of overall dispersion and partial concentration. This pattern takes the expressway as the axis, showing the planned urban development belt along the expressway, forming a growth pole; according to the terrain and landform of Guangyuan and the spatial distribution of carbon sink and carbon source, the layout of urban land in low-carbon industries, residential, public services and trade services will reduce commuting, improve the utilization efficiency of facilities and energy, and build a livable low-carbon ecological city. At present, Guangyuan has formed a "526" ecological pattern, that is, five river valley ecological protection belts, including Nanhe River, Jialing River, Bailong River, Qingjiang River and Donghe River valley ecological protection belts; 2 natural vegetation green belts, the green belt in the east of Guangyuan and the green belt in the southwest of Guangyuan; 6 carbon sink areas, including Qingchuan, Wangcang North, Wangcang South, Cangxi North, Chaotianxi and Jiange carbon sink areas.

Low Carbon Architectures

Guangyuan regards low-carbon buildings as its key work, popularizes energy-saving technologies, enforces energy-saving, material saving, water saving and land saving standards, and promotes the development of green buildings. On the one hand, the original buildings have been renovated. By the end of 2012, 19% of the existing buildings in the main urban area of Guangyuan had been renovated into energy-efficient buildings. Energy saving equipment, household appliances and lighting products were promoted in public facilities, hotels, shops and residential buildings, and the activities of "Green Houses" and "Green Hotels" were carried out. The city implemented the action of benefiting the people with 5 million energy-saving lamps. On the other hand, strictly control the low carbon level of new buildings in terms of construction planning, project approval, and the use of building materials. At present, all new buildings in Guangyuan have achieved the standard of 50% energy conservation; 41,700 LED lamps are installed; of the 2,412 projects registered for energy-saving design, the completed projects all adopt thermal insulation technology and new lamps.

Low-Carbon Transportation

Guangyuan City focuses on urban planning, improving public transport, promoting new energy vehicles, advocating low-carbon travel, and improving low-carbon transport capacity through low-carbon facilities investment to achieve low-carbon transport. In 2011, Guangyuan added 6 bus lines, all of which are dual fuel vehicles; 274 new oil to gas taxis were added; 1859 CNG transport vehicles will be developed; invest 5.7 million yuan to build 4 km bicycle riding greenway; 33 urban public bicycle stations will be built and 1000 bicycles will be put into use to ensure low-carbon travel for citizens.

Forest City Construction

Guangyuan municipality attaches great importance to ecological construction and environmental protection. As early as 1985, when the city was established, it established a long-term development strategy of establishing an ecological city. In 2005, it proposed the goal of building an "Ecological Guangyuan" and an ecological barrier in the upper reaches of the Jialing River. By now, the urban and rural ecological environment of the city has been significantly improved. The forest coverage rate has increased from 48% at the beginning of the establishment to 53.6%. The green coverage rate in built-up areas has reached 41.2%, the green space coverage rate in built-up areas has reached 40%, and the per capita park green area has reached 10.4 square meters.

Low-Carbon Culture Construction

During the construction of "Low-Carbon Guangyuan", Guangyuan attaches great importance to the construction of low carbon culture, and actively uses the guiding role and integration function of culture to promote the low carbon development of

Guangyuan through laws and regulations construction, low carbon research, low carbon publicity and other measures.[18]

5.7.3 The Insights of the Low Carbon Guangyuan Model of "Three Modernization Linkages" to Cities in Underdeveloped Regions

As an underdeveloped area and post disaster reconstruction, Guangyuan City has its representativeness and particularity in developing low-carbon economy. On one hand, Guangyuan's economic development level is relatively low, and the post disaster recovery and reconstruction task are arduous. Guangyuan is in the early stage of industrialization and urbanization and is moving towards the middle stage of development, which needs to consume a lot of energy resources; on the other hand, Guangyuan is a green ecological barrier in the upper reaches of the Jialing River and shoulders the responsibility of protecting the ecological environment of the Yangtze River basin. Guangyuan makes good use of its own resource advantages and sticks to the path of low-carbon reconstruction, which will bring inspiration to the development of other underdeveloped regions and cities in response to climate change.[19]

5.7.3.1 Realization of the Symbiotic Development of Economy and Ecology through Low-Carbon Economy

Guangyuan, which "integrates three districts" (contiguous poverty-stricken areas, old revolutionary base areas and earthquake-stricken areas), promotes low-carbon reconstruction, develops low-carbon economy, and places the starting point and foothold on development. It not only accelerates economic and social development and eliminates poverty, but also actively takes effective measures according to its own capabilities to contribute to coping with climate change. After more than three years of hard practice, Guangyuan's low-carbon development has achieved good results. In 2011, the GDP of Guangyuan City exceeded 40 billion yuan, reaching 40.354 billion yuan, nearly double that of 2007. The city's economy (GDP) grew by 15.6%, 6.4 percentage points higher than the national average and 0.6 percentage points higher than that of the Sichuan Province, ranking the fourth in the Sichuan Province. The added value of industries above designated size was 13.87 billion yuan, with a year-on-year growth of 30.4%, 8.1 percentage points higher than that of the whole province, ranking first in the province. The total number of days with excellent ambient air quality in Guangyuan is 365, with the proportion of excellent days reaching 100%. The number of days with excellent ambient air quality in the urban area of Guangyuan is 222, accounting for 60.8% of the whole year. The two sets of data illustrate a fact: while Guangyuan is developing rapidly in industrialization and urbanization, its environmental quality has not deteriorated, but has shown a steady and positive trend. At the same time, it has "Golden Mountain" and "Green Mountain", realizing a win–win situation of economic and ecological benefits.[20]

5.7.3.2 The Capacity of Cities in Underdeveloped Areas to Develop Low-Carbon Economy

The industrialization and urbanization of underdeveloped regions started late, and the economic model and industrial system have not yet been fully finalized. The adjustment and transformation of industries to low-carbon economy have the advantages of low cost, small resistance and quick action; developing a low-carbon economy, vigorously cultivating new energy, new materials, new technologies and other economic growth points, and vigorously promoting new industrialization and new urbanization can avoid taking the detour of one-sided pursuit of economic growth or even pollution before governance, and achieve leapfrog economic and social development. The practice of developing low-carbon economy in Guangyuan has proved that low-carbon economy is not the "patent" of developed regions (cities). Less developed regions (cities) are fully qualified and capable of developing low-carbon economy and building low-carbon cities.[21]

5.7.3.3 Adaptation to Develop Low-Carbon Economy

Low carbon economy has just started in China, and there is no successful model for reference. All localities must give full play to their comparative advantages, formulate practical development goals, policies and measures, and realize the path to develop a low-carbon economy according to their own actual conditions, natural conditions, resource endowments, geographical location, industrial structure, financial level, citizens' quality, etc. To develop low-carbon economy in underdeveloped areas, we should give play to the advantages of backwardness and build a low-carbon economic model from a high starting point and in a forward-looking manner. Guangyuan City gives full play to its comparative advantages, bases itself on the reality of Guangyuan, and takes the lead in proposing low-carbon reconstruction in Sichuan Province in accordance with the requirements of the Scientific Outlook on Development, chooses a low-carbon development path, and develops a Guangyuan model of low-carbon economic development with Chinese characteristics, which is typical for other cities in China. The "Low-Carbon Guangyuan" development model is worthy of reference for similar regions and cities.

5.8 Forest City—Guiyang Practice

5.8.1 The Foundation of Guiyang to Build a Forest City

Guiyang City is located in the east of Yunnan Guizhou Plateau in southwest China. It is named after "being in the south of Guizhou Mountain". Guiyang is a modern city with plateau characteristics that "there are cities in the mountains, mountains in the city, surrounded by forests, cities in the forest, forests in the city, and green belts", and it is also the first national forest city and circular economy pilot city in China. In August 2007, Guiyang was awarded the title of "Cool City of China in Summer" by China Meteorological Society; in June 2009, it was included in the national pilot city of ecological civilization construction by the Ministry of Environmental Protection.

Geographical conditions. The karst landforms in Guiyang are widely distributed, accounting for about 85% of the city's land area. The Guizhou Plateau is one of the three karst development areas in the world, the largest and most concentrated karst area in the world, and the most typical, complex and landscape type karst area in the world. In view of the special natural and geographical environment of Guiyang, it determines the urgency, importance, difficulty and durability of the ecological construction of Guiyang, which determines that the ecological environment construction of Guiyang is not only related to the sustainable development of Guiyang, but also related to the ecological security of the middle and lower reaches of the Yangtze River.[22]

Climatic conditions. Guiyang is a plateau area with low latitude and high altitude. The city center is located near 106° 27 east longitude and 26° 44 north latitude, with an altitude of about 1100 m. It is located in the Fidel circulation circle and is controlled by the westerly belt all the year round. It belongs to the subtropical humid temperate climate, with both plateau and monsoon climate characteristics; the annual average temperature of Guiyang is 15.3°C, the annual extreme maximum temperature is 35.1°C, the annual extreme minimum temperature is - 7.3°C, the annual average relative humidity is 77%, the annual average total precipitation is 1129.5 mm, and the annual average sunshine hours are 1148.3 h; there is no heat in summer, no cold in winter, the air is not dry, and there is no wind and sand in the four seasons. It can be said that "there is so-called paradise in China, such as Suzhou and Hangzhou, and Guiyang is famous for pleasant climate".

In addition, due to the fact that Guiyang's heavy industry is basically far away from the urban area, the urban pollution is relatively light, and there are fewer days of mild pollution throughout the year. The air quality is good, there is no haze weather, and the weather is pleasant and comfortable; Guiyang has a forest belt around the city with complete vegetation, known as the "forest city". The forest belt around the city also provides abundant negative oxygen ions. The content of negative oxygen ions in the air of the scenic spot is high, with an average of more than 2,700 per cubic centimeter, several times higher than the normal value. It ranks the forefront of major scenic spots in China, and can be called the "natural oxygen bar".[23]

5.8.2 Current Situation of Forest Economy Development in Guiyang

5.8.2.1 General Situation of Forest Resources

Guiyang has always been known as a "city of forests" and a "national garden city". The land area of the city is 8034 square kilometers, of which the forestry land area is about 3,241 square kilometers, accounting for 40% of the land area of the city. With a forest coverage rate of 44.2%, the first ring forest belt is 9066.7 hectares, and is 70 km long and 1–7 km wide, and the second ring forest belt is 88,000 hectares and with a length of 304 km, a width of 5–13 km, which makes people feel the green charm and refreshing atmosphere in summer all the time. This is also the basic guarantee for Guiyang to develop and build a forest city. First of all, forests provide a practical basis for an appropriate human settlement environment. It ensures the lasting freshness of the urban air in Guiyang, and also points out the key points for the construction of the forest city in Guiyang: while continuing to plant trees to protect the environment, more attention should be paid to how to divide and manage forests, how to make rational use of existing forest resources, so as to achieve a virtuous circle between people and forests.

5.8.2.2 Development of Forest Economy

Guiyang has outstanding advantages in forest resources. It is an urban forest area with the largest amount of living things. Guiyang is an extremely rich natural resource base in the city and an important part of the urban ecosystem. Forests widely participate in the efficient use of materials and energy in the ecosystem, and in the coordinated development of urban society and nature, and plays a role and has special and irreplaceable functions in many aspects, such as the "general scheduling room of natural ecology", and in maintaining urban ecological balance.[24] Guiyang uses its unique natural conditions to build a forest city, build ecological protection gardens, and drive the comprehensive development of tourism in the forest economy.

First, building the Forest Park and Guiyang Forest Wildlife Park. Guiyang Forest Park is located in Tuyunguan, Guiyang City, only 2.5 km away from downtown Guiyang. The mountains are continuous, the land is fertile, stretching for tens of kilometers, and the total area is 3900 mu, of which the forest covers 90% of the area. There are more than a dozen forest areas including catalpa, camphor, pomelo, oak, sandalwood, pine, fir, poplar, camellia oleifera, etc. The resources are very rich. There are more than 1000 species of valuable trees under the first level national protection, such as Davidia involucrata, pine, camphor, grapefruit, oak, sandalwood, apricot, and rare flowers and trees, such as camellia, osmanthus, azalea, etc. Guiyang Forest Wildlife Park is a project that attracted investment through Guiyang Pan Pearl River Delta in October 2004. The park is located in Zhazuo Forest Farm, Xiuwen County, about 35 km away from Guiyang, covers an area of about 5000 mu, and has a total investment of about 160 million yuan. There are more than 5000 wild animals in the Wild Animal Park, a total of more than 200 kinds of wild animals. Relying on the gentle slope, col, wide valley, stone forest and other karst landforms in the park, according to the requirements of the park's natural ecological environment and landforms and different animal ecological habits, the park adjusts measures to local conditions and makes a reasonable layout to fully display the wild, animal and spiritual nature of animals in a rich and colorful natural environment, thus forming a wonderful ecological space full of vitality and wild interest.

Second, the sustainable growth of tourism under the forest economy. The construction of forest parks has gradually become one of the important driving forces of GDP growth in Guiyang. According to statistics, Guiyang has really achieved "green GDP" in recent years due to the tourism and forest theme income of 5.7 billion yuan. According to the Statistical Bulletin of Guiyang's National Economic and Social Development, the city's total tourism revenue in 2013 was 72.866 billion yuan, including tourism foreign exchange revenue of 52.2979 million dollars; it received 60,090,800 domestic tourists and 134,200 foreign (overseas) tourists. With the continuous growth of tourism under the forest economy, Guiyang's ecological and environmental advantages are changing into economic advantages.

5.8.3 *Main Measures for the Construction of Guiyang's "Circular Economy Ecological City"*

5.8.3.1 Integration of Forests into Urban Construction Through Scientific Decision-Making

Guiyang is a city with mountains around and inside, which is very suitable for building a forest city. The construction of forest city in Guiyang can be traced back to the 1950s. Since 1954, Guiyang has been building a forest belt around the city; in 1959, parks and forests within 8 km of the urban area were further connected to form a green belt; in 1979, the decision was made to build a forest belt around the city within ten years, and the construction of the forest belt around the city was included in one of the important contents of urban construction. The leadership was strengthened, the planning was formulated, and the investment was increased. The construction of the forest belt around the city within 10 km was accelerated, and the forest belt around the city was built into the environmental protection forest belt and scenic forest belt of the city. By 1990, a forest farm, scenic spot, park and urban mountain green land will be integrated, and the forest belt around the city will have a variety of tree species, a combination of trees and shrubs, a landscape in the forest, and a forest in the landscape. It is a unique forest landscape in provincial capital cities across China. As the landmark landscape and green ecological barrier of Guiyang, the forest belt around the city has played a great role in improving the ecological environment of Guiyang, developing eco-tourism, and promoting economic and social development.

In the twenty-first century, "let the forest enter the city and let the city integrate into the forest" has become a new concept to enhance the image and competitiveness of Guiyang and promote the sustainable and healthy development of regional economy; in accordance with the basic idea of urban forest construction, Guiyang adheres to the principle of people-oriented and harmonious coexistence between people and nature, highlights the urban construction concept of ecological construction, ecological security and ecological civilization, establishes the development strategy of "building a city by environment" and "building an ecological economic city", positions Guiyang as a "forest city", and creates "a national green model city" and "a national garden city". Strive for the goal of "National Habitat Environment Award" and "United Nations Habitat Environment Award".

Guiyang adheres to the principle of scientific planning, department promotion, government implementation, and public participation, and focuses on building an urban forest ecosystem with reasonable layout, complete functions, and significant benefits. While focusing on key forestry construction projects such as natural forest protection and returning farmland to forests, Guiyang also pays attention to the protection of the forest belt around the city and the construction of the second forest belt around the city, and does a good job of greening and beautifying the old city and Jinyang New District. The implementation of the "Three Year Clearing of Nanming River" project and the landscape reconstruction along the river, and the construction of green channels for high-grade highways such as Airport Road, Huaxi Avenue, Guizun Road, have significantly improved the urban environment and further enhanced the city image.

5.8.3.2 Project Driven Green Ecosystem Construction

In the process of building a forest city, Guiyang takes the implementation of engineering construction as the carrier to coordinate the configuration into a "green ecosystem" in the central area, the suburbs and the outer suburbs of the city.

First, implement the Second Ring Forest Belt Construction Project. Centering on the urban area scope determined in the Overall Urban Planning of Guiyang (Revision), the second ring forest belt focuses on channel greening, watershed management, and urban surrounding environment construction. According to the overall goal of laying a foundation in three years and achieving results in five years, 300,000 mu of new forests will be planted, and six parks featuring bamboo, osmanthus, cinnamomum camphora, cherry blossom, magnolia, plum blossom and other trees will be built, forming the second ring forest belt with a total area of 1.32 million mu and 304 km in-length, 5–3 km in width. Through the construction of the second ring forest belt, we will strengthen the greening of the suburbs and rural areas, introduce forests into the city, and lct the countryside under the garden to form a green ecological circle of urban and rural areas that integrates urban and rural greening, synchronizes economic construction with environmental construction, and harmonizes people and nature. We will build the second ring forest belt into an urban forestry ecological economic system with reasonable layout, complete functions, and diverse landscapes. At present, according to the new afforestation mechanism of government guidance, market operation and open bidding, the Second Ring Forest Belt has completed the afforestation of 230,000 mu of public welfare forests, including 110,000 mu of bidding afforestation, 110,000 mu of bundling afforestation with the conversion of farmland to forests and natural forest protection projects, and 10,000 mu of compulsory afforestation. The project construction has achieved phased results.

Second, implement the ecological forest construction project. Since 2001, in combination with the national project of returning farmland to forests and the construction of natural forest resources protection project, we have managed water and soil loss, improved the ecological environment, promoted the adjustment of rural economic structure, promoted local economic development and increased farmers' income. 490,000 mu of farmland has been returned to forests, and 180,000 mu of natural forest protection project has been planted. At the same time, the State Forestry Administration seized the opportunity of taking Guizhou Province as the provincial contact point, introduced Korean aid funds to carry out a demonstration project of stone desertification afforestation in Xiuwen County, and introduced Japanese aid funds to implement a Sino Japanese cooperative afforestation project in Huaxi District, which accelerated the pace of ecological construction in Guiyang and improved the management level of forestry construction.

Third, implement the compulsory tree planting project. The registration card system and inspection and acceptance system of compulsory tree planting for the whole people were implemented. The Municipal Green Committee uniformly printed the Registration Card of Compulsory Tree Planting for the Whole People and issued it to all units. After the compulsory tree planting is completed, the handover procedures were handled according to the ownership relationship, so as to institutionalize the compulsory tree planting for the whole people. First, the suburban units shall contract barren mountains nearby for voluntary tree planting, and be responsible for the planting, living and protection of trees. Second, the Green Committee Office shall collect the "capital for labor" fees in accordance with the provisions, and arrange professional teams to plant trees on the mountain or conduct street greening on its behalf. The third is to establish a voluntary tree planting base for the whole people, list Leihua Road, Guihuang Road and barren hills around Guiyang New Airport as municipal voluntary tree planting bases, organize provincial and municipal Party and government organs and troops to plant trees on the mountain, and establish 9702 mu of voluntary tree planting bases such as "Youth Forest", "Bayi Forest", "CPPCC Forest" and "Party Member Forest".

Fourth, implement the greening construction project along the Nanming River and the green space expansion project in the central area. Since 2002, in order to make the Nanming River, the mother river, clearer, the banks greener, and the scenery more beautiful, we have implemented comprehensive water and soil conservation management in the upper reaches of the Nanming River basin, covering nearly 80 square kilometers, and planted 82,500 mu of trees, effectively curbing the water and soil loss and source pollution in the upper reaches of the Nanming River. Large scale landscape greening construction has been carried out along both banks of the river in the urban central area, with a greening area of nearly 450,000 square meters, which has formed an urban green landscape corridor along the Nanming River. Since 1999, Guiyang has increased the transformation of old urban areas, released urban space, and ensured that urban green space has increased by more than 300,000 square meters every year. The 24 main (secondary) roads in the urban area were adjusted and replanted with large-sized street trees, which increased the per capita green area of the central area from less than 3 square meters to 5.15 square meters.

Fifth, implement the park construction project. In 1960, Tuyunguan Forest Park, the earliest and largest urban forest park in China, was built. In recent years, a total of 160 million yuan has been invested in the construction of Changpoling National Forest Park and Luchongguan Forest Park, the transformation of Riverside Park from a closed park to an open park, the transformation of Qianling Park Qixingtang Scenic Area, and the implementation of forest transformation projects in Tuyunguan Forest Park and Qianling Park. At the same time, the infrastructure and environmental greening of the parks have been reconstructed to make the park layout more reasonable and the facilities further improved. By now, there are 7 urban parks, 4 forest parks and 1 medical botanical garden in the city.

5.8.3.3 Accelerated Afforestation Through Innovative Mechanism

In the process of the construction of the second ring forest belt in Guiyang, the way that used to rely solely on financial allocations and administrative orders has been changed. With the improvement of afforestation quality and the formation of landscape as soon as possible as the core, Guiyang has innovated the mechanism, and explored a new afforestation model that is guided by the government, planned first, operated by the market, and invited public bidding. First of all, the method of attracting investment was adopted to introduce businessmen from inside and outside the province to establish a 500-mu seedling base for the Second Ring Forest Belt in Guiyang, which provided sufficient qualified seedlings for the smooth implementation of the Second Ring Forest Belt. Secondly, in the process of construction, we will adopt public bidding to attract competent afforestation construction enterprises from all over the country to participate in the construction of the second ring forest belt. According to the provisions of the contract, the construction enterprise shall complete the afforestation task in the same year and conduct the completion acceptance after two years of management and maintenance. Thirdly, in order to meet the requirements of the contract, the construction enterprises strictly control the quality in all aspects of land preparation, afforestation, management and protection, and generally use new forestry technologies such as rooting powder, water retaining agent, soil disinfection and sterilization to improve the scientific and technological content of afforestation. The mechanism innovation of forest belt construction in the Second Ring City not only alleviates the pressure of financial fund allocation in the year, but also greatly improves the survival rate and conservation rate of afforestation, and truly achieves the goal of creating a forest and leaving a green area.[25]

5.8.3.4 Improvement the Legal System and Legal Guarantee

In terms of environmental protection, Guiyang has basically formed a relatively complete system of local environmental management laws and regulations. Relevant environmental protection laws and regulations have been issued successively, providing legal guarantee for Guiyang to realize forest city construction, and various forms of legal documents also have their own characteristics and priorities. At present, Guiyang is more actively implementing and forming a complete legal security system, so that all construction projects have laws to abide by, and at the same time, provide security for residents' lives. The Regulations of the People's Republic of China on Nature Reserves fundamentally emphasizes and focus on cornerstones of forest work, which have become one of the bases for Guiyang to formulate laws and regulations. The implementation of the Measures for the Prevention and Control of Air Pollution in Guiyang has fully implemented the environmental work call for more blue sky and clearer water. As an important part of the water cycle, the atmospheric cycle has ensured the healthy circulation of air and water resources throughout the process, reduced the adverse effects of solid wastes on forest resources and soil, and thus formed a virtuous cycle of forest protecting air and air protecting forests. The Regulations on the Prevention and Control of Water Pollution in Guiyang regulates in detail the construction and discharge arrangements of various sewage pipelines in Guiyang; further detailed regulations and punishment measures for enterprises at the end of pollution discharge are made to ensure the health of water quality for normal industrial and agricultural production and provide favorable legal protection for the water cycle in the forest economy. The Measures for the Management of Guiyang's Deadline Control put forward a strict time requirement for the protection of forest work and the control of pollution, which provides a favorable guarantee for enhancing the working efficiency and effectiveness of government agencies. The introduction of this method has brought urban governance into the government's work process, which has become an important issue that brooks no delay.

5.8.4 Experience of Guiyang in Building a Circular Economy Ecological City

5.8.4.1 The Municipal Party Committee and Government Determined the Main Work Objectives and Took the Lead in Completing the Environmental Project Construction

1. Formulate measures to tackle the difficulties. In view of the difficulties in building a national environmental protection model city, Guiyang has tackled five key indicators, including water source, geological pollution, forest construction, key industrial enterprises' stable compliance and safe disposal of hazardous waste according to law. In this process, the regulations are used to lead the actual results,

repeatedly compare the differences between the established project requirements in practice, analyze the feasible schemes, eliminate the wrong schemes, and analyze and discuss the excellent schemes, so that the measures can finally be implemented smoothly.

2. To investigate openly and secretly and strengthen supervision and inspection. The combination of open inspection and secret visit, regular and irregular inspection and other methods were adopted to focus on the construction of hazardous waste center, which effectively promoted the development of the city's model building work. Supervision is always the guarantee for the correct operation of administrative power, and also the most effective way to supervise the government's work. To ensure the performance and transparency of the government during the implementation, the publicity of performance and the supervision of media and public opinion are also cited in environmental protection and construction.
3. Integrate media resources and increase model creation publicity. Through holding a model promotion topic selection meeting with the participation of media editors and journalists, we actively integrated media resources to do a good job of model promotion, creating a good atmosphere for the general public to know, participate in and support model creation.
4. Strive hard and comprehensively renovate. The water quality of centralized drinking water source is up to the standard, which is the one vote veto indicator for model creation. In accordance with the rectification requirements for the existing problems of centralized drinking water sources, Guiyang organized and implemented the optimization and adjustment of centralized drinking water sources in 14 counties and above in the city, improved the centralized drainage system of pipelines, actively promoted the ban of all sewage outlets in the primary and secondary protection areas, and completed the ultra-low emission project. 9 projects were completed in the third and fourth phases of the two lakes environmental protection project.

5.8.4.2 Strictly Implement the Environmental Impact Assessment System According to the Requirements of Ecological Civilized Cities

1. Strictly control project approval and pollution from the source. We will lead economic development with the ecological concept, and strictly control investment projects that consume high energy, are highly polluting, and are inefficient. Open green channels for environmental protection approval of major projects and key projects in line with industrial policies, accelerate the progress of environmental assessment approval, and promote the progress of projects.
2. Earnestly implement the work tasks of the environmental protection objective responsibility statement. Complete the quantitative assessment of the comprehensive improvement of the urban environment, organize the assessment of the environmental protection objective responsibility statement of each district (city, county), and continue to carry out the emission reduction of major pollutants,

strictly control the emission of various pollutants, and complete the emission reduction of major pollutants.

3. Establish the "12th Five Year Plan" emission reduction work system. The "12th Five Year Plan" for the Control of the Total Amount of Major Pollutants in Guiyang was prepared to make arrangements for the control of the total amount of chemical oxygen demand (COD), sulfur dioxide (SO_2), ammonia nitrogen (NH_3-N) and nitrogen oxides (NO_X) from the following eight aspects: increasing investment in emission reduction, promoting industrial restructuring, strengthening environmental law enforcement and supervision, strictly controlling new pollution sources, strengthening policy guidance, and establishing an effective incentive mechanism.

The Implementation Plan for the Reduction of Major Pollutants in Guiyang has been prepared. There are 391 projects to be implemented, with a total investment of more than 30 billion yuan, mainly from eight categories of reduction projects, such as sewage pipe network construction and sewage treatment facilities projects, drinking water source protection projects, and domestic waste treatment projects.

Prepare documents such as Comprehensive Rural Environment Improvement Plan of Guiyang (2010 ~ 2015) and the Outline of Pilot City Planning for Ecological Civilization Construction in Guiyang, and strive for more than 5.8 million yuan of central, provincial and municipal awards for comprehensive rural environment improvement and ecological creation. Carry out rural environmental ecological restoration and comprehensive environmental improvement in six townships, including Dangwu Village, Dangwu Township, Huaxi District and Dashi Village, Dashi Township, Xiuwen County Rural constructed wetland sewage treatment project and other environmental comprehensive improvement projects have effectively improved the rural ecological environment.

5.8.4.3 Strengthen Environmental Law Enforcement and be Strict with Environmental Violations

Strengthen supervision and inspection efforts and frequency, carry out daily inspection and night inspection on key pollution sources and hot and difficult environmental issues of public concern. In the whole year, 2918 enterprises were inspected on the spot, 245 key industrial enterprises in the city were comprehensively inspected for law enforcement, 56 heavy metal enterprises were investigated for potential pollution hazards, 288 provincial and municipal key construction projects were supervised under the principle of "three simultaneity", 148 boilers (using gas and electricity) in 123 bathing industries and hospitals in the city were inspected on the spot, 281 rectification notices were issued for illegal acts, and 13 cases were recommended to be reported for administrative punishment. Two provincial-level designated supervision cases were handled, eight enterprises violating the "three simultaneous" management were ordered to rectify within a time limit, and five illegal enterprises were subject to administrative penalties.

In order to further regulate enterprises' pollution discharge behavior and effectively control the city's pollutant discharge, the city's environmental protection departments at all levels continue to strengthen the issuance and management of pollution discharge permits, strictly comply with the requirements of total pollution discharge control, review the types, concentrations and quantities of pollutants declared by enterprises item by item, and issue pollution discharge permits to enterprises that achieve standard discharge and meet the requirements of total emission control. For enterprises that fail to meet the discharge standards, a temporary discharge permit shall be issued, and rectification and renewal of the permit shall be completed within three months.

5.8.4.4 Focused on the Construction of "Forest City", Comprehensively Achieve the Objectives and Tasks

Guiyang always adheres to the ecological environment construction as the center, focuses on urban and rural greening, and takes the opportunity of creating "China Habitat Environment Award" and "National Forest City" to make great efforts to implement and promote the regional landscape greening of forest city construction to a new level. Expand greening space and vigorously implement three-dimensional greening project. In order to ease the tension of land use for urban greening construction, roof greening, vertical greening of walls and other structures, and green wall construction should be taken as the main content, and the idea of "government guidance, social participation, demonstration and driving, and practical results" should be adopted to widely carry out urban space greening construction, so as to achieve the goal of "increasing the amount of urban space greening from the stock". For the central urban area of the city, the density of trees on the road is increased by planting tall arbors such as Sijiyang, Ginkgo, Luan and so on to achieve shade in summer. Create a batch of landscape sketches at the main nodes, parks and blocks of the main and secondary trunk roads in the urban area to improve the urban cultural taste and create the urban landscape image with a beautiful natural ecological environment.

5.9 Garden City— Shenzhen Practice

Shenzhen, a coastal city in the south of China, is located in the south of the Tropic of Cancer, 113°46' to 114°37' east longitude and 22°27' to 22°52' north latitude, with a total land area of 1,991.64 square kilometers. Shenzhen, also known as "Pengcheng", is not only an important international gateway for China's foreign exchanges, but also a wonderful epitome of China's reform, opening up and modernization drive. It is located in the south of Guangdong Province, bordering Daya Bay and Dapeng Bay in the east, Pearl River Estuary and Lingding Bay in the west, Shenzhen River connects Hong Kong in the south and, and Dongguan and Huizhou in the north. The vast sea area connects the South China Sea and the Pacific Ocean, and many deep-water ports can be built, with rich aquatic resources. Shenzhen has a subtropical marine climate, warm and pleasant, with abundant rainfall; the annual average temperature is 22.4°C, the frost free period is 355 days, the average annual rainfall is 1,933.3 mm, and the sunshine duration is 2,120.5 h. The terrain of Shenzhen is high in the southeast and low in the northwest. Most of the land forms are low mountains.

Shenzhen is the first special economic zone established since China's reform and opening up. In just 30 years of construction and development, Shenzhen has developed from a border town with a population of 30,000 and two or three small streets to a modern city with a population of tens of millions, economic prosperity, social harmony, complete functions, and beautiful environment. It has created a miracle in the history of industrialization, urbanization, and modernization in the world, and is known as "Shenzhen Speed". In 2013, the permanent population of the city was 10,628,900, the built-up area was 871.19 square kilometers, and the green coverage rate of the built-up area was 45.1%. The GDP of the whole year was 1,450 billion yuan, an increase of 10.5% over the previous year. Among them, the added value of the primary industry was 525 million yuan, down 19.8%; the added value of the secondary industry was 629.684 billion yuan, up 9.0%; the added value of the tertiary industry was 819.814 billion yuan, up 11.7%. The added value of the primary industry accounts for less than 0.1% of the city's GDP; the added value of the secondary and tertiary industries accounted for 43.4% and 56.6% of the city's GDP respectively. The per capita GDP was 136,947 yuan/person, an increase of 9.6%, which was converted to 22,112 US dollars at the average exchange rate in 2013.[26] The total economic output of Shenzhen ranks the fourth among large and medium-sized cities in China, and the comprehensive economic competitiveness of Chinese cities ranked the second in 2013. Shenzhen's urban planning and construction place the complementarity of resources and functions with Hong Kong in an extremely important position. It has made proper arrangements in ports, transportation, large-scale cross-border infrastructure, urban functions, environmental protection, etc., while promoting the coordination and connection between Shenzhen and Hong Kong in terms of resource allocation, regional division of labor, and municipal infrastructure. An export-oriented and internationalization have been significantly improved, and an international city that has begun to take shape has emerged.

Shenzhen is an ecological garden city. Nearly half of the city's total land area is included in the "basic ecological control line", and any construction project is prohibited. In 2000, Shenzhen won the title of "International Garden City", which is the first time that a city in China has won this honor, and it is also an international certification of Shenzhen's ecological environment construction and landscaping.

5.9.1 *Shenzhen Urban Construction and Development History*

Shenzhen is the first special economic zone in China and also an emerging city. Due to the rapid development of social economy, the rapid expansion of population, the narrow area, the shortage of land resources, the increasingly prominent contradiction between social and economic development and urban ecological environment protection, and the rapid expansion of urban construction in an extension way, the excessive pursuit of speed and short-term benefits, there is a shortage of developable land. Therefore, the demand for urban function upgrading and urban ecological environment protection is urgent.[27] Shenzhen's urban problems, accompanied by large-scale urban construction, have emerged as early as the late 1990s. So far, Shenzhen's urban construction, urban ecological environment protection and urban sustainable development have gone through the following three main stages.[28]

The first stage: spontaneous urban construction oriented by the market and dominated by enterprises. In the middle and late 1990s, a large number of enterprises in the Special Zone moved out, many industrial zones and factories were vacant, and a large number of people gathered, urbanization accelerated, and there was a great demand for the service industry. Some enterprises, keenly aware of the new changes in urban development, have spontaneously invested in the transformation of the old industrial zones and factories in the Special Zone, and developed services such as commerce and catering, which has promoted the urban renewal and upgrading of Shenzhen. The successful cases of this period were Vanke's transformation of Huaqiangbei and the later transformation of Chegongmiao area and Bagualing area.

The second stage: the urban construction with the focus on the transformation of villages in cities, which is promoted and organized by the government. At the beginning of this century, the problems of villages in cities became increasingly prominent. The low standard and disorderly construction and the gathering of a large number of unregistered citizens brought about many problems such as security risks and crisis. The government began to realize the urgency of the renewal and transformation of urban villages, and the urban governments at both levels promoted the transformation of urban villages as an important work. A typical case of this period is the cooperation between the municipal and district governments in the transformation of the fishing villages in Luohu District.

The third stage: government led, comprehensive promotion of urban construction focusing on urban ecological environment protection and urban sustainable development. In recent years, in the face of various urban development needs, Shenzhen has attached great importance to comprehensive urban construction. Corresponding institutions have been established in the urban area, and various government departments have begun to fully participate in the construction of urban ecological environment protection and urban sustainable development according to their respective responsibilities. Typical cases include: Shenzhen Futian Mangrove Nature Reserve, which was built in 1984 and was designated as a national nature reserve in 1988. At present, the nature reserve covers an area of 367.64 hectares, including 70 hectares of natural mangroves, 22 species of mangrove plants, 189 species of birds, 23 of which are rare and endangered birds under national protection. By now, the Reserve has bird watching pavilion (about 2 hectares) and Xiaoshahekou Ecological Park (about 19 hectares) available for ecological and environmental education. Once the construction of the proposed "Ecological Exhibition Hall", "Mangrove Garden", "Bird Paradise", "Bird House", "Green Corridor" and other projects is completed, it will provide better conditions for ecological environment education. Mangrove Nature Reserve has been named Shenzhen Environmental Education Base.

5.9.2 *Garden City—Practice of Shenzhen Urban Ecological Environment Construction*

With the rapid development of modernization and urbanization in China, many urban ecological environment problems have become increasingly prominent. Therefore, China has carried out large-scale urban ecological environment construction in recent years. Compared with other cities in China, Shenzhen has strong economic strength, superior geographical conditions and higher awareness of environmental protection.[29]

5.9.2.1 Advantages and Challenges of Shenzhen's Ecological City Construction

While vigorously developing Shenzhen's local economy, Shenzhen has made good achievements in ecological environment construction. In 1992, Shenzhen won the United Nations "World Habitat Award"; in 1994, it won the title of "National Garden City"; in 1997, it was awarded the title of "National Environmental Protection Model City"; in 2000, it won the title of "International Garden City"; in 2002, it won the "China Habitat Environment Award" and the "Global 500 Best Environments" awarded by the United Nations Environment Program. In the same year, Shenzhen and other international organizations jointly hosted the "Fifth International Eco City Conference", which adopted the "Shenzhen Declaration" aimed at promoting global eco city construction; in 2003, it was formally proposed to build a high-grade ecological city, namely "Garden City". However, over the past 20 years of extraordinary and rapid development has also accumulated a large number of urban ecological and environmental problems in Shenzhen, which have threatened the ecological security of Shenzhen and become a major obstacle to the realization of sustainable urban development. Relevant research shows that the actual population (fixed population and floating population) of Shenzhen has reached 10 million, the remaining land is only enough for about 10 years of development, and the four major reservoirs are polluted to varying degrees. In particular, compared with the national eco city construction indicator system, Shenzhen's surface water quality, nature reserve area, noise pollution level, urban life classification system and other indicators fail to meet the requirements, and it is very difficult to achieve the goal of ecological city construction in the next few years. How does Shenzhen control its rapidly growing population in the process of rapid development? How to control and restore the water environment pollution that has plagued Shenzhen for a long time? How to achieve sustainable development on the limited land resources and so on will be a series of problems that Shenzhen's ecological city construction planning should focus on solving.

5.9.2.2 Ecological Shenzhen Urban Construction Goals

Shenzhen strives to use about 20 years to build the city into a high-level ecological city with reasonable spatial layout, complete infrastructure, strong natural ecosystem services, developed ecological economy, beautiful ecological environment, harmonious ecological human settlements, prosperous ecological culture, developed modern industrial system, highly international and open pattern, and strong Pengcheng characteristics.

According to the experience of other cities at home and abroad in the planning of ecological city construction and in combination with the foundation and characteristics of Shenzhen's urban construction, Shenzhen's ecological city construction planning should highlight the three development stages of the ecological Shenzhen construction process, aim at the three system levels of ecological Shenzhen construction, weave a triple safety network of ecological Shenzhen construction around the three supporting aspects of ecological Shenzhen construction, and focus on the three core tasks of ecological Shenzhen construction.

The "three stages" refer to Shenzhen's construction of an ecological city: primary, intermediate and advanced. The ultimate goal is to build Shenzhen into a high-level and high-quality ecological city. The main basis for this stage division is that Shenzhen has a relatively good ecological environment foundation in China, a strong economic strength and a high degree of urban openness. Therefore, compared with other cities, Shenzhen can achieve some basic characteristics and functions of an ecological city through relatively short period of centralized recovery and construction, that is, become a primary ecological city; on this basis, through further improvement and targeted construction, the main hardware requirements of eco city can be completed, that is, to reach the intermediate stage of eco city construction; then, by strengthening the construction of the soft environment of the ecological city and combining the traditional ecological concepts and cultural characteristics of the Chinese nation, we can gradually bring Shenzhen into the advanced stage of ecological city construction, so as to fully fulfill the requirements of Shenzhen's international, high-level and high-quality ecological city construction plan.

"Three levels" refers to the three main levels of building a complete ecological city construction system, namely, ecological community, ecological town and ecological city. Among them, the ecological community is the lowest level of the system, the most important level of the ecological city construction system abroad, and also the most innovative and dynamic level; on the basis of ecological community, the middle level of the system—ecological town can be built, which is the most distinctive level in the system and bears a part of specific ecological city functions; the system integrates the above two levels and optimizes the combination and function collocation to form the top layer of the system—ecological city. This level is built on a solid foundation and has various system structures, functions, services and features required by the ecological city. Systematicity, comprehensiveness, openness and complexity are the biggest characteristics of this level. At the same time, a sign of the maturity of this level is that it has the function of self-regulation and self-improvement, so it is the ultimate level of ecological city construction planning.

The "three aspects" are mainly aimed at the three basic aspects of urban sustainable development: society, economy and nature, combined with the high grade urban ecological connotation that should be highlighted in the construction of Shenzhen's ecological city, to form three supporting aspects of the ecological city construction planning with urban ecological sustainable development as the core. These three supporting aspects systematically reflect the relationship between urban economic development, social progress, environmental protection and urban ecological construction in the process of ecological city construction, which both restrict and promote each other. Only by fully understanding and solving the relationship between them can we build an economic-social-natural urban composite ecosystem with high economic efficiency, social harmony and excellent ecology, and build a solid support for the construction of ecological Shenzhen.

The "triple network" refers to the "water network", "road network" and "green network" needed to build Shenzhen's three-dimensional ecological security network. The "water network" mainly refers to the urban water system that guarantees the urban water ecological security and improves the urban water ecological function; "road network" refers to the network of urban roads and their supporting safety facilities (such as traffic pollution monitoring and control measures) that meet the urban ecological traffic construction objectives; "green network" refers to the urban (green) landscape security pattern including various urban greening, ecological belts, urban parks, nature reserves, etc. By rationally planning and building these triple networks and integrating the ecological security objectives into the construction of the "three networks", we can build a three-dimensional ecological security network for ecological Shenzhen, thus ensuring the ecological security of Shenzhen.

The "three constructions" refer to the three basic tasks that must be completed in the construction planning of Shenzhen's ecological city, namely, "the construction of urban sustainable development capacity", "the restoration and construction of urban ecological functions" and "the construction of urban ecological security". Among them, the urban sustainable development capability includes many factors that can promote the sustainable development of Shenzhen, such as urban ecological economy, ecological environment, ecological culture, etc. The improvement and enhancement of these factors can comprehensively enhance the sustainable development capability of Shenzhen; the restoration and construction of urban ecological function is a fundamental task for the construction of an ecological city. The restoration of urban ecosystem function can not only lay a solid foundation for the construction of an ecological city, but also provide improved ecosystem functions and services for urban production and life. One of the basic signs of an ecological city is that the urban ecosystem is healthy and can function normally; urban ecological security refers to the ability of a city as an open composite ecosystem to resist external interference and risks, which is necessary for Shenzhen to build as an international ecological city. It emphasizes the health level and vitality of urban ecosystem, which is characterized by urban ecological risk awareness, urban ecosystem security pattern and urban ecological crisis emergency response capacity.

5.9.3 The Construction Effort of Garden City

Since the construction of the "Garden City", Shenzhen has adhered to the scientific concept of development to guide the overall economic and social development, accelerated the transformation of the development mode and the adjustment of the economic structure, and made great efforts to improve the quality and efficiency of urban construction and development.[30] The sound and rapid development of the national economy has been achieved, and new development has been achieved in various social undertakings. While successfully completing various indicators of economic and social development during the "11th Five Year Plan" period (2006–2010), the construction of "Garden City" in Shenzhen has also made remarkable achievements.

In 2010, Shenzhen's GDP was 951.091 billion yuan. Among them, the added value of the primary industry was 600 million yuan, down 14.3%; the added value of the secondary industry was 452.336 billion yuan, up 14.1%; the added value of the tertiary industry was 498.155 billion yuan, up 9.9%. The ratio of industrial structure is 0.1:47.5:52.4.

Among modern industries, the added value of modern service industry was 336.286 billion yuan, up 10.0%. In the tertiary industry, the wholesale and retail industry increased by 15.4%, the accommodation and catering industry increased by 9.3%, and the real estate industry decreased by 5.4%. The added value of private economy was 251.056 billion yuan, up 11.8% (Fig. 5.19).

In terms of urban construction and environmental protection, Shenzhen invested 74.174 billion yuan in urban infrastructure in 2010, an increase of 5.9%; the power consumption of the whole city was 66.354 billion kWh, up 13.3%; the domestic electricity consumption of urban and rural residents is 8.269 billion kWh. The city's daily supply capacity of tap water is 6.920 million cubic meters, and the total annual water supply is 1.565 billion cubic meters, an increase of 4.2%; the household water consumption was 502 million cubic meters, up 3.0%; the city's tap water coverage rate reached 100%.

By the end of 2010, the city had 758 bus lines, 180 more than the end of the previous year; the total length of public transport lines is 16,987.00 km, an increase of 4,049.30 km; at the end of the year, there were 26,796 bus operating vehicles, an increase of 5.8%, including 12,456 buses, an increase of 4.4%; 14,340 taxis, up

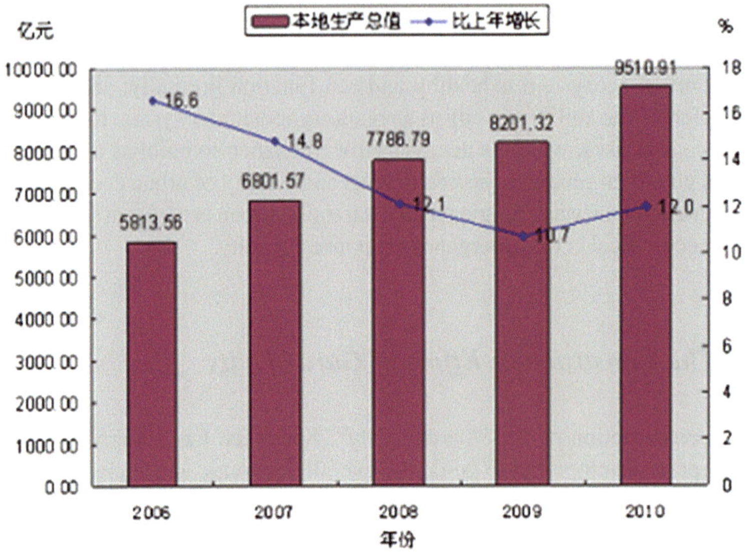

Fig. 5.19 2006–2010 GDP and growth rate

6.9%; the total number of bus passenger transport in the year was 2.281 billion, up 6.8%; the length of rail transit lines was 63.50 km, an increase of 154.0%, and the total passenger volume of rail transit was 163 million person times, an increase of 17.7%.

In 2010, the built-up area of the city was 830.01 square kilometers, the green coverage rate of the built-up area was 45.0%, the harmless treatment rate of the city's garbage was 94.6%, the water quality of the main drinking water reservoirs reached the standard rate of 100%, and the urban sewage treatment rate (secondary treatment) was 88.8%. The number of days to reach the air quality levels I and II throughout the year was 356.

5.9.4 Prospect of Shenzhen's Garden City Construction

2011 is the first year of the "12th Five Year Plan". Focusing on the theme of scientific development and the main line of accelerating the transformation of the economic development mode, Shenzhen has worked hard to promote transformation, stabilize growth, improve quality, and benefit the people's livelihood. It has completed the main objectives of economic development throughout the year. New development has been achieved in various social undertakings, and the urban ecological environment is in good condition, realizing a good start to the "12th Five Year Plan" period.

The annual GDP of Shenzhen was 1,150.206 billion yuan, among them, the first industrial added value was 570 million yuan, the added value of the second industry was 534.333 billion yuan; the added value of the tertiary industry was 615.303 billion yuan. The added value of the primary industry accounts for less than 0.1% of the city's GDP; the added value of the second and third industries accounted for 46.5 and 53.5% of the city's GDP respectively. The per capita GDP was 110,387 yuan/person, an increase of 7.3%, which was converted to US $17,084 at the average exchange rate in 2011.

In terms of urban construction and environmental protection, the investment in urban infrastructure in 2011 was 71.902 billion yuan, and the city's electricity consumption throughout the year was 69.602-billion-kilowatt hours, including 8.942 billion kilowatt hours for urban and rural residents. The city's daily supply capacity of tap water is 6.920 million cubic meters, and the annual total water supply is 1.615 billion cubic meters, including 522 million cubic meters of household water consumption. The city's tap water coverage rate reached 100%.

At the end of 2011, there were 825 bus lines in the city, 67 more than at the end of the previous year. The total length of public transport lines is 17,596.00 km, an increase of 609.30 km. At the end of the year, there were 29,608 bus operating vehicles, up 10.5%. Among them, 14,873 buses, up 19.4%; there were 14,735 taxis, up 2.8%. The total number of bus passengers in the year was 2.364 billion, up 3.6%. The length of rail transit line is 177.00 km, an increase of 178.7%, and the total passenger volume of rail transit is 345-million-person times, an increase of 111.8%.

In 2011, the green coverage rate of the city's built-up areas was 45.1%. The harmless disposal rate of domestic waste in the city was 95.0%. The water quality standard rate of main drinking water source reservoirs is 100%. The urban domestic sewage treatment rate (secondary treatment) is 94.0%. 362 days of reaching Grade I and Grade II air quality throughout the year.

In 2011, the environmental quality of Shenzhen maintained a good level on the whole. The ambient air quality meets the national Class II standard; the water quality of main drinking water sources is good and meets the requirements of drinking water source quality; ammonia nitrogen, total phosphorus and other indicators of main rivers exceeded the standard in some periods, and other indicators met the national Class V standard for surface water; the urban acoustic environment is slightly polluted; the radiation environment is in a safe state. The harmless disposal rate of domestic waste in the city was 95.0%. The water quality standard rate of main drinking water source reservoirs is 100%. The urban domestic sewage treatment rate (secondary treatment) is 94.0%. 362 days of reaching Grade I and Grade II air quality throughout the year. Completed the preparation of the "12th Five Year Plan" for human settlement environmental protection and construction, the "12th Five Year Plan" for pollution reduction in Shenzhen, and the "12th Five Year Plan" for comprehensive improvement of Shenzhen's water environment; promulgate and implement the Shenzhen Environmental Quality Improvement Action Plan; complete the tasks of pollution reduction in the "11th Five Year Plan" and 2011; successfully passed the review and assessment of national environmental protection model cities.

In 2011, the green coverage rate of the built-up area in Shenzhen was 39.15%, and the per capita green area was 16.5 square meters. The proportion of arbors and shrubs in the green coverage area of the built-up area was 81.2%. Shenzhen will promote the creation of a national ecological garden city. Based on municipal parks, the construction of comprehensive urban parks will be increased, forest (countryside) parks outward will be actively developed, and background mountain forests and suburban mountains will be turned into forest (countryside) parks. There are 106 new parks, 220 upgraded parks, and 789 parks of all kinds in Shenzhen, A three-level park system of "forest (country) park - comprehensive park - community park" has been initially formed. The construction of 335 km of provincial greenways has been completed, including 303 km of urban greenways and 506 km of community greenways. The total length of greenways in Shenzhen has reached 1144 km, and the construction mileage and density are among the best in nine cities in the Pearl River Delta; efforts were made to improve the service value of the greenway network, and 38 post stations were built, 31 of which were assembled with waste containers, fully reflecting the concept of low-carbon and environmental protection; eight key exhibition sections including Meilin'ao, the management line of the special zone, were built. The total length of all the key exhibition sections reached 40 km, accounting for 11.9% of the total length of provincial greenways, which improved the livability of the city.

Since December 2000, when Shenzhen won the first place in the international "Garden City" recognized by the United Nations with a population of more than one million, the Shenzhen Special Economic Zone has maintained its economic development and urban construction since its establishment 20 years ago, insisting that "the ecological environment is limited and must be protected according to law. Economic development and ecological protection are complementary and symbiotic. As long as we do not rush for quick success and instant benefit and adhere to the sustainable development strategy, we can achieve win–win development, scientifically formulate the urban planning, and fully consider the ecological environment protection in the planning." In recent years, Shenzhen has focused on 38 environmental quality construction projects, including comprehensive river regulation, urban sewage treatment, atmospheric environment improvement, and environmental noise treatment, aiming at environmental weaknesses. In 2012, the total investment was about 10 billion yuan, of which some key projects have been completed ahead of schedule. Shenzhen focuses on long-term development, takes ecological environment protection as the premise, scientifically formulates urban planning, construction is subject to planning, and planning is subject to environmental protection. In doing so, it has produced comprehensive benefits of rapid urban economic development and ecological environment optimization. At present, the city's ambient air quality, water quality of major drinking water sources, surface water environmental quality, urban noise and traffic trunk road noise all meet the national environmental protection model city standards.[31]

With Singapore's landscaping and Hong Kong's operational efficiency as the target model, Shenzhen has built a greening network with parks as the point, road green belts as the line, cluster green separation belts as the piece, and public green space, residential greening, production greening, protective greening, and scenic belt as the area, forming a garden city with colorful and blossoming flowers all the year round. Today, Shenzhen has 47.5% forest coverage, 45% urban green coverage, and 13.89 square meters of public green space per capita, ranking the highest in China.[32]

To sum up, the current urban economic and social development in China does not match the carrying capacity of resources and environment. The constraints on resources and environment in some urban intensive areas in the east are intensifying. The urbanization potential of areas with strong carrying capacity of resources and environment in the central and western regions needs to be tapped. The development of a city should focus on quality. The structure of the city itself and the capacity of resources and environment should be considered. Without a good internal structure of the city and the coordinated role of various environments, it is difficult to achieve sustainable development. Therefore, the development of low-carbon economy and the construction of REEFCR city should be implemented in specific actions. From a macro perspective, the government plays a strong leading and promoting role in urban construction, which requires government leadership, including institutional innovation, improving the market competition mechanism, introducing policies to encourage technological innovation, energy conservation and emission reduction, and developing low-carbon economy, actively carrying out international cooperation, and leading and boosting the development of low-carbon economy. At the medium level, we should adjust the urban industrial structure and vigorously develop strategic emerging industries such as low-carbon and environmental protection. From a micro perspective, it also requires the social participation of enterprises and citizens to change the traditional consumption concept of high carbon and waste, advocate a low-carbon lifestyle and production mode, and promote the "National Action" of low-carbon economic development. Guided by the spirit of the 18th National Congress of the Communist Party of China and the Scientific Outlook on Development, taking population, resources, environment and development as the fundamental means, taking low-carbon economy, circular economy and green economy as the development model, and taking the construction of a REEFCR city featuring resource efficient, environmental friendly and climate resilient as the goal, it is a strategic choice and realization path for China's urban construction of ecological civilization and sustainable development. In accordance with the principle of balanced population, resources and environment, and unified economic, social and ecological benefits, we should build a scientific and reasonable pattern of urbanization, economic development, and ecological security, ensure national and regional ecological security, and achieve urban construction and sustainable economic and social development.

Notes

1. "The Air Quality Rate in Ningbo Urban Area Dropped by 7% in 8 years", *Qianjiang Evening News*, February 4, 2010.
2. Yaguai Yu, and Pan Hanqing, "Climate Change, Geological Disasters and the Construction of Urban Disaster Reduction and Prevention System - Based on the Perspective of Urban Vulnerability in Ningbo", *Journal of Southwest University for Nationalities (Humanities and Social Sciences Edition)*, Issue 12, 2012.

3. Yaguai Yu, and Jianhui Gao, "Urban Vulnerability and Climate Change Adaptability in Urban Construction", *Business Era*, Issue 5, 2011.
4. Ibid.
5. Ibid.
6. Ibid.
7. Yanhua Yang, "A Brief Discussion on the Development of Low-Carbon Economy in Baoding", *Reform and Opening Up*, Issue 2, 2013.
8. Qun Yu, "Baoding: 'Low Carbon' Concept Boosts Ecological Civilization", *Urban Housing*, Issue 5, 2008.
9. Wenli Yang, "Chasing the Wind and the Sun - Rise of the New Energy Industry Cluster in Baoding High Tech Zone", *China High Tech Industry Guide*, November 2, 2009.
10. Fangjie Wang, and Hongsheng Wang, "Baoding Strives to Create the 'China Electric Valley'", *China Economic Weekly*, Issue 3, 2008.
11. "Nanchang will become a Global Low-Carbon Practice Benchmark City", *Gateway for China's Development*, available at http://cn.chinagate.cn/zhuanti/ditannanchang/2012-07/17/content_25929304.htm.
12. "Nanchang National Low Carbon Pilot Work Implementation Plan", *Baidu Library*, available at http://wenku.baidu.com/link?url=9apXua4iioQ1XrkIqKtySLY4 -F18Nc4ey5llynV1LUbQvej3-aSzTHY4V0mmHdInpPq5No4fFsCjmylCCGS1rOAYW9ym9RmU2lxQOJwJb9i.
13. Yi Ding, and Yaguai Yu, "Research on the Development of Low Carbon Agriculture for Post Disaster Reconstruction under Climate Change - Based on the Perspective of 'Low Carbon Guangyuan'", *Rural Economy*, Issue 10, 2012.
14. Xiaojie Yang, and Shouhu Du, "Research on the Development Model of Low-carbon Economy in Late Developing Areas - Taking Guangyuan City, Sichuan Province as an Example", *Rural Economy*, Issue 8, 2012.
15. Yi Ding, and Yaguai Yu, "Research on the Development of Low Carbon Agriculture for Post Disaster Reconstruction under Climate Change - Based on the Perspective of 'Low Carbon Guangyuan'", *Rural Economy*, Issue 10, 2012.
16. Xiaojie Yang, and Shouhu Du, "Research on the Development Model of Low-carbon Economy in Late Developing Areas - Taking Guangyuan City, Sichuan Province as an Example", *Rural Economy*, Issue 8, 2012.
17. Ibid.
18. Yi Ding, and Yaguai Yu, "Research on the Development of Low Carbon Agriculture for Post Disaster Reconstruction under Climate Change - Based on the Perspective of 'Low Carbon Guangyuan'", *Rural Economy*, Issue 10, 2012.
19. "Low-Carbon Economy is not the 'Patent' of Developed Regions - a Survey on the Development of Low-Carbon Economy in Guangyuan, Sichuan Province", *Netease News*, available at http://news.163.com/10/0428/07/65BEGIPA000146BD.html.
20. Research Group of Macro Department of Development Research Center of the State Council, "Low-Carbon Economy is not the 'Patent' of Developed Regions", *People's Daily*, April 28, 2010.
21. Yi Ding, and Yaguai Yu, "Research on the Development of Low Carbon Agriculture for Post Disaster Reconstruction under Climate Change—Based on the Perspective of 'Low Carbon Guangyuan'", *Rural Economy*, Issue 10, 2012.
22. Guiyang Municipal People's Government, "Building a Forest City and Promoting Sustainable Development", *Guiyang Daily*, November 19, 2004.
23. "The Situation of Guiyang", *the Website of Guiyang Municipal Government*, available at http://www.gygov.gov.cn/col/col13141/index.html.
24. Guiyang Municipal People's Government, "Building a Forest City and Promoting Sustainable Development", *Guiyang Daily*, November 19, 2004.
25. Ibid.
26. "Shenzhen Municipal Statistical Bulletin on National Economic and Social Development", 2013.

27. Research Group of the Policy Research Office of the Shenzhen Municipal Party Committee, "Several Important Issues of Urban Renewal in Shenzhen", *Special Zone Practice and Theory*, Issue 7, 2008.
28. Ibid.
29. Wei Li et al., "Research on the Framework of Ecological City Construction Planning in Shenzhen", *Environmental Science and Technology*, Issue 12, 2005.
30. "Shenzhen National Economic and Social Development Statistical Bulletin", 2011.
31. "12th Five Year Plan Proposal of the Shenzhen Municipal Committee", Sina.com, available at http://city.sina.com.cn/focus/t/2010-11/25-110110942.html.
32. "Optimizing the Ecological Environment and Promoting Economic Development in Shenzhen", *People's Daily*, December 10, 2000.

Chapter 6
Policy System of REEFCR City

Policy is the institutional arrangement for achieving strategic objectives, and policy tools are the bridge and link between achieving policy objectives and policy measures. Based on the basic national conditions, combined with the specific characteristics of the economic development stage, the policy system is formed through the optimal combination of diversified policy tools, which is the legal basis and institutional guarantee for achieving the strategic goal of REEFCR city.

Climate change has become the primary issue threatening the survival and development of human beings nowadays, and has attracted strong attention from governments of all countries. In December 1997, the Kyoto Protocol was adopted at the Third Conference of the Parties to the United Nations Framework Convention on Climate Change, aiming at limiting greenhouse gas emissions of developed countries to curb global warming.[1] In November 2006, Dr. Stern, former senior vice president of the World Bank, published the "Economics of Climate Change", which became an important basis for the EU to carry out actions to address climate change. In November 2007, the report "Progressive Growth, Promoting the Transformation of the United States to a Low Carbon Economy" proposed by the "Center for American Progress" for the new US government has become an important basis for a series of major US decisions to address climate change. The report of the 17th National Congress of the CPC in 2007 also proposed that "we should build ecological civilization and basically form an industrial structure, growth mode and consumption mode that can save energy and resources and protect the ecological environment", which provided a policy basis for the construction of REEFCR city in China. The report of the 18th National Congress of the CPC put the construction of ecological civilization in a prominent position and became an important part of the "Five in One" overall layout of the cause of socialism with Chinese characteristics. It required that the construction of ecological civilization should be implemented in specific aspects such as objectives, evaluation, and mechanisms, which greatly enriched the content of the REEFCR city policy system.

S. Du and H. Du, *The Green Transformation of Urban Areas in China Under Global Warming*, https://doi.org/10.1007/978-981-95-1005-4_6

It is understood that building a REEFCR city to guide and guarantee the sustainable development of cities and the construction of ecological civilization in China has become an important public affair, and the government should play a leading role in it. It is necessary for the government to carry out comprehensive planning and design as well as formulate corresponding laws and regulations. Only from the institutional arrangement of REEFCR city construction can we achieve twice the result with half the effort and ensure the realization of the goal of REEFCR city construction from the source and implementation effectiveness.

Starting with the selection and combination of diversified policy tools, drawing on the relevant policies and measures of successful international cases, this section analyzes the core content and regional differences of China's policy system for building REEFCR city, introduces the concept of participatory management in the process of policy formulation, implementation and supervision, and puts forward corresponding policy recommendations.

6.1 Diversified Policy Options and Portfolio

6.1.1 Theoretical Basis

6.1.1.1 Organic Evacuation Theory

In order to alleviate the drawbacks caused by the excessive concentration of cities, such as traffic congestion, heat island effect, and domestic garbage siege, Finnish architect E. Saarinen proposed a theory on urban development and its layout structure, namely, the organic evacuation theory. In 1942, Saarinen systematically expounded the theory of organic evacuation in his book City, Its Growth, Decline and Future.[2]

Saarinen believes that the reason why the city is paralyzed is not the massive use of modern transportation tools, but the imperfect urban spatial layout, which makes people working in the city tired of going back and forth in their workplaces and living places every day, thus causing urban traffic congestion. The healthy development of cities requires scientific and long-term urban planning in order to optimize urban structure and improve urban quality. This scientific and long-term urban planning reflects the organic evacuation of urban development mode, which integrates the advantages of both urban and rural areas. It not only conforms to the human nature of living together, but also facilitates people to live a common social life and feel the prosperity of urban development. People will not be separated from nature, and will have fresh feeling of countryside and fell the vitality of life.

Saarinen believes that there are two basic principles for organic evacuation: one is to arrange the daily life and work areas of individuals intensively; second, it is not necessary to stick to a certain position and make scattered arrangements in places where occasional activities are organized. He suggested that daily activities should be concentrated in a certain range as far as possible, so as to minimize the traffic volume required by activities, and it is not necessary to use all mechanized vehicles. It doesn't matter if the journey to and from the place of accidental activities is long, because there is a smooth traffic trunk road in the green space outside the daily activities, which can use a higher speed to travel.[3] It is highly promoted that the daily travel should be mainly based on walking and cycling, and vigorously develop modern public transport such as subway, high-speed rail, intercity railway, etc.

6.1.1.2 Urban Life Cycle Theory

The urban life cycle theory was developed by the American scholar Luis Suazervilla, which proposed that cities, like biological organisms, have processes of birth, incubation, development, decline, etc. Urban development has different stages, and urban elements have different manifestations in each stage of urban development, which can be used as a sign of urban occurrence, development and evolution. These development stages are called urban life cycles.[4] If this theory is applied to space, the phases of urban spatial expansion can be explained by the phases of urban industrial development and economic growth. For example, when a city develops to a certain stage, it will be restricted by its carrying capacity. In order to seek development, a city must develop land, water and other resources, plan and build new districts, and improve its carrying capacity.[5]

6.1.1.3 Green City Theory

The theory of green city was first proposed by Le Corbusier, a French master of modern architectural movement. He believed that we should focus on planning and use technology to improve the limited space of the city. He designed a green city with high-rise buildings in the "Guangming City" plan in 1930: the bottom floor of the house is empty, the roof is set with gardens, the underground is connected to the subway, and the space 5 m high from the ground is set with a network of automobile transportation trunk roads and parking lots. The location of residential buildings relative to the "solar thermal axis" is handled properly, forming a spacious and open space. He was very passionate about the beauty of nature and tried to oppose the phenomenon that urban residents were separated from the natural environment.[6] He advocated that "the city should be built into a vertical garden city", with a residential density of up to 3000 people per hectare of land, and hoped that trees, sky and sun could be seen among houses.

Since the United Nations Conference on Human Environment in Stockholm in 1972, the concept of green city has been recognized and vigorously promoted by western developed countries such as Europe and the United States. The development of green city is not limited to the construction of urban green space, but combines the landscape construction, ecological construction and natural protection of urban green space, with multiple functions and benefits.

The practice of green cities has achieved many successful cases worldwide. More and more cities around the world have begun to pay attention to the organic integration of urban planning and construction and natural environment, especially the use of forest land and rivers to form the basis for urban greening.[7] For example, Moscow in Russia uses green belts, water systems and road networks to form the framework of eco city construction, Melbourne in Australia uses water systems to form a green space ecosystem, Cohen in Germany uses forests and waterside terrain to form a circular green space system, and a circular city around the "green center" agricultural area has emerged between Chicago and Mindy Polly in the United States.

6.1.1.4 Low-Carbon City Theory

Low carbon city is a concept based on the proposition of low-carbon economy. The core of low carbon city is to promote low carbon economy in all areas of the city. Through the adjustment of industrial structure and the transformation of development mode, low-carbon cities that characterized by "low emissions, high energy efficiency and high efficiency" will not slow down economic growth, but will promote a new round of high economic growth, increase employment opportunities, improve living standards and promote sustainable urban development.[8] The basic content of the low carbon city theory is: enterprises take low carbon economy as their development mode and direction, citizens take low carbon life as their concept and behavior characteristics, and the government official management takes low carbon society as its construction goal and blueprint, so that the city can maintain low energy consumption and CO_2 emissions under the premise of rapid economic development.[9]

6.1.1.5 Government Regulation Theory

The theory of government regulation, also known as economics of regulation, is a new branch of economics. It was first proposed by famous American economist Stigler in 1971. Government regulation refers to the management and restriction carried out by the government to maintain and achieve specific public interests. It is the general term of government intervention in the market. In economics, government regulation is divided into economic regulation and social regulation. Government regulation theory includes public interest theory, group interest theory, public choice theory and incentive theory.

6.1.2 Diversified Policy Tools

Policy tools are the economic and social variables used by the government to affect policy variables, and are the basic elements to form the policy system. For example, "interest rate" is a policy tool → "interest rate increase" is a specific policy measure

→ in the case of inflation, "interest rate increase" is one of the moderately tight monetary policies to curb economic overheating, and together with other policies, it forms a macroeconomic regulation policy system to curb inflation. Its logical relationship is policy tools → policy measures → policy system.

The policy tools are diversified, and the combination of different policy tools will produce different policy effects. For example, interest rate, discount rate, reserve ratio, open market business, etc. in monetary policy are all policy tools. Different combinations of these policy tools will change the regulatory strength and scope of monetary policy, resulting in different policy effects.

In general, diversified policy instruments fall into four categories[10]:

The first type of tools—"Using markets", including subsidy reduction, environmental taxes on emissions, input and output, user fees (taxes or fees), bonds, deposit refund system, targeted subsidies, returned emissions fees and credit subsidies.

The second type of tool—"Creating market", consists of a mechanism to define rights. The most important mechanism has a special connection with the developing and transitional economies: the creation of private property rights over land and other natural resources. A relevant mechanism at the local level is the management of public property resources. The special property rights in environmental and resource management are pollution discharge permit and mining permit. Within the international framework, such a mechanism is often referred to as the "international compensation mechanism".

The third type of tool—"Environmental regulations", including standards, prohibitions, (non-tradable) licenses or quotas, and regulations related to the space–time expansion of an activity (such as zoning planning). License and liability rules also belong to this category of tools, which link environmental regulation with broader legislation and policy implementation. These instruments, such as liability bonds, execution bonds and more generally execution insurance and compensation, are part of the tool library.

The fourth type of tool—"Engaging the public", includes some mechanisms in environmental or natural resource management: information disclosure, community participation, etc. Dialogue and cooperation exist in environmental protection institutions, and the public and polluters may reach voluntary agreements.

Specifically, the policy tools commonly used in environmental economics are as follows:

6.1.2.1 Direct Regulation of Environment

The direct regulation of environment includes two substantive tools, namely, the direct regulation of national supply of public goods and technology.

The supply of infrastructure such as roads, ports, airports, railways and telecommunications has a considerable impact on the quality of the environment. Therefore, in building a REEFCR city, the government needs to follow the principles of "resource efficient, environment friendly and climate resilient" when building infrastructure. In addition, the state should also provide other public products conducive to the establishment of REEFCR city, such as cleaning public streets, building and maintaining urban green belts, parks, urban sewage treatment and waste management.

The direct regulation of technology refers to the regulation that the economic behavior of enterprises, families, institutions and other economic entities needs to have certain technology or meet certain conditions. For example, specify the energy conservation and emission reduction goals of enterprises, compulsorily install catalytic exhaust purifiers on transportation vehicles, implement protective farming (no tillage farming) in the urban suburbs and rural areas, and specify the use standards and quantities of pesticides and fertilizers.

6.1.2.2 Emission Trading

Emission trading means that within a certain area, under the premise that the total amount of pollutant emissions does not exceed the allowable emissions, the internal pollution sources adjust the emissions through currency exchange, so as to reduce emissions and protect the environment. Its main idea is to establish a legal right to discharge pollutants, that is, the right to discharge pollutants (usually in the form of emission permits), and allow this right to be bought and sold as a commodity, so as to control the discharge of pollutants.[11]

As an economic institutional arrangement based on the market, the economic incentive of emission trading for enterprises is that the seller of emission rights has surplus emission rights due to excessive emission reduction, and then obtains economic returns by selling the surplus emission rights, which is essentially the compensation of the market for enterprises' environmental protection behavior. The buyer has to pay a price for the new emission right, and the cost it pays is essentially the cost of environmental pollution. The significance of emission trading system is that it promotes enterprises to improve pollution control for their own interests, so that the goal of total pollution control can be truly achieved. In this way, pollution control has changed from the government's mandatory behavior to the enterprise's conscious market behavior, and its transaction has also changed from the government and enterprise's administrative transaction to the market's economic transaction. It can be concluded that the emission trading system is an effective means to implement the total amount control.[12]

The main methods of emission trading are: (i) First, the government departments determine the environmental quality objectives of a certain region, and then evaluate the environmental capacity of the region. (ii) The maximum allowable emission of pollutants is calculated, and the maximum allowable emission is divided into a number of specified emissions, that is, a number of emission permits. (iii) The government can choose different ways to allocate these rights, and through the establishment of emission trading market, this right can be legally traded. (iv) In the emission right market, the polluter decides the degree of pollution control independently from his interests, so as to buy or sell the emission right.[13]

6.1.2.3 Taxation

Economists often regard environmental taxes and fees as the most powerful tool for environmental and natural resource policies. For example, enterprises that effectively implement energy conservation and emission reduction will be given certain tax incentives or subsidies, and will be fined for acts that damage the urban ecological environment.

China can start with levying ecological compensation tax and regulating pollution charge system to establish ecological tax system and better serve for environmental protection. The first step is to reform the current tax system and improve the degree of "green"; the second step is to replace the original urban construction and maintenance tax with "ecological compensation tax" according to the principle of "beneficiaries pay", and to collect special funds for ecological construction in the form of universal collection for the beneficiaries of the use of ecological environment. At the same time, according to the principle of "polluter pays", the polluter of the environment is charged for pollution discharge.[14]

6.1.2.4 National Policy and Planning

The framework of environmental planning and policy formulation, together with administrative organizations and systems (such as government departments and environmental protection bureaus), can be seen as a "tool" in itself. Policy plays an important role in building REEFCR city, and planning is the carrier of strategy implementation. Whether the planning is scientific directly affects the effectiveness of strategy implementation and even whether the strategy can be realized. To build REEFCR city, we should first formulate a scientific and reasonable plan and determine the effective implementation of the plan.

6.2 Domestic Policies Evaluation and Insights from International Policies

In the face of the ecological environment problems in urban construction and resource development in China, the government has taken many countermeasures aimed at promoting pollution prevention, treatment and ecological construction, and accelerating energy conservation and emission reduction. These policies have achieved good results in the implementation process. However, with the acceleration of urbanization, urban environmental pressure, pressure on energy conservation and emission reduction are emerging to varying degrees, and the shortcomings of these policies are becoming increasingly obvious.

6.2.1 *Comments on Relevant Policies of REEFCR City in China*

6.2.1.1 Deficiencies of Relevant Policies in Legislation

First, the supply of legislation is insufficient. In some important areas of environmental protection and resource development, there is a lack of special laws and regulations. In the environmental legislation system, there is a situation that the pollution prevention legislation and the resource protection legislation are isolated from each other, and the system is not comprehensive and complementary.[15] For example, although the Mineral Resources Law of the People's Republic of China, adopted in 1986, clearly stipulates the reclamation and restoration of abandoned mining areas, the Measures for the Administration of the Use of Mineral Resources Compensation jointly issued by the Ministry of Finance and the Ministry of Land and Resources in 2001 did not include the reclamation of mining areas and the compensation for the production and living of people in mining areas in the use of mineral resources.[16]

Second, the legislative principle is not perfect. Influenced by the concept of planned economy system, the principle of legislation in China is still government led. In terms of principle guidance, principle establishment, system design, system construction and law enforcement, we are used to playing the role of the government and adopting the administrative enforcement mechanism. However, the direction, strength and effect of administrative enforcement are limited, and we lack experience in making rational use of the market mechanism.[17]

Third, the existing laws and regulations on pollution prevention are basically carried out around large and medium-sized cities and large and medium-sized enterprises, lacking attention to small towns and small enterprises, and not seriously studying and formulating legal systems that adapt to the construction of small towns and the environmental management of rural and township enterprises.

Fourth, the setting of environmental legal principles and systems, rules and regulations on energy conservation and emission reduction is basically dominated by "end control", with the control of construction projects and production links, as well as the "emission control" of pollution treatment and disposal as the basic requirements, focusing on "control" rather than "prevention".[18] The former is a passive act after the event, and the latter is a proactive act in advance. At present, enterprises lack the initiative to prevent and control environmental pollution.

Fifth, the environmental legal principles and systems are based on the "point source control". Although in recent years, the requirements of "up to standard emissions" have been put forward for enterprises, the focus is on emphasizing and highlighting the individual responsibility of enterprises as the source of pollution, ignoring the entrepreneurial responsibility of enterprises to undertake environmental protection tasks.

6.2.1.2 Deficiencies in the Formulation and Implementation of Relevant Policies

First, urban policies on resource efficient, environment friendly and climate resilient are government led in formulation and implementation. Compared with the government behavior running through all fields and links of environmental protection, enterprises are passive recipients of these policies, and there are fewer ways and channels for the public to participate in environmental protection.[19]

Second, China's environmental policy is based on the response to environmental issues, not on the priority of environmental protection. This is determined by China's national conditions and the requirements of development at this stage. China is a developing country rather than a developed country. Economic development is a solid foundation and basic guarantee for China's national rejuvenation, national prosperity and solid national defense. Development is the first important thing. It takes into account the coordinated development of resources and environment, but it is by no means an environmental priority.

Third, the implementation of urban policies related to resource efficient, environment friendly and climate resilient is not effective. Part of the reason is that most of these policies are mandatory by the government, and there are few incentives economic policies. The trend of world development is that mandatory policies are supplemented by guiding and incentive economic policies. China should also strengthen the proportion of incentive economic policies.

6.2.2 *International Policy Reference for Building REEFCR City*

In the face of severe ecological degradation and environmental pollution, more and more countries in the world have taken positive attitudes and comprehensive countermeasures from the following aspects.

6.2.2.1 Policy Reference of Resource Saving Cities—Transformation of Resource Based Cities

From the exploration and practice abroad, the economic transformation of resource-based cities is a worldwide problem. Countries in the world have both successful experiences and lessons from failure. For example, Houston has developed from a single oil resource-based city into a comprehensive metropolis integrating capital, technology and intelligence through extending the industrial chain and introducing scientific and technological projects; Lorraine, France, made a high starting point transformation to improve its international competitiveness.

Column 6.1 Houston, USA

Houston is a huge oil center in the United States and a typical resource-based city. Since the 1960s, Houston's oil exploration industry has declined as a whole, and the situation of resource depletion has emerged. Relevant departments have decisively introduced a series of policies and measures to promote the transformation of urban development mode. Its main policies and measures include:

First, corresponding incentive policies and financial support were provided to accelerate oil research and development according to the extension and expansion of the industrial chain, and drive the development of machinery, cement, electricity, steel and other industries serving them.

The second is to set up a space center in Houston, driving the development of more than 1300 high-tech enterprises around.

It is through this kind of vertical industrial development, technological progress and industrial transformation of the original dominant resource development industry of a single resource city that the original industrial chain is expanded and the processing depth of products is increased, thus driving the transformation of regional industries and regional sustainable development. The urban nature of Houston has also undergone fundamental changes, from the original oil city to a comprehensive base consisting of oil-based industries and multiple industrial clusters, to a modern metropolis integrating capital, knowledge, technology intensive and high-tech.

Source: International Experience and Reference for the Transformation of Resource-Based Cities, Economic Research Reference, Issue 71, 2009, by Han Fengqin, Li Chengwei, and Liang Liangcong.

Column 6.2 Lorraine, France

Lorraine, France, used to be an old industrial base dominated by coal, steel and other traditional industries. In the late 1960s and early 1970s, when faced with the problem of the decline of traditional industries, Lorraine began to make great efforts to implement the economic transformation strategy. They formulated a high starting point transformation goal to improve international competitiveness. Their main policies and measures are as follows:

First, completely shut down coal mines, iron mines, steel mills and other enterprises with high production costs, high resource consumption and heavy environmental pollution. For example, although there are resources for coal, because the mine is deep and the cost of mining a ton of coal is much higher than the world market coal price, the policy of gradually giving up was adopted, and by 2005 all the coal mines had been shut down. Although iron resources are rich, due to the high cost of the steel industry, the sales price of per ton steel is far higher than that of imports, so Lorraine simply shut down all mining, iron making and steel making enterprises.

Second, according to the needs of the international market, Lorraine focus on the development of nuclear power, computers, lasers, electronics, biopharmaceuticals, environmental protection machinery, automobile manufacturing and other high-tech industries.

The third is to transform traditional industries with high and new technologies, vigorously improve their technological content and increase the added value of products.

Fourth, to formulate preferential policies to attract foreign investment and bring economic transformation and structural adjustment into line with international standards.

Fifthly, combine the transformation of the coal industry with the land consolidation, and include it in the regional planning. A special department for land improvement has been set up to deal with and solve the problems of land pollution left by aging mining areas and the re-effective use of idle sites. Since 1979, Lorraine has set up a special fund to assist the affected industries. After the closure of the enterprise, the land shall be rebuilt into residential buildings or entertainment centers, or parks with trees and grass to beautify the environment.

Sixthly, to establish incubation parks to support the unemployed to set up small businesses, and provide them with various services at the initial stage and growth stage. In Lorraine, small enterprises with less than 10 employees founded after transformation are scattered, accounting for more than 90% of all enterprises. Lorraine regards training workers as an important way to arrange for the unemployed to find new jobs. After training, there are more than 100 kinds of jobs to choose from. At the same time, the Municipal Government has also implemented tax and credit incentives for enterprises that settle the surplus coal miners, and subsidized 30,000 francs for each person employed by companies that employ laid-off miners.

After more than 30 years of efforts, Lorraine has gradually transformed into a new industrial zone with a beautiful environment dominated by high-tech industries and complex technology industries.

Source: Transformation has Laws and Different Models—Economic Transformation of Mining Cities in Developed Countries, Seeking Truth, Issue 2, 2007, by Chen Yuchuan and Zhang Yicheng.

6.2.2.2 Policy Reference for Environmentally Friendly Cities—Water Environment Optimization and Domestic Waste Treatment

Environmentally friendly cities have high requirements for city image. First of all, they need beautiful scenery, ecological balance, cleanliness and hygiene. Optimizing the use of urban water environment and effectively disposing of urban domestic waste are very important for creating a high-quality urban environment. Many countries have made demonstrative explorations in this regard, which provides a reference for us to build REEFCR city policy system.

Column 6.3 Optimization and Utilization of Urban Water Environment

In 1990, the United States proposed and implemented a huge water landscape ecological restoration plan to strengthen the leisure and tourism utilization of urban water areas.

By 2010, 640,000 KM^2 of damaged rivers, 670,000 KM^2 of lakes and 4 million KM^2 of wetlands will be restored. For example, by building water level lifting facilities and gates, Chicago reversed the flow of the Chicago River that originally flowed into Lake Michigan, making it flow southward into the Illinois River. Urban sewage no longer flows into Lake Michigan. The blue Lake Michigan has become a world model of harmony between the city and the water area. On the basis of protecting the clean water of the lake, Chicago has developed recreational tourism along the lake to build children's museums, three-dimensional theaters, open-air stages, gardens and other recreational complexes along the lake.

Source: International Experience in Urban Water Issues and Leisure Tourism, Regional Research and Development, Issue 12, 2011, by Quan Hua.

Column 6.4 Urban Domestic Waste Treatment

1. Clarify the extension of producer responsibility (EPR). Japan found that the waste packaging of products accounted for 60% of household waste, so it issued the "Container and Packaging Recycling Act" in 1995, which stipulated that the "extended producer responsibility" product range was mainly paper, plastic and glass (at that time, the recovery rate of steel and aluminum in Japan was already high), and then included scrapped vehicles, household equipment and computers. Through the implementation of the Act, the recovery rate of waste products has been improved and a relatively stable source of funds has been provided for recovery activities. In order to reduce the harm of electronic waste, the European Union has promulgated the Administrative Directive on Waste Electronic and Electrical Products, the Provisions on Prohibiting the Use of Hazardous Substances in Electronic and Electrical Products and other decrees to clarify the extended management responsibility of producers.
2. Levy environmental tax. Studies in Ireland and Australia found that the weight of plastic bags accounted for 5% ~ 7% of the weight of street garbage. In order to reduce the use of plastic bags, Ireland began to levy an environmental tax on plastic bags in 2002, with a tax of 0.15 pounds per bag. In 2007, it increased to £ 0.22. In 2009, the plastic bag tax charge reached 23.4 million pounds, and the management cost was about 397,000 pounds, accounting for 17% of the revenue in 2009. The Irish government invests most of its income in the construction of waste management and recycling system. Compared with the initial implementation of environmental tax on plastic bags, the use of plastic bags in Ireland has decreased by more than 90%. Belgium not only imposes an environmental tax on plastic bags, but also on beverage bottles, glue, ink and disposable lunch boxes.
3. Classified collection and volume charging. In 1990, San Francisco, the United States, set the goal of achieving 50% of the classified recovery rate by the year 2000, or face the risk of a fine of 10,000 dollars a day. The government requires all San Francisco residents to divide their garbage into three categories: recyclable, food waste and non-recyclable. The municipal government has signed a contract with "recycling" company named Recology, which is responsible for the collection,

classification and disposal of garbage. Recology provides residents and enterprises with three garbage recycling bins free of charge. Residents and enterprises directly pay the garbage collection service fee to the Recology company. The charge for normal residents is 27.55 dollars per month, and the charge for active recyclers is 21.21 dollars per month. Low-income people can enjoy 25% discount. Enterprises pay according to the weight of discharged garbage. The municipal government also rewarded the Recology company for reaching the recycling goal, which enhanced the company's enthusiasm. In 2009, San Francisco began to implement the policy of punishment for violation of garbage classification rules, with a maximum fine of $100/time for residents and $1,000/time for enterprises. At present, San Francisco's garbage recycling rate has reached 77%, while the average recycling rate in the United States is 29%, making it the city with the highest recycling rate in the United States.

In order to improve the garbage classification collection rate and solve the problem of disorderly work of garbage collectors, Brazil requires residents to divide garbage into dry garbage and wet garbage. Dry garbage is transported to garbage collectors' cooperatives for manual sorting. At present, there are 610 garbage collectors' cooperatives in Brazil, and local governments provide free workplaces for them, as well as tax exemption and electricity free. Garbage collectors' cooperatives not only improve the recycling rate of garbage, but also provide a healthy and safe working environment for garbage collectors.

In 1995, Seoul, South Korea, began to implement the system of volume-based pricing, and achieved remarkable results. The amount of domestic garbage decreased from more than 15,000 tons/day in 1995 to more than 11,000 tons/day in 2009.

4. Limit landfill. Landfill may cause harm to the environment, especially the waste contains organic and toxic substances. In order to protect the environment and improve the recycling rate of garbage, many countries restrict or prohibit some kinds of materials from entering landfills. The EU Waste Landfill Technology Directive prohibits liquid waste, combustible waste, toxic waste, medical waste, waste tires and other materials from entering the landfill.
5. Priority heating. One of the international best practices to improve the incineration efficiency of incineration plants is to give priority to heating, which is twice as efficient as power supply. In March 2011, the UK introduced the world's first renewable thermal energy incentive plan (PHI) in order to encourage the priority of heating and increase the proportion of renewable thermal energy applications, giving tax incentives to renewable thermal energy producers. It plans to achieve the target of 12% renewable thermal energy by 2020, which is seven times that of 2009.

Source: International Experience, Chinese Problems and Optimization Strategies in Urban Domestic Waste Management, Ecological Economy, Issue 5, 2012, by Xu Jinlong, Zhu Yuezhao, Chen Hongxi, and Wang Xiao.

6.2.2.3 Policy Reference of Climate Resilient Cities—Low-Carbon City Construction

From a worldwide perspective, the exploration of climate resilient cities has just started. Low carbon is an important part of climate resilient. The construction of low carbon cities has been promoted worldwide and has gained some experience.

Column 6.5 Development of Low-Carbon Cities Through Demonstration: Taking Freiburg, Germany as an Example

In 1986, the Freiburg government planned to give up nuclear energy, use solar energy as the main energy of the city, and set up the first environmental protection office in Germany. In 1992, Freiburg was named the "German City of Environment" for its outstanding achievements in environmental science. As early as the environmental issues had not entered the global vision, the Freiburg government had already regarded environmental protection as an important task of the government. Its climate policy has three pillars: saving energy, improving energy efficiency and using renewable energy to replace fossil fuels. When formulating and implementing environmental policies, the government pays attention to continuously exploring new development areas and steadily promoting the implementation of the plan through key projects, even the construction of demonstration areas.

In terms of development demonstration areas, Freiburg's Freban District is known as the benchmark of Germany's sustainable development community. This area is a southern community 3 km away from the downtown of Freiburg, about 600,000 square meters. Formerly a military base, it has been transformed by the government into a low-carbon and energy-saving sustainable development community. Freban District is famous for its housing cooperative system. The 2,000 households and 5,000 residents living in Freban District are the owners and designers of the community. They formed a group by themselves to apply to the government for the purchase of construction land, and designed and built houses in strict accordance with the concept of high efficiency and energy conservation proposed by the government. Such houses can save at least 30% of energy. The community also has its own thermal power plant (with 80% wood chips and 20% natural gas as energy sources). Good thermal insulation and effective heating reduced carbon emissions by about 60%.

Source: The Role of Government in the Development of Low Carbon Cities - International Experience and Its Implications for China, Open Guide, December 8, 2009, by Guo Wanda and Liu Yiping.

Column 6.6 Development of Low Carbon Cities Through Sustainable Action Plans: Taking Sweden's Vicshur as an Example

Vicshur, a small Swedish city with the lowest carbon emission per capita in Europe, was awarded the "European Sustainable Energy Award" by the European Commission in 2007. As early as 1969, the Vicshur government unanimously adopted the decision to implement relevant environmental policies. In the 1980s, bioenergy entered the urban heating system. In 2005, renewable energy accounted for 88% of the heating system. At present, the environmental policy of Vicshur is mainly in the charge of Sweden's first climate committee established by the city. Its climate policy framework mainly includes three areas: daily life, natural environment and "Vicshur Zero Fossil Fuel Plan".

"Vicshur Zero Fossil Fuel Plan" is a world leading project issued by the city in 1996. It stops the use of fossil fuels in heating, energy, transportation, commerce and households, reduces carbon emissions, and makes energy consumption have no impact on climate change. The goal of the plan is to reduce carbon emissions by 50% in 2010 compared with 1993, and by 70% in 2025. It is expected to become the first city in the world with zero fossil fuel in 2015. To achieve the goal, the government has launched a series of actions: (1) Reaching a national consensus in the political field to influence the formation of public opinions; (2) Gradually eliminate direct heating by electricity; (3) Adopt environment-friendly motor vehicles in the procurement or leasing process; (4) Environmental friendly motor vehicles can be parked in urban parking lots for free; (5) Stimulate the demand for energy economy; (6) Provide energy advice to citizens; (7) The traffic design and road command system should be conducive to the use of pedestrians, bicycles and public transport systems.

"Zero fossil fuel plan" includes a series of well-designed action plans, with complete schedules in the following areas: (1) biofuels support district heating/cooling systems; (2) Energy efficiency; (3) Motor vehicles; (4) Traffic congestion and public transport; (5) Biofuels; (6) Bicycle.

Source: The Role of Government in the Development of Low Carbon Cities - International Experience and Its Implications for China, Open Guide, December 8, 2009, by Guo Wanda and Liu Yiping.

6.3 The Core of REEFCR City Policy Systems

6.3.1 The Scientific and Rational Planning and Designing of REEFCR City

6.3.1.1 Overall Planning and Designing Strategy

The preparation of the overall planning of REEFCR city must be based on the local natural, economic and social conditions, reasonably allocate resources, determine the urban capacity and population density according to the environmental carrying capacity, reasonably plan the architectural style, floor height and density according to the urban development positioning, strengthen the building of urban green belts, corridors and wetlands, guide and regulate the development direction of the city, and strive to create a harmonious human and natural living environment.

1. Plan the area where the REEFCR city is located as a whole.
   The overall planning of the REEFCR city must emphasize the spatial integration of urban and rural areas, and the coexistence and co-prosperity of the city and the region, that is, the integration and development of the city and the suburban areas. With the development and expansion of the city, the urban space will inevitably gradually cover the suburban areas. Whether from the perspective of urban–rural integration or the overall development of the city, the suburban areas need to be included in the REEFCR urban overall plan for unified consideration.
2. Comprehensively analyze and reasonably determine the urban capacity to ensure the dynamic balance between the urban construction area and the supply area.
   The development of cities is strictly restricted by the "environmental capacity" and "ecological carrying capacity" of nature. If the operation and development of a city break through these limits, a chain reaction will occur, leading to the destruction of the entire urban ecosystem. The overall planning of an eco-city must systematically analyze the carrying capacity of the urban ecosystem, the capacity of construction land, the supply capacity, the industrial capacity, and the environmental capacity of basic natural elements such as water, atmosphere, soil, etc., and then conduct a feasibility study on the development and construction of the city, so as to ensure that the development and construction of the city are coordinated with the environment, and that the long-term supply capacity and long-term bearing capacity of the city and its supply area are balanced. In short, we must always keep in mind that only a balanced and coordinated region can have a balanced and coordinated city.[20]
3. Emphasize the combination of urban overall planning and socio-economic development planning.
   The overall planning of REEFCR city should be multidisciplinary and multi type of work and interdisciplinary cross research. In particular, it is necessary to combine with the urban socio-economic development planning, systematically explore the countermeasures for the social and economic sustainable development of REEFCR city through planning means, so that social benefits, economic benefits and ecological benefits are comprehensively considered in the planning.
4. Ensuring broad public participation.
   Residents are the main actors in the fields of urban economy, society, culture, ecology, etc. Only when the public widely participates and fully adopts the public's suggestions can the urban planning and design have vitality. In the formulation, implementation and construction of the plan, it is necessary to give the public the opportunity to participate in varying degrees, so as to truly achieve the goal of "people's construction and people's management in people's cities".

6.3.1.2 Specific Implementation Policies

1. Establishment of the strategic concept of "planning first".
   Urban planning is the basis of urban construction and management and the direction and goal of urban development. To build a REEFCR city, it is necessary to have a long-term, scientific, high-level and advanced overall plan. The planning and design of REEFCR city should make full use of all kinds of urban landscapes, reasonably allocate seascape, mountain view, river view and pastoral scenery, display beautiful and unique natural ecological landscape, and integrate local unique folk culture and farmhouse culture. In the preparation of the overall plan, it is necessary to fully draw on international experience, combine regional conditions, and constantly innovate to highlight the "personalized" characteristics of the city in the planning. Listen to experts' opinions widely, hire well-known experts at home and abroad to help prepare the plan, and serve as urban planning consultants. Especially those important planning, urban design, large-scale projects and projects that have an important impact on the landscape must be demonstrated repeatedly. Listen to the opinions of the masses, let the citizens participate in the preparation of the plan, supervise the implementation of the plan, and maximize the positive role of the masses.
2. Urban green space system design with organic combination of "point, line and surface".
   A complete urban green space system will integrate natural landscapes. The REEFCR urban green space system should make full use of the topographic characteristics of the city, incorporate the natural mountain system, water system and vegetation into the urban structure, combine with urban buildings, and organize the urban green space system. This requires REEFCR city to strive to create urban green space landscape with combination of "point" (greening sketch, courtyard greening), "line" (road greening), and "surface" (parks, scenic tourist areas, garden clusters), forming a large urban and rural green pattern. The planning and design of REEFCR urban green space landscape should have its own characteristics. The layout of garden greening construction should be derived from nature and higher than nature. It should focus on natural layout, highlight plant landscape, and reflect the style of "transparent, bright, beautiful and generous".[21] In terms of spatial layout, it is necessary to combine urban architectural style, make full use of mountains and water, strictly control the intersection and transition zone between the built-up area and the external natural landscape, maintain good contact between the city and nature, and integrate the complete natural landscape into the city.
3. Well prepared in disaster prevention planning.
   The construction of REEFCR city requires a high level of disaster prevention. We should combine disaster prevention planning with landscape design, integrate tourism value with practical value, combine peacetime with wartime, and combine peacetime with disaster, so as to gradually establish a complete urban overall disaster prevention system. Urban construction should reflect the

centralized and decentralized spatial pattern, set aside green space, squares and evacuation routes, and make full use of underground space for refuge.

6.3.2 *Resource Development and Ecological Environment Protection of REEFCR City*

The ecological environment is a part of the natural environment and the basis for human survival and development. The construction of REEFCR city, as the goal of encouraging people to move towards the era of globalization, informatization and ecology, requires that cities neither sacrifice the ecological environment for development, nor give up development for simple environmental protection. The construction of REEFCR city should first accomplish the protection and construction of the ecological environment, rely on the sustainable development of the economy and society, take the ecological environment protection and construction and accelerating development as the goal of integration, and essentially achieve the internal unity of economic benefits, social benefits and ecological benefits.

6.3.2.1 Development and Protection According to Different Resource Types

1. Land resources
   Strengthen the ecological environment management of the land used in the development and construction process. It is strictly prohibited to borrow soil, dig sand and quarrying stones in areas along highways, railways and rivers that are prone to damage the landscape; the second is to strengthen the ecological environment protection of major projects such as highways, bridges, railways, ports, navigation channels, power transmission, oil (gas) transportation, and water supply (reservoir and river water diversion).[22]
2. Water resources
   The development and utilization of water resources must start from the whole basin, comprehensively consider the ecological interests and development interests of the upper, middle and lower reaches, make overall arrangements for the regional cooperation between the left and right sides of the straits, attach equal importance to open water source and saving water, combine water control with pollution control, and comprehensively balance the wet and dry seasons, so as to achieve scientific and efficient utilization of water resources.
   First, strengthen the protection of natural water bodies, rural water networks and fishery waters. In particular, the ecological environment of water conservation areas should be effectively protected, and the surrounding water conservation forests should be absolutely protected. Improve urban water environment, increase water surface, and increase urban ecological landscape.

Second, strengthen reservoir construction. The reservoir construction should be comprehensively planned and scientifically demonstrated, taking into account the water demand of the drainage basin and the reservoir in terms of building large reservoirs and a number of medium and small reservoirs. The ecological environment around the reservoir must be effectively protected.
Third, save water and prevent water pollution. Promote planned water use, implement water conservation, and establish a management system for high water consumption projects in water shortage areas; accelerate the construction of environmental protection infrastructure such as urban sewage treatment plants, improve the sewage treatment rate in cities and towns, especially in counties and townships, strictly implement the total pollutant discharge control system, and focus on protecting drinking water sources and main water function areas.

3. Mineral resources
The exploration and exploitation of mineral resources shall follow the principles of unified planning, comprehensive exploration, rational exploitation and comprehensive utilization. In particular, when developing new mining areas, it is necessary to implement corresponding ecological environment protection measures, and try to avoid and reduce the pollution and damage to cultivated land, grassland, forest land and water sources.
First, strengthen the control of ecological damage in mineral resources development zones. Any ecological damage caused by mineral development must be reconstructed or reclaimed within a time limit; the waste gas and waste water generated must be treated in accordance with the national pollution control requirements and discharged up to the standard; the discharged topsoil, tailings and waste residue must be disposed according to the requirements of water and soil conservation and pollution prevention[23]; mines, pitheads and brick yards (kilns) that have been decommissioned or closed must be treated in a timely manner to ensure ecological restoration and comprehensive utilization.[24]
The second is to further strengthen the rectification of mining order and prevent pollution and ecological damage. We should focus on rectifying the order of hot spot mines, and strictly investigate and punish illegal activities such as unauthorized mining, indiscriminate mining, pollution and mining that damage the ecological environment.
4. Biological resources
The development of biological resources must adhere to the principle of attaching equal importance to development, utilization, protection and proliferation, ensuring the population and quantity of wildlife and protecting biodiversity.[25]
First, actively participate in the National Biodiversity Protection Action Plan. Proceeding from the actual situation of the city, we should define our own specific protection objectives, tasks, priorities and priority protection fields and projects, actively carry out systematic investigation and research on biodiversity, establish biodiversity information and monitoring networks, and protect, research, save and utilize the biodiversity of the city.[26]

Second, the development of biological resources must ensure biological security. Accelerate the construction of biodiversity gene bank; strengthen the environmental management of biotechnology development and utilization, and establish the corresponding risk assessment system; the introduction of alien species must be subject to ecological environment impact assessment to prevent the invasion of alien species.

5. Agricultural resources

   The agricultural form of REEFCR city basically belongs to suburban agriculture and urban modern agriculture. It undertakes the functions of providing safe and pollution-free agricultural and sideline products and ecological environmental protection for the main urban areas. Therefore, it focuses on the development of ecological agriculture, low-carbon agriculture and circular agriculture.

   First, protect and rationally use agricultural resources in the process of urban development. Adhere to the strictest cultivated land protection system, adhere to the national red line of cultivated land, give full play to and comprehensively utilize the advantages of agricultural resources and ecological advantages, and comprehensively plan and rationally organize agricultural production on the basis of ensuring the sustainable development of water resources, cultivated land, grassland, forests, etc. In particular, we should focus on forestry as a special industry and develop fruit forests and economic forests according to local conditions.

   Second, strengthen the environmental management of agricultural development projects. Environmental impact assessment system shall be implemented for reclamation of barren mountains, reclamation of tidal flats, agricultural regional development, and construction of commodity bases, so as to control the adverse effects of various agricultural construction on the ecological environment.

   The third is to prevent and control agricultural pollution. Promote pesticide and biological control with low residue, high efficiency and low toxicity to reduce the environmental pollution caused by agricultural chemicals; develop water-saving agriculture and improve the effective utilization rate of water; strengthen the comprehensive utilization of straw and develop the recycling of waste; promote the use of degradable agricultural film to reduce "white pollution" in agriculture; actively develop clean energy such as biogas, solar energy and wind energy.

   Fourth, create a safe, pollution-free, green agricultural product brand. Build organic agricultural product production bases, develop modern agricultural parks, extend the industrial chain, improve added value, and produce high-end and high-quality characteristic agricultural products.

6.3.2.2 Promotion of the Construction of Ecological Demonstration Areas

The construction of REEFCR city should be promoted from point to area. First, pilot projects should be selected for demonstration, and then their experience should be promoted. Therefore, the construction of REEFCR urban ecological demonstration areas is the first choice. REEFCR cities should, according to the overall goal of ecological city construction, focus on protecting and improving the ecological environment, realizing the rational development and sustainable use of resources, and carry out the construction of ecological demonstration areas in an organized, planned and step-by-step manner in areas with good ecological conditions. REEFCR city should build a large number of ecological demonstration areas with various types and characteristics to summarize experience, explore laws, optimize models and display directions for the construction of REEFCR city.

The REEFCR urban ecological demonstration area can choose different construction tasks according to different regional characteristics, basic conditions and development priorities. For example, build ecological demonstration plants, ecological tourism demonstration areas, ecological demonstration communities, etc. in urban areas; build ecological demonstration villages, ecological agriculture demonstration areas, agricultural industry and trade integration demonstration areas, and rural environment comprehensive improvement demonstration areas in the urban suburbs; build demonstration areas for ecological damage restoration and treatment, and demonstration areas for comprehensive improvement of land degradation in resource-based cities.

To promote the construction of ecological demonstration areas, we need to strengthen leadership, management and publicity. First, strengthen leadership. The construction of the ecological demonstration area will be included in the national economic and social development plan, and a leading group for the construction of the ecological demonstration area headed by the main responsible person of the party and government will be established, and a technical steering committee that absorbs a large number of experts and scholars will be established to organize and coordinate the construction of the REEFCR urban ecological demonstration area. Secondly, strengthen management. For various types of ecological demonstration areas, unified planning, classified management and regular inspection shall be carried out. In particular, the competent department of environmental resources shall formulate relevant rules and regulations, prepare technical specifications, organize inspection and acceptance, and be seriously responsible for the daily management of the construction of ecological demonstration areas. Finally, strengthen publicity. Mobilize the enthusiasm of Party members, cadres and the masses to build an ecological demonstration zone; mobilize the whole society to make efforts to form a situation where the whole people run ecological demonstration areas; in particular, we should make good use of the policy guidance and market mechanism to raise funds for the construction of the demonstration zone through multiple channels.

6.3.2.3 Specific Implementation Policies

1. Strengthen the leadership of ecological environment protection and construction. Governments at all levels, departments and industries have included the protection and construction of the ecological environment in their daily work, set feasibility indicators, and included the protection and construction of the ecological

environment as an important part of their work performance assessment. Establish a comprehensive decision-making mechanism and technical steering committee for ecological environment protection and construction, conduct environmental impact assessment and tracking assessment for major economic and technological policies, key resource development, economic and social development plans, ecological construction projects, regional development, etc., summarize experience and training in time, and improve decision-making management level.

2. Strive to integrate the protection and construction of the ecological environment into the rule of law.
   First of all, we should attach importance to the construction of the rule of law and strengthen the law enforcement of ecological environment protection. Strictly implement the existing national and provincial laws and regulations on environmental protection and resource management, crack down on criminal acts that damage the ecological environment, and truly ensure that there are laws to abide by, law enforcement must be strict, and violations must be prosecuted.[27] Secondly, local laws and regulations on ecological environment protection should be established and improved according to specific conditions to form a system of environmental protection laws and regulations. Based on the actual situation, we should formulate some stricter, more specific and more operable local regulations and government rules that are compatible with national laws and administrative regulations, especially strengthen the legislation in areas lagging behind environmental protection, such as the regulations on supervision and management of ecological environment protection, the methods for compensated use of resources and ecological environment compensation, and the regulations on key resource development and environmental restoration. Third, strengthen the innovation of supervision and management system. Establish a regular inspection system, and implement the review and review system of law enforcement, reward and punishment system, department law enforcement responsibility system, and regular reporting system; establish and improve the supervision mechanism of the news media, social organizations and the masses on ecological environment protection; fully implement the veto system for ecological and environmental protection.
3. Establish an input mechanism for ecological environment protection and construction to adapt to the market economy system.
   First, increase investment in ecological environment protection and construction and broaden financing channels. Adhere to the joint participation of the state, local governments, collectives, enterprises and individuals, and raise funds for ecological environment protection and construction in various forms and channels.[28] Second, we should establish economic policies oriented to protecting and improving the ecological environment. The preferential policies of industrial policies and priority projects should be used to guide the flow of social productive forces to the direction conducive to the protection and construction of the ecological environment; Explore the compensation mechanism for natural resources and ecological environment, realize the paid use of resources, and levy resources development compensation taxes on major natural resources and important

natural resources; use consumption policies to guide social consumption trends, and use economic methods to reduce the consumption of environmental pollution goods.

4. Improve the environmental awareness of the whole society through publicity and education.
   On the one hand, give full play to the positive role of the news media and various publicity tools, and more widely and deeply carry out multi-level, all-round and diversified environmental protection publicity activities. Pay attention to the participation of the masses in the publicity activities, fully mobilize the enthusiasm and initiative of the masses to participate in environmental protection, and arouse the environmental awareness of the masses in consumption, life, travel and other aspects. Strengthen the supervision of news and public opinion, praise advanced models, and expose illegal acts; continuously improve the system of letters and visits, reports and hearings[29]; establish public participation mechanism and supervision mechanism. On the other hand, we should integrate environmental protection related knowledge into education and institutionalize, standardize and normalize environmental protection education. Strengthen the training of Party and government cadres at all levels and enterprise managers on ecological environment protection, and constantly improve their comprehensive decision-making ability on ecological environment protection; strengthen the ecological environment education of primary and secondary school students, and constantly improve the professional education of ecological environment protection.

6.3.3 *Climate Security and Disaster Prevention and Reduction in REEFCR City*

6.3.3.1 Promotion of Urban Climate Mitigation Program

The city is the center of economic and social development, and also the region with the most concentrated carbon emissions. This region has its special climate characteristics, such as the "Heat Island Effect". At present, the countermeasures for urban climate security mainly focus on four aspects: urban development mode, urban building environment, urban infrastructure and urban transportation.

1. Urban development model
   With the continuous development of urban productivity and rapid economic growth, cities will inevitably face ecological and environmental problems such as increasingly serious pollution and increasing environmental load. This is the general law of the relationship between urbanization and ecological environment consumption, and we can do nothing about it. However, different urban development models, different development concepts, environmental policies and technical levels, etc., have different ecological and environmental effects.

The extensive urban development mode has increased the intensity and quantity of ecological environment consumption in the economic development, and has emphasized development over protection, construction over management and protection, which leads to deteriorating ecological environment; the intensive urban development model has reduced the intensity and quantity of ecological environment consumption in economic development, the negative effect of urban development on the ecological environment has been weakened and the positive effect has been strengthened. The comprehensive benefits of urban economy, society and ecological environment have been maximized. It can be seen that if we choose an intensive urban development model, change the mode of economic growth and resource utilization in the process of urbanization, and achieve the harmonious development of economy and environment, even if the urban economy and society develop rapidly, the urban ecological environment will not deteriorate, and the environmental pollution can be effectively treated in a timely manner.

2. Urban building environment
   The energy consumption of urban construction industry accounts for 1/3 of the final energy consumption of the city, and accounts for a larger proportion of electric energy consumption. Therefore, the design and utilization of urban building is an important field to mitigate climate change. The technology level of developed countries is leading and mature, energy efficiency technology and alternative energy technology are often used in urban building, which can basically achieve the purpose of building energy conservation. The developing countries started late and their technology is relatively backward. At present, they mainly adopt methods such as installing energy-saving equipment in buildings and using energy-saving materials to reduce energy consumption.
3. Urban infrastructure
   Urban infrastructure, especially energy (electricity and gas) networks and water supply and sanitation systems, are critical to shaping the current and future trajectory of greenhouse gas emissions. The type of energy supply, the carbon concentration in water supply, environmental sanitation and waste disposal, and the methane emission level at landfill sites are important elements of local greenhouse gas emissions. At present, urban climate change mitigation infrastructure projects mainly focus on new energy development, waste to energy and other aspects. There are few projects dedicated to reducing the carbon concentration in water supply, sanitation and waste disposal. To achieve the goal of resource efficient, environment friendly and climate resilient of urban infrastructure, we can start from two aspects: one is to transform the existing infrastructure system and establish a new network through new technology and engineering design; the other is to select some communities and implement pilot projects to reduce carbon emissions from water supply, environmental sanitation and waste disposal.
4. Urban transportation
   With the development of cities and the explosive growth of the number of cars, many families have more than one car, and vehicle exhaust emissions are one of the main sources of urban air pollution, which leads to the urban air quality often

falling into a serious pollution situation. At present, most countries in the world are aware of the traffic congestion and air pollution problems caused by automobiles, and actively take measures to mitigate climate change in transportation. The most common measures are to develop public transport (including intercity express rail, rail transit, BRT, etc.), adopt clean energy technology, encourage the use of non-motor vehicles, and encourage green travel (including walking, using bicycles).

6.3.3.2 Establishment of Urban Comprehensive Disaster Prevention and Reduction System

In addition to conventional disasters such as car accidents and fires, cities will also face sudden disasters such as earthquakes, urban waterlogging, toxic substances, etc. Therefore, establishing an urban comprehensive disaster prevention and reduction system and improving the city's emergency response capacity to sudden disasters is one of the important contents of the REEFCR city, and is also the goal that distinguishes the REEFCR city from the "Resource Efficient and Environment Friendly" city.

1. Establishment and improvement of the mechanism and system for dealing with sudden disasters, and change the management mode to a comprehensive one.
   A national comprehensive disaster reduction system under the unified management of ministries and commissions will be established, and local emergency and disaster reduction institutions led by mayors will be established to take charge of the comprehensive disaster reduction work in cities. Establish and improve a disaster emergency management system featuring unified command, comprehensive coordination, classified management, hierarchical responsibility and territorial management, form a disaster prevention decision-making command system with strong organization and coordination, scientific and effective decision-making, which can centralize leadership and mobilize all social forces to participate, coordinate orderly and operate efficiently, avoid overlapping government functions, multiple government departments and multiple management, and improve the administrative efficiency of disaster prevention and mitigation, Reduce the cost of repeated construction. Such a comprehensive disaster reduction management mode is not only more efficient, more organized, more powerful, orderly and effective than the temporary headquarters or leading group when disasters occur, but also more forward-looking in the daily construction of disaster prevention and reduction system.[30]
2. Strengthen the construction of urban disaster emergency sites.
   Emergency shelters are the most common way to deal with and prevent urban disasters. From the perspective of urban safety, their role cannot be replaced, and they have been highly valued by various countries. In the Plan for the Construction of the National Emergency Response System for Public Emergencies during the Eleventh Five Year Plan period, the Chinese government clearly proposed that provincial capital cities and cities with a population of more than

one million should speed up the construction of emergency shelters in accordance with relevant plans and standards. Emergency shelters can be built in open places such as parks and squares, or the previously built air raid shelters can be expanded and reinforced as emergency shelters. Attention should also be paid to the construction of rapid evacuation channels near the emergency shelters.

3. Disaster reduction and prevention drills in communities.
   At the time of a disaster, although the country can fully mobilize resources from all over the country to support the disaster-stricken area, the self-rescue of the disaster-stricken area is extremely important. If the defense capacity at the grassroots level is perfect, it will take the initiative in disaster prevention and effectively reduce the disaster damage rate.[31] The community is the spatial unit of urban development and the best carrier for implementing the plan of benefiting the people. The slogan of the International Day for Disaster Reduction in 2001 is "develop a community centered disaster reduction strategy", which is to mobilize all residents to participate in the construction of community disaster prevention and reduction, organize community residents to exercise, and improve the ability of residents to reduce and prevent disasters.

6.4 Regional Differences of REEFCR City Policy Systems

6.4.1 Policy Focus of Building REEFCR Cities in Main Functional Areas

The policy of building REEFCR city in the main functional areas mainly covers four aspects: optimized development zones, key development zones, restricted development zones, and prohibited development zones (Table 6.1).

6.4.1.1 Optimized Development Zone

The optimized development zone is an advanced area in China's development and has good conditions in the construction of REEFCR cities. The total population of the optimized development zone accounts for about 20.6% of the country, and the land accounts for 1.1%. The natural endowment conditions are superior, and it will still play a very important role in the factor gathering and economic and social development in the future.

First, strengthen ecological environment governance and reduce carbon emissions.

The land development density of the optimized development zone is high, and the carrying capacity of resources and environment is reduced. To build a REEFCR city in the optimized development zone, it is necessary to effectively solve the contradiction between environment and development, and achieve a win–win situation

Table 6.1 Key policies for the construction of REEFCR city in main functional areas

	Optimized development zone	Key development zone	Restricted development zone	Prohibited development zone
Features	1. Good economic foundation 2. Mindset of ecological civilization construction 3. New achievements have been made in ecological governance	1. Undertake the ecological consumption brought by the industrial transfer of the optimized development zone 2. Undertake ecological consumption brought by population transfer in restricted and prohibited development zones 3. Coordination between economic development and ecological construction goals	1. Related to the ecological security of the country or a large area 2. Due to degraded ecosystem, large-scale and high-intensity industrialization and urbanization development need to be limited in the land and space development	1. National legal nature reserves 2. Establish an industrial system compatible with the functions of the prohibited development zones
Key points	1. Strengthen ecological environment governance and reduce carbon emissions 2. Improve the ability of independent innovation and promote the development of ecological economy 3. Strengthen the cultivation of ecological culture and promote the all-round development of human beings	1. Establish new ecological values of people in key development zones 2. Establish an appropriate circular economy operation system	1. Establish and improve the ecological compensation mechanism 2. Develop ecological agriculture 3. Develop green economy 4. Develop featured economy	1. Strengthen transfer payment 2. Develop featured industries

in economy and ecology. First, control the source of pollution, terminate existing pollution projects, and prohibit any production and operation activities that produce new pollution. Develop cleaner production, strengthen the purification and treatment of waste water, waste gas and other pollutants for existing energy consuming industries, and maximize the effectiveness of environmental protection industries such as sewage treatment plants and garbage treatment stations. The second is to promote the implementation of energy conservation and emission reduction projects in line with local conditions, strictly supervise enterprises with high pollution, high energy consumption and high emissions, and order them to accelerate technological transformation to reduce energy consumption and reduce waste gas and wastewater emissions. Establish a long-term reward and punishment mechanism, implement the responsibility system for energy conservation and emission reduction, and regularly check the energy conservation and emission reduction goals of local governments and enterprises. The third is to repair the ecological environment, strengthen the construction of urban green belts and gardens, and put an end to such phenomena as green space giving way to parking spaces, real estate occupying green space, and green space becoming a sanitary blind corner.

Second, enhance the ability of independent innovation and promote the development of ecological economy.

The economic development level of the optimized development zone is higher than that of other main functional zones. To achieve a win–win situation in economy and ecology and alleviate the environmental development contradiction, the development of ecological economy is an inevitable choice. The optimized development zone has strong scientific and technological strength and a large number of innovative talents. It should give full play to its innovation advantages, focus on promoting the innovation of green science and technology, and develop the ecological economy. Encourage enterprises to improve their independent innovation ability, advocate the green design concept with the core principle of "3R", research and develop new and high technologies such as efficient energy-saving technology, pollution treatment technology, cleaner production technology, recycling, etc., effectively reduce the over development of nonrenewable resources, reduce the emission of harmful substances, enable products to achieve classified recycling and reuse, and promote the effective use of resources.[32]

Third, strengthen the cultivation of ecological culture and promote the all-round development of people.

Optimized development zone is the area with the highest level of economic development and the largest population density. Human behavior directly affects economic, ecological and other fields. Therefore, strengthening the cultivation of ecological culture and promoting the all-round development of people are particularly important for optimized development zone to build a REEFCR city. Strengthen the public education of environmental ethics in the optimized development zone to improve the level of ecological civilization awareness, encourage people to consume green, low-carbon and circular, tap people's enthusiasm and initiative for environmental protection, and let people care about, pay attention to, participate in and supervise environmental protection projects around them.

6.4.1.2 Key Development Zones

First, establish new ecological values of people in key development zones.

The economic growth rate of key development zones is very fast, so it is particularly necessary to change the value of putting interests first, form a new ecological value of harmonious coexistence of urbanization and ecological civilization, and integrate this new ecological value into all areas of economic and social development, throughout the whole process of urbanization. With the realization of harmonious coexistence between human and nature as the core content, pay close attention to the bearing capacity of resources and environment in the process of regional industrialization and urbanization, ensure the coexistence and co-prosperity of social economy and natural ecology, the harmonious development of man and nature, and the reasonable coordination of ecological environment and resource utilization, thus promoting the city to embark on a sustainable and civilized development path with highly developed productivity, good ecology, and improved people's quality of life.

Second, establish an appropriate circular economy operation system.

The operation system of circular economy consists of two components, one is "import" and the other is "export". First of all, solve the problem of economic "entrance" of key development zones in a way of resource conservation and ecological protection. At present, the mode of resource development and utilization is extensive and the comprehensive utilization rate of resources is low. Under such conditions, the sustainable development of regional economy and society must be achieved by reducing the total input of energy resources. For example, reduce the use of nonrenewable energy, try to use renewable resources and energy, develop new energy, and develop technologies for cascade utilization, recycling of resources and energy. Secondly, solve the "export" problem of key development zones by recycling. Corresponding to the goal of investment minimization is emission minimization. Form a circular production system among enterprises in the region, form a circular network and industrial chain among industries, reduce waste, and improve the utilization efficiency of resources and energy.

6.4.1.3 Restricted Development Zone

The development of restricted development zones is based on the maintenance of ecological balance, and its ecosystem is of great significance for maintaining the balance of the entire large ecosystem. The construction of REEFCR city in restricted development zones needs to coordinate economic construction with resources and environment, achieve sustainable development, and take a civilized development path of production development, prosperous life and good ecology.

First, establishment and improvement of the ecological compensation mechanism.

Restricted development zones relate to the national ecological security and the supply security of agricultural products, the improvement of the people's quality of life and the sustainable development of the country. Accelerating the establishment and improvement of the ecological compensation mechanism, and providing reasonable compensation for the contributions made by these regions to ensure the national ecological security are the key to promote the formation of the main functional zones.[33] Due to the restriction of economic development and the focus on protecting the ecological environment, the restricted development zone is in a weak position in protecting ecological construction, maintaining the basic operation of local power, equalization of basic public services, and supporting and cultivating the development of characteristic industries. Mainly through ecological compensation mechanisms, the central and provincial governments provide financial transfer payments and increase investment in the restricted development zone in terms of funds, materials, technology and talents.

Second, development of ecological agriculture.

Ecological agriculture is an agricultural form with low consumption, low pollution and high efficiency, and it is also the main industrial form of restricted development zones. Restricted development zones should follow the principle of "integration, coordination, recycling and regeneration", actively build an ecological agricultural recycling system, and gradually realize the rationalization of agricultural industrial structure, the ecological production technology, and the harmless production of products.[34] In the development of agricultural industry in restricted development zones, it is necessary to return farmland to forests and pastures as soon as possible, adjust measures to local conditions, develop rationally, and vigorously develop ecological animal husbandry and forest, fruit, bamboo, vegetable, tea, herbal medicine and other industries. At the same time, actively explore the model of small and medium-sized ecological agricultural parks, develop ecological agricultural parks combining planting and breeding, and constantly promote the transformation of traditional agriculture to ecological agriculture. Based on the rural reality of restricted development zones, the biogas project is taken as the link to closely combine the recycling of waste resources in agricultural production with the energy construction project, and strive to achieve the win–win goal of developing clean energy, reducing waste, improving rural living environment, extending the agricultural ecological industry chain, and promoting rural economic development.[35]

Third, development of green economy.

Green economy is an economic form that is market-oriented, based on traditional industrial economy, taking ecological environment construction as the basic industrial chain, and aiming at the harmony between economy and environment. It is a state that industrial economy shows to meet the new needs of mankind. The green economy transforms many technologies beneficial to the environment into productive forces, and takes full account of the capacity of the ecological environment and the carrying capacity of natural resources through environmentally friendly economic behavior, so as to achieve long-term stable economic growth. Developing green economy and cultivating new economic growth points characterized by low emissions play an important role in speeding up the formation of an industrial structure and growth mode that can save energy and resources and protect the ecological environment in restricted development areas.

Fourth, development of characteristic economy.

In restricted development zones, we should fully explore and utilize high-quality local products, unique landscape resources, unique folk culture, exquisite characteristic buildings and other characteristic resources to develop environmental protection tertiary industries such as culture and tourism.[36] The local government should give support to the development of characteristic advantageous industries such as ecological agriculture, ecological forestry, eco-tourism and renewable energy development in the restricted development area, and explore the application of a series of preferential policies such as bank credit, loan guarantee, financial discount, investment subsidies, tax reduction and exemption, and technical transformation support.

6.4.1.4 Prohibited Development Zone

First, strengthen transfer payment.

Most of the prohibited development zones are regions with ecological and environmental significance. Except for a few in economically developed administrative regions, most of them are economically underdeveloped. And in the short term, with the promotion of its main function positioning, its own financial resources will be further reduced before the establishment of the emerging characteristic industries. At present, the focus of transfer payment is to ensure that these regions have the financial resources to provide basic public services, strengthen ecological investment and construction, and improve supporting policies and measures for ecological migration.[37]

Second, development of characteristic industries.

The ecological function orientation of the prohibited development zone is based on the overall situation of the ecological security of the whole country. In this area, the development of any industry cannot damage its own main function.[38] The development policy of the state for the prohibited development zones is to implement compulsory protection, control the excessive interference of human factors on the ecology, and prohibit all development activities that do not conform to the national regulations. The development of this region must focus on ecological construction, actively develop characteristic agriculture and tourism, and realize the ecological transformation of characteristic agriculture and tourism.[39]

6.4.2 Policy Focus of Different Types of Cities in Building REEFCR City

Generally speaking, cities can be divided into different types according to different characteristics of cities and certain standards and methods. According to different main functions, cities can be divided into industrial cities, resource cities, tourism cities, service cities and other different types of cities.[40] Different types of cities have different characteristics in their REEFCR city construction.

6.4.2.1 Industrial City—Urban Circular Economy Development

The construction of industrial cities into REEFCR cities should follow the concept of circular economy, which is characterized by the coordinated development of economy, society and environment, as well as the efficient use of materials, energy and information. The sustainable development of eco industrial cities advocates the material recycling production mode of "resources - products - renewable resources", with the basic principles of "reduce, reuse, and recycle"; follow the clean production path of "low mining, low investment, high utilization and low emission", and avoid the end of pipe governance paradigm.[41] The eco industrial system can not only provide the society with a large number of industrial products with many varieties, advanced technology and good quality with less labor input, but also make rational use of natural resources, constantly improve the quality of the city's ecological environment, provide a good living environment for residents, create favorable conditions for the sustainable development of eco industrial cities, and then achieve the simultaneous improvement of industrial economic benefits, social benefits and ecological benefits.

6.4.2.2 Resource-Based City—Urban "Transformation" Realization

Establish a compensation mechanism for resource development. According to the principle of "who develops, who protects, who benefits, who compensates, who pollutes, who governs, who destroys, who repairs", it is clear that the responsibility subjects for resource compensation, ecological environment protection and repair are all kinds of mining enterprises.[42] The government should provide resources exhausted cities with appropriate funds and policy support to help solve the problem of insufficient funds in ecological environment, social security and infrastructure construction.

Foster continuous alternative industries. For resource-based cities, we should cultivate and strengthen their alternative industries, develop diversified industries, so as to enhance their own development ability, help resource-based cities out of difficulties, and help the construction of REEFCR cities.[43]

6.4.2.3 Tourism City—Eco Tourism City Building

An eco-tourism city is a modern new type city that uses the principles of ecology, economics and tourism, follows the ecological laws and urban development rules, takes the construction of an ecological city as the basis, takes the development of urban eco-tourism as the main line, takes the virtuous cycle of natural ecology and the harmony between human and nature and society as the core, and takes the realization of sustainable development of the city as the goal to plan, build and manage.[44] For tourist cities, reasonable urban planning is particularly important. From the reality, within the scope of the overall balance of the urban ecological economic system, the ecological economic balance should be taken as the priority principle to reflect the characteristics of the city. At the same time, comprehensive design and planning of urban buildings, public facilities, garden communities, etc. shall be carried out in combination with urban customs, regional culture, etc. to fully reflect the urban characteristics and create a city tourism brand.

6.4.2.4 Service City—Modern Ecological Service City Building

In the process of urbanization, the development of cities should be closely linked with the development of people and the harmonious coexistence of people and nature. By rationally adjusting the industrial structure of the city, we can realize the service of the city and promote the sustainable development of the city. The "12th Five Year Plan" of China proposes to vigorously develop the productive and living service industries, expand the service sector, develop new business formats, cultivate new hot spots, and promote large-scale, branded and networked operations. In the transition period of China's urbanization process, we must rely on large cities with fast service industry development as the main force, transform the urban economic development mode, take the service industry as the new power of urban development, and gradually build a modern ecological service-oriented city.

6.5 The Application of Participatory Management Approach in REEFCR City Policy Systems

6.5.1 Basic Concept of Participatory Management

Participatory management has several definitions in the construction of REEFCR cities: "people's voluntary and democratic involvement in the decision-making process, including setting development goals, formulating development policies, planning and implementing development plans, monitoring and evaluation; contribute to development efforts; share the benefits of development." "Participation can bring the following benefits: a high degree of commitment and ability to implement and execute decisions; greater innovation, many new thoughts and ideas; creativity, motivation and sense of responsibility." "For urban development, participation includes people's involvement in the decision-making process, project implementation, benefit sharing of development projects, and involvement in evaluation." "Urban participation is a positive process for beneficiaries to influence the implementation and direction of development projects. This influence is mainly to improve and strengthen their own living conditions, such as income, self-reliance and the value they pursue in other aspects."

Participatory management method is to build the content discussed on the thinking mode, concept and understanding level of the managed object. Its purpose is not limited to exploring problems. It can enable people to actively participate in the process of discussing and telling their known problems, so that they can feel that they are not ignorant and passive respondents, but masters who are knowledgeable, active, and able to prove and change their own situation. In this way, participatory management creates a positive atmosphere for "research". In this atmosphere, the previously distinct boundaries between the government departments and those who are managed under the government departments have been broken. In principle, the participatory management method aims to establish a new knowledge structure by creatively integrating the different knowledge and experiences of participants. This process requires the government departments to change their roles, attitudes and behaviors, and become facilitator, guidance and advice seekers. Through this process of role transformation and mutual learning, participants can have the skills to research problems and explore solutions.

Participatory management emphasizes the process. The main participants of sustainable urban construction are the public of the city. Their participation in the project should be the whole process. The public should participate in the investigation, planning and design implementation, monitoring and evaluation of urban construction projects. In this process, their participation is not limited in labor contribution but also includes broader content, such as participation in decision-making and selection process; motivation and responsibility; life knowledge and innovation; control and utilization of resources, etc. By participating in the project, the public will not only be able to develop themselves and become rich through employment, but also benefit from it.

6.5.2 Levels and Types of Public Participation in the REEFCR City Policy System

Participation is an interactive process. The public has different forms and degrees of participation in different projects and activities, and different forms and degrees of participation will lead to different results. Due to different forms and processes of participation, it is generally divided into participation in investigation and planning, participation in management, participation in mapping, participation in monitoring and evaluation, etc.

1. Participate in investigation and diagnosis. As main stakeholders, the public, together with government officials, outsiders and other stakeholders, use tools such as event review, resource utilization map drawing, advantages and disadvantages analysis, rich poor classification, and problem ranking to summarize the development of all aspects of the REEFCR city construction, and find out the main problems and solutions.
2. Participation in planning and decision-making. It is the main content and symbol of participation. Participation in decision-making on the basis of planning is the highest level of participation. The public generally discuss and vote on major urban issues democratically through the NPC or CPPCC and other deliberative bodies.

3. Participate in implementation. The public use their own and family members' funds, technology and other resources to participate in the whole process of development project implementation.
4. Participation benefits. It is the purpose, starting point and destination of the participatory concept. The benefits of public participation include ecological benefits, economic benefits and social benefits; the income can be obtained by prior contract agreement or by enjoying public goods. However, no matter what method is adopted, it must be fair, just and open, and let the public discuss and decide.

According to the willingness, degree and scope of participation, participation can be divided into directive participation, passive participation, consultative participation, incentive participation, functional participation, mutual participation and autonomous participation. (Table 6.2).

Table 6.2 Types of participatory management

Type	Features of participation
Directive participation	False participation. The public is forced to participate, without selectivity and any power
Passive participation	Tell the public what has happened or been decided. The management department or the project government department will participate unilaterally. The public will participate according to the decision of outsiders. Information sharing is only for outsiders
Consultative participation	External institutions have made decisions and controlled the whole process. The public only answers questions, and does not share decisions and benefits. The outsiders do not think they should consider the suggestions of the public
Incentive participation	Outsiders decide what to do and how to do it. At the same time, local people are encouraged to participate by means of rewards and punishments. The public's participation is rewarded with food, cash or other material incentives by contributing resources, such as labor and land. The public can contribute their own resources, but they do not have a process of evaluation or learning, and do not have a long-term perspective. When the project ends, the material stimulus will also end
Functional participation	The public is regarded as a means of participation to achieve the project objectives, especially in terms of cost reduction. People form groups to participate to meet the established objectives of decision-making projects. Once the objectives are achieved, the public will be forgotten
Mutual participation	The public and outsiders make decisions together. The public and external institutions learn from each other in their participation. The disadvantage is that they still do not regard the public as the main body
Autonomous participation	The public make their own decisions and carry out activities independently. Determine to establish the contact they need with the outside world, and obtain any resources and technical advice they need. The public independently implements urban development projects, emphasizing the independent participation of the public, so that the development is ultimately sustainable

6.5.3 The Characteristics of Public Participation in the REEFCR City Policy System

Extensiveness. The "participatory" theory emphasizes the participation of the masses, not to exclude the participation of the government or scientific and technological personnel, but to make sure that all parties should play their due roles in the sustainable development of urban construction activities. The participation of the public in urban development must be extensive to ensure that all the public enjoy rights and interests fairly.

The whole process. Social public participation in sustainable urban development includes the whole process of investigation, decision-making, planning, implementation, control, benefit-sharing, distribution, etc. The interruption or obstacle of a certain link will directly affect the degree of public participation, and sometimes may lead to the withdrawal of the public from the process, thus making sustainable urban development projects far away from the set goals, or even fail.

6.5.4 Basic Principles of Public Participation in the REEFCR City Policy System

First, establish an equal "partnership". The process of participatory development is the joint efforts of government departments and the public which is mutual benefit, and the relationship between government departments and the public is equal and cooperative. Mutual respect, mutual trust, exchange and communication, and mutual learning are important prerequisites for establishing a "partnership" relationship. Participatory style can guide people to express their opinions on their own thoughts and feelings and issues of concern, and can lay a foundation for more proactive communication activities. In this form of exchange activity, participants will no longer play the role of the silent and passive receiver, on the contrary, they and the government will build equal "partnership" and work together to achieve mutual goals.

Second, attach importance to the process rather than the result. According to past experiences for many years, urban development projects were result-oriented, but in fact, such development results are usually not satisfactory. However, any urban development practice is a process, result-oriented or process-ignored will affect the success of the results. Participatory style should provide a correct consciousness to guide people's behavior without affecting the self-organization and development ability of local people. In the process of participation, all participants should not only pay attention to how many tall buildings have been built, how many factories have been constructed, and how much GDP has increased, but also consolidate the knowledge learned by the participants and the public in this process to promote the sustainable development of the city.

Third, improve the comprehensive ability of participants. The target group of general projects is the general public in the city, even the poorest citizens. One of the main purposes of participatory activities is to enable these people to fully participate in all activities of the project, and in this process, enhance their self-confidence and improve their comprehensive ability. At the same time, the staff of the project management and implementation agency can also learn from the public in this process to improve their management and action capabilities. It is also a process of building self-confidence and self-esteem for urban residents to conduct dialogue and exchange information with outsiders as active participants (rather than passive research objects). It is necessary for the urban public to see that their opinions have attracted attention and are listed as topics of conversation. Helping marginalized people to build self-confidence is a crucial link in the process of participation, which creates conditions for people to know their knowledge level and ability.

6.5.5 The General Thought of Public Participation in the REEFCR City Policy System

The construction of REEFCR city is related to building a prosperous society for the whole people. We must closely follow the macro strategy of the Party and the country, and make steady progress under the guidance of the spirit of the 18th National Congress of the CPC.

According to the characteristics of the urban public in China, the key point to promote the public's participation in the construction of REEFCR city is to ensure the right of public participation and promote ecological civilization.

6.5.5.1 Thought One: The Power and Ability of the Public to Participate in the Construction of REEFCR City

As the REEFCR city construction is closely related to the production and life of the public, the public themselves pay close attention to the construction of sustainable cities. Therefore, the key to promote public participation is to ensure their right to know information and participate in decision-making.

The right to information means that every public has the right to obtain information related to urban construction from the government. This information should not only include the state of the atmosphere, drinking water, noise, phenology, biodiversity, etc., but also include relevant policies and projects and the possible impact on people. The public should be able to obtain such information as long as they apply, no matter for what reasons or motives. Government departments are also responsible for regular information disclosure.

The right to participate in decision-making refers to the power of the public to participate in decision-making related to sustainable urban construction. The government departments should encourage individuals or groups of the public to participate in the government's decision on sustainable urban construction, and comment on the policies that have been implemented to promote the further improvement of the policies.

6.5.5.2 Thought Two: Urban Ecological Civilization Promotion in an Open and Targeted Way

The concept of ecological civilization is "respecting nature, conforming to nature and protecting nature". The 18th National Congress of the Communist Party of China put forward "vigorously promoting ecological civilization", and pointed out the construction path of "integrating economic construction, political construction, cultural construction, and social construction in all aspects and the whole process".

To promote urban ecological civilization in an open way is to expand our thinking and integrate the concept of ecological civilization into all aspects of economic, political, cultural and social construction, so that the public can obtain information about ecological civilization in their daily production and life and carry out actions of ecological civilization. The openness also reflects that the construction of urban ecological civilization should closely follow the nature, genuinely link the city with the countryside, and establish the concept of great ecological civilization.

To promote urban ecological civilization in a targeted way, the first thing is to highlight the key points, closely follow the characteristics of the city, and start from the two aspects of industrial development and resource conservation; Secondly, fully recognize the high degree of differentiation of the urban public, and adopt different strategies and methods for different groups.

In a word, the essence of public participation in the construction of REEFCR city is to practice the ruling concept of "development for the people, development depends on the people, and development results are shared by the people" in urban construction, and to reflect the participatory idea in urban construction and management.

6.6 Policy Recommendations for REEFCR City Development

6.6.1 Compilation Model of REEFCR City Master Plan in innovative Way

The construction of REEFCR city involves many fields such as urban economy, society, culture and ecology, and is related to the vital interests of urban residents. From the perspective of the previous planning formulation model, the top-down formulation model excludes residents, and residents do not have right to participate. When preparing the master plan of REEFCR city, we should innovate the traditional top-down planning preparation method, use the participatory method of bottom-up and top-down combination to prepare the plan, and mobilize and organize residents to participate in the whole process of REEFCR city construction. This organization model is people-oriented, takes the community as the basic unit, fully respects the voice of residents, maximizes the enthusiasm of residents, more in line with local reality, and better meets the development needs of urban residents.

6.6.2 Creation of City Management Mechanism—"Government Guidance, Market Dynamics and Public Involvement"

In the whole process of REEFCR city construction, try to create a city management mechanism of "government guidance, market dynamics, and public involvement". Under the guidance of the government, through the fair participation of relevant stakeholders in the management process, the formulation and arrangement of systems and rules, so that all parties affected by the system can benefit from the new institutional arrangements, and obtain economic, social, ecological and other comprehensive benefits from the construction of REEFCR city, so as to achieve a win–win outcome. This diversified management mechanism is also conducive to raising funds needed for environmental protection technology research and development, clean energy production, ecological environment construction, etc., and forming a multi-directional, multi-level, multi-channel fund raising model.

6.6.3 The Pilot Work of REEFCR City

At present, China has determined the pilot cities of ecological civilization and low-carbon cities in batches. These pilot cities have made remarkable achievements in resource conservation, environment protection, climate resilient and other aspects.

Their infrastructure, technology, capital, talent and other conditions are mature, and they are the best carrier for the implementation of the REEFCR city pilot. The competent government departments can choose these existing pilot projects to guide, supervise, inspect and evaluate relevant projects in combination with the construction of REEFCR city, summarize experiences in a timely manner, refine characteristics, play a demonstration role, promote them according to local conditions, and promote the rapid, healthy and sustainable development of REEFCR city in different urban agglomerations from point to area.

6.6.4 Compilation of the REEFCR Urban Ecological Planning

Different from traditional environmental planning and economic planning, urban ecological planning is a bridge connecting urban master planning, environmental planning and socio-economic planning.[45] Urban ecological planning mainly includes high-quality environmental protection system, efficient operation system, high-level management system and completed green land ecosystem.[46]

First, high-quality environmental protection system. The urban air pollutants, wastewater, waste residue and various wastes discharged from the catering industry, slaughtering industry, agricultural and sideline markets, public entertainment places and other systems should be treated and disposed in a timely manner according to their respective characteristics. At the same time, the management of noise should be strengthened. All environmental quality indicators should meet the highest standards of national advanced cities, so as to make the urban ecological environment clean and comfortable. Second, efficient operation system. It includes a smooth road traffic system, an adequate energy flow, logistics and passenger flow transportation system, a fast and orderly information transmission system, a corresponding supporting and guaranteed material supply system (main and non-staple food, vegetables, materials, water, electricity, fuel, etc.), a suburban ecological support circle, a complete professional service system, sewage and waste discharge and treatment system, etc.[47] Third, a high-level management system. Including population control, resource utilization, social services, medical insurance, labor employment, public security and fire prevention, urban construction, environmental improvement, etc., should be managed at a high level to ensure the reasonable development and utilization of water, soil and other resources and the appropriate population size, and promote the harmony between man and nature, man and the environment. Fourth, perfect green land ecosystem. Not only should there be high green space indicators, such as green space coverage, per capita green space area and per capita public green space area, but also the layout should be reasonable, the points, lines and surfaces should be organically combined, and there should be a high biodiversity to form a perfect multi-level green space system. The United Nations Biosphere Ecology and Environmental Protection Organization stipulates that the urban green space coverage rate should reach 50%, and each urban resident should have 60 square meters of green space. At present, most cities in China are far from the above requirements. In the process of urban ecological construction, efforts should be made to develop towards a high standard of greening, so as to improve the quality of urban ecological environment, enrich and beautify the urban landscape.[48]

6.6.5 *Establishment and Improvement of the Emission Trading System*

At present, many first-tier cities in China are actively exploring the establishment of emission trading system. As a means of market economy, emission trading can give full play to the role of the market in allocating resources and is conducive to the macro-control of pollutant emissions. If the enterprises need to reduce pollution level, they should enter the market to buy and hold emission rights, so that the pollution level will be reduced. If environmental protection facilities such as sewage treatment plants are built and the environmental capacity increases, the government can issue more pollution discharge licenses to reduce the cost of enterprises and help economic growth.[49]

6.6.6 *The Urban Lifeline System Building*

The urban lifeline system is an indispensable support system in the daily life of the public, an important infrastructure to ensure the normal operation of urban life, and a basic project to maintain the functions of the city, focusing on: urban transportation, urban power, urban water supply, urban drainage, urban communication (urban network), urban gas supply, urban sanitation and other systems. The ability of urban lifeline system to resist disaster damage directly determines whether a city can maintain its normal function.[50]

1. Establish an advanced information system. Establish a sound public information platform using remote sensing technology, geographic information system, global positioning system, real-time monitoring technology, radar image, optical satellite image and aerial photography, and integrate them into a unified digital city framework. It is used for real-time monitoring and effective control of each key link of the lifeline system, which will control the danger in the bud or in the smallest possible range. The information system is used to conduct hierarchical management according to the city, district, department and community, and establish a community based urban safety management model. The advanced technology of information science is adopted to effectively manage the urban lifeline system, ensure its safe operation, and improve its disaster resistance.

2. Build a comprehensive early warning and emergency mode for urban multi disaster. Change the single urban disaster early warning and emergency management mode of different departments and disaster types, and establish an emergency response mechanism to deal with major public security emergencies with "smooth information, quick response, strong command and clear responsibility". Starting from urban communities, we will establish a city level disaster management and rescue system, and formulate scientific emergency plans to deal with various major urban disasters.

6.6.7 Strengthen the Safety Layout of Urban Space

The urban space is limited. It is very important for the future development of the city to reasonably arrange the living space, production space, ecological space and security space in the limited space.

On the one hand, intensive living is combined with moderate dispersion. In terms of space, urban construction and layout should form a spatial system with clear functions, organic links, high coordination and ecological security in the form of "dense layout" that combines intensive living with moderate dispersion. Intensive living can make the residential space and industrial space realize intensive utilization and compact development in the region, complement the functions of residential space and industrial space, and simultaneously optimize the spatial structure and industrial structure; Moderately dispersed living is convenient for "green and safe space" (ecological space and safe corridor) to blend in, so that "green and safe space", residential space and industrial space can achieve an open layout in the region.[51]

On the other hand, the living, production, ecology and security space develop in a balanced way. The urban spatial layout must take into account the four goals of production development, living improvement, ecological restoration and disaster prevention and reduction, and form a spatial pattern of reasonable, appropriate and balanced development of living space, production space, ecological space and security space. In the process of spatial adjustment and optimization, ecological green belts should be built within and between small towns to restore and strengthen the urban ecosystem functions, improve the ecological environment, reserve safe space according to geological structure and population distribution, and build urban safe corridors to evacuate residents and reduce casualties in case of natural disasters.

Notes

1. Hongqiang Yang, and Xiaoxin Zhang, "Coordination of Carbon Trade and Environmental Protection Constraints under the Kyoto Protocol Mechanism", *International Trade Issue,* Issues 10, 2005.
2. Min Zhao, "Source of Sustainable City Thought", *Journal of Changsha University*, Issue 3, 2003.

3. Ibid.
4. Yaoyu Lin, and Guosheng Chen, "FRP Theory on Urban Design Combining Ecology: Concepts, Values, Methods and Achievements", *Journal of Southeast University (Natural Science Edition)*, No. 12, 2005.
5. Xiangrong Wang, *Urban Ecology* (Shanghai: Fudan University Press, 2011) 19.
6. Min Li, "From Garden City to Land Garden and Forestry: The Development of Green Space Planning Thought in Human Settlement Environment", *Journal of Architecture*, No. 6, 1995.
7. Jun Yang, "Taiyuan Urban Green Space System Planning", *Taiyuan Science and Technology*, Issue 6, 2003.
8. "The Climate Organization will Develop at Least 15 'Low-Carbon Cities' in China within 5 years", *Resource Conservation and Environmental Protection*, Issue 2, 2009.
9. Guomei Zhou et al., "How to Achieve Low-Carbon Transformation in Resource-Based Cities", *Environmental Economy*, Issue 10, 2009.
10. Thomas Steiner(Sweden), translated by Weiwen Zhang and Zuhui Huang, *Policy Tools for Environment and Natural Resources Management* (Shanghai: Shanghai People's Publishing House, 2005) 34.
11. Jingge Wang, "Reflections on the Emission Trading System - Establishing an Emission Trading System with Chinese Characteristics", *Journal of Liaoning University of Administration*, Issue 11, 2010.
12. Xiaodong Wang, "International Comparison and Reference of Emission Trading Systems", *Taxation and Economics*, Issue 3, 2009.
13. Jingge Wang, "Reflections on the Emission Trading System - Establishing an Emission Trading System with Chinese Characteristics", *Journal of Liaoning University of Administration*, Issue 11, 2010.
14. Xing Li, "Construction of China's Ecological Tax Framework", *Tax Research*, Issue 6, 2005.
15. Ailin Jiang et al., "Problems and Governance in Urban Environment", *Journal of Changchun Municipal Party School*, Issue 8, 2008.
16. Huali Wang, and Chunling Pu, "Defects and Countermeasures of Compensation Mechanism for Land Resources Utilization in Tarim Basin", *Xinjiang Social Science Forum*, Issue 8, 2008.
17. Longxiang Tang, and Jin Min, "New Ideas for Environmental Legislation in China under the Sustainable Development Strategy", *Lanzhou Academic Journal*, Issue 6, 2005.
18. Ibid.
19. Man Zhang, "Adjusting Environmental Policies and Developing Environmental Protection Industry", *China's Environmental Protection Industry*, Issue 2, 2002.
20. Guangyu Huang, and Yong Chen, "Research on the Concept, Planning and Design Methods of Ecological City", *Urban Planning*, Issue 11, 1997.
21. Xu Qin, "Sanya: Building a Garden City in the South", *China Construction Information*, Issue 7, 2003.
22. Hesheng Wang, "Research on Ecological Environment Construction and Protection in the Yangtze River Basin", *Science and Technology Management of National Land Resources*, Issue 4, 2000.
23. Ibid.
24. Dan Dan, and Xiao Han, "Research on Ecological Environment Protection Planning of Hunchun City, Jilin Province", *China's Comprehensive Utilization of Resources*, Issue 2, 2014.
25. Zixue Zhang, "Inner Mongolia Ecological Environment Protection Strategy", *Inner Mongolia Environmental Protection*, Issue 3, 2000.
26. "Outline of the Construction Plan of Hainan Ecological Province", *Hainan Daily*, July 18, 2005.
27. Hesheng Wang, "Research on Ecological Environment Construction and Protection in the Yangtze River Basin", *Science and Technology Management of National Land Resources*, Issue 4, 2000.
28. Wenliang Yin, and Kaiting Ji, "Discussion on Biodiversity Conservation Planning in Lu'an City", *Anhui Agricultural Bulletin*, Issue 3, 2012.

29. "Notice of the State Council on Printing and Distributing the National Ecological Environment Protection Program", *Bulletin of the State Council of the People's Republic of China*, January 30, 2001.
30. Junzan Guo, "Preliminary Study on the Construction of Urban Disaster Prevention and Reduction System", *City*, Issue 10, 2009.
31. Ibid.
32. Ling Deng, "Research on China's Ecological Civilization Development Strategy and its Regional Realization", *Research Report of Sichuan University*, 2013.
33. "Establishing an Ecological Compensation Mechanism to Promote the Transformation of Development Mode", *China Finance*, Issue 2, 2010.
34. Biqiu Mei, "Strengthening Ecological Civilization Construction and Promoting the Development of Hanshou Forestry", *China Forestry*, Issue 9, 2008.
35. Yunwen Song, "Ways to Strengthen the Construction of County Ecological Civilization", *Leadership Science*, Issue 3, 2008.
36. Fujia Li et al., "The Development Model of Restricted Development Zones in Liaoning Province during the Transitional Period under the Main Functional Zoning", *Progress in Geographic Science*, Issue 9, 2008.
37. Yimiao Song, *Research on Management of Main Functional Zones* (Sichuan: Southwestern University of Finance and Economics, 2008).
38. Rong Pu et al., "Exploration of the Development Model of Tourism Industry in Restricted and Prohibited Development Zones - Taking Yunnan Province as an Example", *Yunnan Geographical Environment Research*, Issue 11, 2008.
39. Rong Pu, and Xiuyu Hu, "Exploration on the Development of Tourism Industry in Restricted and Prohibited Development Zones - Taking Yunnan Province as an Example", *Journal of Kunming University*, Issue 12, 2008.
40. Wenhui Xie, and Wei Deng, *Urban Economics* (Beijing: Tsinghua University Press, 2008) 123.
41. Yudong Li, "Clean Production and Governance of Eco Industrial City Construction", *Journal of Xinjiang University (Philosophy, Humanities and Social Sciences Edition)*, Issue 7, 2005.
42. Yun Zhou, *How to Choose the Sustainable Development Path for Resource-based Cities - Interpretation of "Several Opinions on Promoting the Sustainable Development of Resource-based Cities"* (Beijing: China New Technology and New Products, 2008).
43. Wenzhong Zhang, "Research on the Development Path and Mode of the Continuous Alternative Industry of Resource-based Cities", *Journal of the Chinese Academy of Sciences*, Issue 2, 2011.
44. Yihua Jin, "Urban Tourism Resources Development and Protection for Eco Tourism Cities in the Context of Circular Economy", *Mall Modernization*, Issue 4, 2007.
45. Xiangrong Wang et al., "Basic Theory and Empirical Research on Urban Ecological Planning - Taking Maluanwan in Xiamen as an Example", *Journal of Fudan University (Natural Science Edition)*, Issue 12, 2004.
46. Xiangrong Wang, and Wu Renjian, *Report on Urban Ecological Environment Issues in China* (Jiangsu: People's Publishing House, 2006) 87.
47. Shu Dong, "Approaches and Measures for Sustainable Ecological City Construction", *Science and Technology Today*, Issue 6, 2003.
48. Xiangrong Wang, "Concept, Connotation, and Empirical Research on Urban Ecological Planning", *Planner*, Issue 5, 2002.
49. Zhuo Du et al., "Property Rights Market: Exploring Emissions Trading", *Property Rights Guide*, Issue 11, 2007.
50. Hanwu Yu et al., "Analysis of Security Measures for Urban Lifeline Systems", *Chinese Journal of Safety Sciences*, Issue 5, 2008.
51. Xiaoyan Li, "Research on the Spatial Layout of Villages and Towns' Reconstruction after the Wenchuan Earthquake", *Economic System Reform*, Issue 4, 2009.

Chapter 7
Monographic Study

7.1 Institutionalization of Experience of Adapting to Climate Change, Disaster Prevention and Mitigation

2010 was the year with one of the most serious geological disasters since the founding of the People's Republic of China, and with 2150 geological disasters occurring in Sichuan Province. The towns and villages that have just completed reconstruction after the Wenchuan devastating earthquake have been hit again by natural disasters such as continuous heavy rainfall, floods, mudslides, and landslides. The vast number of cadres and masses in Sichuan Province adhere to the people-oriented scientific development concept, and with the support of the ideological, organizational, material, technical and other aspects accumulated in the Wenchuan earthquake relief and post-disaster reconstruction, Sichuan Province has achieved success in combating geological disasters. A total of 181 cases were successfully avoided in the province, and 39,000 casualties were avoided.

The special geological landforms make Sichuan Province an area prone to various geological disasters in history. The Wenchuan earthquake caused the loosening of the rock and soil mass on the slopes of the disaster area and the deterioration of the geological environment, which not only induced and aggravated the major geological disasters in 2010, but also experts estimated that the secondary disasters after the major earthquake would last for at least 10 years, of which, the first 5 year is the peak period. In addition, due to the frequent occurrence of various extreme weather events caused by global warming, it is completely foreseeable that natural disasters with geological disasters as the main content in Sichuan Province will present a trend of frequent and repeated occurrences in the future. Geological disasters featured by suddenness, concealment and strong destructiveness have seriously damaged the prosperity of economic and social development in Sichuan Province, posed a huge threat to the safety of people's lives and properties, and have become the most prominent environmental problems and people's livelihood in Sichuan Province.

S. Du and H. Du, *The Green Transformation of Urban Areas in China Under Global Warming*, https://doi.org/10.1007/978-981-95-1005-4_7

A nation that is good at summarizing and drawing lessons from natural disasters is bound to become increasingly strong and invincible. According to the situation of high and frequent occurrence and tendency of geological disasters in Sichuan Province, it is necessary to carefully summarize and sort out Sichuan Province's experience and lessons in the prevention and control of geological disasters, and improve and institutionalize them, provide guidance and norms for strengthening the ability of Sichuan Province to prevent and control geological disasters, and accelerating the construction of a comprehensive system and long-term mechanism.

According to our investigation and research, it is necessary to advance from the following aspects:

1. Establishment of mechanism for investigation and assessment of geological hazards. Make full use of modern technology and information technology to carry out a comprehensive survey of geological disasters in the province to find out various hidden dangers. Take the impact of geological disasters as an important part of environmental impact assessment, and strictly carry out geological disaster risk assessment and risk control for the site selection of post-disaster reconstruction, including towns, houses, and major projects. For the projects that have passed the EIA in the past, the course of geological disaster prevention should be supplemented, and the projects that are currently undergoing the EIA and will be under construction in the future should be strictly assessed. Adjust and improve the fortification standards for geological hazards accordingly according to the assessment results. Establish a system of supervision, notification, etc. supporting geological disaster risk assessment. In particular, it is necessary to publicize and supervise the assessment of geological hazards of projects under construction and mining enterprises, identify problems in a timely manner, rectify within a time limit, and implement preventive measures.
2. Establishment of monitoring and early warning system and mechanism for geological disasters that combine native and technical experience and local and foreign specialties. In key areas of geological disasters, a six-level linkage monitoring and group prevention system will be established at the provincial, city, county, township, village, and community levels. The responsibility for early warning and prediction and the responsibility for monitoring hidden dangers of geological disasters will be implemented at different levels. Identify the monitoring responsible person and the disaster prevention responsible person, and implement the inspection, investigation, reporting and other systems. Establish a team of geological disaster monitors, set up full-time monitors in hidden danger areas of geological disasters, and set up scientific instruments in key areas to monitor changes in geological disasters. Formulate emergency plans including information platforms, personnel, communication facilities, traffic vehicles, emergency clothing, signs and other preventive technical standards. Equip the counties and towns in the high-incidence areas of geological disasters with necessary emergency basic equipment such as automobiles.
3. Multi-level, multi-industry, multi-department linkage emergency response mechanism. Strengthen the linkage and cooperation among departments of land and

resources, meteorology, water conservancy, transportation, etc.; communicate with enterprises, monitoring leaders and monitors in a timely manner through multiple channels in the disaster-stricken areas; inform the people in production and living areas and the society about the changes in the disaster. Unremittingly carry out publicity, education and drills on the prevention and control of geological disasters, and make the content of geological disaster prevention and control, including early warning signals, evacuation routes, and disaster shelters, well-known and known to everyone.

4. In accordance with the principles of combining underground remediation with above-ground remediation, combining prevention and governance, and combining economic development with ecological and environmental protection, establish a long-term mechanism for disaster prevention and mitigation. Restricted by the existing technical means of forecasting and early warning, the most effective and feasible measure to deal with geological disasters is to avoid. Avoidance plans should be formulated in key areas, and construction should not be carried out on earthquake fault zones, areas prone to geological disasters, and flood channels. For the inescapable areas, resettlement and reinforced engineering would be the solutions. For cities and towns that are located in areas with fragile ecology and frequent geological disasters, and whose infrastructure construction is lagging and aging, and which have long needed to be relocated and renovated, those towns that have not been relocated in the past due to financial constraints, etc., must take firm measures to relocate.
5. Increase investment in geological disaster remediation through multiple channels. Just as the Central No. 1 document stipulates that the investment in water conservancy construction should increase rigidly, it is necessary to propose an increase in the proportion of financial investment in the prevention and control of geological disasters. In addition to increasing fiscal funds year by year, a considerable part of the land transfer fee should be allocated to the relocation of cities and towns in ecologically fragile areas and the reconstruction of the original urban infrastructure.
6. Strengthen international cooperation in the prevention and control of geological disasters, learn from the management experience of disaster prevention and mitigation in other countries, absorb international funds, technologies, and facilities, and improve the province's disaster prevention and mitigation capabilities.
7. The frequency of geological disasters is the result of the destruction of the ecological environment. The frequency and intensity of geological disasters are closely related to the degree of ecological environment damage. Humans' plundering of nature beyond its limits will eventually be punished by devastating natural disasters. Therefore, in order to deal with geological disasters, in addition to focusing on the construction of systems such as disaster prevention and avoidance, fundamentally, we should start from improving the ecological environment, correctly handle the relationship between economic development and environmental protection, and manage and protect the ecological environment of Sichuan Province, which is the most fundamental long-term mechanism for disaster prevention. With the goal of building an ecological barrier in the upper

reaches of the Yangtze River, it is necessary to consolidate and improve the ecological construction achievements implemented in Sichuan Province, such as natural forest protection, returning farmland to forests, and returning grazing to grasslands, speed up the transformation of Sichuan Province's economic development mode, and accelerate the paid use of resources and the construction of ecological compensation mechanism. The "12th Five-Year Plan" will be a critical period for Sichuan Province to speed up its development and build the western economic highland and transportation hub. Many major construction projects will be implemented, and the contradiction between economic development, resource utilization and ecological protection will become more prominent, and it is even more necessary for us to develop conservation and protection strategy for the whole process of development to achieve the synergy of production development, affluent life, and good ecology.

8. Strengthen the construction of the rule of law for disaster prevention and mitigation, make sure disaster prevention and mitigation has a legal basis. The construction of the rule of law related to disaster prevention and mitigation has lagged far behind the needs of practice. There is no basis for disaster prevention and mitigation, and the lack of norms is common scene. Most of the people are unfamiliar with the few relevant laws and regulations that have been promulgated, and there is a situation of non-compliance with the laws. The progress of disaster prevention and mitigation legislation should be accelerated, and the effective policies, systems, and regulations that have been proven in Sichuan Province's fight against the Wenchuan earthquake and geological disasters should be elevated to laws and regulations, and disaster reduction and prevention work should be brought into the legal track.

7.2 Lifeline System Construction in Chinese Cities: Lessons Learned from the "3.11" East Japan Earthquake

In the twenty-first century, with the influence of climate change and extreme weather, the frequent occurrence of various natural disasters makes urban ecological security more and more risky. Due to the acceleration of industrialization, urbanization, and informatization, the population and economy are increasingly concentrated in cities, and the functions of cities are more complex, important and indispensable. The larger the city and the higher the level of modernization, the higher the dependence on transportation, communication and other infrastructure. Therefore, cities, especially megacities, have increasingly become the center and focus of disaster prevention and mitigation in the international community and the country. Establish and improve the "Lifeline System for Disaster Prevention and Mitigation", has become an effective way and an international trend for cities to improve their emergency rescue capabilities and ensure urban safety.

The so-called "Lifeline System" of the city is to treat the city as an organism, and the support system to maintain the normal operation of this organism is the concrete realization of the principle of "Safety First" in urban construction. The city's "Lifeline System" is mainly composed of shelter system, transportation system, source power system, information dissemination system, and life supply system. In the event of a catastrophe, it highlights the irreplaceable special role of the city's "Lifeline System" in emergency rescue and urban security. The construction level of a city's "Lifeline System" directly determines the safety level of a city. The concept and practice of urban "Lifeline System" originally originated from developed countries such as Germany and Japan. At present, the city's "Lifeline System" is becoming more and more mature from theory to practice, and has been widely used in urban disaster reduction and prevention to ensure urban safety.

The "3.11" catastrophe in Japan has tested the ability of Tokyo's "Lifeline System" to resist and reduce disasters, and exposed problems such as the gap of the construction level of Tokyo's "Lifeline System". Learning from the lessons of Tokyo, Japan in the "3.11" catastrophe, accelerating the construction of a "Lifeline System" for urban disaster prevention and mitigation with Chinese characteristics is obviously of great significance to improve China's urban disaster prevention and mitigation capabilities, strengthening urban ecological security, and promoting the healthy development of China's urbanization.

7.2.1 *Tokyo's Experience and Lessons in Dealing with Catastrophes*

Japan has always been a disaster-stricken country. It is in a leading position in the world in dealing with various natural disasters from hardware to software, from technology to facilities. Under such a complex disaster, Tokyo, with high population density, the reason that suffered few casualties directly from the disaster, and the transfer and evacuation of personnel is the "Lifeline System". However, the "3.11" catastrophe also exposed the existing problems in disaster prevention and mitigation in Tokyo, mainly:

1. The catastrophic disaster caused the closure of the Tokyo Expressway, and the subway was also basically paralyzed due to the lack of electricity and have to reduce frequency and capacity. Vehicles on the main road in urban area travel at a speed of less than 10 km per hour, or even less than 3 km. The traffic jam caused the chairman and general manager of Tokyo Electric Power Company to fail to return to their posts in time. It took the general manager 20 h to return to the headquarters, which delayed the critical opportunity to deal with the nuclear power crisis and was an important reason for the subsequent tragedy of the nuclear power plant.
2. In the center of Tokyo, the population density is very high during the day. Most office workers live in satellite cities, with a large commuter population. People travel mainly rely on rail and ground transportation networks with a total length of more than 1000 km. On the day of the earthquake, 3.92 million of the 11.44

million people in Tokyo's central urban area were unable to go home due to traffic obstructions. They were stranded in the center of the city, and sheltering and housing for these people became prominent problems.

3. The disaster makes all kinds of institutions in the city unable to perform their daily functions, which are related to the lifeline of the country and the operation of society. For example, Mizuho Bank, one of Japan's three largest banks, suffered a wide-ranging system failure after the disaster, resulting in a large number of ATMs and business outlets being unable to withdraw cash or process deposits, resulting in a backlog of 1.16 million transactions at most. At that time, it was at the peak of panic caused by nuclear radiation, because people could not withdraw cash in time, which in turn amplified social panic and affected social stability.
4. The urban lifeline projects including energy which will damage in the disaster may cause secondary disasters will have an impact on urban security during the nuclear crisis. Nuclear energy accounts for more than one-third of Tokyo's electricity supply and is an important part of the city's energy system. The nuclear crisis is a secondary disaster of an earthquake, but in comparison, the impact on Tokyo, whether in scope, degree or duration, obviously far exceeds that of the main disaster.
5. The control and stability of post-disaster social emotion is an important part of the role of the city's "Lifeline System". Post-disaster social panic and instability are also secondary disasters caused by the loss of the city's "Lifeline System". For example, the nuclear power crisis has caused panic and chaos in society, as well as concerns about food safety, and even triggered a chain reaction such as panic buying of iodized salt around the world.

7.2.2 Suggestions on Accelerating the Construction of "Lifeline System" for Disaster Prevention and Mitigation in Cities with Chinese Characteristics

1. Take the construction of the city's "Lifeline System" as an important content and index system to implement the scientific concept of development and the sustainable development of the city, and incorporate it into the national disaster prevention and mitigation and the city's "12th Five-Year Plan". Learn from the international theories, experiences and models of building "Lifeline System", combine China's national conditions, and successful experiences in fighting against disasters such as the "5.12 Wenchuan Earthquake" to accelerate the theoretical research and exploration of technologies and methods for the construction of "Lifeline System" with Chinese characteristics.
2. Integrate the city's "Lifeline System" project, reasonably configure the functions of the "Lifeline System" in peacetime and during disasters, and improve the safety and availability of the lifeline system. Improve the shelter system with reasonable urban layout and complete structure, including temporary shelters established in densely populated areas where people can take refuge nearby;

larger space, more people can be accommodated, and can be used in the event of collapse of surrounding buildings or fires, a wide-area evacuation place that leaves a safe enough distance for evacuees, and a shelter and evacuation place that is mainly used for temporary use by those who cannot return home due to disasters. Incorporate the air defense system into the shelter system, and implement the strategies of resource sharing, combination of peace and war, and the co-management of the military and the land. Accelerate the relocation of flammable, explosive, radioactive or poisonous enterprises and engineering facilities that are likely to cause secondary disasters. For ecologically fragile areas such as earthquake fault zones, geological disaster-prone areas, and flood passages, where the effect of project governance is very poor or need to be relocated and renovated for a long time should be relocated and avoided.

3. Enhance the "Lifeline System" with new technologies and new equipment to improve its intelligence level. Establish the automatic disposal system to ensure that the lifeline project can decide which emergency plan to adopt through rapid assessment of disasters, including automatic shutdown, remote control to shut off gas and electricity, etc., to avoid secondary disasters. Establish a unified urban water supply, gas supply and other underground pipeline network, establish network management information system and information sharing mechanism; establish and improve the city's "Lifeline System" to call for an emergency comprehensive rescue system; coordinate "above and underground" in urban construction to avoid "zipper roads" construction mode to prevent accidents. To make sure most lifeline projects, especially pipelines, are underground and corridor-like, combine them with the construction of "common ditch".
4. Strengthen the capacity building of disaster prevention and mitigation of lifeline key systems. Although the "Lifeline System" is composed of various systems and links with strong correlation, the function of disaster relief and emergency rescue can only be realized when the systems work in synergy. However, the positions and functions of the "Lifeline System" are not parallel, and there are lifeline systems that are in a key and dominant position, such as traffic and information system. The increasingly developed urban media and networks are an important part of the urban information system. They are an important platform for transmitting relevant information after a disaster, guiding people to evacuate popularizing disaster relief information, eliminating panic, and communicating among people. The city's radio, television and network departments should formulate complete and detailed disaster prevention plans and conduct regular drills to ensure that facilities and equipment can respond to various disasters in a timely manner. The construction of the power supply system should aim at the least loss, the fastest repair, and the timely availability of backup power after a severe disaster. Due to the rapid increase in energy demand, the development of clean energy, the response to climate change and other considerations, China is already in the stage of nuclear power development, and nuclear power has increasingly become the

main energy source for cities. For example, 11 nuclear power units have been built in Jiangsu, Zhejiang and Pearl River Delta regions to supply power to big cities such as Hong Kong, Macau, Shenzhen and Guangzhou. Take into consideration that China's nuclear power plants are located in urban areas with such a dense population and economy, and learn from Japan's nuclear crisis, it is necessary to suspend the approval of new nuclear power projects, while re-examine and assess nuclear power development plan, nuclear power plant layout, technology, and safety.

5. Strengthen the overall coordination of the "Lifeline System" and the construction of the rule of law. The construction of urban "Lifeline System" already has a certain foundation in terms of material, organization and management, but in general there are problems like divisions of departments, repeated construction, multi-headed command, single function, lack of overall planning, and difficulty in forming synergy and the low level of emergency rescue. Deepening the reform of the social rescue mechanism, coordinating the city's "Lifeline System", and establishing an efficient and economical emergency rescue mechanism are necessary and urgent to strengthen the construction of "Lifeline System". The construction of urban "Lifeline System" and the construction of the rule of law for safety management are lagging behind, and there is coexistence of non-compliance with laws. Learning from successful international experience, and previous proven and effective policies, systems and regulations in fighting earthquakes and floods in China, to speed up the construction of urban disaster prevention and mitigation systems and legislation for safety management schedule.
6. Increase funds for the construction of "Lifeline System" through multiple channels. It is necessary to form a financing pattern for the construction of the "Lifeline System" led by the government, social participation, and market operation. Just as the Central No. 1 document stipulates that the investment in water conservancy construction should increase rigidly, the proportion of financial investment in the construction of "Lifeline System" should be proposed. In addition to increasing fiscal funds year by year, a considerable part of the land transfer fee should be allocated to the relocation of cities and towns in ecologically fragile areas and the construction of urban "lifeline systems". Use more of market mechanisms and means to attract social funds into the construction of the "Lifeline System".
7. Strengthen the construction of urban safety culture, including daily disaster prevention plans, training and education, so that people can understand how to use the "Lifeline System" to rescue themselves and help each other in times of disaster. Raise the public awareness of "Lifeline System", and everyone should be a model for protecting the "Lifeline System".

7.3 Urban Air Pollution Control Through Regional Cooperation

Air pollution has become a prominent problem affecting the sustainable development of urban economy and society. Since urban atmospheric pollution is the result of the dual effects of atmospheric circulation and atmospheric chemistry, its governance must be coordinated regionally. Below we analyze the air pollution situation and put forward seven countermeasures and suggestions.

7.3.1 The Situation

Since 2010, the atmospheric environment of Chengdu has shown the characteristics of pollution in the stage of accelerated development of industrialization and urbanization, and the air quality has declined seriously.

In the national air quality rankings of 31 provincial capital cities, Chengdu ranked from 16th in 2010 to 19th in 2011, and dropped to 28th in 2102. In 2011, the World Health Organization released the urban outdoor air pollution database. Among the surveyed 1,082 cities in the world, Chengdu ranked 1,025. Among the listed 32 cities in China, Chengdu ranked the 8th from the bottom.

The annual number of days with good air quality decreased. In 2011, the number of days with air quality above Grade II in Chengdu reached more than 320 days, but in 2012 it dropped to 280 days. From January to May 2013, the pollution days were 114 days, and only 21.2% of the days reached the standard, while the number of days that met the standard in the first batch of 74 key cities that implemented air quality standards in the same period was 54.8%, and that of Chengdu was 23.6 percentage points lower.

Among the 14 cities in Sichuan Province that are included in the national key areas for air pollution prevention and control, Chengdu is the only city with severe air pollution.

The air pollution in Chengdu shows some new features:

The type of pollution has changed from a single type of soot to a complex type of pollution including photochemical pollution;

PM2.5 and ozone have become the primary pollutants. The smog with PM2.5 as the main component has become the main meteorological disaster and extreme weather and climate event in Chengdu, and the PM2.5 environmental capacity of Chengdu has reached the limit value.

From a single city air pollution to contiguous, regional air pollution. The mutual influence of air pollution among urban agglomerations in the Chengdu Plain is increasingly obvious, and the influence of pollution transmission between adjacent cities is extremely prominent. Exogenous pollution has accounted for a large proportion.

Pollution sources have changed from point sources to non-point sources, and pollution factors have changed from one-time pollutants to secondary pollutants. The contribution rate of secondary particulate matter represented by sulfate, nitrate and secondary organic carbon to the formation of PM2.5 has exceeded 40%, and there is an increasing trend year by year.

7.3.2 Suggestions

1. Establish a rational code of conduct for dealing with urban air pollution.

   It is important to pay attention to the seriousness of air pollution in Chengdu and the urgency of rectifying air pollution, while also face up to its complexity and arduousness. Developed countries such as the United States and the United Kingdom have struggled for at least 30–50 years with urban air pollution. Chengdu is at the stage of accelerated development of industrialization and urbanization. In addition, the geographical location of Chengdu in terms of atmospheric environmental quality control are inherently difficult, and the problems encountered are more complicated; secondly, the long-term accumulation of urban air pollution problems is a complex system issue. Furthermore, the source and formation mechanism of PM2.5 which is the main pollutant that affects the air environment quality in Chengdu, have not yet been scientifically concluded. Therefore, it is difficult to distinguish the responsibilities and the plan cannot be determined. All of the above factors determine that the prevention and control of atmospheric pollution is very difficult and arduous, and it is impossible to achieve immediate results. Secondly, in accordance with the requirements of "government-lead, corporate-implement, market-driven, and public-participation", the government, enterprises, and citizens perform their duties and responsibilities accordingly. The government takes overall responsibility for urban air quality, and takes effective measures to improve urban air quality, including promoting corporate responsibility for pollution control, advocating economical and green consumption patterns and living habits, and mobilizing all citizens to participate in environmental protection and supervision. Enterprises must abide by the social responsibility of energy conservation, emission reduction, and environmental protection, and strive to realize the internalization of external costs and take into account of the social costs. While supervising enterprises and governments to fulfill their environmental responsibilities, citizens should also change their lifestyles and consumption patterns, walk the talk, and actively participate in the actions to protect the atmospheric environment of the city.
2. Improve the legal and standard system to provide a legal environment and norms for the governance and protection of the urban atmospheric environment.

   A common experience learned both from developed country or an advanced city in China, including Shanghai to manage the atmospheric environment, is that the legal system should go first. Based on conditions below: Chengdu's special natural geographical and meteorological conditions, atmospheric environmental capacity, pollution conditions and other realities. There are four suggestions: firstly, it is necessary to step up the formulation and improvement of more stringent local comprehensive emission standards for air pollutants and for key industries. Secondly, it is to formulate environmental protection policies that are conducive to the improvement of atmospheric environmental quality, and strictly enforce environmental access. Implement special emission limits for air pollutants. High-pollution projects will no longer be approved; new pollutant emissions will be strictly controlled, the total amount of atmospheric pollutant emissions will be taken as a precondition for EIA approval, and projects will be determined based on the total amount. The amount of active sources within the region will be replaced by newly built projects that discharge half of the pollutants. Thirdly, it is to formulate supporting policies, such as adjusting energy resource prices, taxation and credit policies, and form an incentive and restraint mechanism that encourages enterprises to take the main responsibility for pollution control. Fourthly, it is to speed up the promulgation of the "Urban Heavy Air Pollution Emergency Plan", the "Chengdu Ambient Air Quality Compliance Plan" and other regulations and the revision of the "Chengdu Air Pollution Prevention and Management Regulations".

3. Pay attention to the impact of the new national air quality standards on the economic and social environment of Chengdu, and regard the new air quality standards as a forceful mechanism and an important starting point for Chengdu's energy conservation, emission reduction and economic upgrading.

Since 2013, China has replaced the original air pollution standard (PQA) with the air quality index (AQI), and Chengdu is one of the first cities to implement the new standard. In contrast, the pollution factors monitored by the new standard have increased, the concentration limit has been tightened, and the standard has been raised. In the first half of 2013, Chengdu met all the standards according to the old standards in many time periods, but according to the new standards, it was all polluted weather. In addition, Chengdu is also listed as a national key area for air quality prevention and control, requiring that by 2015, in addition to the substantial reduction of traditional pollutants such as sulfur dioxide, the PM2.5 concentration will decrease by 5% annually.

The new national air quality index will obviously pose rigid constraints and severe challenges to the economic and social development of Chengdu. Chengdu should turn crises into opportunities, turn pressure into driving force, and use the new national air quality index as a pushback mechanism to optimize Chengdu's economic structure and speed up the transformation of its development model.

Chengdu's technology and industrial energy conservation and emission reduction have reached a relatively high level, and there is no room for major breakthroughs and changes in the short term. The way out is to open up energy conservation and emission reduction space by optimizing the economic structure, free up environmental capacity, and contribute to the quality of the city's atmospheric environment. To lay a good foundation for improvement, we should promptly complete the city's energy and industrial development planning and its environmental impact assessment, reasonably determine the industrial development layout, structure and scale, and provide a scientific basis for optimizing the economic structure.

4. Strengthen the joint prevention and control of air quality in the Chengdu Plain urban agglomeration, and incorporate air quality into the assessment objectives of each city.

   Affected by the atmospheric circulation, the air pollution situation in Chengdu cannot be changed only by efforts of Chengdu along, the regional joint prevention and control is also necessary. Incorporate air quality into the assessment objectives of the provincial Party Committee and the provincial government for each area of the Chengdu Plain urban agglomeration. According to the "Main Functional Zoning of Sichuan Province" and the functional orientation and development direction of each city in the Chengdu Plain City Cluster, it can be divided into plains, hills, mountainous areas and other types of air quality management areas, and different air quality goals can be determined. The specific content of the assessment may include the number of days when the air quality is better than or equal to Grade 2 or above, the emission intensity of major pollutants affecting urban air quality, straw burning and comprehensive utilization, etc. And decompose the national goal of improving air quality in key regions into different types of cities and regions, and assign different scores.

5. Pay attention to the prevention and control of volatile organic compounds, which is an important source of PM2.5.

   Volatile and semi-volatile organic compounds (VOCs) in the air are not only the precursors of PM2.5, but also have the effect of increasing atmospheric oxidation and promoting the formation of PM2.5. The prevention and control of volatile organic compounds is not only for strengthening the control of PM2.5 precursors, but also for promoting the coordinated control of multiple pollutants. Chengdu should take the monitoring and control of volatile organic compounds as the focus of prevention and control of air pollution on the basis of measures to prevent and control urban air pollution such as "coal pressure, vehicle control, and dust reduction".

   In accordance with the requirements of the National Plan for Key Areas of Air Pollution Prevention and Control, a thorough investigation and monitor of volatile organic compounds shall be carried out, and a basic database shall be established; carry out pilot work on total emission control of volatile organic compounds in key industries. Improve the VOC pollution prevention and control system to reduce VOC emissions in the petrochemical industry; promote the control of VOC in the organic chemical industry and other industries; strengthen the control of VOC emissions in surface coating processes; and promote the treatment of VOC in solvent use processes. Complete the city's gas stations, oil storage depots and oil tanker oil and gas recycle management; strict environmental protection approval for new catering service business sites; catering service business sites should install high-efficiency oil fume purification facilities, and strengthen operation supervision; strengthen the open-air barbecue without oil fume purification facilities.

6. Implement urban motor vehicle increment control, and timely introduce a policy of restricting the purchase of cars.

   The results of the analysis of pollutant sources in Chengdu by the Chengdu Environmental Protection Bureau and Nankai University show that the direct and indirect contribution rates of motor vehicle emissions to air pollutants are about 20%. Tsinghua University conducted a comparative analysis of motor vehicle pollutant emissions in 22 cities in China. The per car emission level in Chengdu ranks in the bottom third, while the total emissions are in the top 6, which also shows that the high ownership of motor vehicles is an important source of air pollution in Chengdu. In recent years, urbanization and motorization in Chengdu have been advancing rapidly. By the end of 2012, the number of motor vehicles in the city had exceeded 3 million, and the number of vehicles increased by nearly 300,000 every year. The impact of motor vehicle exhaust pollution on urban air quality is more and more severe. It has become increasingly evident that the control of motor vehicles should be a focus of air pollution control in Chengdu.

   Based on the prevention and control of urban air pollution, many cities in China are reforming urban motor vehicle and traffic management models, especially taking the strengthening of traffic demand management as a new direction. However, different traffic demand management ideas and policies have different effects. Beijing and Shanghai have adopted unlimited and restricted purchases of private cars respectively. As a result, by 2009, the number of private cars per 100 people in Beijing reached 15.8, while Shanghai is 4.5. Originally, Shanghai has a larger population than Beijing, and its per capita disposable income is relatively higher. However, the air pollution level caused by automobile exhaust in Shanghai is lower, and the traffic control is more controllable. Therefore, Beijing has recently begun to implement restrictions on the purchase of private cars. In view of the above situation, Chengdu should consider controlling the increase in motor vehicles and adopting a policy of restricting the purchase of private cars, in addition to continuing to take measures such as restricting traffic, eliminating yellow-label vehicles, improving oil quality, and developing new energy vehicles. Formulate relevant regulations, plans, and supporting policies as soon as possible to ensure that the purchase restriction policy is introduced timely and promoted in an orderly manner.

7. Develop the energy-saving and environmental protection industry into a pillar industry for controlling atmospheric pollution and promoting economic upgrading.

   The energy-saving and environmental protection industry provides equipment, technology and services for air pollution control. The development of energy-saving and environmental protection industry is the genuine need of Chengdu to control air pollution. The energy conservation and environmental protection industry has multiple benefits of ecology, economy and socicty. Thc energy conservation and environmental protection industries in developed countries and domestic advanced regions are their pillar industries and foreign trade fist products. Especially because the energy conservation and environmental protection industry is a technology-intensive industry that can carry and accommodate high-tech achievements in various fields, the energy conservation and environmental protection industry is also a leading industry that promotes technological innovation. Accelerating its development can receive multiple benefits of optimizing the industrial structure, saving resources and energy, and promoting the construction of ecological civilization.

Chengdu has a huge market potential for developing energy-saving and environmental protection industries, and is facing a good opportunity for upward development. It is predicted that by 2020, only major pollutants such as COD, ammonia nitrogen, sulfur dioxide and nitrogen oxides will increase by 13.59 million tons in Sichuan Province. For this reason, there will be a market demand of 420 billion yuan for pollution control in the province. On the other hand, Chengdu's energy-saving and environmental protection industry already has a good foundation and huge development potential. In 2012, Chengdu had 20 energy-saving and environmental protection projects of more than 100 million yuan, and has formed a production capacity including providing complete sets of technology and equipment for industrial waste gas, comprehensive utilization of sewage, supermagnetic separation water treatment, and new high-efficiency solid waste sludge treatment equipment, and has formed the Jintang energy-saving and environmental protection industry base, Qingbaijiang low-carbon economy demonstration park and other platforms for the development of energy-saving and environmental protection industry.

It is suggested to take measures such as the government giving priority to purchasing energy-saving and environmentally-friendly products produced in this city, financial subsidies to promote energy-saving and environmentally-friendly products, and promoting the upgrading of the consumption of energy-saving and environment-friendly products by ordinary people, so as to expand the market consumption demand for energy-saving and environmentally-friendly products. Promulgate supporting policies and supporting measures for production factors such as capital, technology, talents, land, and information. Encourage technological innovation in energy conservation and environmental protection, enhance engineering and technical capabilities, and stimulate the growth of social investment in energy conservation and environmental protection, and promote the growth of Chengdu's energy conservation and environmental protection industry at an average annual growth rate of more than 15%. By 2015, the total output value will reach 100 billion yuan, with profits and taxes of 20 billion yuan, becoming a new growth pole and pillar industry in Chengdu and Sichuan Province.

7.4 Low Carbon Economy Development to Meet National Greenhouse Gas Emission Reduction Target

China has always attached great importance to the issue of climate change. Following binding national targets such as reducing energy consumption per unit of GDP, decreasing emissions of major pollutants, and increasing forest coverage during the

"11th Five-Year Plan" period, guidelines for controlling greenhouse gas emissions by 2020 Action Objective has been formulated, thus forming a scientific linkage target system of energy saving, pollution control and carbon reduction, and a complete national plan for addressing climate change.[1]

Achieving goal of controlling greenhouse gas emissions is a strategic task for China to deal with climate change at present and in the future. The goal of reducing greenhouse gas emissions as a binding indicator is included in the medium and long-term planning of national economic and social development, requiring all localities to unify their thinking and clarify their tasks, implement responsibilities, and do solid work to ensure the realization of the goal of controlling greenhouse gas emissions. It is foreseeable that the national greenhouse gas emission reduction targets will be broken down into various localities, industries, and key areas, and corresponding statistics, monitoring, and assessment methods will be introduced one after another.

Compared with other indicators in the national plan for addressing climate change, China's target of reducing carbon dioxide emissions per unit of GDP by 5% annually by 2020 is more stringent. The author has recently modeled and calculated the relationship between the reduction of greenhouse gas emissions per unit of GDP and the reduction of total greenhouse gas emissions; the reduction of greenhouse gas emissions per unit of GDP and the reduction of energy consumption per unit of GDP, and concluded that the reduction of emissions is more difficult whether compared with the reduction of total emissions or the reduction of energy consumption per unit of GDP. This is because the target China set is incremental emission reduction, while the Kyoto Protocol sets stock emission reduction for developed countries. During the period of rapid economic development and regions with an average annual GDP growth rate of over 6%, incremental emission reduction is clearly much more arduous and challenging than stock emission reduction.

The next ten years will be an important stage for the accelerated development of industrialization and urbanization in Sichuan Province. The tasks of economic development, disaster rehabilitation, and improvement of people's livelihood will be arduous, and there will inevitably be a great demand for resources, environment, and emission space. With the accelerated upgrading of the consumption structure brought about by the improvement of people's living standards in the province, the fields of production, consumption and circulation will still be in a high-carbon economy. The three major challenges that developed countries and regions have gradually experienced–economic growth, environmental pollution and climate warming–will be presented for Sichuan Province in a compressed and centralized state at the same time. On the other hand, the economic development level of Sichuan Province is still relatively low, the economic structural contradiction is prominent, and the economic development mode needs transformation. Sichuan Province is still at the low end of the industrial chain and value chain in terms of the national division of labor and global economic integration. The coal-dominated energy structure (the carbon dioxide emissions per ton of coal burning is 30% and 70% more than that of oil and natural gas, respectively) and the energy efficiency that is lower than the national average has all contributed to the increase in Sichuan's energy consumption, and the arduousness and complexity of implementing the carbon reduction targets assigned by the state to Sichuan Province.

To implement the national emission reduction action target will not only be pressure, challenges, and comparative disadvantages for Sichuan Province, but also motivation, opportunities and potential. Sichuan Province has abundant low-carbon resources including a variety of renewable energies, and has the industrial foundation and technological advantages to develop a low-carbon economy. Sichuan is the largest hydropower energy base in China, a major province of nuclear energy technology, and the conditions for large-scale development of solar energy and wind energy are becoming more and more mature. Forest carbon sink resources are among the best in China. Through the implementation of the ecological barrier strategy in the upper reaches of the Yangtze River with the construction of the Yangtze River shelterbelt, natural forest protection, conversion of farmland to forest and other projects as the main content, Sichuan province's forest area has accounted for 48% of the province's total area.

It is necessary to conduct early analysis of the impact of the national greenhouse gas emission reduction action targets on the economic and social development of Sichuan Province, in the preliminary study of the formulation of Sichuan Province's "12th Five-Year Plan", fully considered the feasibility of implementing indicators such as energy conservation, emission reduction renewable energy, forest carbon sinks, and greenhouse gas emission reduction in Sichuan Province; through the analysis of the industrial structure, energy structure and consumption structure of Sichuan Province, study the difficulties, priorities and potential of Sichuan Province to realize the national plan to address climate change; study the changing trend of key carbon sources and carbon sinks in Sichuan Province, and formulate the assumption and framework of Sichuan Province's "12th Five-Year Plan" carbon budget; study the basis, current situation and prospect of developing low-carbon industry, circular economy, ecological economy and renewable energy in Sichuan Province; it is urgent and important to study the changes in consumption structure, the situation of building a low-carbon culture, lifestyle, and society, and on this basis, put forward the countermeasures for Sichuan Province to implement the national action goal of controlling greenhouse gas emissions and develop a low-carbon economy.

Low-carbon economy is a low-carbon development model, and it is the main means and measure for human beings to deal with climate change. The development of a low-carbon economy is of course also a practical starting point and a key measure for Sichuan Province to achieve the national greenhouse gas emission reduction action goal, and it is also a huge engine for adjusting the economic structure and accelerating the transformation of the economic development mode.

7.4.1 Adjustment Acceleration of Economic Structure and Transformation the Model of Economic Development as the Strategic Entry Point for Developing a Low-Carbon Economy and Implementing the National Emission Reduction Target

Climate change is the direct cause of the low-carbon economy, while the decrease of non-renewable energy and the unsustainable production and consumption patterns of human beings are the root causes of the low-carbon economy. The unreasonable industrial structure and energy structure are an important and direct cause of high energy consumption and serious environmental pollution.[2] The United Kingdom and other countries have achieved sustainable development of "double decoupling" between economic growth, environmental pollution and greenhouse gas emission through the strategic transition from an industrial-led economic model to an advanced service-led economic model. It has fully proved that adjusting the economic structure and changing the economic growth mode are the key strategic measures to develop a low-carbon economy and implement the national greenhouse gas emission reduction goals.

Sichuan Province has an unreasonable economic structure and extensive development methods, and faces enormous challenges in energy conservation, pollution control, and carbon reduction. Even in Chengdu, the most developed area in the province, heavy chemical industries such as smelting, medicine, and chemical industry still accounted for more than half of the city's industrial structure in 2008; secondly, the overwhelming automobile development threaten the sustainable development of the city. Since 2000, the average annual growth rate of motor vehicles in Chengdu has exceeded 13%. In 2009, the number of vehicles has reached more than 2 million, ranking No. third in the country. Rapidly growing vehicle exhaust has become the main "carbon source" in Chengdu, which not only seriously affects Chengdu's air quality, but also increases the city's carbon intensity and pressure to achieve emission reduction targets.

Seizing the favorable opportunity of the country to accelerate the transformation of economic development mode, based on the development of a low-carbon economy and the implementation of national emission reduction targets, the recent economic restructuring and development mode transformation in Sichuan Province should focus on the following aspects:

1. Strengthen the adjustment of industrial structure and layout, and shift the focus of industry from smelting, automobile, medicine and other industries with high pollution and high energy consumption to clean energy. Guide enterprises to clean production.
2. Develop modern service industries including finance, insurance, logistics, tourism, education, culture, scientific research, technical services, etc.

3. Develop public transportation, build a green public transportation system, and curb the excessive growth of motor vehicles through the development of public transportation, thereby reducing dust and carbon dioxide emissions.
4. Accelerate the implementation of key projects for energy conservation and emission reduction, so that the industrial structure tends to be low-carbon and circular.
5. Increase the utilization of solid waste, support the research and development, promotion and application of energy-saving and environmental protection technologies such as landfill recycling, crop straw power generation, harmless treatment of livestock manure, and calcium carbide slag replacing limestone to make cement.
6. Guide green consumption. Promote low-carbon life style, clean production methods, advocate green travel, green life, green consumption patterns, and reduce carbon emissions.

7.4.2 Applying Both "Addition" and "Subtraction" Strategies to Advance Low-Carbon Development Across the Province

The so-called addition and subtraction are simply to increase carbon sinks and reduce carbon sources. In other words, through energy conservation and emission reduction, the development of clean production and circular economy, the low-carbon transformation of traditional industries, products, and process technologies, and the development of low-carbon technologies, industries, and products, make them new economic growth points. The simultaneous promotion is essentially to promote the technological transformation of traditional industries, develop strategic emerging industries, and promote the coordinated development of energy conservation, pollution control, and carbon reduction.

Whether doing addition or subtraction, technological innovation is the key. Sichuan Province should strengthen the promotion of scientific and technological innovation to promote the low-carbon development of products and industries, and accelerate the establishment of a technical system that includes technologies such as energy efficiency improvement, energy conservation, renewable energy and greenhouse gas emission reduction as the main content. In particular, it is necessary to give full play to the advantages of Sichuan Province in the manufacture of new energy and renewable energy equipment. The high-frequency electrodeless fluorescent lamp independently developed by Chengdu Times Light Source Co.; Ltd. belongs to the fourth-generation new light source. It is 40–50% more energy efficient than traditional light sources, and the price is one-half to two-thirds lower than that of LEDs. It is estimated that if the product is used in highway tunnels, urban roads and enterprise lighting in Sichuan Province, it can save 3.3 billion kWh of electricity, reduce 1.32 million tons of standard coal, and reduce nearly 2 million tons of carbon dioxide emissions. Only this enterprise and a new product can complete the task of forming an energy-saving capacity of more than 1.4 million tons of standard coal per year proposed by the provincial government. It shows the huge potential and role of scientific and technological innovation in the province's realization of the national emission reduction action target.

7.4.3 Low-Carbon Economy Promotion

The so-called low-carbon economy means that low-carbon technologies, industries, and low-carbon lifestyles are both technically and economically feasible. It includes adopting more economic means and incentive measures to make the departments, institutions and enterprises that produce low-carbon products, R&D and promotion of low-carbon technologies profitable and become profitable industries and technologies, and also includes the improvement of cost-efficiency of low-carbon products and technologies, service, so that consumers can afford.

At present, most low-carbon technologies and products in Sichuan Province are expensive, far below the basic rate of return that the market is pursuing, and have become a bottleneck for the development of low-carbon industries and technologies. It not only seriously restricts the development of low-carbon enterprises, but also seriously restricts the promotion and application of low-carbon technologies, equipment and service products. Reducing costs and realizing economic feasibility is the way out for developing a low-carbon economy.

The photovoltaic industry is a rapidly developing low-carbon industry. Sichuan Province has formed a huge production capacity of polysilicon, the upstream product of the photovoltaic industry. Only Leshan City's polysilicon production capacity and scale account for a quarter of China's capacity. Constrained by the high cost of the main raw material, silicon wafers, the price of photovoltaic power generation is $1 per kilowatt-hour, which is 15 times the price of thermal power; purchasing a set of photovoltaic power generation equipment requires at least 50 years of electricity savings to offset the purchase cost. Reducing the cost and making it economic feasible is the key for Sichuan's polysilicon industry to be competitive and invincible in the market among the many polysilicon manufacturers and excess capacity in China.

For another example, with the rapid development of large-scale livestock and poultry breeding in the province's rural areas, the use of microbial technology to harmlessly treat a large amount of livestock and poultry manure, processing and producing organic fertilizer is a good way to develop low-carbon agriculture. However, it is very difficult, and Chengdu handles nearly one-thousandth of livestock and poultry manure each year. The main reason is still that the price of organic fertilizer is 4–5 times higher than that of traditional farmyard manure and chemical fertilizer. Even if it is comparable to the price of chemical fertilizer, the latter is small in size, relatively low in shipping costs, and easy to use. Farmers are only willing to accept chemical fertilizers.

The government plays an irreplaceable role in the process of promoting low-carbon economy. Low-carbon products, technologies, and services are, to a large extent, public goods with high ecological benefits. In addition, each link from early-stage research and development to large-scale production to product promotion and application are risky and requires a lot of investment. Since the market conditions are not yet mature, it is necessary to have the support of corresponding economic policies, especially fiscal policies. Through the guidance and support of public finance, the government should improve relevant supporting policies in investment, price, finance and taxation, financial credit, etc., and form an incentive mechanism for the development of a low-carbon economy. Set up a special fund for low-carbon economic development, provide on-grid price subsidies for new energy and renewable energy power generation, and propose to reduce the subsidy standard year by year to encourage renewable energy power generation enterprises to reduce costs and eliminate high-cost forms of power generation; stimulate consumers' willingness to purchase low-carbon products and equipment by directly subsidizing. In addition, the government should also adopt market mechanisms such as Contract Energy Management to guide social funds to invest in the development of low-carbon industries and technologies.

7.4.4 Institutional Mechanisms for Innovative Development of Low-Carbon Economy

To develop low-carbon economy, it is necessary to innovate systems and mechanisms, and use multi-pronged means and diversified policy tools to achieve the goal of reducing greenhouse gas emissions.

The rise of carbon trading in response to climate change provides us with a new mechanism called the property rights approach. That is to define the property rights of the emission space of carbon dioxide and other greenhouse gases, make it a valuable asset and tradable, and form a price discovery mechanism. Compared with the traditional management methods of environmental protection and emission reduction, this form provides a power mechanism and operation mechanism driven by green interests. Let the environmental protection and the provision of public goods change from previously the simple top-down to nowadays bottom-up approach; the funds for public goods are mainly provided by the government and are provided together with social funds.

Carbon trading is ostensibly a financial activity, but it is closely linked to the green real economy. Through carbon trading, financial capital is directly or indirectly invested in enterprises or projects to promote technological innovation and optimization and transformation of the low-carbon economy, thereby leading energy conservation and emission reduction, driving the transformation of economic growth patterns, and promoting the healthy development of the low-carbon economy.

Carbon trading can be carried out not only between countries, but also between different regions and enterprises within a country. Its operating mechanism can either stipulate the upper limit of the total amount of greenhouse gas emissions in each region or industry under the mandatory constraints of the government, and allocate it to relevant enterprises or institutions according to the quota, and through market-based transactions, which allow participants to meet the specified emission requirements by paying as little as possible. Through project cooperation, buyers and sellers provide financial or technical support to obtain greenhouse gas emission reduction credits.

Sichuan Province can implement the national greenhouse gas emission reduction target as an opportunity and basis to develop carbon emission trading in the region. The specific method is to allocate the greenhouse gas emission reduction credits granted by the State to each city on an annual basis, and each city redistribute credits to counties, districts, and finally to key enterprises to use it every year on a decreased basis. Through the establishment of a provincial carbon fund, counties and districts that fail to meet their greenhouse gas emission reduction targets will pay the fund and subsidize cities and prefectures that have exceeded their emission reduction targets. This approach can not only promote the national goal of reducing greenhouse gas emissions in Sichuan Province, but also use this mechanism to subsidize the loss of industries that are difficult to develop in the backward regions, thereby driving the establishment and improvement of the ecological compensation mechanism in the province. On this basis, gradually linked with the international carbon trading market, and packaged Sichuan hydropower, forest carbon sink, biomass energy, biogas development, rural livestock and poultry manure recycling and other projects into CDM projects in exchange for international funds and technology to support Sichuan's energy conservation, environmental protection, and low-carbon economic development.

7.4.5 Establishment of "Climate Exchange" in Sichuan Province

The Climate Exchange, the carbon emission rights exchange, is a platform for carbon trading. The purposes to establish a Climate Exchange, firstly is to find buyers for domestic companies engaged in CDM project development and develop carbon dioxide emission reduction futures; secondly is to find suitable prices. It is not only conducive to the country and region where it is located to get more shares in the international carbon emissions trading to support its technological transformation and environmental protection, but also conducive to the country and region's carbon emission reduction rights to obtain reasonable price benefits. More importantly, it will broaden horizons and provide new impetus for the development of low-carbon economy in Sichuan Province, and provide a starting point and support for building the province into a financial center in the west and an economic highland in the west.

At present, countries in the world, including Australia, Japan, and Canada, are actively establishing policy frameworks and preparing for the establishment of domestic carbon emission markets. Beijing, Shanghai, Tianjin and other cities have successively established Climate Exchanges.

Sichuan Province should seize the opportunity and strive to establish the first Climate Exchange in the western region, specifically start from the following aspects:

1. Sichuan's Climate Exchange should be positioned to cover to the west, serve the whole country, and face the world. The types of transactions can be either emission reduction quotas or approved emission reduction rights under the clean mechanism, as well as provincial sulfur dioxide emission rights and chemical oxygen demand emission rights. It can be both spot and futures contracts. The organizational form can be either an independent establishment or a branch that cooperates with the World Bank, the Chicago Stock Exchange, and the European Exchange.
2. Establish a special working organization to organize and coordinate relevant departments and institutions, formulate a work schedule, and speed up the progress. Communication with national climate change authorities and international climate trading agencies, and fully grasp all aspects of information. At the same time, an expert committee consisting of experts in finance, environment and economy should be established to provide technical advice.
3. Improve the environment and strengthen system construction. Adjust relevant policies, simplify approval policies and procedures, and introduce and establish carbon emission trading projects and international intermediaries. Establish carbon emission trading guidelines, evaluation indicators, calculation methods of carbon credits, and regulations on emission rights acquisition, trading licenses, and fee collection; provide consulting services for enterprises to participate in carbon emission trading.
4. Strengthen capacity building and personnel training. Organize exchange visits to Climate Exchange in Europe, in Beijing, Shanghai, Tianjin, etc. to strengthen capacity building and human resource development.

7.5 Demonstration and Guiding Role of Guangyuan in Regional Development by Improving Low Carbon Model

Low-carbon economy is a huge change in economic development mode, energy consumption mode and human life style. It has become the commanding height of regional economic competition at home and abroad. Whoever grasps the opportunity of low-carbon economy will have the advantage of strategic competition in the future. The development of a low-carbon economy is the most effective form of transforming ecological advantages into economic advantages, and is the best choice for promoting ecological civilization. It is also an inevitable strategic choice for implementing the scientific concept of development, building a resource-saving and environment-friendly society, optimizing the economic structure and transforming the economic development mode.

7.5.1 *Advantages and Potential of Guangyuan to Develop Low-Carbon Economy*

1. The construction of ecological Guangyuan has laid a good economic and social foundation for the development of low-carbon economy.

   Focusing on the strategic goal of building an ecological Guangyuan, the city promotes ecological restoration and reconstruction, earnestly implements ecological projects such as returning farmland to forests and natural forest protection, actively creates a "National Forest City", comprehensively conducts urban and rural environmental management, and actively promotes environmental protection and green development in the community, transportation, and waste utilization, etc. The city's forest coverage rate is as high as 53.60%, the green coverage rate in the city's built-up areas is 41.20%, the green space rate is 40%, and the per capita park green space area is 10.4 square meters; the road greening rate is 93%, and the waterfront greening rate is 90%. Guangyuan's energy structure quality rate is higher than the national average. Through the implementation of the "Gasification Guangyuan" strategy, Guangyuan's use of clean energy accounts for 20% of its energy consumption structure.
2. Guangyuan is endowed with unique energy resources.

   Guangyuan is rich in wind and solar energy; it is rich in natural gas, hydropower and other clean energy and renewable energy, of which the proven natural gas reserves are 230 billion cubic meters, and the proven reserves are over 400 billion cubic meters in 10 years, and the prospective reserves are particularly huge. Rural household biogas is being promoted at an annual rate of 50,000 households (each household has a biogas pool of 8 to 10 cubic meters). Guangyuan is rich in tourism resources and has great potential for development, and tourism is a low-pollution industry. Renewable energy resources are the material basis for Guangyuan to develop a low-carbon economy, but the current development and utilization are only a small part of the total resources, and a large number of renewable energy resources such as wind energy, geothermal energy, solar energy, biomass energy, etc. have not been fully developed.
3. Guangyuan's low-carbon economy has a first-mover advantage.

   Guangyuan was the first to put forward "low-carbon reconstruction" in the post-disaster reconstruction, firmly established the concept of low-carbon development in the reconstruction, adhered to the low-carbon energy structure, low-carbon industrial development and ecological construction as the main lines, promoted the low-carbon economic and social recovery, low-carbon reconstruction and low-carbon development. Focusing on the main line of reducing "carbon sources" and increasing "carbon sinks", Guangyuan city explore and practice from nine aspects such as advocating the concept of low-carbon development and building a low-carbon energy system through adjustments of energy structure, industrial structure and consumption structure. Focusing on technological innovation, management innovation and ecological construction, Guangyuan has explored a path for developing a low-carbon economy and transforming growth patterns in late-developing regions, and preliminary results have been achieved.

Guangyuan won the title of "Low-Carbon China Contribution City" in 2009, and was awarded the title of "Low-carbon Development Outstanding Contribution City" in 2010. In 2011, Luo Qiang, secretary of the Guangyuan Municipal Party Committee, was invited to attend the Durban Climate Conference, which was recognized by the international community.

7.5.2 *Aspects of Improving Low-Carbon Guangyuan*

1. Low-carbon industrial system needs to be improved.

   In 2011, Guangyuan's three industrial structure was adjusted from 23.8:39.0:37.2 in 2010 to 20.8:44.6:34.6. Although the "231" industrial pattern was initially formed, the overall development of the industry was still dominated by traditional raw material industries, and the proportion of heavy industry reached 70%; the proportion of modern service industry is less than 40%, and the proportion of service industry in GDP continues to decline. Low-carbon development is in the shape of "dots", the development of low-carbon economy in urban and rural areas is unbalanced, and there is a lack of full integration among industries, which is prominently reflected in the lack of close links between industry and the tertiary industry, agriculture and service industries. The low-carbon industrial chain effect has not yet emerged, the adjustment of the industrial structure is difficult, and the construction of a low-carbon industrial system has a long way to go.
2. Strengthening scientific and technological support for low-carbon economy.

   Science and technology are motivation for low carbon economy development. By now, the bottleneck of Guangyuan's low-carbon economy is the lagging behind development of science and technology. Most enterprises have not been able to develop key technologies to greatly improve resource utilization efficiency, reduce pollution emissions and comprehensive utilization of waste. A considerable number of small and medium-sized enterprises lack the skills and talents to develop a low-carbon economy.
3. Low-carbon marketization needs to be followed up.

   Although Guangyuan took the lead in establishing an environmental exchange in the province, with a total transaction value of 175 million yuan, there are problems such as excessive price fluctuation, long project execution cycle, high transaction cost, and complicated application for certification procedures. In addition, the content of the transaction has not yet involved the inter-regional transaction of major pollutant emissions. At the beginning of 2012, 7 of the more than 20 emission reduction exchanges in China will be selected to carry out the pilot work of carbon emission trading. Guangyuan Exchange should actively apply to be included.

4. Improve low-carbon economic policy guarantees.

   At present, the laws and regulations and policy system to promote the development of Guangyuan's low-carbon economy are not completed, and the supporting policies such as industrial policies, tax policies, land policies, credit policies and market access need to be further formulated, improved and put into place.
5. Form a synergy for the development of a low-carbon economy.

   The development of a low-carbon economy requires the joint efforts of the government, enterprises and the general public. At present, Guangyuan has done a lot of effective work at the level of government promotion. For example, in 2009, the leading group for low-carbon economic development (the leading group for addressing climate change) was established, and in 2011, the municipal low-carbon development bureau was first established in the country. However, some enterprises and a few departments and regions are not very aware of low carbon, and they only look at immediate interests and ignore long-term plans. Many public consumption methods are still traditional high-carbon methods.[3]

7.5.3 Countermeasures for Low-Carbon Guangyuan Development

1. Actively support Guangyuan's declaration to become a national low-carbon pilot area and a low-carbon pilot city.

   In August 2010, the National Development and Reform Commission has selected "five provinces and eight cities" as the first batch of low-carbon pilot areas. The provincial party committee and the provincial government should attach great importance to the current general trend of low-carbon economic development at home and abroad, establish strategic cooperation with international organizations such as the International Climate Organization and WWF, seize opportunities, and strive to include Sichuan in the second batch of national low-carbon pilot areas. On this basis, cities with low-carbon development advantages and potential, such as Guangyuan, are selected as pilot areas for low-carbon economy, leading and driving the accelerated and scientific development of the province.
2. Make the low-carbon industry solid and strong, and prevent the hollowing out of the low-carbon development industry.

   The ultimate goal of low-carbon economy is low-carbon economic development, and economic development provides material basis for low-carbon, and realizes the benign interactive development of the two. Economic development requires industrial support. Without solid low-carbon industry support, it is difficult to achieve low-carbon development. Guangyuan is located at the junction of Sichuan, Shaanxi, and Gansu provinces, and is on the edge of Sichuan and Chengdu-Chongqing economic zones. Once the post-disaster reconstruction investment is completed, the investment in Guangyuan will show a downward trend, and Guangyuan's low-carbon development may show a trend of industrial hollowing out. It is necessary to further strengthen the counterpart cooperation mechanism, make use of the aided provinces and cities and their own resources to build a low-carbon industry, and further accelerate the industrialization of Guangyuan National Advanced Electronic Products and Supporting Materials Industrialization Base, an Energy Base Supported and Developed by Sichuan Province, and a National Construction of Circular Economy Industrial Demonstration Parks. Vigorously cultivate strategic emerging industries such as energy conservation and environmental protection, new materials. Make full use of the advantages of Guangyuan's rich tourism resources, and develop the tertiary industry represented by the tourism industry.[4]

3. Organizing the promotion of low-carbon technologies and low-carbon demonstration projects.

   Sum up the good experience of Guangyuan's existing low-carbon economy practice, track the frontier of low-carbon technology innovation at home and abroad, and actively introduce advanced and applicable low-carbon technology at home and abroad through multiple channels, promote Guangyuan's low-carbon technology innovation. Actively track and pay attention to the new direction, new measures and new policies of low-carbon economic development at country level, provincial level and in other cities, make full use of relevant industrial policies successively issued by the state, and help relevant enterprises apply for project funds. Coordinate multi-channel resources such as finance and banks, coordinate the funds for technological transformation of enterprises, special funds for the development of small and medium-sized enterprises, innovation funds for small and medium-sized technological enterprises, and funds for agricultural industrialization. Actively apply for funds from the central government for special transfer payments for energy conservation, environmental protection, and new energy in the western region. Actively apply for public welfare construction projects. At the same time, on the basis of summarizing the successful pilot projects, expand the pilot industries, regions or units, and promote them to a larger scale.

4. Establish and improve the ecological compensation system and trading platform, and promote low-carbon marketization.

   It is necessary to deeply study the international and domestic emission reduction situation and market dynamics, and make further full use of the forestry carbon sink mechanism. Further study the status and role of Guangyuan ecological resources in the ecosystem of the whole province and the upper reaches of the Yangtze River; further study and master international emission measurement methods, financing methods, market mechanisms, project application procedures, etc.; further study the potential of Guangyuan greenhouse gas emission reduction, cost and efficiency, so as to know not only the needs of the market, but also the content of natural resource, and timely conduct international and inter-regional communication according to the actual situation of the region.

   Take Guangyuan as a platform to speed up the construction of the ecological and environmental protection compensation system. As an ecological upstream area, Guangyuan undertakes the important task of protecting the ecological environment in the upstream area, and has made huge sacrifices in the overall development of the country. Therefore, an ecological compensation mechanism for cities like Guangyuan in the downstream area should be established. It is suggested that the provincial government establish a major pollutant emission trading platform as soon as possible, so that developed regions can purchase major pollutant emission credits from underdeveloped regions. On the one hand, it will not affect the industrial development of developed areas, and on the other hand, through transactions, less developed areas will get more funds for economic and social development and ecological and environmental protection projects. Actively participate in the construction of the carbon market, strive to explore voluntary emission reduction standards, establish corporate low-carbon indicators, promote and package new energy companies to go public, and participate in the construction of the National Environment Exchange Voluntary Emission Reduction (VER) Trading Platform.

5. Further establish and improve the incentive mechanism of low-carbon policy.

   The development of a low-carbon economy requires policy and institutional innovation. Guangyuan should study and formulate preferential policies such as: the government can gradually establish a low-carbon fiscal and tax preferential policy system from the perspective of improving energy efficiency and promoting energy conservation. Promote the development of a low-carbon economy through financing incentives, tax incentives and other mechanisms. Formulate and implement a low-carbon certification system, and the government implements a low-carbon procurement policy. At the same time, it is necessary to increase the publicity and promotion of low-carbon economy products, increase the marketing of low-carbon economy products, and support the promotion and application of low-carbon economy products in terms of finance, environmental protection, energy conservation and consumption reduction. Violations of low-carbon regulations must be punished in accordance with the law. Promote energy management contracts (EMC) on a pilot basis. Encourage shopping malls, restaurants and other large public buildings to implement energy-saving renovations by adopting contract energy management methods. Accelerate the transformation of the government's energy management mechanism, and use the market to drive energy efficiency.

6. Establishing a tripartite cooperation low-carbon economic governance structure.

   The development of a low-carbon economy requires tripartite cooperation between the government, enterprises, and the public, and the government should undertake the leadership and management functions of coordinating the development of a low-carbon economy; enterprises should take the initiative to assume social responsibility and become the main body of low-carbon industry and low-carbon product development; society should become the main body of low-carbon consumption and low-carbon life, establish a green and low-carbon lifestyle, reduce high-carbon purchases, and determine reasonable per capita CO_2 peak index to guide the masses to carry out carbon budget management. Create a low-carbon community in the way of "government guidance, enterprise participation, and technology integration", realize low-carbon benefits for the people, and elevate the low-carbon development of Guangyuan to a new level.

7.6 Construction of Ecological Shelters in Upper Reaches of Yangtze River as an Engine for Promoting Ecological Civilization in Sichuan Province

Sichuan Province locates in important strategic position of the entire Yangtze River Basin and plays an important role in the national ecological security, since at the beginning of the new century, the Sichuan Provincial Party Committee and the Provincial Government have consistently made the construction of an ecological barrier in the upper reaches of the Yangtze River as one of the province's important goals. In the critical period of building a moderately prosperous society in an all-round way, accelerating the construction of ecological barriers in the upper reaches of the Yangtze River will not only lay a good ecological foundation and provide industrial support for Sichuan Province and the whole country, but also provide industrial support for the middle and lower reaches of the Yangtze River and even the whole country.

Ecological construction projects such as returning farmland to forests and natural forest protection, which were first implemented in Sichuan Province, are the main body of the construction of the Yangtze River ecological barrier, and have produced huge ecological benefits. The forest coverage rate of the province has increased by more than 20 percentage points to 35.3%, and the forest ecological service value reached 1.6 trillion yuan, ranking first in China. The sediment input into the Yangtze River from Sichuan Province has been reduced by 46%, effectively curbing the threat of the Yangtze River becoming the second Yellow River, and safeguarding the safety of the Three Gorges Reservoir area.

During the critical period of building a moderately prosperous society, the construction of the ecological barrier in the upper reaches of the Yangtze River faces some new situations and new problems. First of all, the trend of ecological environment deterioration in Sichuan Province has not been fundamentally curbed. The existing soil erosion area is 220,000 square kilometers, and the sandy and rocky desertification land is 36 million mu. The whole province's river ecosystem is degraded, the water level has dropped, and the total amount of water resources has decreased by 6% in the past five years. In addition, Sichuan Province will enter a period of accelerated development of industrialization and urbanization, which will be accompanied by a peak period of resource consumption and environmental pollution. According to the forecast of relevant departments, by 2020, the total amount of sewage discharged in Sichuan will double on the basis of 2010. The second is that the "National Main Function Zone Plan" has designated 39 counties (cities) in the northwestern Sichuan plateau and the mountainous areas around the basin as restricted and prohibited development zones. These areas are rich in natural resources. More than 90% of the province's forest resources and 63% of water resources are distributed in these areas. These areas are also designated by the National Program for Poverty Alleviation and Development as concentrated and contiguous areas with special difficulties in the new 10-year period. As these areas are restricted and prohibited from development, the development gap with the downstream areas will widen. These areas are also key areas for natural protection and conversion of farmland to forests. In a short period of time, ecological construction achievements such as returning farmland to forests are difficult to become the pillar industries for farmers' income and regional tax increases in these areas. Thirdly, most of the farmland to forests in Sichuan Province are still in the stage of young forests or undeveloped forests, and more investment is needed to strengthen the management and protection of forests. On the other hand, since 2007, the state has stopped issuing targets for returning farmland to forests. However, according to the statistics of the forestry department, there are still nearly 10 million mu of steep-slope farmland in Sichuan Province that needs to be converted into forests. The diminishing financial support from the state level is also a serious challenge to the construction of the ecological barrier in the upper reaches of the Yangtze River in Sichuan Province.

How to promote the development of key ecological function areas in Sichuan Province in accordance with the national main function orientation? How to coordinate the construction of ecological barriers in the upper reaches of the Yangtze River with the goal of doubling the regional economy and the income of urban and rural residents? This is not only related to the consolidation of ecological construction achievements, but also to the major issues of building a moderately prosperous society in Sichuan Province and China. The following countermeasures are proposed for these problems:

1. Use the new concept that "lucid waters and lush mountains" can be transformed into "gold and silver mountains" to speed up the construction of ecological barriers in the upper reaches of the Yangtze River. Relying on the newly increased ecological productivity from the construction of the ecological barrier in the upper reaches of the Yangtze River, to develop the ecological economy. Through the development of forest cultivation, forest tourism, biomass energy, biomass materials, biopharmaceuticals and other means to cultivate new regional pillar industries and important sources of farmers' income, and transform ecological advantages into economic advantages.
2. Develop forest carbon sinks to provide financial support for the construction of ecological barriers in the upper reaches of the Yangtze River. Lack of funds is still the main constraint on the construction of ecological barriers in the upper reaches of the Yangtze River. The "Kyoto Protocol" has listed the indirect emission reduction of forests as an important measure to combat climate change. Various carbon sink resources, including forest carbon sinks, have become increasingly scarce and value-added resources. The annual carbon storage of forest vegetation in Sichuan Province has reached 77 million tons, accounting for 29% of the annual fixed carbon dioxide in forests in China, ranking first in all provinces. Sichuan Province should seize the opportunity that carbon emission reduction trading

will be carried out in 2015, and make full use of the successful experience of the forest carbon sink project in Sichuan Province and platforms such as the Sichuan Environment Exchange to establish and improve the carbon emission trading mechanism in Sichuan Province in a timely manner. It will realize the economic value of the rich forest carbon sink resources in Sichuan Province, and provide financial and technical support for the construction of ecological barriers in the upper reaches of the Yangtze River. Secondly, combined with the promotion of "forest reform", strengthen the intensive management and utilization of the converted forest land, develop the under-forest resource economy, and the under-forest planting and breeding industry economy to improve the output and economic benefits of forest land. Increase income, replace and transform inefficient forest varieties, and improve the quality and carbon sequestration capacity of forests.

3. Promptly promote major ecological restoration projects. Funds have been raised from various parties to give priority to the implementation of returning farmland to forests for more than 10 million mu of steep-slope cultivated land with a slope of more than 25 degrees in the province, especially 6 million mu of severely desertified and rocky desertified cultivated land and ecologically fragile areas around lakes and reservoirs. Natural restoration is the most effective ecological protection. During the time period that the large number of rural population in Sichuan Province to go out to work, a large amount of land have been abandoned due to lacking of working force, and the adjustment of concentrated rural settlements, it is the good opportunity to implement the return to forests and forests in ecologically fragile areas such as the Ruoergai grassland in northwestern Sichuan, the Jinsha River, and the dry-hot valleys in the upper reaches of the Minjiang River by implementing projects such as closure of mountains and afforestation and other ecological restoration.
4. Build energy saving and environmental protection industry as pillar industry to facilitate the construction of ecological civilization in Sichuan Province. Development of energy saving and environmental protection industry provide material and technical guarantee for the construction of ecological barriers in upper reaches of Yangtze River. The energy saving and environmental protection industry has multiple benefits of ecology, economy and society, which are pillar industries and foreign trade fist products in developed countries and domestic advanced regions. Especially because the energy conservation and environmental protection industry is a technology-intensive industry that can carry and accommodate high-tech achievements in various fields, and also a leading industry that promotes technological innovation and a strategic emerging industry supported by the State. On the one hand, with the advancement of industrialization and urbanization in Sichuan Province and the need to build an ecological barrier in the upper reaches of the Yangtze River, Sichuan Province has an increasingly strong market demand for energy conservation and environmental protection industries. It is predicted that by 2020, major pollutants such as COD, ammonia nitrogen, sulfur dioxide and nitrogen oxides will increase by 13.59 million tons. For this reason, there will be a market demand of 420 billion yuan for pollution

control in Sichuan Province. On the other hand, although the energy conservation and environmental protection industry in Sichuan Province currently accounts for less than 3% of the province's GDP, it only accounts for 4.37% of the output value of the national environmental protection industry. However, the province's energy-saving and environmental protection industry already has a good foundation and huge potential for development. Not only has the world's leading "Supermagnetic separation water purification technology", but also the first company in the country to manufacture PM2.5 monitoring instruments and the company that produces the country's largest waste treatment equipment. The environmental protection products of Dongfang Boiler, Hainuoer and other enterprises have entered international markets such as Southeast Asia. Jintang, Zigong, Panzhihua, Mianyang and other environmental protection have formed industry bases. Through policy-oriented, financial and other support measures, Sichuan Province's energy conservation and environmental protection industry can fully reach 100 billion yuan in output value and 20 billion yuan in profits and taxes by 2020. It will become a pillar industry to support Sichuan Province and the whole country to build a moderately prosperous society.

5. Coordinate urban and rural areas to promote the construction of ecological barriers in the upper reaches of the Yangtze River. Comprehensive management of urban and rural environment is a new important content and historical task of coordinating urban and rural development. Due to the long-term unbalanced development of urban and rural areas in China, during the process of environmental construction in vast rural areas, the non-point source pollution that is extremely difficult to control, and has seriously restricted the sustainable development of China's agriculture and rural areas, threatened the health of the majority of farmers.[5] Excessive application of chemical fertilizers and pesticides will lead to a decline in the quality of crops, reduction of production or even no harvest, decreasing farmers' income and endangering food safety. Environmental governance and protection in rural areas is not only related to the development of rural areas, but also directly related to the development of cities and the whole society. The externalities and spillovers of environmental protection determine that environmental protection and sustainable development can only be achieved through coordinated urban and rural development.[6]

At present, the management of excrement and sewage from large-scale farms in rural areas and the management of rural straw burning should be promoted as the key tasks of comprehensive management of urban and rural environment. In the medium and long term, it is necessary to integrate urban and rural environmental protection planning, build a new investment and financing system for rural environmental protection, integrate urban and rural environmental protection institutions, fully cover urban and rural areas with environmental monitoring, build a modern agricultural production system that is resource-saving, environmentally friendly, ecologically safe, and develop clean production, food safety, etc. Using the construction of ecological villages, ecological towns and ecological counties as a platform to further promote the overall planning of urban and rural areas in the province's environmental governance and protection.[7]

7.7 The Global Trend of Emission Reduction After the Copenhagen Climate Conference and China's Strategic Choice to Address Climate Change

Professor Christian Azar is a senior expert of the UN Intergovernmental Panel on Climate Change (IPCC) Expert Committee and one of the main authors of the Third Assessment Report. He is also member of the Swedish Government's Sustainable Development Committee, special adviser to the former European Union Vice-President and Environment Minister Margot Wallstrom, and adviser to the former Prime Minister and Environment Minister of Sweden. Professor Christian held a scientific, rigorous attitude and an objective and fair position toward the studying of climate change, and his views have wide influence and representativeness in the world. He put forward the following suggestions on the global emission reduction trend after the Copenhagen Climate Conference and China's strategic choice for addressing climate change:

7.7.1 Emission Reduction Trend after the Copenhagen Climate Conference

The Copenhagen Accord is one of the world's biggest climate outcomes to date. If our expectations were not so high, the outcome of this consultation might not have been so unexpected.

The Copenhagen Conference reached a consensus on reducing emissions to keep the global temperature rise within 2 °C, and reached some consensus on tropical rain forests and financial support for developing countries. However, there is still no binding emission reduction obligation. Instead, countries have chosen and announced their voluntary non-binding emission reduction targets. A year later, at the UN-led climate conference in Cancun, Mexico, these non-binding emission reduction targets became a formal part of the United Nations Framework Convention on Climate Change, but these targets are still not legal emission reduction obligations. Moreover, many believe that such a voluntary goal looks weak if global temperature rise is to be safely kept within 2 °C.

The results of Copenhagen and Cancun mean that the Kyoto Protocol is drifting away. Although the Kyoto Protocol is still on paper, and while a new round of climate conference will begin in Durban, South Africa in late 2011, and some rescue packages may be proposed, the meeting is unlikely to pass any regional binding emission reduction targets other than Europe. Because many countries have announced in advance that they will not accept any binding emission reduction targets. What's the point of extending the Kyoto Protocol since Europe is the only region to accept a binding target?

From Copenhagen to Cancun, countries in both the "northern hemisphere" and "southern hemisphere" have pledged their own voluntary emission reduction targets, and all have agreed to work to keep global temperature rise below 2 °C. The world is already further on the road to reducing emissions than was thought possible a decade ago. Of course, there is still a long way to go to solve this thorny problem, and more work needs to be done. How to provide human civilization with energy that does not emit carbon dioxide, how to gradually reduce emissions every year? Those issues need to be addressed and it is indeed a journey of thousands of miles. But the project team believes that the total global greenhouse gas emissions should be reduced by 21% by 2020 compared to 2005.

7.7.2 The U.S. Role and Shifts in Reducing Emissions

As early as 1997, when the Kyoto Protocol was still under negotiation, the US Senate announced by a vote of 95 to 0 that the US would never accept binding emission reduction obligations unless major developing countries accepted similar emission reduction obligations. President Obama also decided to accept non-binding emission reduction targets outside the Kyoto Protocol system, which was the best option under the circumstances.

In 2010, the U.S. Congress failed to pass a proposal for an emissions trading system. For the world's emission reduction, the significance of this matter can be compared with the Copenhagen Conference, and the weight of the former is even higher than that of the latter. The reason is that while international agreements pave the way for emissions reductions around the world, putting pressure on countries to move forward, it is ultimately through the domestic policies of individual countries that emissions reductions actually happen.

If the United States passes the proposal, it will be more willing to urge other countries to reduce emissions. The failure of the U.S. emissions trading proposal has huge implications for the global landscape, as it is the world's largest economy and the country with the highest per capita emissions. It's hard to expect other countries to start cutting emissions without a real commitment from the US.

Although the emissions trading system was not passed by the U.S. Senate, it was passed by the House of Representatives in a vote in 2009, and many states in the U.S. still insist on reducing their own emissions. The U.S. is actually one step closer to implementing an effective national policy to reduce emissions.

7.7.3 Global Emission Reduction Trends

Over the past decade, the increase in global emissions has climbed at an unprecedented rate, reaching 33 billion tons per year, a 50% increase since the signing of the United Nations Framework Convention on Climate Change in 1992. After the 2008–2009 financial crisis, emissions fell slightly, but in 2010 they rebounded sharply to new highs.

If the world is to meet the 2 °C warming target, global emissions must drop significantly over the next few decades. Emission levels more than halved by 2050, reaching 15 billion tons of carbon dioxide per year. Assuming that this emission space is equally distributed to each person on earth, then by 2050 each of us will only be able to emit 1.5 tons of carbon dioxide per year. Since then, the per capita allowable emissions will be further reduced. For Americans or Europeans who emit about 20 tons per capita, this is an extremely huge challenge. This is also a huge challenge for China and most countries in the world. Because people in developed countries are richer, have higher historical and per capita emissions, and are more advanced in science and technology, it is reasonable to infer that the primary responsibility for reducing emissions lies with developed countries. However, the development of many developing countries, including China, has raised a very important question: when should developing countries begin to undertake the task of reducing emissions? Many countries like Saudi Arabia, Singapore, South Korea, South Africa and many others have higher per capita emissions than many developed countries. In general, the boundaries between "south" and "north", poor and rich, and those who are responsible for reducing emissions and those who do not need to be responsible are becoming increasingly blurred. The world is no longer simply composed of a few rich countries and many poor countries, it has become more multidimensional.

7.7.4 China's Evolving Impact and Global Leadership in Cutting Emissions

7.7.4.1 An Important Role Played by China in Reducing World Emissions

More than half of the increase in global carbon dioxide emissions since 1990 has come from China. Emission from China now accounts for 25% of global total. China's rapid rise in income and energy use has impressed the world. In 2006, China surpassed the United States to become the world's number one carbon dioxide emitter. By 2010, China's emissions had risen by another 30 percent, while in the U.S., partly because of the financial crisis, emissions have actually fallen somewhat. In recent years, China has become the same heavyweight player as the U.S. in the international climate game.

In the past few decades, China has lifted millions of people out of poverty. From this perspective, China's rapid transformation is gratifying and admirable. But each coin has two sides, there are also problems behind the achievements, such as the environmental pollution caused by industry and coal power plants, which seriously affects the lives of millions of people in China.

7.7.4.2 China's Clear Stance and Responsibility on Climate Change

In China, more and more people aware the importance of reducing carbon emission globally, and it is not the only responsibility of the developed countries. "Climate change is a major challenge facing the world today. It is the common mission of all human being to combat global warming and save the earth. Every country and nation, every enterprise and individual, should act with responsibility." China has also announced a pilot program for emissions trading and will introduce stringent policies to promote energy efficiency.

7.7.4.3 China's Carbon Intensity Reduction Goals: Crucial and Challenging

China has voluntarily pledged to "reduce CO_2 emissions per unit of GDP by 40–45% by 2020 from 2005 levels". While this is an important step, we also need to recognize that this is likely to mean an increase in absolute emissions. If GDP grows by an average of 7% over the 15-year period, total carbon dioxide emissions will rise by 65% during this period. On the other hand, emissions have increased by 40%, (referring to the total national carbon emissions in 2010 has reached 8.332 billion tons, an increase of 40% over 2005); if emissions grow by 6–7% per year by 2013, this target implies a freeze on carbon dioxide emissions from 2013 onward s(based on a 40% reduction in carbon intensity and an average annual GDP growth of 7%, the country's total carbon emissions in 2020 can only be increased by 65% compared to 2005, reaching 9.788 billion tons of carbon dioxide. However, at an average annual growth rate of 7%, it is estimated that the national emission will reach 9.525 billion tons by 2012, and will reach more than 10 billion tons by 2013, which has obviously exceeded the control value of 9.788 billion tons. Therefore, in order to achieve the goal of reducing carbon intensity by 40% on the basis of 2005, the total national carbon emission must be controlled above the level of 2012). It will be an extremely important but extremely difficult breakthrough.

7.7.4.4 Regional Carbon Intensity Inequality in China: A Significant Challenge

Maybe ten years from now, China's per capita emissions will reach the European average. In 2010, the average annual per capita emission of Western Europe was

8.4 tons of carbon dioxide, and China was 6.2 tons, which has surpassed Sweden. While the per capita emissions in different provinces in China are also differentiated. In 2007, less developed areas in western China, such as Sichuan Province, had an annual per capita emission of 2.6 tons, while Shandong Province reached 7.3 tons. Hundreds of millions of people in China's coastal provinces enjoy the same standard of living as Europe and the United States, and emit similar levels of carbon dioxide, but their data is hidden by the data of hundreds of millions of people in the western provinces.

7.7.5 *Strategic Options for Tackling Climate Change*

7.7.5.1 The Dilemma Between Economic Growth and Emission Reduction

Huang Ming, an entrepreneur from Dezhou, Shandong Province, China, who has won Sweden's "Right Lifestyle Award", known as "another Nobel Prize", and others offer the first tentative insights into the most crucial dilemma in the climate debate. They argue that many developing countries are in desperate need of economic growth. But if it grows in the same way as the developed world, the growth of emissions will push the limits and we are risking our climate, ecosystems and the lives and homes of hundreds of millions of people.

Is there any way to break through the siege? The answer is YES. The potential of renewable energy technologies represented by solar energy and wind energy is tremendous that we are fully capable of taking into account the contradiction between growth and emissions, and taking a path of energy development that not only integrates global well-being, but also reduces or even achieves zero carbon dioxide emissions.

The good news is that wind and solar have continued to grow rapidly over the past few years. In 2000, the installed capacity of wind energy in the world was about 18GW (18 million kilowatts), and by 2010, it increased to 200GW (200 million kilowatts), an increase of 10 times. The installed capacity of solar photovoltaic power generation has reached 40GW (40 million kilowatts), an increase of 27 times compared with 2000. For EU countries, most of the increase in electricity supply in 2009 came from solar and wind energy. China is a major producer and installer of windmills, as well as a major producer of solar photovoltaic cells (mostly for export).

7.7.5.2 A Revolution in the Transformation of the World's Energy Supply

The rapid growth of solar and wind is encouraging in many ways, both proving the viability of these technical solutions, enabling learning by doing (the more you do, the more proficient), and the ability to build on a larger scale factory facilitate mass production and attract more and more talented engineers and researchers, and of course entrepreneurs, all of which help keep costs down. This is important because the cost of solar and wind is still too high, (most of the time) it is insufficient by itself to compete with fossil fuel-based grid electricity prices. When the cost is reduced, the technology will be more competitive and the application will be more widespread.

Despite rapid growth, wind power and solar photovoltaic cells account for only a few percent of global electricity generation. Therefore, if wind energy and solar photovoltaic cells are to completely change the world's energy system and reduce carbon dioxide emissions, this rapid growth must be maintained, or even accelerated. We also need to recognize that it will take a long time to change the energy system, not a few years or ten or twenty years, but half a century to a century.

7.7.5.3 Biomass Energy's Promise and Challenges

Solar and wind are not the only answers to zero-carbon energy supply technologies, but also nuclear, carbon capture and storage, and biomass. Biomass has grown rapidly over the past few years, but so have concerns about its large-scale use, in large part due to the use of corn to expand ethanol production in the United States (which will led to an increase in greenhouse gas emission, and also rising of food prices). On the other hand, biomass can also have very little CO_2 emissions (biomass from understory residues or efficiently managed short-rotation plantations or sugar cane). This depends on the choice of feedstock and its transformation. In addition, biomass energy can be paired with carbon capture to achieve negative carbon emissions. This could even undo some of the mistakes of our past emissions spree, and increase the likelihood that atmospheric carbon dioxide levels will drop from the current level of 390 PPM to the target of 350 PPM by 2100.

The key question is the scale. If the plantation model to develop biomass energy is to have a seat in the global energy system, say 10–20% of the total supply, it will need land use as large as the current global agricultural system. Considering the various environmental problems caused by current agriculture, such as deforestation, the use of pesticides, and the possible impact of forest plantation on food prices, we cannot help to ask if it is a wise choice. Second, once a hard and meaningful price for carbon is established, we will certainly protect existing forests and priceless ecosystems by taxing—not subsidizing—biomass energy.

7.7.5.4 Concerns About Nuclear Power

For nuclear energy, the nuclear leak in Fukushima, Japan is the biggest disaster in recent years. A huge earthquake accompanied by a devastating tsunami is an extreme scenario that is unlikely to occur in most places on earth. But this series of events has awakened a renewed focus on the risks of nuclear power itself. Germany has decided to phase out the development of nuclear power across the board, and China has temporarily frozen approvals for new nuclear power projects, as well as more careful analysis and verification of the safety of existing or future nuclear power plants. There is no doubt that new nuclear power plants need to meet higher safety requirements, which will inevitably increase costs, thereby diluting the profits in the future. However, it is too early to tell how the Fukushima incident's blow the confidence in nuclear power will affect the long-term development of nuclear energy.

In the long term, energy can be obtained sustainably from solar energy or from nuclear fission. If we use solar energy, we need 10% of the world's deserts, and if we use nuclear power, we need to build 10,000 nuclear reactors. Yet the risk of a nuclear accident and concerns that civilian nuclear energy programs could provide cover for the development of nuclear weapons are ever-present. So, it's hard to convince people that nuclear energy will provide humanity with a bright future. The future represented by solar energy, wind energy, biomass energy, water energy and ocean energy are easier to accept.

While scientists are pretty sure we can reduce carbon dioxide emissions while still providing enough energy for a growing world population, they are also sure it won't be easy. We need a 100-fold effort to improve solar and wind energy systems, develop more energy-efficient technologies, electric vehicles, hydrogen storage and conversion technologies, batteries, and more. We also need to protect Earth's sensitive ecosystems, such as tropical rain forests, as agriculture and biomass farming continue to expand.

7.7.5.5 Policy Formulation and International Cooperation: Key Solutions for Global Challenges

Global warming is caused by hundreds of countries, millions of companies, and billions of people around the world. Choices big or small will all affect energy use and carbon dioxide emissions. People, companies and countries should gradually adopt technologies and lifestyles that emit less carbon dioxide. For the transformation to happen, policy comes first. People should consciously recognize that this is a problem that needs solutions, and that policymakers need to demonstrate leadership. Common problems require common solutions, both domestic policies and international collaboration, consultations and treaties are needed.

Notes

1. Shouhu Du, "The Impact and Countermeasures of National Greenhouse Gas Emission Reduction Goals on Sichuan", *Party Building in Sichuan (Urban Edition)*, Issue 4, 2010.
2. Dan Li, "How to Solve the Problem of Building a Low Carbon City", *Sichuan Daily*, February 2, 2010.
3. Ruidong Li, and Houmei Zhang, "Post Disaster Low Carbon Reconstruction - Interview with Luo Qiang, Secretary of Guangyuan Municipal Party Committee of Sichuan Province", *Environmental Protection*, 2011.

4. Qiang Luo, and Wei Jiang, "Poverty Stricken Areas can Also Take the Lead in Low-carbon Development - Low-Carbon Reconstruction Practice in Guangyuan Disaster Area", *Environmental Protection*, Issue 6, 2010.
5. Chuanhao Wen, and Yan Tie, "The Theory of Ecological Civilization Construction needs to be Continuously Deepened", *China Environmental News*, November 13, 2012.
6. Shouhu Du, "New Goal of Urban Rural Integration: Urban Rural Integrated Construction of Ecological Civilization", *Decision Consultation Communication*, Issue 7, 2009.
7. Shouhu Du, "Promoting the Construction of Ecological Civilization in Chengdu with the Goal of Building REEFCR City", *Journal of Chengdu University of Administration*, Issue 6, 2013.

Chapter 8
Park City: Harmony and Coexistence of Mountains, Waters, and People

Park city is a new goal in urban modernization, a new paradigm in urban governance, and a new platform for urban ecological civilization construction.[1] The key features of park city are green, ecological, and sustainable; the core values of park city are prioritizing people, livability, harmony between humans and nature. Ecological priority and green development are the guiding principles of park cities. Balancing the coordinated development of the economy, society, and ecological environment is a crucial challenge that worth to be addressed in the construction of a park city. The saying "lucid waters and lush mountains are invaluable assets" profoundly illustrates the dialectical unity between economic development and environmental protection, serving as the fundamental guiding principle for the high-quality construction of a park city. Climate resilient and low-carbon development are important characteristics of a park city. It is essential to integrate with the green economy and circular economy, combine carbon reduction with pollution control, and coordinate the advancement of low-carbon development with addressing prominent environmental issues such as air pollution. Advocating and practicing a low-carbon lifestyle and consumption concept is crucial. Building an urban industrial ecosystem, promoting urban industrial transformation and upgrading, enhancing urban economic competitiveness are key points for building park city. Industrial greening (i.e., green transformation and upgrading of traditional industries) and green industrialization (i.e., transforming intangible ecological assets into tangible benefits) serve as the foundation for constructing an urban industrial ecosystem. Both urban and rural areas play indispensable roles in park city development.

Since the 19th National Congress of the Communist Party of China, Xi Jinping, the General Secretary of the Communist Party of China, has visited Sichuan Province twice, he elaborated important instructions on ecological civilization construction. During his visit to Sichuan in February 2018, Xi Jinping emphasized the importance of enhancing ecological civilization by making the skies bluer, the land greener, and the water clearer, promoting the harmonious coexistence of beautiful urban and rural areas, as well as integrating beautiful landscapes with livable environments.

S. Du and H. Du, *The Green Transformation of Urban Areas in China Under Global Warming*, https://doi.org/10.1007/978-981-95-1005-4_8

He specifically addressed that Chengdu should highlight its characteristics as a park city and incorporate ecological values. In June 2022, during his visit to Yibin, which was known as the "First City on the Yangtze River", Xi Jinping emphasized the importance of Sichuan being located in the upper reaches of the Yangtze River, it is necessary to enhance the overall awareness, firmly establish the upstream mindset, and resolutely implement the policy of prioritizing ecological conservation over large-scale development to build a solid ecological barrier in the upper reaches of the Yangtze River and safeguard its clear waters. This chapter, based on a thorough study of General Secretary Xi Jinping's important instructions during his visits to Sichuan Province, aims to clarify the characteristics and scientific connotations of park city, explore how to consider ecological values, and discuss the pathways and mechanisms for high-quality construction of park cities to present the theoretical value and practical significance of Xi Jinping's ecological civilization ideology.

8.1 Park City: Urban Governance Paradigms in the Era of Ecological Civilization

The twenty-first century is the century of cities. Rapidly growing metropolises have become symbols of the world's rapid development. The Asian Development Bank predicts that by 2025, there will be 37 mega-cities worldwide with populations exceeding 10 million, with 20 of them located in Asia. By 2050, two-thirds of the population in Asia will be living in urban areas, whereas in 1970, only 20% of Asia's population was urbanized. Engels once pointed out that where does history begin, the process of thought should also begin. Cities are the places where modern industrial civilization is concentrated, but they are also the places that suffer from many modern problems.[2] With the development of the economy and society, the expansion of social division of labor, and the increasing demand for population in urban development, the scale of cities continue to expand. Cities' demands for transportation, energy, construction, and information are rapidly increasing. At the same time, issues such as traffic congestion, inadequate public resource supply, and environmental problems in the air and water are becoming more prominent. Urban management and the sustainable development of cities are facing increasingly severe challenges. The traditional urban governance paradigm is clearly insufficient to address these increasingly serious "urban diseases". Therefore, since the early twentieth century, many countries around the world have been exploring new paradigms of urban governance in theory and practice.

The history of urban governance is a history of paradigm shifts. Looking back at the history of urban governance corresponding to different stages of human civilization development, various theories, doctrines, and models have emerged. The paradigms that can be considered are only the garden city, compact city, and park city. Garden city is the paradigm of urban governance in the agricultural civilization era; while compact city represents the paradigm of urban governance in the industrial civilization era; the park city, on the other hand, signifies the modernization of urban governance in the ecological civilization era. Thomas Kuhn believes that paradigms are essentially theoretical systems, divided into three types or aspects: philosophical paradigms, sociological paradigms, and artificial paradigms. A paradigm is a model representing a stage of scientific development, based on a specific scientific theory as an example. It is a recognized model or pattern. A paradigm should not only have established patterns and consensus, integrity, and other specific regulations, but also new ideas, theoretical systems, distinguishing it from mere patterns.

The concept of an ecological civilization in urban governance, known as the park city model, is primarily based on the idea that "building an ecological civilization is an important feature of socialism with Chinese characteristics in the new era". Since the 18th National Congress of the Communist Party of China, there have been historical turning and overall changes in China's ecological environment with the creation of practice models including forest city and ecological city. More importantly, it is supported by the new concept and theory of "harmonious coexistence between human and nature" and "people's city".

"Harmonious coexistence between human and nature" is an important concept of park city. Xi Jinping emphasized that China's construction of socialist modernization has many important features, one of which is that China's modernization is a modernization in which human beings coexist harmoniously with nature, focusing on the simultaneous advancement of the construction of material civilization and ecological civilization."[3] "Human beings and nature are a community of life. Human beings must worship nature, respect nature, adapt to nature and protect nature." "Let's join hands, uphold the concept of ecological civilization, take responsibility for future generations, and together build a global community of life on Earth, work together to construct a clean and beautiful world." "To integrate pollution control, ecological protection and climate change response, promote the sustainable improvement of the ecological environment, and strive to build a modernized environment in which human beings live in harmony with nature." The above elaborations are the core ideas of harmonious coexistence between human beings and nature.

"People's city" is another important concept of park city. During his visit to Shanghai in 2019, Xi Jinping proposed that "people's cities are built by the people, and the people's cities are for the people." "Whether it's urban planning or urban construction, whether it's the construction of a new city or the renovation of an old one, people-oriented should be the center of the city." When Xi Jinping visited Sichuan in 2022, he said, "Focus on tackling the outstanding ecological and environmental problems around the common people, so that they can actually feel the improvement of the quality of the ecological environment". These statements form the core of the "people's city".

Park City has raised the rich practical experience and model of modern urban governance and ecological civilization construction since the 18th National Congress of the CPC to a theoretical level, and has become a new paradigm for the modernization of urban governance and a new platform for the construction of urban ecological civilization.

8.2 Ecological Priority and Green Development: Primary Characteristics and Goal Orientation of Park City

The classification and naming of cities can be based on various dimensions. It can be from natural climate, geographical location, resource endowment, ecological environment dimensions, such as tropical cities, western cities, forest cities, ecological cities, etc.; or from human society, political economy, historical culture, functional planning dimensions, such as political centers, historical cities, livable cities, harmonious cities, hub cities, and so on. Compared with other types of cities, the most significant feature of a park city is its emphasis on greenery, ecology, and sustainability; with a value orientation towards livability, suitability for business, and harmony between people and nature. Xi Jinping has emphasized that Chengdu should highlight its characteristics as a park city and incorporate ecological values, which is the most important basis for the above judgment. Furthermore, as supporting evidence, there is the national nature reserve system aimed at protecting the ecological environment and promoting harmony between people and nature, divided into national parks, nature reserves, and natural parks.

Cities make life better, and the urban lifestyle is a constant driving force behind urbanization. However, with the changing times, the concept of a happy life has undergone significant changes. On October 8, 2021, the United Nations Human Rights Council declared that having a clean, healthy, and sustainable environment is a human right. This fully demonstrates that "a good ecological environment is the fairest public good and the most inclusive well-being for the people"; the increasing need of the people in the new era for a better life is evidently no longer limited to material and cultural needs, but a good ecological environment and living a sustainable life have become the new expectations and pursuits of the people for a better life.

The beautiful ecological environment is the most important characteristic of urban livability, which in turn is the primary indicator of a city's happiness index. Whether in terms of livable cities or citizens' happiness index, Chengdu has consistently ranked at the top of national urban rankings for many years. This not only deeply reveals that livability, characterized by a beautiful ecological environment, is the source of citizens' happiness and sense of achievement, but also fully reflects citizens' recognition of the Party Committee and government's efforts to improve the city's ecological environment and enhance its livability and business-friendliness.

Prioritizing ecology and promoting green development can not only meet the growing need for a beautiful ecological environment among the people but also drive the green transformation and upgrading of the city's production methods, lifestyles, and consumption patterns, comprehensively enhancing the city's governance capabilities and the modernization level of its systems.

8.3 Development and Conservation: The Primary Concern that Park City Must Address

In the new era, cities in China, especially mega-cities like Chengdu, are facing the dilemma and distress of being "both troubled by fast development and stagnant development." On one hand, measured by population size, economic volume, and other factors, Chengdu has become an important growth pole and a national central city; on the other hand, the city continues to expand, facing homogeneous competition in production capacity, unreasonable spatial resource allocation, uneven population density, and a series of urban problems that have seriously eroded the city's livability and business quality. How to implement Xi Jinping's strategy on the Yangtze River Economic Belt of "Embrace large-scale conservation, avoid large-scale development"; how to meet the environmental requirements nationwide for large cities above the prefecture level to have over 80% of days with excellent air quality; how to improve the water quality at the Tuojiang River outfall—a major tributary of the Yangtze River in the region? As a key area for the ecological barrier in the upper reaches of the Yangtze River, all those questions challenge Chengdu's wisdom and capability in addressing the contradictions between insufficient development and imbalanced development.

The coordinated development of the economy, society, and ecological environment to achieve a harmonious coexistence between humans and nature is the key challenge that must be addressed in the construction of park cities. The contradiction between conservation and development is a common issue in human society, stemming from the dual nature of the relationship between humans and the environment, as well as the mismatch between human needs and the Earth's supply capacity. The crises of resources, environment, and development are often interconnected. To overcome this mismatch, it is necessary to find a compromise to bridge the gap, explore and resolve the organic integration and enhancement of the "Nature-Society" interaction mechanism in the name of development, and strive for the harmonious coexistence of human society and the environment.

Domestic and international experiences have shown that protecting the environment does not necessarily slow down economic development. Rapid economic growth does not have to come at the expense of the environment. Firstly, "green, low-carbon, and circular development can not only meet the increasing need for a beautiful ecological environment among the people, but also promote a higher quality, more effective, fairer, more sustainable, and safer development, leading to a path of civilized development with prosperous production, affluent living, and a good ecology." Secondly, green development is an organic unity of development and protection. On one hand, protection and development are a contradiction that runs through the construction of ecological civilization. Different stages of development, different levels of economic development, different ecological zones, different positioning of the main functions, the manifestation of this pair of contradictions shows great differences. On the other hand, not engaging in large-scale development does not mean inaction, but rather avoiding the kind of development that sacrifices resources and the environment. It involves breaking free from old concepts and path dependencies, using "intensive protection" as the starting point to drive regional economies towards an ecological priority and green development path.[4]

The fundamental guiding ideology of building a park city is that "lucid waters and lush mountains are invaluable assets," which profoundly reveals the dialectical unity between economic development and environmental protection. "A sound ecology itself contains infinite economic value, continuously creating comprehensive benefits, and achieving sustainable economic and social development." In the construction of a park city, it is essential to comprehensively grasp the ecological and economic benefits revealed by the saying "lucid waters and lush mountains are invaluable assets," emphasizing the interactive and dialectical unity between ecological benefits and economic benefits, protection, and development. It is crucial not only to focus on the transformation from lucid waters and lush mountains to tangible assets, converting ecological benefits into capital; but also, to consider the transformation from invaluable assets to lucid waters and lush mountains, expanding the increment of green capital, where economic benefits support ecological benefits, promoting sustainable development.

8.4 The New Characteristics of Park City: Climate Resilient, Low-Carbon Development

One of the unique features of park cities is climate resilient and low-carbon development. Firstly, global warming is the largest and most destructive environmental issue, posing the most severe challenge to the sustainable development of human society. It is the main culprit behind the increasingly threatening storms, floods, droughts, forest fires, and other disasters that constantly endanger lives and livelihoods. Climate change also leads to the destruction of biodiversity, seriously damaging the stability of ecosystem and reducing the ability to supply high-quality ecological products. Secondly, global warming is also an energy issue. Since the Industrial Revolution, humans have excessively used fossil fuels such as coal, emitting large amounts of greenhouse gases, which are the main cause of global warming. Energy conservation and emission reduction are the most crucial paths to address climate change. Thirdly, addressing climate change is also a development issue. With the increasing level of urbanization in our country, cities will significantly increase their demand for energy and greenhouse gas emissions. Cities must maintain a balance between decarbonization and energy security, livelihood security, and between development and protection.

Cities play a crucial role in addressing climate change and maintaining climate resilient. Firstly, urban low-carbon development best demonstrates a city's proactive response to climate change and global ecological security, making it easier to gain international recognition and cooperation, showcasing a responsible city image.

Secondly, green and low-carbon development is essential for promoting comprehensive green transformation of urban economy and society, addressing urban ecological environmental issues at their core. Thirdly, urban green and low-carbon development is a vital stronghold and guarantee for achieving the "Dual Carbon Target". For these reasons, green and low-carbon development should clearly be integrated into the overall strategy of urban ecological civilization construction, becoming one of the key development objectives of park city.

Urban low-carbon development aims to adopt a model of "Resource Efficient, Environment Friendly, and Climate Resilient". It serves as a starting point and operational platform to change spatial layout, optimize economic structure, transform development modes, lifestyles, and consumption patterns. It integrates and coordinates with green economy, circular economy and low-carbon economy. It serves as a platform for promoting energy revolution, energy conservation, emission reduction, increasing the proportion of non-fossil energy, developing new energy sources like hydrogen, and modern strategic industries with low carbon as a primary feature. This development provides robust support in economic, technological, and institutional aspects to enhance resource and energy efficiency. Low-carbon development combines carbon reduction with pollution control, coordinating the advancement of low-carbon development with addressing prominent environmental issues like air pollution. Strategic adjustments in urban economic structure shift from heavy industries to modern service industries, emphasizing the development of public transportation and promoting energy-efficient and environmentally friendly transport vehicles. It also promotes the decoupling of regional economic growth from high energy consumption and pollution.[5]

Promoting and practicing a low-carbon lifestyle and consumption concept involves integrating the requirement of "low-carbon" into various aspects of life and consumption. Consumption is a fundamental human activity for survival and development, a crucial part of the social reproduction process, and a vital foundation for the existence and development of a market economy. Consumer demand determines changes in social production and consumption patterns, guiding the transformation of social production methods. On one hand, optimizing residents' consumption structure, improving their living standards, and enhancing access to public services are essential goals for building park city. However, blind consumption and wastefulness can lead urban consumption habits and lifestyles astray from sustainable development, resulting in sharp contradictions between economic development and energy resource supply, severe ecological damage, and a decline in urban living standards, deviating from the original intention of creating park city. Therefore, raising public awareness of the severe consequences and urgency of the "greenhouse effect" and "climate crisis", transforming urban consumption habits and lifestyles, and promoting energy conservation, moderate consumption, and pollution reduction concepts are essential. Encouraging urban residents to start from themselves, pay attention to daily life details, and promote a "low-carbon lifestyle". This shift aims to turn "rational consumption, green consumption, and low-carbon consumption" from concepts into consciousness actions for every citizen.

8.5 Industry Greening and Green Industrialization: Building a Park City Industrial Ecological Circle

Industry is an important foundation for the economic and social development of cities, and the prosperity of industries is a significant indicator of a city's level of development. The suitability for industries is an important indicator of a city's competitiveness and soft power beyond livability. In addition to features such as perfect infrastructure, convenient transportation, complete industrial chains, and supply chains, the suitability for industries in a park city is reflected in the increasingly upgrading of industrial ecological circle of the city.

Building a city's industrial ecosystem will create a new image for the city, greatly improve the city's investment environment, enhance its attractiveness and aggregation of various production factors such as technology, talent, information, and capital, and achieve the goal of making the city a desirable place for business and innovation. Constructing a city's industrial ecosystem is not only a symbol of high-quality development for park city but also promotes the transformation and upgrading of urban industries, increasing the city's economic competitiveness and reducing the environmental impact. The construction of a city's industrial ecosystem should be problem-oriented, efficiency-centered, and focus on promoting the green transformation and upgrading of urban industries, accelerating the shift from low value-added to high value-added, and from extensive to intensive models, advancing the high-level development of urban industrial foundations and modernizing industrial chains, continuously enhancing the comprehensive strength and international competitiveness of industries. Establishing a city's ecological industrial circle means establishing green production methods, integrating the requirements of ecological priority and green development into all aspects and stages of production activities, consciously promoting green, low-carbon, and circular development, building a green industrial structure with high technological content, low resource consumption, and minimal environmental pollution, creating new growth points for economic and social development, nurturing and expanding energy-saving and environmental protection industries, clean production industries, clean energy industries, and achieving the circular connection of production and living systems.

Industrial greening and green industrialization are key drivers for building urban industrial ecosystems. Industrial greening involves upgrading and comprehensively managing traditional industries that are high-energy consuming and highly polluting, aiming to minimize their impact on energy consumption and environmental pollution.[6] It also promotes the intelligent and clean transformation of traditional industries, fostering the deep integration of advanced manufacturing and modern services, accelerating the development of new infrastructure, supporting the transformation and upgrading of industries towards networked, digitized, and intelligent operations, and nurturing new industries, new business models, and new patterns for development momentum. Green industrialization is about transforming the ecological productivity and ecological benefits of cities into tangible productivity and economic benefits, promoting the development of eco-friendly industries. It is not only a crucial aspect of constructing urban industrial ecosystems but also a significant approach to reconciling the contradiction between conservation and development, turning ecological resources into economic prosperity.

8.6 Urban–Rural Collaboration in Building Park City

The close relationship between large cities and vast rural areas is a significant characteristic of super large and mega cities in China. Both urban and rural areas play indispensable roles in the construction of park cities. A beautiful city alone, without beautiful countryside, is insufficient to qualify as a park city. An essential aspect of building a park city is to promote the coordinated development of urban and rural economies and societies over the years, while simultaneously advancing green and low-carbon development in both urban and rural areas.

Rural areas are focal point and difficulty point for ecological and green development. They serve as the ecological base for cities, providing water sources, absorbing pollutants, and preserving natural ecosystems crucial for urban ecological security. However, rural areas pose challenges for ecological civilization construction. The Overall Urban–Rural Development Strategy has largely alleviated the urban–rural economic and social development gap. However, while the urban–rural environmental governance gap has not narrowed, it is even showing signs of widening. The construction of environmental infrastructure in rural areas, such as rural sewage, garbage disposal, and sanitary toilets, lags far behind that of cities, with limited network coverage and financial difficulties. The phenomenon of "shifting pollution from cities to rural areas" worsens the rural environment further.

Rural ecological environment protection requires integrated planning and coordinated efforts between urban and rural areas. There is a high degree of interdependence between rural and urban areas in ecological civilization construction and environmental protection. The governance and protection of rural environment not only affect the protection of farmers' environmental rights and the enhancement of their sense of well-being but also directly impact the development of cities and the entire society, as well as the overall planning of building park city. The effective supply of agricultural products and food safety are significant livelihood issues. Urban pollution affecting rural water and air, rural pollution impacting urban food and vegetables, the vicious cycle of rural environmental pollution and urban pollution seriously threaten agricultural products and food safety. Coordinated urban–rural governance of rural environments should closely integrate the construction of park cities with the strategy of rural revitalization aiming for the goals of "strengthening agriculture, beautifying the countryside, and enriching farmers", in conjunction with ongoing initiatives such as rural sewage treatment, waste management, and toilet revolution.

In the comprehensive planning of urban and rural areas and the coordinated promotion of rural ecological environment governance, firstly, it is essential to adhere to the actual conditions of rural areas, avoiding the misconception of "urban–rural homogenization" and "one look for all villages". "The integrated development of urban and rural areas should preserve the original appearance of villages by being cautious with tree felling, lake filling, and house demolition, and improving residents' living conditions as much as possible within the original village layout". "There is no need to spend great efforts on massive land reclamation; many mountainous and riverside cities have unique characteristics that can be leveraged to enhance residents' quality of life, allowing them to see mountains, rivers, and remember their hometown nostalgia".[7] Chengdu's "Five Golden Flowers Program" take the lead nationwide by utilizing the local excellent ecological and cultural resources to develop rural tourism, homestays, agritourism, agricultural experiences, and leisure agriculture. This meets the increasing demand of citizens for tourism, vacation, and leisure, creating new job opportunities and additional income sources for farmers, transforming intangible ecological assets into prosperous economic capital. The promotion of this model should continue in the construction of park city. Secondly, it is also essential to protect scarce high-quality arable land resources. Xi Jinping pointed out that "urbanization does not necessarily have to be contiguous; it can expand outward in a linked and satellite city development manner. Connecting in a contiguous manner will inevitably occupy a large amount of highly productive farmland that has been painstakingly built over a long period of time. The best farmland is often located in the suburbs, where the most investment has been made. If we turn them all into urban areas, we will have to spend money again to build high-yield farmland. How much money will that cost? Has anyone calculated it!"[8] Park city construction must follow Xi's requirements, cherish and protect arable land resources, promote the modernization of agriculture, enhance the ability to ensure the supply of agricultural products, and take a leading role in realizing Xi Jinping's instructions to Sichuan Province to "enhance the reputation as a leading agricultural province".

Notes

1. Shouhu Du, and Heng Du, "Park City: Harmony and Coexistence of Mountains, Waters, and People", *Social Science Research*, Issue 5, 2022.
2. Shouhu Du, "Green Transformation of Urban Areas in China under Climate Change", *Social Science Research*, Issue 6, 2014.
3. Jinping Xi, "Endeavoring to Build a Modernization in which Human Beings Live in Harmony with Nature", *The Turth Monthly*, No. 11, 2022.
4. Shouhu Du, "Suggestions for Promoting the Construction of an Ecological Barrier on the Upper Reaches of the Yangtze River in Sichuan", *Decision-Making Consultation*, Issue 3, 2016.
5. Shouhu Du, "Promoting the Construction of Ecological Civilization in Chengdu City with the Goal of "REEFCR" City", *Journal of Chengdu Institute of Administration*, Issue 6, 2013.
6. Keli Liu, "The Construction of REEF Society: 'Bend the Road to Overtake the Car' is the Right Time -- Reflection on REEF Society Reading Book", *Hunan Social Science*, Issue 4, 2009.
7. Jinping Xi, "Speech at the Central Urbanization Work Conference", December 12, 2013.
8. Ibid.

Chapter 9
Game Theory of Climate Change

Climate change poses a substantial challenge that humanity must confront. It ties the international community together, facing a shared future. Climate change touches on the economic and security interests of all nations and its impact cannot be underestimated. Under the influence of international conventions and organizations such as the United Nations Framework Convention on Climate Change and the Intergovernmental Panel on Climate Change, climate change has evolved into a unique form of multilateral relationship. Countries all over the world need to participate in open cooperation concerning climate change discussions and domestic actions. Bilateral dialogues and policy coordination are crucial for enhancing and refining existing international climate governance schemes, political frameworks, systems, and mechanisms. However, the urgent need lies in exploring new solutions in areas lacking corresponding norms that are acceptable to all countries worldwide.[1]

9.1 Ecological Challenges and Sino-US Relations

Owing to their vast territories and extensive coastline, both China and the United States face acute climate change threats. China's National Report on Climate Change discloses that it is severely affected by climate change, experiencing higher-than-average increases in annual temperature and sea level rise. The United States, on the other hand, is also seriously affected by global warming. NASA's 2013 report states that the decade's average temperature was the highest in ten years since the US began meteorological recordings. Since 1880, 9 out of the 10 hottest years in the United States have occurred within the last decade. In 2012, hurricane Sandy—a strong storm—hit the eastern United States, affecting a vast area of 1600 square kilometers, and brought heavy rainfall and even snow, resulting in power outages and 125 deaths.

S. Du and H. Du, *The Green Transformation of Urban Areas in China Under Global Warming*, https://doi.org/10.1007/978-981-95-1005-4_9

Moreover, China and the United States hold critical position in global climate governance. Both nations are the top energy consumers and greenhouse gas emitters, their energy use and greenhouse gas emissions accounting for over 40% of the global total. Coal predominantly fuels the energy structure of both nations. In 2013, China consumed 3.65 billion tons of coal, accounting for 67% of its energy consumption. Although coal is one of the most polluting energy sources, it is one of the most important industries in the United States, with coal power generation accounting for 37% of its energy consumption, surpassing natural gas and nuclear power.

The economies, energy consumption rates, and emissions of China and the United States influence their climate governance strategies. To set an example or to intensify the crisis of curbing climate change, their actions cast a significant impact on the world's response. The International Energy Agency reported that from 2004 to 2013, global carbon dioxide level increased annually by 2.4%. However, in 2014, despite a global economic growth of 3%, the annual carbon dioxide emissions remained at the 2013 level of 32.3 billion tons, marking the first time in 40 years that such a situation occurred without an economic crisis. The World Energy Agency attributes this to two main causes: Firstly, China's reduction of coal usage and increase the installed capacity of hydropower, wind and solar power generation; Secondly, the United States and other organizations for economic cooperation and development (OECD) have begun to decouple economic growth from increased carbon emissions.

Evidence underpinning this assertion includes the global increase in hydropower generation by 5.3% in 2010, of which 60% was attributed solely to China. The share of biofuels in global renewable energy increased by 13.8%, mainly from the United States (17%). Global renewable energy for power generation rose by 15.5% with the wind power sector recording a 22.7% increment most predominantly in China and the United States, which accounted for 70% of worldwide growth. In 2012, wind power constituted 43% of new electricity generated in the United States. Compared to a 50% contribution in 2007, coal-fired power dropped to providing only 37% of the United States' electric supply in 2012. During the 11th Five Year Plan period, China's energy consumption per unit of GDP decreased by 19.1%, reducing nearly 1.5 billion tons of carbon dioxide emissions, equivalent to about 5% of global greenhouse gas emissions in 2012.

China and the United States, both early signatories of the United Nations Framework Convention on Climate Change and the Kyoto Protocol, play pivotal roles in climate change negotiations. As per Professor Christian Azar, a renowned Swedish climate economist, the prospect of resolving climate issues could radically transform once the U.S. decisively commits to emission reductions. If the U.S. achieves this, it could catalyze other nations to follow suit. Conversely, absent firm U.S. commitments, other countries might be disinclined to initiate similar actions. The joint statement on climate change by the heads of China and the U.S. in 2014 substantially bolstered the multilateral process of addressing global climate change, particularly anticipated negotiations at the forthcoming Paris Climate Conference in 2015.

9.2 The Delicate Balance of Emission Reduction: Power and Pressure

Both China and the United States face immense challenges to reduce emissions. According to the report of the Intergovernmental Cooperation Committee on Climate Change (IPCC) in 2013, global emissions must remain under the threshold of 300 billion additional tons of carbon dioxide to prevent a temperature rise of more than 2°C compared to the late 1980s.The increasing scarcity of permissible atmospheric greenhouse gas emissions prompts more heated negotiations and power struggles among nations, China and the United States included. Concurrently, a 3/4 reduction in fossil fuel usage worldwide is necessary to maintain the temperature increase below 2°C. Once emission reduction becomes the decision of governments of all countries, domestic factories and equipment, including coal and carbon dioxide emissions, will face significant depreciation, and there will be a large number of economic disorders represented by so-called "stranded assets", which will also put great pressure on the upgrading of energy and economic structure and the transformation of development mode, including China and the United States. Moreover, historical emissions of greenhouse gases by developed nations, particularly the United States, contribute 70% of total global emissions, whereas developing countries accounted for less than 30% in the same instance. According to the principle of "Common but Differentiated Responsibilities", the "Kyoto Protocol" requires that the United States and other developed countries should provide $100 billion in financial support to developing countries by 2020, which will also put pressure on the United States.

The Warsaw Climate Negotiation Conference in 2013 concluded with an agreement to adopt a new international treaty at the Paris Climate Conference in 2015, which discards the traditional division of climate change responsibilities between developed and developing countries. The future allocation of emission reduction tasks will factor in each country's individual responsibilities and capabilities. Both China and the United States, as responsible global powers, seek to uphold their image and relationship, and this common aspiration is made apparent at diverse international platforms. Several nations have articulated their commitment to mitigating climate change. For instance, the 2007 National Plan for Addressing Climate Change issued by China explicitly vowed to uphold its obligations under the Kyoto Protocol and the Global Framework Convention on Climate Change. Similarly, former U.S. President Obama recognized the United States' significant role in both contributing to and mitigating climate change, declaring that despite being home to only 5% of the global population, the U.S. is responsible for 17% of the total cumulative greenhouse gas emissions. This equates to 20% of the global annual greenhouse gas emissions. This proportionate disparity underscores that the U.S. should carry a greater responsibility than other countries in addressing this issue and leading the global effort towards seeking viable solutions.

The enhancement of climate change cooperation can yield mutually benefits. Lowering greenhouse gas emissions can stimulate economic growth, foster job creations, and bolster national energy security. Although China and the United States are in different development stages, they share common interests and potential in green, low-carbon development and energy conservation initiatives. In response to the climate challenge, both nations have taken strategic decisions turning danger into opportunity and transforming pressure into power. Through the energy revolution, the United States transitioned from being energy-dependent to becoming an energy exporter. This measure has bolstered national energy security while significantly contributing to the global fight against climate change. On the other hand, China has taken climate change as an opportunity to establish an ecological civilization, by fostering low-carbon industries such as renewable energy and electric vehicles as strategic sectors, and promoting the domestic expansion of energy conservation, emission reduction, and environmental protection industries.

9.3 Historical Accounting of Energy Conservation and Emission Reduction

Energy conservation and emission reduction remains the objective, although the obligations are differentiated due to the significant disparities among nations in terms of national conditions, developmental stages, historical responsibilities, per capita emissions, and governance capacity. The per capita carbon footprint in the United States is the highest globally and thrice that of China. Furthermore, China's per capita emissions and historical emissions are considerably below those of the United States. Nevertheless, China's aggregate energy consumption and greenhouse gas emissions have escalated swiftly, thus surpassing the United States and leading the world. From a development perspective, the United States has ventured into a post-industrialization phase, thereby transcending peak energy consumption. The energy revolution has greatly reduced the proportion of coal in the energy consumption structure and subsequently, the emissions of greenhouse gases. Conversely, China is still in a rapid phase of industrialization and urbanization where a rise in energy consumption and greenhouse gas emissions is inevitable. A coal-dominated energy consumption structure might remain unchanged in the short run.

There are significant differences between the United States and China's perceptions on core issues, such as the understanding of climate change, the division of contribution of responsibilities and sharing of duties. For an extended period, the United States has expressed skepticism starting from government authorities down to the public, and has evaded climate responsibility by citing the "uncertainty of global warming". Concerning the principle of "Common but Differentiated Responsibilities", fairness, and the principle of respective capabilities in addressing climate change as stipulated by the Kyoto Protocol, the United States has displayed either negativity or opposition. Instead, it has counter-proposed the idea that "all major emitters should participate in absolute emission reduction". The United States also suggested the formulation of a new global emission reduction agreement to override the Kyoto Protocol, even resulting in its withdrawal from the Kyoto Protocol in 2001.

However, China holds divergent views and has displayed firm support and execution of the aforementioned principles.

9.4 Exploration and Establishment of a New Mechanism for Climate Governance

1. The role of dominant national governance in driving new mechanisms for global governance has become apparent. Throughout the twentieth century, the world successfully averted the threat of nuclear war and established the World Trade Organization. These events underscore the constructive role of multilateral mechanisms in accelerating economic globalization. A potent strategy would entail initiating problem-solving efforts in countries that bear the primary responsibility for the problem at hand. Once these countries commit to problem resolution and response, they may incorporate other countries into a cohesive agreement and concerted action. In this light, Global Climate Governance, fueled by prominent national governance, should serve as a supplementary mechanism augmenting the comprehensive political strategy addressing climate change undertaken by the United Nations.
2. There is an urgent need for a coordinate growth mechanism incorporating energy conservation, environmental protection, and low-carbon practices. China, for instance, is currently grappling with the trifold challenges of economic development, environmental pollution and climate change. The escalating issue of haze pollution is a consequence of over 30 years of rapid development and is intimately linked to China's energy infrastructure and effectiveness. Coal is not only a high-carbon, dirty energy source but also significantly contributes to smog formation. It is responsible for generating over 70% of sulfur dioxide, more than 60% of nitrogen oxides, and approximately 70% of the soot in China's total air pollutant emission. Climate change and haze contamination share common origins and a high degree of correlation. It is obvious that solving the haze problem requires comprehensive treatment and coordinated promotion of energy, environmental protection and low-carbon practices. Historical parallels can be drawn to challenges faced by the United States, such as photochemical pollution in Los Angeles. It is very important to establish and improve the coordinated promotion system of coal and carbon reduction and avoid the occurrence of conflicted policies and behaviors in terms of environmental protection and low-carbon.
3. New energy development and promotion mechanism. Climate change primarily originates from energy-related issues. Thus, a fundamental solution to climate change is lies in enhancing energy efficiency and driving the development of alternative energy sources. The United States has made significant strides in this regard, concentrating on the research, promotion, and deployment of technological innovations appealing to the energy revolution. Notable examples include shale gas exploitation, solar energy, wind energy, and biomass energy. Policy

measures like the Wind Energy Production Tax Credit Act (PTC) have been invaluable, where tax rebates for wind energy, closed-loop biomass energy, and geothermal power in 2010 were set at 2.2 cents per kWh. Eligible technologies were granted 50% of the wind power rebate. Moreover, wind power projects initiated before the year-end of 2012 were guaranteed a 10-year tax rebate and the agreement for renewable energy technologies was extended by another year, that is, projects put into operation before the end of 2013 can get a 10-year tax rebate. In the three years of PTC cancellation (i.e. 2000, 2002 and 2004), the growth rate of wind power installed capacity has stagnated significantly, while in the years before the scheduled expiration, wind energy development projects have increased significantly, which is a very convincing case.

4. Carbon emissions trading system is recognized as the most important and effective policy instrument for Climate Governance. Studies and experiences from countries like the United States have demonstrated that carbon emission trading can offer significant institutional and financial support for countries towards a low-carbon transition. The United States, in fact, is a pioneer in the implementation of carbon emission trading with the establishment of the Chicago Climate Exchange in 2003. It is currently the world's second-largest carbon trading market, extending trading services to 10 states and commercial enterprises undertaking voluntary emission reduction commitments. China is also actively exploring carbon emissions trading as a strategy to catalyze its transition towards low-carbon and ecological civilization. At present, China has a national carbon emission trading plan and implementation strategy in place and has initiated pilot carbon trading schemes in 8 regional cities. This measure has facilitated the foundational work of carbon trading, such as the establishment of monitoring systems, calculation systems, and the formulation of a carbon inventory and budget. Potential avenues for mutual beneficial cooperation exist between China and the United States in the establishment of a carbon trading system, formulation of carbon pricing scheme, as well as development and refinement of potential climate governance solutions. The employment of both international and domestic carbon emission trading markets is critical. Equally significant are the establishment of carbon emission trading institutions, the formulation of governing rules, the training of skilled personnel, and the enhancement of overall capacity.

Note

1. Shouhu Du, and Heng Du, "Game Theory of Climate Change", *Guangming Daily*, November 29, 2015.

Bibliography

Azar, Christian (Sweden), translted by Heng Du, and Ke Du. *Solving the Climate Challenge.* Beijing: Social Sciences Academic Press, 2012.

Bai, Yunwen, Fuqiang Yang. "Double Efforts to Make Up for Inherent Shortcomings." *China Environmental News*, May 14, 2013.

Bai, Zhipeng, Baoqing Wang, Shiyong Du. "How to Prevent and Control PM2.5." *China Environmental News*, February 21, 2012.

Bi, Jun. "Low Carbon Cities Cannot be Built on High Carbon Development." *People's Daily*, October 12, 2011.

Chen, Hongbo, Jiahua Pan. "Progress in Theory and Practice of Ecological Civilization Construction in China." *Journal of China University of Geosciences (Social Sciences Edition)*, Issue 10, 2012.

Chen, Hongwan, Lei Zhang. "Thoughts on the Feasibility of China's Current Greenhouse Gas Emissions through Carbon Tax." *Collected Essays on Finance and Economic*s, Issue 1, 2019.

Chen, Yumei. "Resolving the Four Major Contradictions is the Key to Enhancing the Vitality of New City Construction." *Economic Crossroads*, Issue 12, 2011.

Cheng, Tianquan and Yang Zhi. "Reflections on Several Issues Concerning the Development of Low Carbon Economy." *Economic Perspective*, Issue 9, 2012.

Cheng, Tianquan, Zhi Yang. "Thoughts on Several Issues of Low-Carbon Economy." *Economic Review*, Issue 9, 2012.

Dan, Dan, Xiao Han. "Research on Ecological Environment Protection Planning of Hunchun City, Jilin Province." *China's Comprehensive Utilization of Resources*, Issue 2, 2014.

Deng, Ling. "Research on China's Ecological Civilization Development Strategy and its Regional Realization." *Research Report of Sichuan University*, 2013.

Ding, Yi, Yaguai Yu. "Research on the Development of Low Carbon Agriculture for Post Disaster Reconstruction under Climate Change - Based on the Perspective of 'Low Carbon Guangyuan.'" *Rural Economy*, Issue 10, 2012.

Ding,Zhongli. "Climate Change and the Game of Interests Behind It." *Liberation Daily*, April 10, 2011.

Dong, Shu. "Approaches and Measures for Sustainable Ecological City Construction." *Science and Technology Today*, Issue 6, 2003.

Du, Shouhu, Heng Du, "Game Theory of Climate Change", *Guangming Daily*, November 29, 2015.

Du, Shouhu, Heng Du. "Park City: Harmony and Coexistence of Mountains, Waters, and People." *Social Science Research*, Issue 5, 2022.

Du, Shouhu. "Advance Eco-Civilization in Chengdu through REEFCR City Development." *Journal of Chengdu Institute of Public Administration,* Issue 3, 2013.

S. Du and H. Du, *The Green Transformation of Urban Areas in China Under Global Warming*, https://doi.org/10.1007/978-981-95-1005-4

Du, Shouhu. "Ecology: Cannot become a 'Short board' of Economic Development." *Sichuan Party Construction (Urban Edition)*, Issue 2, 2008.
Du, Shouhu. "Four Questions on Ecological Civilization Construction." *Open Guide*, December 8, 2007.
Du, Shouhu. "Green Transformation of Urban Areas in China under Climate Change." *Social Science Research*, Issue 6, 2014.
Du, Shouhu. "New Goal of Urban Rural Integration: Urban Rural Integrated Construction of Ecological Civilization." *Decision Consultation Communication*, Issue 7, 2009.
Du, Shouhu. "Promoting the Construction of Ecological Civilization in Chengdu with the Goal of Building REEFCR City." *Journal of Chengdu University of Administration*, Issue 6, 2013.
Du, Shouhu. "Suggestions for Promoting the Construction of an Ecological Barrier on the Upper Reaches of the Yangtze River in Sichuan." *Decision-Making Consultation*, Issue 3, 2016.
Du, Shouhu. "The Impact and Countermeasures of National Greenhouse Gas Emission Reduction Goals on Sichuan." *Party Building in Sichuan (Urban Edition)*, Issue 4, 2010.
Du, Shouhu. *Environmental Economics*. Beijing: Encyclopedia of China Publishing House, 2008.
Du, Zhuo, Yongfeng Gan, Yanxin Lin. "Property Rights Market: Exploring Emissions Trading." *Property Rights Guide*, Issue 11, 2007.
Glaeser, Edward L. "The Greenness of Cities: Carbon Dioxide Emissions and Urban Development." *Journal of Urban Economics*, 2010.
Gao, Cailing, Ge Gao, Xianwen Zhang. "Evaluation of Sustainable City Construction in Zhengzhou Based on PSR Model." *Regional Research and Development*, Issue 4, 2013.
Ge, Zhihao. "The Average Annual Decrease in PM2.5 in the Yangtze River Delta Should be no Less than 6%." *News Morning News*, December 6, 2012.
Giddens, Anthony (UK), Translated by Rongxiang Cao. *Politics of Climate Change*. Beijing: Social Science Academic Press, 2011.
Goodall, Chris. *How to Live a Low-Carbon Life: The Individual's Guide to Stopping Climate Change*. London: Earthscan, 2010.
Gu, Chaolin. "Research Framework of Urban Planning based on Low-Carbon Concept." *Research on Urban and Regional Planning*, Issue 2, 2010.
Guiyang Municipal People's Government, "Building a Forest City and Promoting Sustainable Development." *Guiyang Daily*, November 19, 2004.
Guo, Junzan. "Preliminary Study on the Construction of Urban Disaster Prevention and Reduction System." *City*, Issue 10, 2009.
Guo, Mingfang. "The Lies Behind Global Warming." *English Digest*, Issue 1, 2008.
Guo, Shuang. "A Sample of Future Ecological Cities – Acosandi." *Building Energy Efficiency*, Issue 5, 2013.
Guomei Zhou, Zhipeng Tang, Liping Li. "How to Achieve Low—Carbon Transformation in Resource—Based Cities." *Environmental Economy*, Issue 10, 2009.
He, Jiankun. "China's Energy Development and Climate Change Response." *China's Population, Resources, and Environment*, Issue 10, 2011.
He, Jiankun. "The Only Path to Improve Core Competitiveness." *People's Daily*, October 20, 2010.
Hiroaki Suzuki, Arish Dastur, Sebastian Moffatt Nana. *ECO^2 Cities: Ecological Cities as Economic Cities*. New York: World Bank Publications, 2010.
Hu, Jintao. "Following the Path of Socialism with Chinese Characteristics and Striving to Build a Moderately Prosperous Society in an All-round Way——Report at the 18th National Congress of the CPC.".
Hu, Jintao. *Holding High the Great Banner of Socialism with Chinese Characteristics, Striving for a New Victory in Building a Well—off Society in an All—round Way—Report on the 17th Congress of the CPC*. Beijing: People's Publishing House, 2007.
Hu, Jintao. *Unswervingly Advancing Along the Path of Socialism with Chinese Characteristics and Striving to Build a Moderately Prosperous Society in an All-Round Way—Report at the 18th National Congress of the CPC*. Beijing: People's Publishing House, 2012.

Hu,Yingfei, Rui Wang, Yunjun Yu. "Experience and Prospect of Establishing Carbon Labeling System in China." *Journal of Economic and Management Studies*, 3rd issue, 2010.
Huang, Guangyu, Yong Chen. "Research on the Concept, Planning and Design Methods of Ecological City." *Urban Planning*, Issue 11, 1997.
Huang, Zhaoyi, Dongyuan Yang. "Review of Theoretical Research on Ecological Cities Domestic and Abroad." *Urban Planning*, Issue 1, 2001.
Jiang, Ailin, Haiqiu Chen, Zhihui Zhang. "Problems and Governance in Urban Environment." *Journal of Changchun Municipal Party School*, Issue 8, 2008.
Jiang, Hong. "Tackling Climate Crisis must Rely on Economic Policies." *Chinese Social Sciences Today*, September 14, 2012.
Jiang, Zemin. *Selected Works of Jiang Zemin.* Beijing: People's Publishing House, 2006.
Jin, Yihua. "Urban Tourism Resources Development and Protection for Eco Tourism Cities in the Context of Circular Economy." *Mall Modernization*, Issue 4, 2007.
John Cobb Jr. "The Prospects for achieving ecological civilization in China are more Optimistic." *Chinese Journal of Social Sciences*, September 21, 2012.
Li, Chongyin. "Regarding Several Issues Related to Addressing Climate Change." *Xinhua Digest*, Issue 7, 2011.
Li, Dan. "How to Solve the Problem of Building a Low Carbon City." *Sichuan Daily*, February 2, 2010.
Li, Fujia, Zenglin Han, Lizhu Wang. "The Development Model of Restricted Development Zones in Liaoning Province during the Transitional Period under the Main Functional Zoning." *Progress in Geographic Science*, Issue 9, 2008.
Li, Min. "From Garden City to Land Garden and Forestry: The Development of Green Space Planning Thought in Human Settlement Environment." *Journal of Architecture*, No. 6, 1995.
Li, Qian. "Incorporating the Concept of 'Low—Carbon' into Urban Development Thinking." *Economic Daily*, February 6, 2012.
Li, Ruidong, Houmei Zhang. "Post Disaster Low Carbon Reconstruction - Interview with Luo Qiang, Secretary of Guangyuan Municipal Party Committee of Sichuan Province." *Environmental Protection*, 2011.
Li, Shantong, Yongzhi Hou, Zhiyan Sun, Jie Feng. "The Goal and Indicator System for Comprehensively Building a Moderately Prosperous Society." *Survey and Research Report*, No. 20, 2004.
Li, Songxue, Yibing Xia. "Performance Evaluation of "REEF" City Construction in Wuhan Urban Circle Based on Analytic Hierarchy Process." *Yangtze River Basin Resources and Environment*, Issue 7, 2012.
Li, Wei, Zheng Zhang, Yingying Zhang. "Research on the Framework of Ecological City Construction Planning in Shenzhen." *Environmental Science and Technology*, Issue 12, 2005.
Li, Xiaoyan. "Research on the Spatial Layout of Villages and Towns' Reconstruction after the Wenchuan Earthquake." *Economic System Reform*, Issue 4, 2009.
Li, Xing. "Construction of China's Ecological Tax Framework." *Tax Research*, Issue 6, 2005.
Li, Ya. "Ecological Responsibility of the Government in Economic Development." *Journal of the Central Party School of the Communist Party of China*, Issue 5, 2005
Li, Yudong. "Clean Production and Governance of Eco Industrial City Construction." *Journal of Xinjiang University (Philosophy, Humanities and Social Sciences Edition)*, Issue 7, 2005.
Lin, Boqiang. "The Impact of Resource Tax Reform." *Economic Daily*, November 1, 2011.
Lin, Huocan, Lei Zhu. "Continuing to Implement Sustainable Development is an Inevitable Choice." *Economic Daily*, June 2, 2012.
Lin, Yaoyu, Guosheng Chen. "FRP Theory on Urban Design Combining Ecology: Concepts, Values, Methods and Achievements." *Journal of Southeast University (Natural Science Edition)*, No. 12, 2005.
Ling, Yi. "Chengdu's Air Quality Fully Meets the National Second Level Standard." *Chengdu Daily*, February 8, 2012.

Liu, Keli. “The Construction of REEF Society: ‘Bend the Road to Overtake the Car’ is the Right Time—Reflection on REEF Society Reading Book.” *Hunan Social Science*, Issue 4, 2009.

Liu, Minquan, Jiantuo Yu. “Environment and Human Development: A Literature Review.” *Journal of Peking University (Philosophy and Social Sciences Edition)*, Issue 3, 2010.

Liu, Shujiang. “Ten Hard Measures towards Mist and Haze.” *Earth*, Issue 7, 2013.

Liu, Keli. “Corner Overtaking: No Better Time than Now - Reviews on the Leaders’ Readings for Resource—Efficient and Environment—Friendly (REEF) Society.” *Hunan Academy of Social Sciences*, 7th edition, 2009.

Low-Carbon Economy, Baidu Library available at http://wenku.baidu.com/view/710de9d284254b35eefd3403.html.

Luo, Qiang, Wei Jiang. “Poverty Stricken Areas can Also Take the Lead in Low—Carbon Development—Low—Carbon Reconstruction Practice in Guangyuan Disaster Area.” *Environmental Protection*, Issue 6, 2010.

Ma, Kai. “Global Warming is a Common Challenge Facing Humanity.” *Green Leaf*, Issue 8, 2007.

Managerial Personnel Low-Carbon Economy Manual, Baidu Library available at http://wenku.baidu.com/view/73a8c60d52ea551810a687bf.html

Mei, Biqiu. “Strengthening Ecological Civilization Construction and Promoting the Development of Hanshou Forestry.” *China Forestry*, Issue 9, 2008.

Pan, Jiahua. “Economy Needs Low Carbon, Low Carbon Needs Economy.” *Journal of Huazhong University of Science and Technology (Social Science Edition)*, Issue 2, 2011.

Pu, Rong, Xiuyu Hu. “Exploration on the Development of Tourism Industry in Restricted and Prohibited Development Zones - Taking Yunnan Province as an Example.” *Journal of Kunming University*, Issue 12, 2008.

Pu, Rong, Yingmei Wu, Haixia Bai. “Exploration of the Development Model of Tourism Industry in Restricted and Prohibited Development Zones - Taking Yunnan Province as an Example.” *Yunnan Geographical Environment Research*, Issue 11, 2008.

Qian, Yi, Peng Zhang. “Research on Ecological City Construction.” *Xinjiang Environmental Protection*, Issue 3, 2005.

Qin, Jiangbo, Hongqi Wang. “Construction of a Performance Evaluation Model for Bank Credit Risk Management Based on AHP Method.” *Financial Theory and Practice*, Issue 1, 2009.

Qin, Xu. “Sanya: Building a Garden City in the South.” *China Construction Information*, Issue 7, 2003.

Qiu, Baoxing. “New Urbanization: From Concept to Action.” *Administrative Management Reform*, Issue 11, 2012.

Qiu, Baoxing. “Transforming Development Models and Building Low Carbon Cities.” *China Construction Daily*, December 9, 2009.

Research Group of Macro Department of Development Research Center of the State Council, “Low—Carbon Economy is not the ‘Patent’ of Developed Regions.” *People’s Daily*, April 28, 2010.

Research Group of the Policy Research Office of the Shenzhen Municipal Party Committee, “Several Important Issues of Urban Renewal in Shenzhen”, *Special Zone Practice and Theory*, Issue 7, 2008.

Song, Rongwei. “Discussion on the Construction of Credit Risk Early Warning Indicator System by Commercial Banks.” *Journal of Sichuan Normal University (Social Science Edition)*, Issue. 5, 2007.

Song, Rongxing, Haitao Sun. “Research on Sustainable Development Capability of Urban Ecological Environment.” *Research on Financial Issues*, Issue 7, 2007.

Song, Yimiao. *Research on Management of Main Functional Zones*. Sichuan: Southwestern University of Finance and Economics, 2008.

Song, Yunwen. “Ways to Strengthen the Construction of County Ecological Civilization.” *Leadership Science*, Issue 3, 2008.

Stayler, Achim. “Achim Stayler’s Speech at the World Expo Forum.” *Wen-Hui News*, July 17, 2010.

Steiner, Thomas (Sweden), translated by Weiwen Zhang and Zuhui Huang. *Policy Tools for Environment and Natural Resources Management.* Shanghai: Shanghai People's Publishing House, 2005.
Su, Yun, Shengkui Cheng, Gaodi Xie. "A Preliminary Study on the Ecological Occupation of Urban Residents' Lives—Case Studies of Beijing and Shanghai." *Resource Science*, Issue 11, 2001.
Sun, Xiaowei. "Design and Implementation of a Carbon Tax System." *Guangming Daily*, September 14, 2010.
Tang, Longxiang, Jin Min. "New Ideas for Environmental Legislation in China under the Sustainable Development Strategy." *Lanzhou Academic Journal*, Issue 6, 2005.
Wang, Shuhua, Fengyi Zhang, Zhongjing Wang, Hanying Mao. "Evaluation of Suburban Economic Coordination Based on Ecological Footprint Model – Case Study on Xinle City, Hebei Province." *Geography and Geographic Information Science*, Issue 1, 2003.
Wang, Binbin, Shouhu Du. "ECO^2: The Third Mode of Low-Carbon City." *Journal of Sichuan Normal University (Social Science Edition)*, Issue 6, 2012.
Wang, Fangjie, Hongsheng Wang. "Baoding Strives to Create the 'China Electric Valley.'" *China Economic Weekly*, Issue 3, 2008.
Wang, Feng and Genfu Feng. "Factors Influencing the Low Carbon Development of China's Economy and Its Role in Carbon Reduction." *China Economic Issues*, Issue 5, 2011.
Wang, Guolian. "PM2.5: A Sample for Studying Contemporary Chinese Ecological Politics." *Journal of Qingdao Agricultural University, Social Sciences Edition*, Issue 11, 2013.
Wang, Hesheng. "Research on Ecological Environment Construction and Protection in the Yangtze River Basin." *Science and Technology Management of National Land Resources*, Issue 4, 2000.
Wang, Huali, Chunling Pu. "Defects and Countermeasures of Compensation Mechanism for Land Resources Utilization in Tarim Basin." *Xinjiang Social Science Forum*, Issue 8, 2008.
Wang, Jingge. "Reflections on the Emission Trading System—Establishing an Emission Trading System with Chinese Characteristics." *Journal of Liaoning University of Administration*, Issue 11, 2010.
Wang, Lin. "Marxism has Guiding Significance for the Construction of Ecological Civilization." *China Social Science Daily*, September 21, 2012.
Wang, Xiangrong, Renjian Wu. "Basic Theory and Empirical Research on Urban Ecological Planning - Taking Maluanwan in Xiamen as an Example." *Journal of Fudan University (Natural Science Edition)*, Issue 12, 2004.
Wang, Xiangrong, Wu Renjian. *Report on Urban Ecological Environment Issues in China.* Jiangsu: People's Publishing House, 2006.
Wang, Xiangrong. "Concept, Connotation, and Empirical Research on Urban Ecological Planning." *Planner*, Issue 5, 2002.
Wang, Xiangrong. *Urban Ecology*. Shanghai: Fudan University Press, 2011.
Wang, Xiaodong. "International Comparison and Reference of Emission Trading Systems." *Taxation and Economics*, Issue 3, 2009.
Wen, Chuanhao, Yan Tie. "The Theory of Ecological Civilization Construction needs to be Continuously Deepened." *China Environmental News*, November 13, 2012.
Wen, Jiabao. "Making Energy Conservation and Emission Reduction a Compulsory Task, Compulsory Measures, and Compulsory Indicators." *People's Daily*, September 28, 2011.
Wu, Jiandong. "Rebuilding the United States through Green Economy: Deconstruction of Obama's Energy Strategy." *Science Times*, January 20, 2009.
Wu, Jie, Qi Jiang. "Carbon Labeling in International Trade." *International Economic Cooperation*, 7th issue, 2009.
Xi, Jinping. "Endeavoring to Build a Modernization in which Human Beings Live in Harmony with Nature." *The Turth Monthly*, No. 11, 2022.
Xi, Jinping. "Opening of the 2013 Annual Conference of the Ecological Civilization Guiyang International Forum, Congratulatory Letter from Xi Jinping." *Xinhua Daily Telegraph*, July 21, 2013.
Xi, Jinping. "Speech at the Central Urbanization Work Conference." December 12, 2013.

Xi, Jinping. "Striving towards a New Era of Socialist Ecological Civilization." *Communist Party Member*, Issue 6, 2013.

Xie, Pengfei. "Sustainable City Indicator System Construction and Sustainable City Demonstration Evaluation." *Urban Development Research*, Issue 7, 2010.

Xie, Wenhui, Wei Deng. *Urban Economics*. Beijing: Tsinghua University Press, 2008.

Xin, Zhangping, Yintai Zhang. "Low-Carbon Economy and Low Carbon Cities." *Urban Development Research*, Issue 4, 2008.

Xu, Jianping. *Application of Mathematical Models in Geographic Information Systems*. Beijing: Higher Education Press, 2002.

Yang, Hongqiang, Xiaoxin Zhang. "Coordination of Carbon Trade and Environmental Protection Constraints under the Kyoto Protocol Mechanism." *International Trade Issue,* Issues 10, 2005.

Yang, Jun. "Taiyuan Urban Green Space System Planning." *Taiyuan Science and Technology*, Issue 6, 2003.

Yang, Kaizhong. "Which Province Has a More Civilized Ecology - Ranking of Ecological Civilization Levels in Various Provinces, Districts, and Cities in China." *China Economic Weekly*, Issue 12, 2011.

Yang, Wenli. "Chasing the Wind and the Sun - Rise of the New Energy Industry Cluster in Baoding High Tech Zone." *China High Tech Industry Guide*, November 2, 2009.

Yang, Xiaojie, Shouhu Du. "Research on the Development Model of Low-carbon Economy in Late Developing Areas—Taking Guangyuan City, Sichuan Province as an Example." *Rural Economy*, Issue 8, 2012.

Yang, Yanhua. "A Brief Discussion on the Development of Low-Carbon Economy in Baoding." *Reform and Opening Up*, Issue 2, 2013.

Yin, Wenliang, Kaiting Ji. "Discussion on Biodiversity Conservation Planning in Lu'an City." *Anhui Agricultural Bulletin*, Issue 3, 2012.

Yu, Hanwu Guozheng Wu, Hu Xu. "Analysis of Security Measures for Urban Lifeline Systems." *Chinese Journal of Safety Sciences*, Issue 5, 2008.

Yu, Qun. "Baoding: 'Low Carbon' Concept Boosts Ecological Civilization." *Urban Housing*, Issue 5, 2008.

Yu, Yaguai, Jianhui Gao. "Urban Vulnerability and Climate Change Adaptability in Urban Construction." *Business Era*, Issue 5, 2011.

Yu, Yaguai, Pan Hanqing, "Climate Change, Geological Disasters and the Construction of Urban Disaster Reduction and Prevention System - Based on the Perspective of Urban Vulnerability in Ningbo", *Journal of Southwest University for Nationalities (Humanities and Social Sciences Edition)*, Issue 12, 2012.

Yu, Yue, Haiyun Wang. "Urban Diplomacy and Image Communication in the Context of Subnational Behavior. *Youth Journalist*, Issue 33, 2012.

Zeng, Zuotao, Xun Wang. "Scientifically Studying the Impact of Global Warming on China's Water Resources and Food Production: A Discussion with Professor Park Shilong et al." *Science and Technology Introduction*, Issue 32, 2011.

Zhang, Bin, Qidong Yong, Fangchun Xiao. *Fuzzy Matter Element Analysis*. Beijing: Petroleum Industry Press, 1997.

Zhang, Gaixi. "How to Join Hands for the Five Cities to Promote the 'Prohibition of Burning' Campaign." *Sichuan Daily*, May 2, 2013.

Zhang, Jinsong. "On the Construction of the Ten Major Systems of Ecological Civilization." *Administrative Forum*, Issue 3, 2013.

Zhang, Man. "Adjusting Environmental Policies and Developing Environmental Protection Industry." *China's Environmental Protection Industry*, Issue 2, 2002.

Zhang, Wenzhong. "Research on the Development Path and Mode of the Continuous Alternative Industry of Resource-based Cities." *Journal of the Chinese Academy of Sciences*, Issue 2, 2011.

Zhang, Xiumei, Junying Liu, Xiaoying Zhou. "Review of Network Information Resource Evaluation." *Library Science Research*, Issue 12, 2013.

Zhang, Zixue. "Inner Mongolia Ecological Environment Protection Strategy." *Inner Mongolia Environmental Protection*, Issue 3, 2000.
Zhang,Chunhai. "Climate Philosophy Research Boosts Ecological Civilization Construction." *China Social Science Daily*, November 30, 2012.
Zhao, Jing. *Mathematical Modeling and Experiments*. Beijing: Higher Education Press, 2000.
Zhao, Min. "Source of Sustainable City Thought." *Journal of Changsha University*, Issue 3, 2003.
Zhao, Zan. "Analysis of the Impact Mechanism of Tourism Development on Ethnic Traditional Culture Based on the PSR Model Framework." *Chinese Journal of Agriculture*, Issue 9, 2010.
Zheng, Guoguang. "Enhancing Adaptation to Climate Change and Ensuring Sustainable Development." *People's Daily*, November 21, 2011.
Zhou, Yun. *How to Choose the Sustainable Development Path for Resource—based Cities— Interpretation of "Several Opinions on Promoting the Sustainable Development of Resource-based Cities."* Beijing: China New Technology and New Products, 2008.
Zhu, Konglai, Ruyan Wang. "Research on Comprehensive Evaluation of REEF Society." *China Population, Resources and Environment*, Issue 12, 2011.
Zhuang, Guiyang. "Low-Carbon Economy Leads the Development Direction of the World Economy." *World Environment*, Issue 2, 2008.

MIX
Papier aus verantwortungsvollen Quellen
Paper from responsible sources
FSC® C105338

If you have any concerns about our products,
you can contact us on
ProductSafety@springernature.com

In case Publisher is established outside the EU,
the EU authorized representative is:
Springer Nature Customer Service Center GmbH
Europaplatz 3, 69115 Heidelberg, Germany

Printed by Libri Plureos GmbH
in Hamburg, Germany